HOLY
TEACHING

1775417472 M29l05

WITH

D1005311

HOLY TEACHING

Introducing the
Summa Theologiae
of St. Thomas Aquinas

FREDERICK CHRISTIAN BAUERSCHMIDT

BrazosPress

Grand Rapids, Michigan

Published by Brazos Press
a division of Baker Publishing Group
P.O. Box 6287, Grand Rapids, MI 49516-6287
www.brazospress.com

Printed in the United States of America

Library of Congress Cataloging-in-Publication Data
Thomas, Aquinas, Saint, 1225?–1274.
    [Summa theologica. English. Selections]
    Holy teaching : introducing the Summa theologiae of St. Thomas Aquinas / [edited by] Frederick Christian Bauerschmidt.
        p.   cm.
    Includes bibliographical references (p.   ).
    ISBN 1-58743-035-5 (pbk.)
    1. Theology, Doctrinal. 2. Catholic Church—Doctrines. I. Bauerschmidt, Frederick Christian. II. Title.
BX1749.T515 2005
230'.2—dc22   2005003341

For Stanley Hauerwas, fellow hillbilly Thomist

Contents

THE FIRST HALF OF THE SECOND PART

THE SECOND HALF OF THE SECOND PART

INTRODUCTION

INTRODUCING A WORK THAT NEEDS NO INTRODUCTION

Thomas Aquinas's *Summa theologiae* is undoubtedly a great work of theology.[1] Indeed, it is the only volume of anything like dogmatic or systematic theology among Britannica's *Great Books of the Western World*. If there is a work of theology that needs no introduction, this is it.

But in attempting to teach the theology of Thomas Aquinas, I found that although there were many affordable anthologies of his work in print, none of them contained much in the way of the texts that would be of particular interest to theologians: texts on Christology or the Trinity or the sacraments. We might speculate about why this is the case—why it is that Thomas is viewed in the English-speaking world more as philosopher than a theologian, or why it is that his theology is thought to be of little interest—but the fact remains. One could, of course, have students spend a few hundred dollars on a translation of the entire *Summa theologiae* (which is certainly a good investment), but even with the text in hand, Thomas's theology is not immediately accessible. Terms have to be explained; historical background has to be given; arguments have to be diagrammed.

This book is born partly out of my desire to make some of Thomas's texts more readily available. To that end I have collected a number of texts that are not found normally in anthologies of Thomas's writings, and I have provided a commentary that is designed to help the reader who is not familiar with Thomas's theology (or perhaps even with theology in general).

But this book is also born out of a desire to help people read Thomas Aquinas differently. I hope this book will show that there is much of interest in Thomas

---

1. *Summa theologiae* is "Summary of Theology." It is also called the *Summa theologica* or "Theological Summary."

that for many people remains unknown because it remains unread. Many people think they know what is important in Thomas's *Summa theologiae:* his proofs for the existence of God and perhaps what he has to say about natural law. These things certainly are important, but focusing on them exclusively distorts our image of what Thomas is up to in the *Summa.* He himself describes the *Summa* as an exercise in *sacra doctrina,* which is sometimes translated as "sacred doctrine," but which I think is better rendered as "holy teaching." This is an activity that is first and foremost God's activity of self-revelation through the prophets, the apostles, and preeminently through Jesus Christ. It is secondarily our human activity of passing on that revelation through teaching, which involves not simply rote repetition but a kind of critical reflection by which we seek to understand how to hand on this teaching faithfully.

So in this book I hope not simply to introduce the *Summa theologiae,* but to introduce it in such a way that its character as "holy teaching" is manifest.

THOMAS'S LIFE AND TIMES

When studying some theologians, it seems crucial to understand their lives in order to understand their thought. If one wants to study Augustine, for example, his *Confessions* would seem the logical place to start, not least because his account of his own conversion illuminates the struggle between sin and grace—the earthly and the heavenly cities—that is at the heart of his theology. But not so with Thomas Aquinas. His writing displays little of the passion of Augustine: the tone is measured, the language without rhetorical flourish—reduced to essentials for the sake of clarity. One interpreter, presumably paying Thomas a compliment, went so far as to say that he "is hardly an 'author,' or even a 'man,' but rather a channel connecting us directly with intelligible truth."[2] When confronted with a direct channel to intelligible truth, one is likely to be far more interested in the truth revealed than in the channel's family history. Thus have some viewed Thomas.

But I think this view of Thomas is mistaken. His life, while lacking the drama of Augustine's, is still important for understanding his work. More specifically, although one could remain ignorant of the pious anecdotes that surround Thomas without much loss in understanding his theology, some knowledge of the context in which he lived, taught, and wrote is crucial. Even if Thomas's theology is one for the ages, one cannot properly understand that theology if one does not understand its author's place within his own age.

For those seeking a full presentation of Thomas's life, we now have Jean-Pierre Torrell's authoritative biography, which is the first part of a two-part interpretation of Aquinas. For those who want something briefer, Simon Tugwell

---

2. A. D. Sertillanges, *St. Thomas Aquinas and His Work,* trans. Godfrey Anstruther (London: Burns, Oates & Washbourne Ltd., 1932), 109.

provides an excellent short biography in the introduction to his *Albert and Thomas: Selected Writings*. For those who want to know only the most essential information, I offer the following.

Youth

Thomas Aquinas was born around the year 1225 at the Aquino family castle in Roccasecca, midway between Rome and Naples, in what was then the Kingdom of the Two Sicilies. Thomas was the eighth of nine children of Landulf d'Aquino, born to his wife, Theodora. Landulf was a minor noble, described in the necrology of the monastery at Monte Cassino as a "knight." Thomas was born at the beginning of a time of conflict between Emperor Frederick II and a series of popes,[3] which caused problems for his family, since his father was a vassal of Frederick and their lands lay on the border between imperial and papal lands.

It was customary for the youngest son of a noble family to be offered for service to the church, and so, around the age of five (ca. 1230/31), Thomas was taken to live at the famous Benedictine monastery of Monte Cassino (which was nearby) as what was called a "child oblate." This may sound a bit callous to us, but it was a common practice in the Middle Ages, not unlike sending a child to boarding school. *Oblatio* is different from *professio* (i.e., becoming a monk) in that it does not involve solemn vows. Thomas would have been able to decide for himself if he wanted to profess vows, but it is not unlikely that his family hoped he would eventually become abbot of the monastery. But Monte Cassino was a contested territory between the emperor and the pope, and in 1239 Frederick's troops took it over, turned it into a fortress, and began expelling the monks. Thomas probably left about this time, with a recommendation from the monks to his family that he should go study at the University of Naples.

When he was around the age of fifteen Thomas entered the *studium generale* at Naples to study the liberal arts and philosophy (not theology). Universities were a relatively recent educational innovation, and this one had been founded by Frederick II with the idea of training men to serve the emperor in various official capacities. The education offered in Naples was broader and more secular than in some of the universities. Here Thomas would have studied the seven "liberal arts"—what Vergerius called "those studies . . . which are worthy of a free man." These studies were divided into the *trivium* (grammar, rhetoric and logic) and *quadrivium* (arithmetic, geometry, astronomy, and music) and were the basis for any higher study, whether law, medicine, or theology.

It was at Naples that Thomas encountered two new phenomena that would exert profound influence on him and that are crucial for understanding Thomas

---

3. Honorius III, then Gregory IX, who excommunicated Frederick at least twice, and then Innocent IV, who declared him guilty of heresy and tried to depose him as king.

and his times: the works of Aristotle, and members of the Order of Preachers, more commonly known as the Dominicans.

Aristotle

Boethius, in the sixth century, had conceived a plan to translate all of the works of Plato and Aristotle into Latin, so they would remain available to a Western Europe that was rapidly losing its intellectual ties with the Greek-speaking East. He had gotten only as far as translating Aristotle's *Posterior Analytics,* a work on logic, when this plan was cut short. Boethius ran afoul of the Emperor Theodoric and was executed in 524. As a consequence, up until the thirteenth century most of the works of Aristotle were lost to the West. His logic was available in Boethius's translation, but no one knew anything of his works of natural science, metaphysics, or ethics.

About the turn of the thirteenth century works by Aristotle and by Arab philosophers commentating on his work began to be translated into Latin. This was a revolutionary event. Relatively quickly, the Western intellectual world was introduced to a body of thought that offered a comprehensive interpretation of the world. Most disturbing was the fact that this interpretation seemed to have no need for Christian revelation. Christianity had long before made a kind of peace with Platonic thought (e.g., in St. Augustine), but Aristotle contradicted Plato on many points and seemed to call into question the harmony of natural and supernatural wisdom. For example, Christians had long before appropriated Plato's notion of a realm of "forms" as a way of speaking of the Christian notion of divine ideas in the mind of God. Aristotle, however, conceived of "form" as existing, not in a transcendent realm, but immanently in particular things. In this and numerous other cases, Aristotle's departure from Plato seemed to threaten Christian doctrine. And it did not help Aristotle's cause that many of the first Latin translations to become available were made not from the original Greek, but from Arabic translations made by Muslim infidels.

Because of the threat that Aristotle seemed to pose to faith, the study of his scientific and metaphysical works was banned at many universities, most notably at the University of Paris (the full Aristotelian corpus finally became an official part of the curriculum at Paris sometime between 1252–1255, though it was undoubtedly taught unofficially prior to this). But this ban was not in effect at Naples, and it was here that Thomas first studied Aristotle—not only his logic and ethics, but also his scientific and metaphysical works. Later, in his formation as a Dominican, Thomas continued to study Aristotle under Albert the Great, and toward the end of his life, Thomas wrote a number of commentaries on the works of Aristotle. To anyone who has read Thomas, it is clear that Aristotle's philosophy is one of his chief tools for solving intellectual puzzles, though he frequently ends up making that tool do jobs for which it was never designed.

The Order of Preachers

Dominic Guzman was born in Spain in 1171–1172 and died in 1221. He founded the Order of Preachers in 1215 to combat heresy—specifically the Cathar or Albigensian heresy in southern France—through preaching. The Dominicans were part of a broadly based and diverse movement known as the *vita apostolica,* which sought a return to the kind of life depicted in the Acts of the Apostles: a shared life of preaching, prayer, and poverty. Along with the Franciscans (founded around the same time by Francis of Assisi), the Dominicans were *mendicants,* meaning that rather than living off the income from property, as traditional monastics did, they begged to support themselves. This freedom from income-generating property allowed them to minister in cities, which were undergoing a revival. The mendicant orders emphasized active service and were not strictly contemplative, again differentiating them from traditional monastics. Because of the Dominican emphasis on preaching they also emphasized education, establishing houses of study at major universities.

Just as Aristotle presented a new intellectual way of proceeding, the mendicant orders presented an innovative form of religious life, one that responded to recent developments such as the rise of universities and the revival of urban life. As such, they were the object of much suspicion. The Dominicans had founded a priory in Naples in 1231, although there were only two friars in residence when Thomas arrived (Frederick II had kicked most of the mendicants out of his realm). One of these friars, John of San Giuliano, inspired in Thomas a desire to join the Dominicans and to live their life of prayer and study in the service of preaching.

We are not exactly sure when Thomas entered the Dominicans, though it was probably in early 1244,[4] and it touched off the most obviously dramatic event in his life. His family was not thrilled at his interest in the Dominicans, who seemed to them a bunch of upstart radicals, and certainly not the kind of group with which the son of a nobleman should be associated. Thomas's family no doubt still harbored the hope that he would someday become the abbot of Monte Cassino.

The friars, foreseeing trouble, decided Thomas should get out of Naples, so they sent him first to the Dominican community at Santa Sabina in Rome and then on to either Bologna or Paris (scholars differ as to his destination). His mother, seeking to talk some sense into his head, just missed him in both Naples and Rome.[5] Thereupon she sent a force, which included his brother

---

4. Tugwell inclines toward an earlier date—1242/43—which would indicate perhaps a fuller period of formation for Thomas prior to the events that were to follow.

5. The *Vita* of Thomas by Bernard Gui, written in the early fourteenth century, tells the story slightly differently, perhaps in order to put Thomas's family in a better light. In Bernard's version, Theodora was thrilled that Thomas was joining the Dominicans and went to Naples to congratulate him. The Dominicans, misunderstanding her motive in coming to Naples, secreted Thomas away, thus arousing the ire of his mother.

Rinaldo, to intercept him and take him to the family castle in Roccasecca, so they could persuade him to adopt a more conventional path than that of a Dominican friar. His family kept him under a sort of under house—or castle—arrest for about a year, during which time he is said to have memorized the Bible and studied the *Sentences* of Peter Lombard. John of San Giuliano was able to visit him. Thomas also engaged in discussions with his sister Marotta that eventually led her to become a Benedictine nun. His brothers, frustrated with their lack of progress, smuggled a prostitute into his room to dissuade him from his chosen path, but Thomas kept her at bay with a burning stick, with which he then inscribed a cross on the wall of his room. This scene indicated, at least to his mother, that the case was hopeless. According to legend, she supplied him with a rope that he used to climb out the window of his room to the ground below. Torrell thinks "the truth is no doubt more prosaic" (i.e., they simply let him go).[6]

Legend tends to exaggerate the conflict between Thomas and his family, and it is clear that later in life he had good relations with them; but it *is* important to remember that his decision to join the Dominicans, like his interest in Aristotle, was seen as something radical. Thomas has come to be seen by so many as (for good or for ill) the standard bearer for intellectual conformity that it is worth noting his association with two movements that in his day were seen as dangerously nonconformist.

Student

Upon his release by his family, Thomas first went back to Naples, but then his movements become a bit difficult to track. Apparently the Dominicans sent him to study, first to Paris (1245–1248) and then to Cologne (1248–1252), where he was ordained a priest in 1250/51. In both places he studied with the Dominican theologian Albert the Great, who made extensive use of the philosophy of Aristotle. Apparently neither Albert nor Thomas's fellow students were particularly impressed with him at first. Tall and somewhat stout,[7] Thomas never spoke much and often seemed lost in his own thoughts. His fellow students referred to him as the "dumb ox." Albert, however, recognized fairly quickly Thomas's great intellectual gifts and took a special interest in him. Eventually, his fellow students also came to recognize Thomas's gifts and depended upon Thomas to help them understand Albert's lectures. One of Thomas's earliest works, *On the Principles of Nature,* is thought to be something

6. Jean-Pierre Torrell, O.P., *Saint Thomas Aquinas,* vol. 1, *The Person and His Work,* trans. Robert Royal (Washington, D.C.: The Catholic University of American Press, 1996), 11.

7. Though not, as some have claimed, obese. Like all Dominicans, Thomas would not ride a horse, traveling by foot on his various journeys. If one takes into account all of Thomas's travels, it becomes apparent that he got plenty of exercise—much more so than modern day academics.

like a study guide to Aristotle's natural philosophy that Thomas prepared for his fellow students.

In 1251/52 Thomas went to Paris as a *baccalarus sententarium*—roughly equivalent to a graduate student. His job was to lecture on the *Sentences* of Peter Lombard.[8] Lombard's text was a collection of quotations that represented conflicting authoritative opinions (which is what *sententia* means) from Scripture and the church fathers on a host of topics. Lombard (ca. 1100–1161) had put these conflicting opinions into something like a coherent structure and had then appended his own resolutions. The *Sentences* became the standard theology "text book" for medieval universities. Thomas spent his time lecturing on the *Sentences* and composing those lectures into a commentary, which would serve as the functional equivalent of a modern dissertation and become the first of his comprehensive summaries of Christian doctrine, the *Scriptum super libros Sententiarum.*

One closing comment about Thomas as a student: Thomas was a good student because he was inquisitive and, like all truly inquisitive people, was open minded (though not perhaps in our modern sense). He read voraciously in a time when books were hard to come by (he once said that he would give the whole city of Paris for a copy of John Chrysostom's commentary on Matthew). He sought truth wherever he could find it, whether in Muslim or Jewish or ancient pagan sources. But his fundamental understanding of truth was shaped by his identity as a Christian. Those who disagreed with the Christian faith were worth listening to, but the goal was always the vindication and deeper understanding of Christian truth.

Teacher and Preacher

In the spring of 1256 Thomas "incepted" as a Master of Theology (*Magister in sacra pagina* or "Master of the Sacred Page"), which involved a two-day disputation on four questions as well as an inaugural lecture on a passage of Scripture. Once Thomas was a *magister,* his job was threefold:

> *Legere*: to lecture/comment on Scripture. This task was a significant part of Thomas's responsibilities. From the texts that survive, we know that Thomas lectured on the Old Testament books of Isaiah and Job as well as the first fifty Psalms. Among the New Testament books, lectures on the Gospels of Matthew and John and on the letters of Paul survive. Thomas's role as a commentator on Scripture is worth underscoring since for him this commentary is at the heart of his intellectual enterprise. Indeed, one might say that the whole point of studying the fathers of the church—and even Aristotle—is to understand Scripture better.

---

8. Note that Thomas was not yet allowed to lecture of the Bible, which only the Masters of Theology were allowed to do.

Disputare: to participate in disputations, which were, along with the lecture, one of the chief ways of teaching in the medieval university. In a disputation, a question (e.g., "Whether, besides philosophy, any further teaching is required?") was proposed; a group of students would first present arguments and citations of various authorities for the "no" side; then another group of students would present arguments and authoritative citations for the "yes" side. The next day the Master would offer his own position, resolving the conflicts between the various authorities and responding to the specific arguments. A number of these disputations are preserved, and Thomas uses a modified form of the disputation to structure his arguments in the *Summa theologiae.*

Predicare: to preach. Thomas was, after all, a member of the Order of Preachers. But a reader of the *Summa theologiae,* or one of his commentaries on Aristotle, will find it difficult to imagine what one of Thomas's sermons would have been like. Apparently, however, Thomas did not engage in high-flown speculation in his preaching, which he often did in his native Neopolitan dialect. Bernard Gui notes, "To the ordinary faithful he spoke the word of God with singular grace and power. . . . Subtleties he kept for the Schools; to the people he gave solid moral instruction suited to their capacity; he knew that a teacher must always suit his style to his audience."[9]

In addition to these official duties, Thomas wrote on a variety of topics. It is noteworthy that many of the works for which he is best known, specifically his two *Summae* and his commentaries on Aristotle, were works he accomplished in his "spare time." In 1259, he was given Reginald of Piperno as a *socius:* what we might call today a research assistant. Reginald became important to Thomas in helping him carry out the vast amount of work that he took on. Among other things, Reginald apparently had the task of reminding Thomas to eat, since Thomas seemed prone to forget to do so. It was during this time in Paris that Thomas began writing his second comprehensive work of Christian doctrine, the *Summa contra Gentiles.*

The habits Thomas formed as a *magister* in Paris between 1256 and 1259 in many ways defined the rest of his life, which he lived according to the relatively ordered pattern of lecturing to classes, reading, writing/dictating, and praying. His world was primarily an academic one. He spent many years in Paris at the university, but never learned French, since this was the language of the marketplace, whereas Latin was the language of the university. Thomas rose early, said Mass, attended another Mass, and then spent the rest of the day praying, teaching, reading, and writing.

Between the spring of 1259 and the fall of 1268 Thomas was in Italy, mainly teaching Dominicans. In Rome (beginning in 1265) he was the regent master

---

9. Bernard Gui, *Vita Sancti Thomae Aquinatis* §29, in *The Life of St. Thomas Aquinas, Biographical Documents,* ed. and trans. Kenelm Foster, O.P. (Baltimore, Md.: Helicon Press, 1959), 47.

of the Dominican *studium* (house of studies), where he was given free reign to develop his own ideas about how theologians were to be trained. It was during this time he finished the *Summa contra Gentiles* (1264) and soon after began the *Summa theologiae* (1266), which he describes as a work for "beginners." No doubt, his experience at the *studium* in Rome prompted him to think about how one should proceed in teaching theology, and as students he quite possibly had in mind the kind of men he was teaching at the *studium* in Rome: those preparing for pastoral ministry as Dominican friars.[10]

In 1268 Thomas returned to Paris as a regent master. It is possible that he was sent back to Paris to address the brewing controversy between the arts faculty and the theology faculty. The arts faculty, which instructed the students in the liberal arts prior to more advanced study, was much enamored of Aristotle, particularly as interpreted by the Arab philosopher Averroes. The theology faculty remained suspicious of the Aristotelians. They were willing to employ Aristotle's philosophy for certain purposes, but suspected that the arts faculty was more Aristotelian—or in fact Averroist—than they were Christian.

Thomas had been critical of the so-called Averroists on a number of issues; yet, despite his disagreements with them, he was highly admired by many of the philosophers on the arts faculty—no mean achievement for a theologian, even in Thomas's day. His reputation was more mixed among the theologians, many of whom, particularly the Franciscans, accused him of being a closet Averroist and of holding something like a "double-truth" view of the relationship between philosophy and theology (i.e., the view that something could be true philosophically, but not theologically, and vice versa). This charge would not go away quickly. The secular masters (i.e., those theologians who did not belong to either the Franciscans or the Dominicans) disliked Thomas because he was a mendicant, and mendicants, as noted, were thought to be dangerous innovators.

During his time in Paris, Thomas continued work on the *Summa theologiae* (the *secunda pars*) and began working on commentaries on the works of Aristotle. In addition, he delivered his lectures on the Gospel of John, which are widely considered one of his masterpieces; he also wrote numerous smaller works. In 1272, he was once again sent to Naples, where he was to set up a *studium*, again with freedom to organize it as he wished. Here he delivered his lectures on Paul's letters and continued work on his Aristotelian commentaries and on the *tertia pars* of the *Summa theologiae*.

---

10. This is Torrell's view; see *The Person and His Work*, 144–45, based on the arguments made by Leonard Boyle in *The Setting of the Summa Theologiae* (Toronto: Pontifical Institute of Medieval Studies, 1982). John Jenkins argues, contrary to this, that the *Summa theologiae* was not written for those preparing for pastoral ministry, but for those preparing to become Masters (i.e., teachers) of Theology; see John I. Jenkins, C.S.C., *Knowledge and Faith in Thomas Aquinas* (Cambridge: Cambridge University Press, 1997), 85–90.

Silence and Death

While celebrating Mass on December 6, 1273 (the feast of St. Nicholas), Thomas underwent some sort of extraordinary experience. After Mass, Thomas did not set to work, as was his habit, but returned to his room. Reginald tried to get him to work, but Thomas said, "Reginald, I cannot, because all that I have written seems like straw to me." Thomas seemed as if he were in a daze. A few days later Reginald pressed him about the problem, and Thomas replied, "All that I have written seems to me like straw compared to what has been revealed to me."

What happened? Scholars differ. Thomas had been working at an incredible pace and was undoubtedly under a certain amount of stress, both physically and mentally. Clearly Thomas experienced more than a simple mental breakdown, because the historical sources emphasize his physical weakness after this event. Some scholars have speculated that it was something like a stroke. But was this simply a psychological/physical event, or was there a spiritual component? Thomas's remark about "what has been revealed to me" seems to indicate a spiritual experience. Simon Tugwell notes that Thomas had just finished the section of the *Summa theologiae* dealing with the sacrament of the Eucharist, and whatever it was that happened occurred while Thomas was celebrating Mass. Thomas had always had a strong devotion to Christ as present in the Eucharist, and it is perhaps the case that he was granted some extraordinary insight into this mystery, an insight that made him unwilling or uninterested or unable to continue writing.

Some people wish to see in the words "All that I have written seems to me like straw" Thomas's repudiation of his own writing. However, Tugwell suggests a different interpretation:

> 'Straw' is a conventional image for the literal sense of scripture, which is worth having, even if it is only a beginning. Words can lead us to reality. But if Thomas had, in some way, peered beyond faith and glimpsed something of the reality to which the words of faith point, of course the words would lose their appeal. They had served their purpose.[11]

Despite Thomas's ceasing his scholarly work, he was still a friar in service to the church. So when in February 1274 he was summoned to attend the Council of Lyon, which was seeking to reunite the Eastern and Western churches, he set out, despite his physical weakness. While traveling, he hit his head on a tree branch and was unable to continue. He was taken first to the nearby house of one of his sisters and then, at his request, to the nearby Cistercian monastery at Fossanova, where he died on March 7.

---

11. Simon Tugwell, O.P., "The Life and Works of Thomas Aquinas," in *Albert and Thomas: Selected Writings*, ed. and trans. Simon Tugwell, O.P. (New York: Paulist Press, 1988), 266–67.

THE CHARACTER OF THOMAS'S THOUGHT

I make no pretense that the comments that accompany this selection of texts from the *Summa theologiae* represent anything like a "neutral" interpretation of Aquinas. I have tried to make comments that will help the reader understand Thomas, but I, like all interpreters, have my biases. So I will spell out here what I take to be characteristic of Thomas's thought, noting where I differ from other interpreters.

First, I take Thomas to be a theologian through and through. Though philosophically astute, Thomas does not think of himself as a philosopher. Indeed, he reserves the title "philosopher" for non-Christian lovers of wisdom. Thomas, by contrast, is a Master of the Sacred Page—an interpreter of Christian Scripture who is willing to use whatever tools are at hand, including philosophical ones, to bring out the meaning of God's revelation. Thus the image some people (usually those who have not read much Aquinas) have of Thomas as a philosopher who wrote a bit of perfunctory theology is prima facie incorrect. The more sophisticated view that there is within Thomas's theology a philosophy that can be detached and stand on its own is equally wrong. It is true that for Thomas things can be known about God apart from divine revelation, but he never tries to construct a system of thought out of those things, since he sees them as radically inadequate to true human flourishing.[12] And even when writing his commentaries on Aristotle, Thomas is always writing in service of the Christian faith.

Second, on a related point, I take Thomas's relationship to Aristotle to be a complex one, and hardly one of disciple to master. Thomas is surely an admirer of Aristotle and a brilliant commentator on his writings. In particular, he thinks Aristotle more useful for Christian theology than Plato (of whom he has at best a second-hand knowledge), not least because Aristotle helps him focus on and analyze the concrete particular existing thing, which for him fits well with the Christian ideas of creation and incarnation. But Thomas is *not* an Aristotelian in at least two senses. First, his strong interest in Aristotle must be balanced by the fact that he draws upon a wide range of thinkers, including the two very different forms of Neoplatonic Christian theology represented by Augustine and by Dionysius the Areopagite, both of whom are pervasive influences on Thomas's writings. Second, although he finds Aristotle useful for his theological purposes, he is willing to change Aristotle both when he conflicts with divine revelation and when Thomas judges him to be philosophically inadequate. The common view that Thomas's reconciliation of Christian revelation with Aristotelian philosophy is one of his great achievements is true, in a sense, but

---

12. It can appear in the first three books of the *Summa contra Gentiles* that Thomas does try to build a system out of what we can know of God apart from revelation, but for an argument that this is not the case, see Thomas Hibbs, *Dialectic and Narrative in Aquinas: An Interpretation of the Summa Contra Gentiles* (Notre Dame, Ind.: University of Notre Dame Press, 1995).

we must always keep in mind that Thomas accomplishes this reconciliation only through a fundamental transformation of Aristotle.

Third, whereas some scholars think of Thomas as someone who thinks that we can know quite a lot about God, I take him quite seriously when he says that we can know more easily what God is not than what God is. For Thomas, God's essence—what God is—is ungraspable by created intellects, and his theology always proceeds with this fact in mind. God's essence is ungraspable not because God hides from us, but because when we turn our minds to God there is too much offered to our understanding. We get a sense of this excess in Thomas's words to Reginald, "All that I have written seems to me like straw compared to what has been revealed to me." As Joseph Pieper puts it, "He is silent, not because he has nothing further to say; he is silent because he has been allowed a glimpse into the inexpressible depths of that mystery which is not reached by any human thought or speech."[13]

Fourth, I do not take Thomas to be someone who thinks that the ungraspability of God's essence consigns us to silence. In Christ, God has given us a language to speak, by which we can speak truly about God, even if the concepts to which our words refer are inadequate to the truth we seek to articulate. Some interpreters have taken the fact that Thomas's discussion of Christology is deferred to the third part of the *Summa theologiae* as an indication of a lack of interest on his part. This is, I think, too wooden a reading of the structure of the *Summa*. But whatever opinion one holds about the structure of the *Summa*, careful attention to the actual content that fills that structure reveals that Christ pervades the entire work. Indeed, the whole point of the *Summa* is to help us learn to follow Christ by teaching us the truth that God has revealed in Christ.

READING THE *SUMMA*

The format of the *Summa theologiae* can appear confusing at first, but once you grasp how Thomas proceeds it is in fact a model of clarity.

The *Summa* is structured in three "parts." The *prima pars* (first part) concerns God and the creation of the universe. The *secunda pars* (second part) concerns human action and is subdivided into a theoretical treatment of human action (the *prima secunda,* or first half of the second part) and a detailed treatment of human virtues and human vices (the *secunda secunda,* or second half of the second part). The *tertia pars* (third part) concerns Christ: his person and work; the continuation of his work in the church through the sacraments; and his second coming and the consummation of creation (this last section was never written). There are numerous theories about the structure of the

13. Joseph Pieper, *The Silence of St. Thomas: Three Essays,* trans. John Murray, S.J., and Daniel O'Connor (South Bend, Ind.: St. Augustine's Press, 1999), 38.

Summa, and although they can be illuminating, they should not distract us from its actual content.

Each part contains numerous "questions," which are further subdivided into "articles." Your reading of Aquinas will be greatly helped if you understand how Thomas proceeds in these articles.

As mentioned above, the articles of the *Summa* grow out of a medieval teaching practice known as "disputation." To recall, the pattern of the disputation was as follows:

- A question/thesis is put forward.
- Objections against the thesis are offered (these can be quite numerous).
- Counter-objections that speak for the thesis are offered (these also can be quite numerous).
- The master (usually the next day) offers a response outlining his own position.
- The master replies to any of the objections that remain.

If we look at any of Thomas's collections of disputed questions (e.g., *De veritate* or *De potentia*) we can see that these disputations could become quite unwieldy. After all, some students talk even when they have nothing to say; and so too in the disputed questions some of the objections and counter-objections are quite repetitive, and others are of dubious value. In the *Summa,* Thomas refines this form, boiling it down to its essentials:

- He states the thesis in the form of a question.
- He raises objections against the thesis—usually two or three, but occasionally more.
- He offers a counterposition, introduced by *sed contra* (on the contrary), which is almost always reduced to a single counterpoint and usually cites a biblical passage or other authority, instead of making an argument.
- He gives his own response, introduced by *respondeo* (I answer)—usually inclined toward the *sed contra,* but not always.
- He marshals replies to the objections.

We might note a few key points about reading an article. First, it is never enough to read the *responsio* alone, since Thomas sometimes makes his most important point in the replies to the objections. Second, the objections are not "straw men." Of all the possible objections, Thomas chose those he thought most convincing. Often an objection is at least half way, and some times three-quarters of the way, to the truth. Third, you should not to presume that the *sed contra* is Thomas's position. Sometimes it misses the truth as much as the objections, albeit in a different direction. Finally, we should note how this structure, based as it is on the disputation, is dynamic. There is always an argument that is moving forward through objection and counter-objection. Indeed, we should think of the *Summa* as a vast, extended discussion of the truth of the Christian faith, a discussion we are invited to join.

SUGGESTIONS FOR USING THIS BOOK

For teaching purposes, this book might be used in conjunction with other anthologies of Aquinas's work in order to give a more rounded picture of his thought. In particular, one might want to supplement this book with readings of Thomas's moral theology or of his understanding of the human person (found primarily in the second part of the *Summa*). One might want also to use this text in conjunction with other sorts of writing by Thomas, such as his commentaries on Scripture or Aristotle.

But this book can also stand on its own as an introduction to Thomas's thinking on the principle doctrines of Christianity. One might follow it through in order, which is the order in which the articles occur in the *Summa theologiae*. Alternatively, one might adapt its order to correspond to the typical course in modern dogmatic or systematic theology. Such an order might look like this:

Theological Method: 1.1.1, 1.1.2, 1.1.8

Theological Sources—Faith and Reason: 1.12.12, 1.12.13, 2–2.2.3, 2–2.2.7, 2–2.2.8, 2–2.2.10

Theological Sources—Scripture: 1.1.9, 1.1.10, 2–2.2.10

Theological Language: 1.13.3, 1.13.5

God's Existence and Nature: 1.2.1, 1.2.2, 1.2.3, 1.3.4

The Trinity: 1.27.1, 1.27.3, 1.29.4, 1.32.1, 1.36.2

Creation and Its Goal: 1.45.5, 1–2.3.8, 1–2.5.1

Law, Grace, and Love: 1–2.91.4, 1–2.109.2, 1–2.109.6, 2–2.23.1

The Incarnation: 3.1.1, 3.1.2, 3.1.3

The Person of Christ: 3.2.2, 3.9.4, 3.16.1, 3.17.2

The Work of Christ: 3.40.1, 3.40.3, 3.40.4, 3.46.1, 3.46.2, 3.46.3, 3.46.4, 3.47.1, 3.47.2, 3.53.1

The Church and Mary: 3.8.1, 3.27.2, 3.42.4

The Sacraments in General: 3.61.1, 3.62.1, 3.63.1, 3.65.1

Baptism: 3.66.1, 3.68.2, 3.68.9

The Eucharist: 3.75.1, 3.75.8, 3.80.1, 3.83.1

Eschatology: 1–2.4.6, 2–2.17.2, 3.59.5

SOME TECHNICAL MATTERS

Text and the translation. This translation is something of a hybrid. It is not an entirely new translation, but neither does it correspond to any already existing translation. As mentioned, this book grew out of my own teaching of Aquinas and my desire to make available to my students texts that were not available in the standard anthologies, along with a commentary that could help them understand what they were reading. Originally, I gave my students the translation done by the English Dominicans is the early twentieth century, which was readily available online. Over time, I began to modify this translation, at first only slightly and then more radically, to make it more intelligible to readers today by eliminating archaisms, making the sentences follow the Latin word order less slavishly, and changing the translation of key terms that might be misunderstood (e.g., replacing "satisfaction" with "repayment" and "sensible" with "perceptible"). In making these texts available to a wider audience, I decided to check them in their entirety against the Latin for accuracy. For this purpose I used the 1948 Marietti edition of the *Summa*, occasionally consulting the 1870 Vives edition. In the course of this task I made further modifications to the translation, with the end result that we have here something like a "revised standard" version of the old Dominican translation. Few sentences remain unchanged; indeed, some bear no resemblance to the earlier version at all, but anyone familiar with the original translation will recognize my indebtedness. I hope this hybrid, dictated by my limitations as a translator, will not seem too much a mongrel to readers.

Citations. The *Summa theologiae* itself is cited by part, question, and article, so that 3.24.2 means, third part, question twenty-three, article two. In referring to the reply to an objection, I use *ad,* plus the number of the objection, so that 3.24.2 *ad* 1 means third part, question twenty-three, article two, reply to objection one. Because the second part of the *Summa* is itself divided into two "halves," references to this part begin with an additional numeral to designate the "half"; thus 1–2.5.1 means the first half of the second part, question 5, article 1.

My annotations to Aquinas's text appear as footnotes that are numbered sequentially within each question. In other words, as you move from one of Aquinas's questions to the next, you will see that the numbering of the annotations starts over again with the numeral 1. Cross-references between notes thus rely on the same method of citation just described, although only the part and question number are required. For example, if I say "see 2–2.19, note 5," I mean "see the second half of the second part, question 19, note 5." When I refer to texts from the *Summa theologiae* that are contained in this volume, I add the word "above" or "below" (as appropriate).

I have tried to fill out all of Aquinas's citations, using the common English title of the work (except where the work is better known by its Latin title, for example, Augustine's *De Trinitate*) and giving the book/chapter divisions as they appear in most editions. In the case of Aristotle's works, I have also included the column number of the Berlin edition, which can greatly aid in locating texts in different translations. Perhaps I should also note that Aquinas refers to Aristotle as "the Philosopher," just as he refers to St. Paul as "the Apostle" and to Peter Lombard as "the Master."

Secondary sources are rarely cited unless quoted explicitly, but anyone reading the books listed in my suggestions for further reading will see how little of what I say is original to me.

ACKNOWLEDGMENTS

I would like to thank the various students to whom I have taught these texts over the years, particularly the students in my class on the theology of Thomas Aquinas in the spring of 2004. I would also like to thank my colleague Trent Pomplun, who offered comment on a number of these texts, and David Toole, for his careful and insightful copyediting. Finally, I would like to thank Stanley Hauerwas, to whom I dedicate this book, for his boundless enthusiasm for holy teaching. Some may find this difficult to believe, but Thomas would have found in him a kindred spirit.

PROLOGUE

Because the teacher of Catholic truth should not only teach the proficient, but also instruct beginners (according to the Apostle, "As unto little ones in Christ, I gave you milk to drink, not solid food"—1 Corinthians 3:1–2), we propose in this book to treat of whatever belongs to the Christian religion, in such a way as may be directed to the instruction of beginners.[1]

We have considered how newcomers to this teaching have not seldom been hampered by what they have found written by other authors, partly on account of the multiplication of useless questions, articles, and arguments; partly also because those things they need to know are not taught according to the order of the subject matter, but according as the plan of the book might require, or the occasion of the argument offer; partly, too, because frequent repetition brought weariness and confusion to the minds of hearers.[2]

---

1. There has been a lot of debate over what Aquinas means by *incipientes* (beginners). Some scholars have argued that his intended readers were the students in the various provincial centers of study (i.e., *studia*) of the Dominican order, students preparing not for teaching careers but for pastoral ministry. Thomas began writing the *Summa* while teaching as just such a *studium* (Santa Sabina, in Rome), and the length of the treatment of moral theology in the second part suggests perhaps such a pastoral orientation. On the other hand, even a quick glance at the *Summa* shows that Thomas cannot mean by *incipientes* those with no theological instruction whatsoever. The *Summa* presumes a fairly extensive knowledge not only of Scripture, but also of philosophy. Some scholars have proposed, therefore, that Aquinas's intended readers were those students at the University of Paris who had completed their initial instruction in the liberal arts, philosophy, and theology and were beginning their preparation to become teachers themselves.

2. We can infer what Aquinas has in mind here. We know that theological instruction in the medieval university took primarily two forms: lectures that commented on the books of Scripture or on Peter Lombard's *Sentences,* and "disputations" in which students and faculty debated specific theological questions (see the introduction to this book). It is perhaps these two forms of instruction that Thomas means when he says "those things they need to know are not taught according to the order of the subject matter, but according as the plan of the book [i.e., of Scripture] might require, or the occasion of the argument [i.e., the disputation]

Endeavoring to avoid these and other similar faults, we shall try, by God's help, to set forth whatever is included in this holy teaching as briefly and clearly as the matter itself may allow.

---

offer." Aquinas's point seems to be that in both these cases topics are taken up as they arise rather than presented in an orderly fashion, in which one question presumes and builds upon what has come before.

THE
FIRST
PART

QUESTION 1

THE NATURE OF HOLY TEACHING

1.1.1

Whether, besides philosophical studies, any further teaching is required?

It seems that, besides philosophical studies [*philosophicas disciplinas*], we have no need of any further teaching [*doctrinam*].[1]

1. A human being should not seek to know what is above reason; according to Sirach 3:22, "Seek not the things that are too high for you." But whatever is not above reason is fully treated of in philosophical studies. Therefore any other teaching besides philosophical studies is superfluous.

2. Teaching can be concerned only with being, for nothing can be known, except what is true; and all that is, is true.[2] But everything that is, is treated

---

1. *Philosophicae disciplinae* might also be translated as "the philosophical disciplines," referring to such areas of philosophy as logic or ethics or metaphysics. However, I have translated it as "philosophical studies" in order to include both the activity of accomplished philosophers and that of students of philosophy. *Doctrina* does not refer primarily to a proposition that one is expected to believe (what we today normally mean by a "doctrine") but to an activity: the activity of teaching. This is significant because Thomas is not asking about the legitimacy of some set of propositions but rather about the legitimacy of a particular kind of teaching activity. Thus Aquinas's question is whether there is a need for a teaching other than the teaching associated with philosophy—in other words, why do we need theology or, as Aquinas calls it, *sacra doctrina* (holy teaching)?

2. Like virtually all medieval philosophers, Aquinas presumes what in technical language is called "the convertibility of the transcendentals," which refers to those perfections that necessarily accompany existence, such as goodness, truth, and unity. So inasmuch as something exists, it is

31

of in philosophical disciplines—even God himself, so that there is a part of philosophy called "theology," or "the divine science," as the Philosopher has proved in his *Metaphysics* (bk. 6, chap. 1, 1026ª).[3] Therefore, besides philosophical disciplines, there is no need of any further knowledge.

On the contrary: It is written in 2 Timothy 3:16, "All Scripture inspired of God is useful to teach, to reprove, to correct, to instruct in justice." But Scripture inspired of God is not part of the philosophical disciplines, which are acquired through human reason. Therefore it is useful that besides philosophical studies, there should be other knowledge, namely, that which is inspired of God.

I answer: It was necessary for human salvation that there should be a teaching revealed by God, besides the philosophical studies investigated by human reason. First, because humanity is directed to God as to an end that surpasses the grasp of its reason.[4] According to Isaiah 66:4, "eye has not seen, O God, without you, what things you have prepared for those that love you."[5] But the end must first be known by people who are to direct their thoughts and actions to the end.[6] Therefore it was necessary for the well-being [*ad salutem*] of humanity that certain truths that exceed human reason should be made known by divine revelation.[7]

---

good, true, and one. And the more perfectly the existence of something is realized, the better, truer, and more unified it is. The point of the objection is that because being and truth are "convertible," philosophy, which in metaphysics deals with "being," is all you need for truth.

3. The point of the objection here is that philosophers *also* inquire after God's existence and nature, therefore philosophical inquiry is sufficient for understanding God.

4. This is a basic principle of Aquinas's thought (and, indeed, of all Christian, Jewish, and Muslim theology), namely, that God is the goal or purpose (i.e., the "end") of our existence.

5. Thomas is here conflating Isaiah 64:4, which reads "those who wait upon you," with 1 Corinthians 2:9, which reads "those who love him."

6. That is, you cannot be said to be acting to obtain a particular goal unless you have at least *some* knowledge of the goal. If I went to college but did not know that the college gave out diplomas upon successful completion of the course of study, then one would not normally say that obtaining a degree was the goal of my going to college.

7. How one interprets *ad salutem* here affects how one understands the overall shape of Thomas's thinking on the question of faith and reason. The Latin *salus* has a wider range of meanings than the English word "salvation." The root meaning of *salus* is "health" or "well-being," and although it certainly can, and in this specific case probably does, refer to the ultimate well-being of eternal life with God, it is not restricted to this meaning. If one takes *salus* in the more restricted sense of eternal life with God, then Thomas can be understood to be saying that human reason is sufficient to secure this-worldly well-being, but that we need a truth beyond what reason can give us—the special teaching by God known as revelation—in order to attain eternal life. Put differently, he would be saying that reason suffices for natural fulfillment, but revelation is necessary for *super*natural fulfillment. However, if one takes *salus* in the broader sense of human well-being or flourishing, then Thomas would seem to be saying that a knowledge of divine truths beyond reason contributes to flourishing in all areas of human life, not simply in our religious or spiritual lives. This interpretation would lead to the conclusion that even in the "natural" realms of family and politics and the market there are potentials that are unrealized apart from divine truth. Thus one might say that in the last analysis human beings have no purely "natural" fulfillment, but only a "*super*natural" one. Human beings are fulfilled *as humans* only in going beyond what it means to be human.

Even regarding those truths about God that human reason *could* have discovered, it was necessary that human beings should be taught by a divine revelation; because the truth about God such as reason could discover, would be known only by a few, and that after a long time, and with the mixing in of many errors.[8] But humanity's whole well-being, which is in God, depends upon the knowledge of this truth. Therefore, in order that the salvation of human beings might be brought about more fittingly and more surely, it was necessary that they should be taught divine truths by divine revelation.[9]

It was therefore necessary that, besides philosophical studies investigated through reason, there should be a holy teaching learned through revelation.

Reply to 1: Even if things that are too lofty for human knowledge may not be sought for by a person through reason, nevertheless, once they are revealed by God, they must be accepted by faith.[10] Therefore the text continues, "For many things are shown to you above human understanding" (Sirach 3:25). And in this, holy teaching consists.

Reply to 2: Disciplines are differentiated according to the various means through which knowledge is obtained. The astronomer and the physicist both may prove the same conclusion, that the earth, for instance, is round:[11] the astronomer by means of mathematics (i.e., leaving aside matter), but the physicist by means of matter itself. Therefore there is no reason why those things that may be learned from philosophical studies, so far as they can be known by natural reason, may not also be taught us by another discipline, so far as they fall within revelation. Therefore, the theology

---

Evidence for both interpretations can be found in the writings of Aquinas. Many debates over the proper interpretation of Aquinas, especially in the last century, have centered around this and related questions. Of particular relevance is the question of the relationship between divine grace and human nature (see note 28 and all of 1–2.109.2, below).

8. Aquinas does believe that we can know *some* things about God by simply using our human reason, but he also thinks that such knowledge is quite minimal, and that it can be had only by very smart people who have a lot of time for thinking. And even when they have arrived at some genuine truths about God (e.g., that God exists), they will still be wrong about many other things about God (e.g., that he requires human sacrifices).

9. It is worth noting here that when Thomas says revelation is "necessary," he does not mean that God is in any way obliged to reveal himself to human beings. Rather, he means that given the divine purpose of saving humanity—and not simply the clever and leisured, but also the dull and busy—it was fitting that God teach human beings. On this use of "necessary," see Thomas's discussion in 3.46.1.

10. In response to the first objection Aquinas points out that the discipline of theology is based not on what *we* think about God, but on what God has revealed about himself. At the same time, the human response of faith *is* an intellectual act.

11. Contrary to current popular opinion, educated medieval people knew that the world was round. As early as the sixth century BC the Greek philosopher Pythagoras argued for a round earth, and almost no educated person after this thought that the earth was flat. The widespread belief that Christopher Columbus was the first to "prove" the roundness of the earth apparently originated in the nineteenth century.

included in holy teaching differs in kind from that theology that is part of philosophy.[12]

1.1.2

Whether holy teaching is *scientia*?[13]

It seems that holy teaching is not *scientia*.

1. Every *scientia* proceeds from self-evident premises.[14] But holy teaching proceeds from articles of faith that are not self-evident, since their truth is not admitted by all; as 2 Thessalonians 3:2 says, "For not all have faith." Therefore holy teaching is not *scientia*.

12. What makes one kind of knowledge different from another is not so much the knowledge itself as it is the *means* by which the knowledge is obtained. Aquinas's point is that philosophy and theology might lead us to the same bit of knowledge (e.g., that there exists a first mover of the universe), but they are still distinct ways of pursuing knowledge, since in the case of philosophy we believe something because human reason tells us, whereas in the case of theology we believe something because God tells us.

13. I have chosen to leave the word *scientia* untranslated in order to remind readers that in medieval usage the word *scientia* meant something quite different from its modern English cognate "science." In one way, *scientia* is something much broader than our modern conception of "science." Loosely translated, it simply means "knowledge," in contrast to "opinion" or "faith." More precisely, however, *scientia* names the result of a process by which unknown things are deduced from known things; as Aquinas says, "The nature of *scientia* consists in this, that from things already known conclusions about other matters follow of necessity" (*Exposition on Boethius's "De Trinitate"* 2.2). Normally *scientia* proceeds from premises or "first principles" to certain conclusions; probably the best model for us to think of is how a proof in geometry works (see note 14, below). One can see how *scientia* differs from our modern notion of science, in which knowledge is based on experimentation, not on deduction.

It is also important to note that in order to have true *scientia* of something, it is not enough to accept it as true; one must also grasp *why* it is true. Thus, to use an example from geometry, in order to have *scientia* of the Pythagorean theorem it is not enough to memorize it; one must also be able to grasp how the proof works. Aquinas contrasts *scientia* in its normal sense with both faith and opinion. Unlike opinion, it is certain of what it holds true (because its conclusions "follow of necessity"), and unlike faith it involves a process in which reason gives assent to something that it "sees"—as when, after struggling to understand the Pythagorean theorem, one says, "Ah, *now* I see!"

In addition to referring to the knowledge that one possesses, *scientia* can also have the sense of a body of knowledge, or what we today might call a "discipline." This is the primary meaning it has in 1.1.8, below.

14. The objection is that if *scientia* is to be taken as certain knowledge, then it must begin from certain truths that no one could deny (what Aquinas calls premises or "first principles"). Thus, in geometry we might begin from the truth that a whole is always bigger than its part (which is self-evident to anyone who knows the meaning of "whole" and "part"); and in philosophy we might begin with the truth that the same statement cannot at the same time be both true and not true (which is self-evident to anyone who knows the meaning of "true" and "false"). If someone will not grant these premises, then they have no access to geometric or philosophical truth. The objection here is that in theology there are no premises that everyone accepts, as is evidenced by the fact that not everyone has faith.

2. No *scientia* deals with individual facts.[15] But holy teaching treats of individual facts, such as the deeds of Abraham, Isaac, and Jacob and similar cases. Therefore holy teaching is not *scientia*.

On the contrary: Augustine says in *De Trinitate* (bk. 14, chap. 1, no. 3), "To this *scientia* alone belongs that by which saving faith is begotten, nourished, protected, and strengthened." But this can be said of no *scientia* except holy teaching. Therefore holy teaching is *scientia*.

I answer: Holy teaching is *scientia*. We must bear in mind that there are two kinds of *scientiae*.[16] There are some that proceed from premises known by the natural light of intelligence, such as arithmetic and geometry and the like. There are some that proceed from premises known by the light of a higher *scientia:* thus the *scientia* of optics proceeds from premises established by geometry, and music from premises established by arithmetic. And it is in this way that holy teaching is *scientia,* because it proceeds from premises established by the light of a higher *scientia,* namely, the *scientia* of God and the blessed.[17] Therefore, just as the musician accepts on authority the premises taught to him by the mathematician, so holy teaching is established on premises revealed by God.

Reply to 1: The premises of any *scientia* are either in themselves self-evident, or can be traced back to the conclusions of a higher *scientia,* and such, as we have said, are the premises of holy teaching.

Reply to 2: Individual facts are dealt with in holy teaching, not because it is concerned with them principally, but rather they are introduced both as examples to be followed in our lives (as in moral *scientiae*) and in order to es-

15. The objection expresses the common medieval view that genuine knowledge is first and foremost a knowledge of universals (such as "humanity" of "circularity") and not of concrete particulars ("this human being" or "this circle").

16. Here Aquinas makes a move that you will see him make again and again: he points out that we use the word *scientia* in at least two ways and that the answer to this question lies in properly distinguishing them. Aquinas pays close attention to our use of language and frequently resolves questions by sorting out linguistic confusions. For example, he distinguishes various ways in which we use terms like "necessity," "comprehension," and "temptation."

17. Aquinas points out that not all forms of inquiry proceed from self-evident premises. Some forms (like geometry and mathematics) do, but others (such as optics and music) begin from premises established by a "higher" (i.e., logically prior) *scientia* (cf. the reply to objection 1). Thomas calls the latter forms of inquiry "subaltern" *scientiae*. So, for example, although music is based on premises derived from mathematics, a musician may be a perfectly fine musician without having a firm grasp of (i.e., *scientia*) the premises of mathematics. What Aquinas is saying is that theology is based on premises that are self-evident only to God and the blessed (those who behold God face to face in heaven). Just as the subaltern *scientia* of music must "borrow" knowledge from mathematics, so too the *scientia* of theology "borrows" knowledge from God's own self-knowledge. One point to note here is that the higher *scientia* acts as an "authority" for the lower.

Thus from the perspective of God and the blessed, *sacra doctrina* is *scientia* in the normal sense (see note 13, above); for human beings in this life it is *scientia* only in the sense of a subaltern *scientia*.

tablish the authority of those through whom the divine revelation, on which
Holy Scripture or teaching is based, has come down to us.[18]

1.1.8

Whether holy teaching proves anything through argumentation?[19]

It seems this teaching does not prove anything through argumentation.

1. Ambrose says in his *On the Catholic Faith* (bk. 1, chap. 13, no. 84), "Put
arguments aside where faith is sought." But in this teaching, faith especially is
sought, for it is said in John 20:31, "These things are written that you may believe."
Therefore holy teaching does not prove anything through argumentation.

2. If it is a matter of argument, the argument is either from authority or from
reason. If it is from authority, it does not seem to fit with the dignity of this
teaching, since the proof from authority is the weakest form of proof. But if it
is from reason, this does not seem to fit with the goal of this teaching, since,
according to Gregory (*Homilies on the Gospels,* sermon 26), "faith has no merit
in those things of which human reason offers its own experience." Therefore
holy teaching does not prove anything through argumentation.[20]

On the contrary: It says in Titus 1:9 that a bishop should "embrace that
faithful word that is according to doctrine, that he may be able to exhort in
sound teaching and to convince the unbelievers."

I answer: As other *scientiae* do not argue in proof of their premises [*prin-
cipia*], but argue from these premises to demonstrate other truths in these

---

18. Here Aquinas accepts the objection's presumption that *scientia* is concerned with the
eternal and unchanging, not the contingent and historical. Thus that with which the *scientia*
of holy teaching is primarily concerned is God, who is eternal and unchanging. However, in
a secondary sense the *scientia* of holy teaching *also* knows those historical events by which the
identity of God has been revealed in the world—such as the deeds of Abraham, Isaac, and
Jacob; as Thomas goes on to argue in 1.1.4, theology is a practical inquiry (i.e., concerned
with human action) as well as a speculative inquiry (i.e., concerned with truth). One might
also add, though Aquinas does not argue this here, that Abraham, Isaac, and Jacob can be the
object of *scientia* because they are known by God in an eternal and unchanging manner (since
God exists outside of time).

19. Aquinas here asks a "modern" question: Is it not pointless to talk about theological
questions? Do not different people simply have different beliefs? Is there any way to decide
between conflicting claims about the nature of God? Is it not all a matter of opinion? As we
shall see, Aquinas's answer to the last question, in particular, is an emphatic "No." In saying
that *sacra doctrina* is "argumentative" he is saying that it uses its own sorts of evidence in order
to arrive at truths about God.

20. The objection states that arguments are based either on authority ("you should have
open heart surgery because your cardiologist recommends it") or on reason ("if all human
beings are mortal and Socrates is a human being, then Socrates is mortal"). Since arguments
from authority are generally taken to be fairly weak (they work only if the person accepts your
authority), and since theology deals with things that surpass human reason, theology should
not proceed by way of argumentation.

scientiae,[21] so too this teaching does not argue in proof of its premises, which are the articles of faith, but rather from them it goes on to prove something else. Thus the Apostle, in 1 Corinthians 15:12, argues from the resurrection of Christ in proof of the general resurrection.[22]

It is to be borne in mind, in regard to the philosophical *scientiae,* that the inferior *scientiae* neither prove their premises nor dispute with those who deny them, but leave this to a higher *scientia.* The highest of them, metaphysics, can dispute with one who denies its premises only if the opponent will make some concession; but if he concede nothing, it can have no dispute with him, though it can answer his objections.[23] Therefore Holy Scripture, since it has no *scientia* above itself,[24] can dispute with one who denies its premises only if the opponent admits at least some of the truths obtained through divine revelation. Thus we can argue with heretics from the sources of holy teaching, and against those who deny one article of faith, we can argue from another.[25] If our opponent believes

21. Note that in most of this article *scientia(e)* has the sense of what we today would call a "discipline"—a body of knowledge that is arrived at starting from certain presuppositions and following certain ways of proceeding.

22. As we have seen in the previous article, Aquinas says that every *scientia* presumes certain premises or "first principles," which it does not seek to prove, but which it uses to prove other things. So, for example, physics presumes certain mathematical laws that it does not attempt to prove. We do not generally think that this makes physics a doubtful matter. Similarly, theology also presumes certain premises, which Aquinas describes as "the articles of faith" (more or less equivalent to the articles of the creed). It does not attempt to prove these articles of faith but uses them to prove other things, as Paul uses the resurrection of Christ to prove our resurrection from the dead.

23. "Lower" or "subaltern" *scientiae* can appeal to a "higher" *scientia* to prove their premises (e.g., physics can appeal to mathematics), but the highest *scientiae* cannot prove their first premises. For example, how could one "prove" that a whole is always bigger than one of its parts? Such premises have a compelling obviousness about them that makes proof unnecessary. Thus in the case of metaphysics (which Aquinas takes to be the highest of the philosophical disciplines), one cannot even get started on a metaphysical argument (such as "what is the nature of reality?") if one is arguing with a person who will not grant such basic premises as the law of noncontradiction (i.e., "A" and "not A" cannot both be true in the same way at the same time). At best, one can argue with such a person only on an ad hoc basis—refuting the specific objections that they raise. In other words, there are some people who are so stubborn or obtuse that you will never convince them. What you *can* do with such people, if they are intellectually honest, is to show them that *their* arguments do not work.

24. Here Thomas is using "Holy Scripture" interchangeably with "holy teaching" (*sacra doctrina*), as a way of naming that authoritative body of knowledge that God shares with humanity through divine revelation to prophets and apostles.

25. If someone acknowledges at last some of the premises of *sacra doctrina* (i.e., the "articles of faith") then one can argue with them in order to reasonably prove another article. For example, since both Jews and Christians accept the prophetic writings in Scripture as divine revelation, a Christian might reasonably argue with a Jew over the question of whether Jesus was the Messiah. Likewise, one can debate with Christian heretics who accept some Christian beliefs but reject others. Thus in the debates over the doctrine of the Trinity in the fourth century, the argument between St. Athanasius and his opponent Arius took the form of a debate over which view fit better with other Christian beliefs.

nothing of divine revelation, there is no longer any means of proving the articles of faith by reasoning, but only of answering his objections, if he has any, against faith.[26] Since faith rests upon infallible truth, and since the contrary of a truth can never be demonstrated, it is clear that the arguments brought against faith cannot be demonstrations, but are difficulties that can be answered.[27]

Reply to 1: Although arguments from human reason cannot serve to prove what must be received on faith, nevertheless, this teaching argues from articles of faith to other truths, as has been said.

Reply to 2: This teaching is especially based upon arguments from authority, since its premises are obtained through revelation; thus we should believe on the authority of those to whom the revelation has been made. Nor does this take away from the dignity of this teaching, for although the argument from authority based on human reason is the weakest, yet the argument from authority based on divine revelation is the strongest.

Nevertheless, holy teaching makes use even of human reason, not indeed to prove faith (for thereby the merit of faith would be taken away), but to make clear other things that are put forward in this teaching. Since therefore grace does not destroy nature but perfects it, natural reason should minister to faith as the natural inclination of the will ministers to charity.[28] Therefore the Apostle

26. In the case of those who completely reject the premises of *sacra doctrina,* the options for reasoned argument are more limited. If someone rejects the divine revelation contained in Scripture entirely, then you are not going to get far in a theological argument with them. What Aquinas thinks you *can* do is to answer their objections on an ad hoc basis—that is, show them how their objections do not disprove Christian claims about God (a similar approach would be required in the case of metaphysics when someone rejects such basic premises as the law of noncontradiction; see note 23, above).

27. A Christian should be confident that even if it is not possible to rationally convince someone of the truth of Christianity, he or she can reasonably answer any objections that are raised, since it is *impossible* to offer a genuine demonstration of untruth, and Christian revelation is based on the highest truth, God.

28. In replying to the objection about the inadequacy of human reason to argue about divine things, Aquinas states what is often taken to be one of the key premises of his thought: "grace does not destroy nature but perfects it." It is surely a mistake to think that Aquinas has an abstract theory—to which he must make his theology conform—about the relationship between our natural capacities as human beings ("nature") and the divine gift that enables us to live in God eternally ("grace"). A better way to think about his point would be to say that if one looks at God's dealings with the world—both in the history revealed in Scripture and in the contemporary life of the church—then it appears that God's typical activity does not override our natural capacities but fulfills them in a way that, paradoxically, exceeds them. Thus, to use Aquinas's example, our will desires certain things by nature—food, sex, and so on—and grace does not destroy our willing but perfects it by making us desire God with the love that Christians call *caritas* (charity). Likewise, we know certain things by the exercise of our natural capacity for knowing (reason). We can also know things through God's revelation, which does not contradict human reason but brings it to a fulfillment beyond itself. So what we know through faith does not contradict what we know through reason, but goes beyond it. One might even say that in the act of faith we do not become *un*reasonable, but in fact become *more* reasonable, through coming to know truths that exceed our reason.

speaks in 2 Corinthians 10:5 of "bringing every understanding into captivity to the obedience of Christ." Therefore holy teaching makes use also of the authority of philosophers in those questions in which they were able to know the truth by natural reason,[29] as Paul quotes a saying of Aratus in Acts 17:28, "As some also of your own poets said, 'For we are also his offspring.'"[30]

Nevertheless, holy teaching makes use of these authorities only as inessential and probable arguments. But it properly uses the authority of the canonical Scriptures as an incontrovertible proof, and the authority of the doctors of the church as one that may properly be used, though merely as probable; for our faith rests upon the revelation made to the apostles and prophets who wrote the canonical books, and not on the revelations (if any such there are) made to other teachers.[31] Therefore Augustine says in a letter to Jerome (epistle 82, no. 1), "Only those books of Scripture that are called canonical have I learned to hold in such honor as to believe their authors have not erred in any way in writing them. But other authors I read in such a way as not to deem everything in their works to be true, merely on account of their having so thought and written, whatever may have been their holiness and learning."

1.1.9

Whether Holy Scripture should use metaphors?[32]

It seems that Holy Scripture should not use metaphors.

1. That which is proper to the lowest kind of teaching does not seem appropriate to this *scientia*, which holds the highest place of all. But to proceed by the aid of various likenesses and representations is proper to poetry, the

---

29. Apparently Aquinas reserves the term "philosophers" exclusively for pagan thinkers.

30. Aratus was a Greek poet from the third century BC. In the book of Acts, Paul is depicted quoting from his astronomical treatise *Phenomena*.

31. Aquinas here ranks authorities. The views of pagan thinkers have a certain authority, but of the lowest sort. Having Aristotle on your side adds force to your argument, but, as Aquinas sees things, it does not prove anything (though one of Aristotle's arguments might). Next would come the views of the "doctors"—those Christian teachers (*doctores*) whose views have been widely accepted by the church. But their authority can establish only the *probability* of something being true and, like the views of the philosophers, they are not of final authority. Finally comes the authority of Scripture, which is supreme, resting as it does on the revelation given to the prophets and apostles. Arguments based on the authority of Scripture can attain a certainty that arguments based on the authority of philosophers and theologians cannot.

32. Here Aquinas takes up the question of how we should think about metaphorical statements in Scripture. By "metaphor," Thomas means specifically those statements that use images of material things in order to speak about God. The problem metaphors present in this context is that the knowledge conveyed by Scripture is supposed to be certain knowledge, and yet, as Thomas knows, not every sentence in Scripture can be taken at face value (e.g., the Bible describes God as "my rock and my redeemer" [Psalm 19:14], but we know God's composition is not mineral). If *sacra doctrina* is supposed to be *scientia*, does not the use of metaphors introduce an element of uncertainty into theology?

least of all teachings. Therefore it is not fitting that this *scientia* should make use of such likenesses.

2. This teaching seems to be intended to make truth clear. Therefore a reward is held out to those who do so; as Sirach 24:31 says, "They that explain me shall have life everlasting." But by such likenesses truth is obscured. Therefore, it is not appropriate to this teaching to convey divine matters by likening them to bodily things.

3. The higher creatures are, the nearer they approach to the divine likeness. If therefore things from creatures are to be applied to God, these should chiefly be taken from the higher creatures, and not from the lower, and this is often found in Scriptures.

On the contrary: It is written in Hosea 12:10, "I have multiplied visions, and I have used likenesses by the ministry of the prophets." But to convey anything by means of a likeness is to use a metaphor. Therefore this holy teaching may use metaphors.

I answer: It is fitting for Holy Scripture to put forward divine and spiritual truths by means of comparisons with material things; for God provides for everything according to the capacity of its nature. Now it is natural to a human being to come to intellectual truths through perceptible objects, because all our knowledge originates from sense.[33] Therefore, in Holy Scripture spiritual truths are fittingly conveyed with bodily metaphors,[34] as Dionysius says in *The Celestial Hierarchy* (chap. 1, no. 2), "We cannot be enlightened by the divine rays unless they be hidden within the covering of many sacred veils."

It is also appropriate to Holy Scripture, which is proposed to all without distinction of persons (as Romans 1:14 says, "To the wise and to the unwise I am a debtor"), that spiritual truths be expounded by means of likenesses taken from bodily things, in order that thereby even the unsophisticated who are unable by themselves to grasp intellectual things may be able to understand it.

Reply to 1: Poetry makes use of metaphors to produce a representation, for it is natural to a person to be pleased with representations. But holy teaching makes use of metaphors as both necessary and useful, as explained above.

33. I have translated Aquinas's term *sensibilis* as "perceptible" rather than as "sensible," which has misleading connotations of "practical" or "down-to-earth" in modern English. The view that "all our knowledge originates from sense" is one of the ways in which Aquinas is a follower of Aristotle, rather than Plato (who believed that we possessed a certain innate or inborn knowledge).

34. The point of there being a Bible is for God to teach us, and, like any good teacher, God adapts his methods to the requirements of his students. Since we are the kind of beings who learn from observation of material things, God uses comparisons with material things (i.e., metaphors) to teach us about spiritual things. The word "metaphor" comes from the Greek meaning "to carry from one place to another." It is interesting to note that in this article Thomas speaks of teaching as *tradere*—the act of transferring or "handing over" (here translated as "convey"). In Scripture, God "hands over" God's own self-knowledge, and this knowledge is "carried" by metaphors from the realm of spiritual truth to the realm of material images, so that human beings can be carried back from the material images to the spiritual truth.

Reply to 2: As Dionysius says (*The Celestial Hierarchy,* chap. 1, no. 2), the ray of divine revelation is not extinguished by the perceptible imagery with which it is veiled, but it remains in its truth, so that it does not allow the minds of those to whom the revelation has been made to rest in the metaphors, but raises them to the knowledge of truths.[35] And through those to whom the revelation has been made others also may receive instruction in these matters. Therefore those things that are taught metaphorically in one part of Scripture are taught more openly in other parts.[36] And the hiding of truth in figures is itself useful for the exercise of thoughtful minds and as a defense against the ridicule of the unfaithful, according to the words of Matthew 7:6, "Do not give that which is holy to dogs."

Reply to 3: As Dionysius says in *The Celestial Hierarchy* (chap. 2, no. 2), it is more fitting that divine matters should be conveyed under the figure of lowly bodies than of noble bodies, and this for three reasons. First, because by this human minds are the better preserved from error; for it is clear that these things are not literal descriptions of divine matters, which is something that might have been open to doubt had they been expressed under the figure of noble bodies, especially for those who could think of nothing nobler than bodies.[37] Second, because this is more appropriate to the knowledge of God that we have in this life; for what God is not is clearer to us than what God is. Therefore likenesses drawn from things farthest away from God form within us a truer estimate that God is above whatever we may say or think of God.[38] Third, because in this way divine truths are the better hidden from the unworthy.

35. The metaphors that Scripture uses should not be thought of as barriers that veil the truth from us; rather, they are media through which the truth is communicated to us. Thus metaphors do not undercut our certainty but make certain truths more available to us.

36. What is to keep us from ascribing all sorts of metaphorical meanings to Scripture? For example, "I am the good shepherd" is obviously a metaphor, since Jesus was a carpenter. But how does the metaphor work? What if we take it to mean "I am primarily concerned with animals whose hair can be made into clothing"? Thomas says that everything in Scripture that is taught metaphorically is elsewhere in Scripture taught nonmetaphorically. Since Scripture nowhere teaches that Jesus is more concerned with wool-producing animals than with people, this cannot be the metaphorical meaning of "I am the good shepherd." However, Scripture does teach that Jesus cares for us and is even willing to give his life for us, so this would be an acceptable meaning for the metaphor. See also the reply to objection 1 in the next article.

37. Why not use more exalted metaphors for God, such as "God is the supreme being"? "Supreme being" sounds impressively philosophical, but it is still a metaphor. Aquinas prefers the more down-to-earth metaphors of Scripture, because although we are not likely to think that God is a rock or a sheep herder, we might think that God is literally something called "the supreme being." The advantage of biblical metaphors is that they are so obviously not to be taken nonmetaphorically.

38. In everything that Aquinas says about God it is important to remember that he thinks we have a better grasp on what God is *not* than we do on what God *is*. Aquinas says a great many things about God, but it is important to recognize how often these are *negative* statements about God: God is omnipresent (meaning that God is *not* confined to a particular location, the way that we are); God is eternal (meaning that God's life is *not* lived within the stream of time, the way that ours is).

1.1.10

Whether in Holy Scripture a word may have several senses?

It seems that in Holy Scripture a word cannot have several senses: historical or literal, allegorical, tropological or moral, and anagogical.[39]

1. Many different senses in one text produce confusion and deception and destroy all force of argument. Therefore no reasoned argumentation, but only fallacies, can be deduced from a multiplicity of propositions. But Holy Scripture should be able to state the truth without any fallacy. Therefore in Scripture one word should not convey several senses.

2. Augustine says in the book *On the Usefulness of Believing* (chap. 3, no. 5) that "the writing called the Old Testament has a fourfold meaning: namely, according to history, according to etiology, according to analogy, and according to allegory." Now these four seem altogether different from the four divisions mentioned above. Therefore it does not seem fitting to explain the same word of Holy Scripture according to the four different senses mentioned above.

---

39. Here Aquinas names what is sometimes called the fourfold meaning (or "sense") of Scripture. Prior to the sixteenth century, Christians generally thought of Scripture as having four "levels" of meaning. First, a word or a sentence or a story had its "literal" or "historical" sense, which is simply what the words mean. Then, a passage might have a "spiritual" sense, which was further subdivided into three: the typological (or allegorical) sense, which refers to how things of the Old Testament point forward to their fulfillment in the New Testament; the tropological or moral sense, which refers to what a passage might teach us about our spiritual lives; and the anagogical sense, which refers to what a passage has to say about our ultimate destiny. It was generally thought that the more spiritually adept one became as a reader of Scripture, the more deeply one could penetrate these levels of meaning.

Of course, this way of interpreting the biblical text is confusing to us, since most people today do not read the Bible in this way. An example might help clarify the matter. Consider the word "Jerusalem." Its fourfold sense might be taken to be as follows:

literal:	a city in Palestine
typological:	the church
moral:	the soul
anagogical:	heaven

Now imagine that you are Thomas Aquinas, sitting in church with your fellow Dominicans and chanting the Psalms. You sing Psalm 137: "If I forget you, O Jerusalem, let my right hand wither!" You know that on a literal level "Jerusalem" refers to the city in Palestine and that for the writer of the psalm it was imperative to remember that city because it was there, in the Jewish temple, that God was worshiped by means of animal and other sacrifices. But for you as a Christian it does not seem imperative to remember that city, because Jesus's offering of himself on the cross has made the sacrifice of animals unnecessary. Yet you are praying this psalm, so presumably it means something that you would actually want to say to God, something more than anything you might want to say about the city in Palestine. And so, on the spiritual level, you can take "Jerusalem" to mean the church, the living temple in which God is worshiped through the Eucharist; or you can take it as a reference to your soul, which you must remember and care for, lest you wither and die spiritually; or you can let the word direct your mind to heaven—the eternal vision of God—which must be the constant goal of your life. These levels of meaning make it possible for a Christian like Thomas to give voice to his prayer through the words of the psalm.

3. Besides these senses, there is the parabolical, which is not one of these four.[40]

On the contrary: Gregory says in his *Moralia in Job* (bk. 20, chap. 1, no. 1), "Holy Scripture, by the manner of its speech, transcends every *scientia,* because in one and the same sentence, while it describes a fact, it reveals a mystery."

I answer: The author of Holy Scripture is God, who has it in his power to signify his meaning, not by words only (as a person also can do), but also by things themselves.[41] So, while in every other *scientia* things are referred to by words, this *scientia* has the property that the things referred to by the words also themselves have a reference. Therefore that first kind of referring, in which words refer to things, belongs to the first sense: the historical or literal. That second kind of referring, in which things referred to by words also have a reference, is called the spiritual sense, which is based on the literal, and presupposes it.[42]

This spiritual sense has a threefold division. As the Apostle says in Hebrews 10:1, the Old Law is a prefiguration of the New Law, and the New Law itself, as Dionysius says in *The Ecclesiastical Hierarchy* (chap. 5, no. 2), "is a figure of future glory."[43] Again, in the New Law, whatever acts are done by [Christ] our head are signs of what we should do. Therefore, so far as the things of the Old Law signify the things of the New Law, there is the allegorical sense; so far as the things done in Christ, or so far as the things that signify Christ, are signs of what we should do, there is the moral sense; and insofar as those things related to eternal glory are signified, there is the anagogical sense.

Since the literal sense is that which the author intends, and since the author of Holy Scripture is God, who by one act comprehends all things by his intellect, it is not unfitting, as Augustine says in the *Confessions* (bk. 12, chap. 31, no. 5), if, even according to the literal sense, one word in Holy Scripture should have several senses.[44]

Reply to 1: The multiplicity of these senses does not produce equivocation or any other kind of multiplicity, for these senses are not multiplied because

40. By "parabolical" Aquinas seems to mean the same thing as "metaphorical" (see the example given in the reply to this objection).

41. God speaks to us not simply through words, but through things and events. Thus, for example, through King David and the events surrounding him God speaks to us of Christ. One might say that historical events have God as their "author."

42. Here Aquinas clarifies the rationale for the distinction between literal and spiritual meanings. The "literal sense" is how *words* refer to *things* (i.e., how the word "Jerusalem" is a "sign" pointing to the city in Palestine). The "spiritual sense" is how *things* refer to *other things* (i.e., how the city of Jerusalem is a "sign" pointing to the church or the soul or heaven).

43. When Aquinas speaks of things being "figures" of other things, we might think in terms of "foreshadowing." Thus for Aquinas the animal sacrifices of the Old Covenant are "figures" of the sacrifice of Jesus on the cross.

44. The literal sense is related to the intention of the speaker. If I use the word "Alexandria" intending to refer to a city in Egypt and you take me to be referring to a city in northern Virginia, then you have misunderstood me. However, God can intend to say an infinite multitude of things with the same word or event, even on the literal level.

one word signifies several things, but because the things signified by the words can themselves be signs of other things.[45] Thus in Holy Scripture no confusion results, for all the senses are founded on one—that is to say, the literal—and only from this sense can any argument be drawn, and not from those intended in allegory, as Augustine says in his letter to Vincent the Donatist (epistle 93, chap. 8, no. 24). Nevertheless, nothing of Holy Scripture perishes on account of this, since nothing necessary to faith is contained under the spiritual sense that is not elsewhere put forward by the Scripture in its literal sense.[46]

Reply to 2: These three—history, etiology, analogy—all pertain to the literal sense. "History," as Augustine explains (epistle 93), is when something is simply recounted; "etiology" is when its cause is assigned, as when our Lord gave "the reason why Moses allowed the putting away of wives—namely, on account of the hardness of men's hearts (Matthew 19:8); "analogy" is when the truth of one text of Scripture is shown not to contradict the truth of another. Of the four named, allegory stands by itself for the three spiritual senses. Thus Hugh of St. Victor (*On the Sacraments of the Christian Faith*, bk. 1, prologue, chap. 4) includes the anagogical under the allegorical sense, laying down three senses only—the historical, the allegorical, and the tropological.

Reply to 3: The parabolical sense is contained in the literal, for through words something is signified both properly and figuratively. Nor is the literal sense the figure itself, but that which is figured. When Scripture speaks of God's arm, the literal sense is not that God has such a bodily member, but that which is signified by this member, namely, operative power.[47] Therefore it is plain that nothing false can ever underlie the literal sense of Holy Scripture.

45. If the word itself had multiple meanings, this would be a case of equivocation; but the multiple sense of Scripture is not based on the multiple meanings of words, but on the further meanings of the things and events to which the words refer.

46. As with metaphors, so too with spiritual meanings: nothing is said by means of a spiritual meaning that is not elsewhere said by means of a literal meaning. So, for example, "Jerusalem" in Psalm 137 cannot be taken allegorically to signify the city of Paris, since Scripture nowhere assigns salvific importance to the city of Paris.

47. Aquinas's point is that the spiritual meaning of a text is *not* the same thing as the metaphorical meaning. In fact, a metaphorical meaning is a *literal* meaning, because it is a case of words referring to things and not of things referring to things. Although metaphorical statements do not refer to things in the same *way* as nonmetaphorical statements, they are still cases of "literal" reference. Thus, in the example Aquinas gives here, the words "God's arm" refer to a thing—God's power to act. In our Jerusalem example, the word "Jerusalem" refers *literally* to the city, which in turn refers *spiritually* to the church or the soul or heaven.

THE EXISTENCE OF GOD

1.2.1

Whether the existence of God is self-evident?

It seems that the existence of God is self-evident.[1]

1. Things are said to be self-evident to us when the knowledge of them is naturally implanted in us, as we can see in the case of first principles. But as John of Damascus says (*On the Orthodox Faith,* bk. 1, chap. 3), "the knowledge of God is naturally implanted in all." Therefore the existence of God is self-evident.

2. Things are said to be self-evident when they are grasped as soon as the meaning of their terms is grasped, which the Philosopher says is true of the first principles of demonstration (*Posterior Analytics,* bk. 1, chap. 3, 72ᵇ). Thus, when the nature of a whole and of a part is known, it is at once recognized that every whole is greater than its part. But as soon as the signification of the word "God" is understood, it is seen at once that God exists; for by this word is signified that thing than which nothing greater can be conceived. But that which exists in reality and in the mind is greater than that which exists only in

---

1. It is helpful to think of this article and the one immediately following as something like bookends between which Aquinas wants to position our knowledge of God's existence. In essence, Aquinas argues in these two articles that God's existence cannot be a premise or first principle, but can still be known without going beyond the natural human faculty for knowing.

the mind.[2] Therefore, since God exists in the mind as soon as the word "God" is understood, it also follows that he exists in reality. Therefore the proposition "God exists" is self-evident.

3. The existence of truth is self-evident, for whoever denies the existence of truth grants that truth does not exist; and, if truth does not exist, then the proposition "Truth does not exist" is true; and if there is anything true, then truth must exist.[3] But God is truth itself, according to John 14:6, "I am the way, the truth, and the life." Therefore "God exists" is self-evident.

On the contrary: No one can think the opposite of what is self-evident, as the Philosopher states concerning the first principles of demonstration (*Metaphysics*, bk. 4, chap. 3, 1005[b]; *Posterior Analytics*, bk. 1, chap. 10, 76[b]). But the opposite of the proposition "God is" can be thought, for according to the Psalm 53:1, "The fool said in his heart, 'There is no God.'" Therefore, that God exists is not self-evident.[4]

I answer: A thing can be self-evident in either of two ways: on the one hand, self-evident in itself, though not to us; on the other, self-evident in itself, and to us. A proposition is self-evident because the predicate is included in the meaning of the subject, as in the case of "a human being is an animal," since "animal" is contained in the definition of "human being."[5] If, therefore, the definition of the predicate and subject be known to all, the proposition will be self-evident to all, as is clear with regard to the first principles of demonstration, the terms of which are common things that no one is ignorant of,

2. This objection gives a succinct presentation of what is sometimes called the "ontological argument" for God's existence, which, in essence, says that if "God" is defined as "that than which no greater thing can be conceived" then God must necessarily exist, since it is a greater thing to exist than not to exist. A perfect being that existed only in one's mind would not be the greatest thing that could be conceived, since we can conceive of a perfect being who exists in the mind *and* in reality. A form of this argument is found in Descartes (1596–1650), though it is most famously associated with the *Proslogion* of St. Anselm (ca. 1033–1109). It is worth noting that Anselm's *Proslogion* takes the form of a prayer addressed to God and not of a philosophical argument. Thus, it is not clear that Anselm thinks of himself as offering a "proof" of God's existence so much as a probing exploration of the logic of the term "God," undertaken within the context of faith and prayer.

3. This objection offers the standard refutation of various forms of skepticism and relativism—namely, if I say that nothing can be known with certainty, this sounds like something I am certain about.

4. It is good to bear in mind that in discussing this question Aquinas is speaking of propositions or statements, which consist of a subject and a predicate. So when he asks whether the existence of God is self-evident, what he is really asking is whether the truth of the statement "God exists" is immediately and necessarily grasped by those who hear it, in the same way as, for example, the statement "a whole is bigger than its parts." Another way to put this same point would be to ask whether God's existence can serve as a first principle for human *scientia,* where *scientia* is taken in its normal sense (1.1, note 20). As we shall see in the body of this article, Thomas's answer will be "no."

5. Aquinas, following Aristotle, defines human beings as "rational animals" (i.e., animals capable of abstract thought). So "human beings are animals" is a self-evident proposition since its predicate, "animals," is contained in the definition of the subject ("human beings").

such as "being" and "nonbeing," "whole" and "part," and similar things.[6] If, however, there are some to whom the definition of the predicate and subject is unknown, the proposition will be self-evident in itself, but not to those who do not know the meaning of the predicate and subject of the proposition.[7] Therefore, it happens, as Boethius says in the book *De hebdomadibus,* that there are some mental concepts self-evident only to the learned, such as "incorporeal substances are not in space."

Therefore I say that this proposition, "God exists," is in itself self-evident, for the predicate is the same as the subject, because God is his own existence, as will be shown later (1.3.4). But because we do not know what God is, the proposition is not self-evident to us,[8] but needs to be demonstrated by things that are more known to us, though less known by their nature—namely, God's effects.[9]

Reply to 1: To know in a general and confused way that God exists is implanted in us by nature, since God is the ultimate happiness [*beatitudo*] of human beings;[10] for a human being naturally desires happiness, and what is naturally desired by a person must be naturally known to him. This, however, is not to know absolutely that God exists, just as knowing that someone is approaching is not the same as knowing that Peter is approaching, even though it *is* Peter who is approaching; for there are many who imagine that the perfect good of human beings, which is happiness, consists in riches, and others in pleasures, and others in something else.[11]

Reply to 2: Perhaps not everyone who hears this word "God" understands it to signify something than which nothing greater can be thought, since some

6. Thomas seems to think that a grasp of some concepts (e.g., "whole" and "part") is so basic to the human form of life that we can safely presume that all human beings possess it.

7. Here it is helpful to remember that Aquinas is talking about the structure of propositions. The basic distinction on which this article turns is that between something being self-evident in itself and something being self-evident to us. A proposition can be self-evident in itself, even if no one recognizes it as true, so long as the predicate forms part of the definition of the subject. This understanding, of course, presumes that definitions are somehow written into the fabric of reality and are not simply conventions.

This point is important in order not to misinterpret what follows. Aquinas's point is *not* that God's existence is evident to God but not to us (though this is true), but that the proposition "God exists" is a self-evident proposition, though it is not evident to us. Aquinas is not making a claim about God's self-awareness, but about the status of a proposition.

8. "God exists" cannot be self evident to us because we do not have a definition of "God." This is perhaps Thomas's real concern here: to insure that we do not think that we can grasp what it is for God to be God.

9. Thomas takes up the subject of the knowledge of God through God's effects in the next article.

10. The Latin *beatitudo* can mean either "blessedness" or "happiness," and might loosely be translated as "fulfillment."

11. In other words, although everyone pursues happiness, not everyone identifies that happiness with "God." Therefore, the proposition "God exists" would not be self-evident to such a person.

have believed God to be a body.[12] Yet, granted that everyone understands that something than which nothing greater can be thought is signified by this word "God," nevertheless, it does not follow that they understand that what the word signifies exists in reality, but only that it exists in the mind. Nor can it be argued that it exists in reality unless it be admitted that there actually exists something than which nothing greater can be thought; and this is precisely what is not admitted by those who hold that God does not exist.[13]

Reply to 3: The existence of truth in general is self-evident, but the existence of a First Truth is not self-evident to us.

1.2.2

Whether it can be demonstrated that God exists?
It seems that the existence of God cannot be demonstrated.

1. It is an article of faith that God exists. But what is of faith cannot be demonstrated, because a demonstration produces the knowledge called *scientia;* whereas faith is of the unseen, as is clear from the Apostle in Hebrews 11:1.[14] Therefore it cannot be demonstrated that God exists.

2. The middle term of a demonstration is "that which something is" [*quod quid est*].[15] But we cannot know what God is, but only what he is not,[16] as John of Damascus says (*On the Orthodox Faith*, bk. 1, chap. 4). Therefore we cannot demonstrate that God exists.

3. If the existence of God were demonstrated, this could be only from his effects. But his effects are not proportionate to him, since he is infinite and his

12. A material being (i.e., a "body"), because it is perishable, is inferior to a spiritual being, which is imperishable.

13. Thomas here makes the point that there can be no necessary passage from mental existence to actual existence, unless one already admits that there is a highest actual being. Thomas's rejection of the so-called ontological argument is related to a distinction he makes in his early work *De ente et essentia* between the essence of a thing (*what* it is) and the existence of a thing (the fact *that* it is). The actual existence of a thing is something different from its definition; we can have a definition of a unicorn or the current king of France without there actually existing a unicorn or a current king of France. The existence of unicorns or French kings must be demonstrated. Although Aquinas thinks that God in fact *is* that than which no greater can be thought *and* that God's essence is identical with his existence, he also thinks that these are things that must be demonstrated.

14. On the relationship between *scientia* and "seeing" see 1.1, note 13.

15. What Aquinas here calls a "middle term" (*medium*) is also known as the "minor premise" in a logical argument. The classic example would be:

Socrates is a man. (major premise)
All men are mortal. (minor premise or "middle term")
Therefore Socrates is mortal. (conclusion)

Note that the minor premise offers a partial definition of "man"—to be human is to be mortal.

16. See 1.1, note 38.

effects are finite, and between the finite and infinite there is no proportion. Therefore, since a cause cannot be demonstrated by a disproportionate effect, it seems that the existence of God cannot be demonstrated.

On the contrary: The Apostle says in Romans 1:20, "The invisible things of God are clearly seen, being understood by the things that are made."[17] But this would not be the case unless the existence of God could be demonstrated through the things that are made, for the first thing we must know of anything is whether it exists.

I answer: Demonstration can be made in two ways. One is through the cause, and is called *propter quid,* and this is to argue from what is prior in an absolute sense.[18] The other is through the effect, and is called a *demonstratio quia*; this is to argue from what is prior relative to us.[19] When an effect is better known to us than its cause, we proceed from the effect to the knowledge of the cause. And from every effect the existence of its proper cause can be demonstrated, so long as its effects are better known to us; for if the effect exists, the cause must pre-exist, since every effect depends upon its cause. Therefore the existence of God, insofar as it is not self-evident to us, can be demonstrated from those effects that are known to us.

Reply to 1: The existence of God and other such truths about God that can be known by natural reason, as is said in Romans 1:19, are not articles of faith but are preambles to the articles; for faith presupposes natural knowledge, even as grace presupposes nature, and perfection supposes something that can be perfected.[20] Nevertheless, there is nothing to prevent someone who cannot grasp a proof from accepting as a matter of faith something that in itself is capable of being demonstrated and known with the knowledge of *scientia*.[21]

17. Romans 1:19–20 is a much-used text by those who want to say that we can know God by observing the world because the world is an effect of which God is the cause.

18. *Propter quid* might be translated as "on account of which" and refers to arguments that move from a known cause to an unknown effect.

19. *Demonstratio quia* might be translated as a "demonstration that"—in other words, a demonstration that moves from a perceived effect to the existence of an unperceived cause. A cause, by its very nature, is prior to its effect: there must be smoke in order for there to be fire. But we may know the effect before we know the cause: we see the smoke on the horizon.

20. See 1.1, note 28.

21. In this response to the objection Aquinas distinguishes the *articuli fidei* from the *praeambula fidei*. The articles of faith are those things that cannot be known apart from revelation, whereas the preambles of faith *can* be known simply by the exercise of human reason observing the world. However, two things should be noted about these preambles: the knowledge they give us is limited and defective (see 1.1, note 8, and 1.12, note 5), and some people—indeed, many—come to know the content of these preambles (e.g., God's existence) not through the exercise of natural reason, but through the teaching of revelation. And, of course, those who come to know God's existence through revelation know it differently from those who know it through the exercise of natural reason: those who know God's existence through reason know simply *that* God exists, but those who know God through revelation know, at least implicitly, all that revelation teaches about God.

Reply to 2: When the existence of a cause is demonstrated from an effect, this effect takes the place of the definition of the cause in proving the cause's existence. This is especially the case in regard to God, because in order to prove the existence of anything it is necessary to accept as a middle term "that which the word means," and not "that which it is" [*quod quid est*]; for the question "what is it?" follows after the question "is it?"[22] Now the words applied to God are derived from his effects; consequently, in demonstrating the existence of God from his effects, we may take for the middle term the meaning of the word "God."[23]

Reply to 3: From effects not proportionate to the cause no perfect knowledge of that cause can be obtained. Yet from every effect the existence of the cause can be clearly demonstrated, and so we can demonstrate the existence of God from his effects, though from them we cannot perfectly know God as he is in his essence.[24]

1.2.3

Whether God exists?[25]

It seems that God does not exist.

22. Here Thomas is anticipating the distinction between essence and existence discussed in the notes to 1.3.4, below.

23. Thomas's point here is that in arguing for *why* something is the case, one needs a definition in the middle term of the demonstration. Thus, Socrates is mortal because he is a man and because all men are mortal. However, in arguing *that* something is the case, it is necessary merely to have an effect of that thing in the middle term. Thus a demonstration of God's existence would be something like:

"God" is what the world's cause is called. (major premise)

The world exists. (minor premise or "middle term")

Therefore God exists. (conclusion)

Now it remains to be argued that "God" is something distinct from the world itself (i.e., that the world is not its own cause), and this is what Thomas does in the next article.

24. See note 13, above, and 1.12, note 4.

25. This article contains what have come to be called the "five ways" by which Aquinas proves the existence of God. It is important to have a sense of what Aquinas is and is not doing in this article. Many people overestimate what Thomas *is* doing. He wishes to demonstrate that what we know about the world still leaves us with the question "Why is there anything at all?" and that the answer to that question is what people commonly call "God." This is, in a sense, a fairly modest project. Thomas is simply trying to demonstrate that the question "Why?" is legitimate not simply in reference to this or that thing, but in reference to *every*thing; and it is legitimate because it is a question that has an answer (in the way that a question like "Is the sofa sad?" does not). When we ask why there is anything at all, may not know the answer, but we use "God" (that is, the God who can be known by the exercise of our natural reason) as something like the placeholder for whatever that answer might be. Of course, Thomas also thinks that reason can go on to discern of God such attributes as "simplicity," "eternity," and so forth. Thomas does *not* think, however, that what he is doing in this article is proving the existence of the Christian God. Rather he is pointing to features of the world that indicate that the world cannot account for its own existence. Thomas does this not to prove to the atheist that God exists (though an atheist *may* be convinced by what Thomas says) but to show that the normal way in which people use the word "God" is not nonsensical; indeed, this usage fits with our observation of the kind of world we live in.

1. If one of two contraries be infinite, the other would be altogether destroyed. But the word "God" means that he is infinite goodness. If, therefore, God existed, no evil would ever be encountered. But there is evil in the world. Therefore God does not exist.[26]

2. It is superfluous to suppose that what can be accounted for by a few principles has been produced by many. But it seems that everything we see in the world can be accounted for by other principles, supposing God did not exist; for all natural things can be traced back to one principle, which is nature; and all voluntary things can be traced back to one principle, which is human reason or will. Therefore there is no need to suppose God's existence.[27]

On the contrary: In Exodus 3:14 God is shown saying, "I am who am."[28]

I answer: The existence of God can be proved in five ways.[29]

The first and most obvious way is the argument from motion [*motus*].[30] It is certain, and evident to our senses, that in the world some things are in motion. But whatever moves [*movetur*] is moved [*movetur*] by something else,[31] for nothing can be moved unless it has a potential for that toward which it is moved;

26. At first glance this objection seems to be the rather jejune one of "How can there be a good God when there is so much suffering in the world?" A second glance reveals that the objection is much more subtle than that. The objector points out that "God" is usually taken to mean a being of infinite goodness. Yet if God is *infinite* goodness, then this would leave no "room" for evil in the world. But there is evil in the world; therefore there cannot be a being of infinite goodness.

27. This objection states that for every individual thing in the world we can find a cause—that is, a reason why it exists. Therefore God is a superfluous proposition, very much in the way he is for certain modern Darwinians.

The objections in this article are best understood if taken together. The first says that the existence of an infinite God would overwhelm a finite world, in effect leaving no room for anything that is not God (e.g., evil). The second says that since everything in the world can be accounted for by some finite thing there is no room for an infinite God. Thomas's response to both of these objections is implicit in his conception of the relationship between God and the world: it is a mistake to think of God as an "object" that competes for room with the other objects that make up the world.

28. God's reply to Moses when he inquires after God's name. Étienne Gilson referred to this reply as "the metaphysics of Exodus."

29. The first three of the five ways are similar to each other. I will explain the first in some detail, and then the second and third should be easy to understand.

30. *Motus* does not mean simply "motion," but might also mean, at least in this context, "change." Thomas follows Aristotle (*Categories* 14, 15ª) in seeing at least three distinct sorts of *motus*: any alteration or qualitative change; a change of size; and a change of location. Only the last of these is what we would normally call "motion" in English. However, I have retained the translation "motion," not least because this first argument is often referred to as the "argument from motion."

31. The Latin word *movetur* is the passive form of the verb *movere* and can mean either the intransitive "moves" (as in "Bob moves across the room") or the passive "is moved" (as in "Bob is moved across the room by Sally"). Thomas's use of the passive form introduces some ambiguity into his argument, since it somewhat prejudices him toward the view that whatever moves (*movetur*) is moved (*movetur*) by something else. I have translated it according to my own sense of what best fits the particular context.

whereas something moves [something else] inasmuch as it is actual, since motion is nothing other than the transition of something from potentiality to actuality. But nothing can be moved from potentiality to actuality except by something in a state of actuality. Thus that which is actually hot, such as fire, makes wood, which is potentially hot, to be actually hot, and thereby moves and changes it.[32] Now it is impossible for the same thing to be simultaneously actual and potential with regard to the same thing, but only with regard to different things: for example, what is actually hot cannot simultaneously be potentially hot, but it is simultaneously potentially cold. It is therefore impossible that something should, in the same way and with regard to the same thing, be both mover and moved, that is to say, that it should move itself.[33] Therefore, whatever is in motion must be put in motion by another. If that by which it is put in motion is itself put in motion, then this also must be put in motion by another, and that by another again.[34] But this cannot go on to infinity, because then there would be no first mover, and, consequently, no other mover, because secondary movers do not move unless they are put in motion by the first mover, as with a stick that moves only because it is put in motion by a hand.[35] Therefore it is

32. A novice reader of Thomas is probably thoroughly confused at this point, and a somewhat freer translation might help: "We see things changing. Now anything changing is being changed by something else. For things changing are on their way to realization, whereas things causing change are already realized: they are realizing something else's potential, and for that they must themselves be real. The actual heat of a fire causes wood, already able to be hot, to become actually hot, and so causes change in the wood"; see *Summa Theologiae: A Concise Translation*, ed. and trans. Timothy McDermott (Allen, Tex.: Christian Classics, 1989), 12.

Aquinas draws his account of change from Aristotle: a thing changes by becoming in reality something that it is potentially. So, to use Aquinas's example, a piece of wood is potentially on fire; for it to burn is for it to actualize that potential. So then how is it that some things come to actualize one particular potential rather than another (after all, a piece of wood is also potentially a club)? Only, Aquinas says, when something that has *already* actualized that potential acts upon these things. Thus wood (potential fire) burns because it comes into contact with a flame (actual fire). With respect to its potential to burn, a burning piece of wood is said to be "in act."

33. In other words, nothing changes itself; it is always changed by something else. Things do not really spontaneously combust; they burn because something acts upon them. Being *potentially* something and being *actually* something are mutually exclusive.

34. Here Thomas points out that this account of change is true of *everything* in the world. Everything changes, and nothing changes itself. One might ask, however, whether Thomas has really demonstrated this claim. Wood burning is an example that supports the claim, but what about helium rising? Is something acting upon helium to make it realize its "upward" potential? Examples like this may at least make contestable the claim that all change is accounted for by something with a realized potential acting upon something with an unrealized potential.

35. Two points of clarification: First, Thomas denies the possibility of an infinite regress of causes because, in effect, he thinks that "Why?" is always an appropriate question to ask about features of our world; indeed, he thinks it an appropriate question to ask about the world *as a whole*. To grant the possibility of an infinite regress would be in effect to say that the question "Why is there something rather than nothing?" is a nonsensical question (see note 25, above). Second, despite Thomas's way of putting things, it is misleading to think of a "chain" of movers stretching back until we get to God, who is at the end of the chain as prime mover. In his

necessary to arrive at a first mover, which is not moved by anything else; and this everyone understands to be God.[36]

The second way is from the nature of the efficient cause.[37] In the perceptible world we find that there is an order of efficient causes; but we do not find, nor could we find, anything that is the efficient cause of itself, for in that case it would be prior to itself, which is impossible. Now in efficient causes it is not possible to go on to infinity, because in every ordered series of efficient causes the first is the cause of the intermediate cause, and the intermediate is the cause of the ultimate cause, whether there are many intermediate causes or only one. But to take away the cause is to take away the effect; therefore, if there were no first cause among efficient causes, there would be no ultimate, nor any intermediate, cause. But if efficient causes were to go on to infinity, there would be no first efficient cause, neither would there be an ultimate effect, nor any intermediate efficient causes—all of which is plainly false. Therefore it is necessary to accept some first efficient cause, to which everyone gives the name of God.[38]

---

discussion of whether the idea of "creation" necessarily implies a beginning in time (1.46.2), Thomas makes it clear that he does not conceive of such a chain. He says that what we mean by "creation" is a relationship of existential dependence, which does not necessitate that the creator be temporally prior. So even though (on the basis of revelation) Thomas thinks that God creates "in the beginning," he is not presuming that God is part of the chain of causes. This would be a problem because such a conception would hold that God is an "object" in our world, essentially like other objects, with the exception that he is self-actualizing. Aquinas denies that God is a being like other beings in the world; God is not an object that can be "placed" in our world (see note 27, above).

It is better to think of a chain of movers that is potentially of infinite length. The idea of the unmoved mover (or unchanged changer) is not to be found at the end of the chain, but in the answer to the question, "Why is there a chain of causes at all?" In other words, the reason for there being an actual world rather than simply a potential world must be found outside the world, in something that is itself in no need of being actualized, in a being that is, as Aquinas will put it, "pure act"—completely actualized existence. Of course, as noted above, Aquinas does not think the chain of causes *is* of infinite length, but he believes that it is only possible to know this because of divine revelation: "*In the beginning* God created the heavens and the earth."

36. Each of the five ways concludes in something like this manner. Aquinas is appealing here to the ordinary use of the word "God."

37. An "efficient cause" is that which causes something to occur; it brings about the existence of a state of affairs. In modern thinking, this is typically what we mean when we say that something is a "cause." Thomas, however, has a much richer vocabulary of causation than we do, one taken over from Aristotle. In addition to efficient causality, there is also "material causality," or that matter from which something is made; "formal causality," or the character of a thing by which it is what it is (see 1.12, note 1); and "final causality," or the goal or purpose of something (see note 49, below). Thus a table has a carpenter as its efficient cause, wood as its material cause, "tableness" as its formal cause, and being used for meals (or some other activity) as its final cause.

38. The similarities between this second way and the first one should be obvious. In fact, what is less obvious is how it is *different* from the first way. Étienne Gilson argues in his book *The Elements of Christian Philosophy* (New York: Doubleday and Co., 1960) that Thomas enriches Aristotle's four causes by distinguishing between Aristotle's "moving cause," which is the

The third way is taken from possibility and necessity, and goes like this:[39] we find among things those that have the possibility of existing or not existing, since they are found to be generated, and to corrupt, and consequently have the possibility of existing or not existing.[40] But it is impossible for everything like this always to exist,[41] for that which has the possibility of not existing, at some time is not. Therefore, if everything has the possibility of not existing, then at one time there could have been nothing in existence.[42] But if this were true, even now there would be nothing in existence, because that which does not exist only begins to exist through something already existing. Therefore, if at one time nothing was in existence, it would have been impossible for anything to have begun to exist; and thus even now nothing would exist—which is obviously false.[43] Therefore, not all beings are merely possible, but there must exist something with necessary existence. Now every necessary thing either has its necessity caused by something else, or it does not. But it is impossible to go on to infinity in necessary things that have their necessity caused by another, as has been already proved in regard to efficient causes.[44] Therefore one must posit the existence of something that is necessary in itself, not receiving its necessity from another thing, but rather causing the necessity of other things. This is what everyone speaks of as God.[45]

The fourth way is taken from the gradation to be found in things. One finds among things that there are some more and some less good, true, noble,

---

reason for something that exists undergoing change, and an "efficient cause" strictly speaking, which is the reason for something beginning to exist at all. On Gilson's reading, the first way still operates within the Aristotelian understanding of God as the cause of change in things, whereas the second way moves to a more specifically Christian understanding of God as the cause of the existence of things.

39. Again, the similarity to the first two ways is obvious. Here Aquinas points out yet another feature of the world: everything in it could conceivably not exist.

40. At least some (if not all) of the things we encounter in the world have a *contingent* existence: they can come into existence and pass out of existence.

41. This translates "*impossibile est autem omnia quae sunt talia, semper esse*," which is the reading from the Leonine edition of the *Summa*. The earlier Piana edition, which some scholars favor on this point, reads, "*impossibile est autem omnia quae sunt, talia esse*," which translates as "but it is impossible for everything to be like this."

42. Given an infinite amount of time, all possibilities would at some point be realized. But if everything is contingent, and therefore has the possibility of not existing, then at some point the possibility of every contingent thing not existing would have been realized and at that point there would have been nothing.

43. See the first two ways: whatever comes to be has a cause (which must be some existing thing). But if at some point nothing existed, then there would be no causes to bring about existence.

44. Aquinas grants the possibility that there may be things in this world that have necessary existence (e.g., angels), but he says that they would have a "caused" necessity—that is, even though they might exist in such a way that they do not pass out of existence, this existence would still be derived from something else and therefore might not have been.

45. In other words, there must be something that lacks the possibility of nonexistence. But if everything in the world has that possibility, then something that lacks that possibility must not be an object in our world (i.e., it must be what people call "God").

and so forth. But "more" and "less" are said of different things insofar as they approach, in their different ways, something that is the maximum, as in the case of a thing being said to be hotter insofar as it most nearly resembles that which is hottest. There is, therefore, something that is truest, something best, something noblest, and, consequently, something that is most fully in being, for those things that are truest are most fully in being, as it is written in *Metaphysics* (bk. 2, chap. 1, 993ᵇ).[46] It is said in the same book that the maximum in any genus is the cause of everything in that genus, as, for example, fire, which is the maximum heat, is the cause of all hot things. Therefore there must also be something that is to all beings [*entibus*] the cause of their existence [*esse*],[47] goodness, and every other perfection; and this we call God.[48]

The fifth way is taken from the governance of things. We see that some things that lack awareness—that is, natural bodies—act so as to obtain a goal, which is evident from their acting always, or nearly always, in the same way, so as to obtain the best result. Therefore it is plain that they do not achieve their end by chance, but by intention.[49] But whatever lacks awareness cannot move toward an end unless directed by something endowed with awareness and intelligence, as the arrow is directed by the archer.[50] Therefore, there is something intelligent by which all natural things are directed to their end, and this we call God.[51]

Reply to 1: As Augustine says in the *Enchiridion on Faith, Hope, and Love* (chap. 11), "Since God is the highest good, he would not allow any evil to

46. See 1.1, note 2.

47. On the significance of *esse,* see 1.3, note 1.

48. The fourth way clearly differs from the preceding three. It focuses on the fact that we make qualitative judgments about things—that is to say, we use the language of good and better, less and more. Aquinas notes that this use of language seems to have built into its logic the notion of that which is "highest" or "greatest" or "best." But note also that by the end of the fourth way Aquinas is back to the notion of God as cause, not simply of this thing or that thing, but of *everything* in its totality: "something that is to all beings the cause of their existence, goodness, and every other perfection."

49. Aquinas's view of the world is "teleological," meaning that he thinks of everything in the world as acting so as to attain a goal or "end" (in Greek, *telos*). For example, we might say that a tree grows leaves in the spring for the purpose of performing photosynthesis. Photosynthesis is the point (goal/end/purpose) of growing leaves. Drawing on Aristotle, Aquinas therefore speaks of there being "final causes"—the goal of an action in some sense causes that action to occur.

50. Thomas is well aware that it is strange to speak of a tree having a purpose for growing leaves. There are two different ways in which we might speak of a thing having a purpose: First, we might say that the purpose of an arrow is to hit a target; second, we might say that in shooting an arrow my purpose is to hit a target. The arrow and I have "purposes" in a different sense. As an intelligent being, I can do things "on purpose"; an arrow is not an intelligent being, therefore it cannot. So it is the archer who gives the arrow its purpose and who directs it to its goal. A tree is also unintelligent. So who or what intelligent being guides the tree in fulfilling its purposes?

51. Note here that Aquinas has taken us a bit beyond the first four ways, which have simply demonstrated God as a universal cause. In the fifth way, Aquinas shows God to be an *intelligent* cause, in the sense of being a cause that acts with a purpose.

exist in his works, unless his omnipotence and goodness were such as to bring good even out of evil." Therefore, it is part of the infinite goodness of God, that he should allow evil to exist, and out of it produce good.[52]

Reply to 2: Since nature works for a determinate end under the direction of a higher agent, it is necessary that whatever is done by nature must be traced back to God as its first cause. Similarly, whatever is done voluntarily must also be traced back to some higher cause other than human reason or will, since these can change or fail; for all things that are changeable and capable of failure must be traced back to a first principle that is immovable and necessary by its very nature, as was shown.[53]

52. Like Augustine, Aquinas understands evil to be not a substance, but rather *privatio boni*—an absence of goodness. God can allow evil to "exist" because it has no positive being that could in any way "compete" with God.

53. The reference is to the body of the article.

THE SIMPLICITY OF GOD

1.3.4

Whether essence and existence are the same in God?

It seems that essence and existence are not the same in God.[1]

1. If this were the case, then the divine existence would have nothing added to it. But existence to which no addition is made is existence-in-general [*esse*

---

1. Much of what Aquinas thinks about the nature of divinity comes into play in this article. A great deal hangs on understanding the previously mentioned distinction (see 1.2, note 13) between "existence" (*esse*) and "essence" (*essentia*). Throughout this article it is important to keep in mind Aquinas's understanding of that distinction. In contrast to Aristotle (and drawing on the Muslim philosopher Ibn-Sina, known in Latin as Avicenna, and the Jewish philosopher Moses Maimonides), Thomas recognized that *what* something is differs from the fact *that* it is. In making this differentiation, Aquinas calls the fact of a thing's existence its *esse*—a noun that he forms out of the verb "to be" and that we might translate as "existence" or (loosely) "the activity of existing." This activity of existing is distinct from the *kind* of thing something is.

Ibn-Sina's way of making this point is to say that *esse* is an accidental property of things—that is, a quality that a thing might or might not possess, without changing what it is. Thus, Aaron is bearded, but being bearded is not part of the meaning of "Aaron," so he could cease to be bearded without ceasing to be Aaron. Therefore beardedness is an accidental property of Aaron. Likewise, existence is not part of the meaning of "Aaron," as is witnessed by the fact that Aaron no longer exists.

Though in one place (*Quodlibetal Questions* 2, q. 2.1) Thomas adopts Ibn-Sina's language of *esse* as an "accident," he is on the whole unhappy with this way of putting the matter, since Aaron's existence is not really like Aaron's beard, for if Aaron ceased to be, he would most certainly cease to be Aaron. Therefore Thomas says in another place (*Quodlibetal Questions* 12, q. 4.1) that *esse*, "strictly speaking" (*proprie loquendo*), is not an accident. Thomas recognizes that Ibn-Sina has made a crucial distinction between a thing's essence and the fact of its existence: like an accidental property, existence is not contained within something's essence. Therefore we speak of *esse* in created beings as if it were an accident, even though it is in fact the very "actuality" of created beings. Even things

commune], which is predicated of all things. Therefore it follows that God is the being-in-general [*ens commune*] that can be predicated of everything.[2] But this is false, according to the book of Wisdom 14:21, "They gave the Name that cannot be shared to wood and stone." Therefore God's existence is not his essence.[3]

2. We can know "whether" God exists, as said above (1.2.2), but we cannot know "what" he is. Therefore God's existence is not the same as what he is—that is, as his quiddity or nature.[4]

---

that are unchanging (in Aquinas's worldview, for example, angels and certain heavenly bodies) have their existence "accidentally," in the sense that their unchanging existence is not given with their essence but depends on something else (see 1.2, note 44).

What Thomas is arguing in this article is that the distinction between essence and existence is true of everything in the world, but it *cannot* be true of God, if God is the cause of the world. The shorthand way of making this argument is to speak of God's "simplicity." By divine simplicity Aquinas means, first, that God is not composed of form and matter (see 1.12, note 1). This, however, is also true of the angels, since they are pure form without matter. So God's simplicity is even more radical; for even the angels—like everything that is created—consist in the *possibility* of existing or not existing, to which their *actual* existence is something added (since they might not have existed). God, however, has the radical simplicity of pure actual existence, since God does not have the possibility of not existing.

It is also worth noting here that Thomas distinguishes not only between *esse* and *essentia,* but also between *esse*—the activity of "be-ing"—and *ens*—this or that particular "being" or "entity." All created beings have *esse* by virtue of being an entity, whereas God *is esse,* without being an entity alongside other entities. God is existence itself, or "be-ing" (the activity of existing), but not *a* being. I try to translate *esse* consistently as "existence" rather than "being."

2. "To predicate" (*praedicare*) is, most simply, "to say," though in Aquinas's usage it has the more specific meaning of the act of affirming something of something else. Thomas calls the things that might be affirmed of something "predicates" and groups them into ten categories (borrowed from Aristotle, *Categories* 1[b]):

- substance ("Thomas is a human being.")
- quantity ("Thomas weighs one hundred pounds.")
- quality ("Thomas has blond hair.")
- relation ("Thomas is older than Sophia.")
- place ("Thomas is in New York.")
- time ("Thomas was born in 1992.")
- position ("Thomas is standing.")
- possession/state ("Thomas is wearing a blue shirt.")
- acting on ("Thomas loves Sophia.")
- being affected by ("Thomas is loved by Sophia.")

Thus we would say that being in New York is predicated of Thomas under the category of "place," while being a human being is predicated of him under the category of "substance."

3. The point of this objection is that beyond the being (the simple fact of existence) that all things share, each thing must have an essence (i.e., the specifics that make a thing what it is); otherwise we could not distinguish different sorts of beings. If God had no essence added to, and therefore specifying, his existence, then he would not be distinct from being-in-general and would be a pantheistic God, since his existence would not be distinct from the existence shared by creatures.

4. Thomas speaks of God's "quiddity" (from the Latin *quid*—"what") as a way of speaking about God's essence or definition. If God's existence and essence were identical and if, as Thomas maintains, we cannot know God's essence, then we also cannot know of God's existence. But Thomas's point in the five ways is to show that we *can* know of God's existence. Therefore, so the objection goes, God's existence must be distinct from God's essence.

On the contrary: Hilary says in his *On the Trinity* (bk. 7, no. 11), "In God existence is not an accidental quality, but subsisting truth." Therefore what subsists in God is his existence.

I answer: God is not only his own essence, as shown in the preceding article (1.3.3), but also his own existence.[5] This may be shown in several ways.

First, whatever a thing has besides its essence must be caused either by the constituent principles of that essence,[6] like a property that necessarily accompanies the species (in the way that the faculty of laughing is proper to a human being, and is caused by the essential principles of the species),[7] or by some exterior agent (as heat is caused in water by fire). Therefore, if the existence of a thing differs from its essence, this existence must be caused either by some exterior agent or by its essential principles. But it is impossible for a thing's existence to be caused by its essential principles, for nothing can be the sufficient cause of its own existence, if its existence is caused.[8] Therefore that thing, whose existence differs from its essence, must have its existence caused by another.[9] But this cannot be said of God, because we call God the first efficient cause.[10] Therefore it is impossible that in God his existence should differ from his essence.

Second, existence is that which makes every form or nature actual; for goodness and humanity are spoken of as actual, only because they are spoken of as existing. Therefore existence must be compared to essence, if the latter

---

5. Before proceeding to Aquinas's arguments for this claim, it is important to understand the claim itself. Think of the question "What is x?" If we replace "x" with anything in our world, we can answer the question without any mention of x's existence. For example, What is a human being? We can reply, "A rational animal." We need not reply, "A rational animal that exists." However, if we are asking about God, the cause of the world, then our answer must be, "God is *esse.*" In other words, unlike every being that is caused, in God there is no distinction between *what* he is and the fact *that* he is.

6. What created beings have besides their essence are all their accidents, including their existence.

7. Human beings sometimes laugh and sometimes do not—thus it is an accidental property. Humorlessness is not normally seen as grounds for exclusion from the human species (though it might serve as grounds for exclusion from a social event). At the same time, the ability to laugh is caused by the essential constitution (or definition) of a human being, which is to be a rational animal. Other rational beings, such as angels, do not laugh, not least because one needs a body in order to laugh, and human beings (according to Aquinas) are the only embodied rational beings. Other animals do not laugh because they do not possess rationality and thus do not get our jokes. So, unlike some accidents (such as being in a particular location), the accidental quality of laughter is caused by the constituent elements of what it is to be human.

8. Existence is not a part of the definition of any created thing; even more, it cannot be derived from that definition, as the ability to laugh can be derived from the definition of human beings as rational animals, for the existence of a particular thing's essence presupposes that the thing exist.

9. See the third of the five ways (1.2.3, above).

10. In other words, if "God" is the answer to the question of why the world as a whole exists, then "to be" (*esse*) is not something caused in God by another, nor something derived from God's definition; rather, *esse* must itself be the definition (essence) of "God."

is a distinct reality, as actuality to potentiality.[11] Therefore, since in God there is no potentiality, as shown earlier (1.3.1), it follows that in him essence does not differ from existence.[12] Therefore his essence is his existence.

Third, just as that which is on fire, but is not fire itself, is on fire by participation; so that which has existence, but is not existence itself, is a being by participation.[13] But God, as was shown earlier (1.3.3), is his own essence.[14] If, therefore, he is not his own existence he will be a being by participation and not by nature [*per essentiam*]. He will not therefore be the first being—which is absurd. Therefore God is his own existence, and not merely his own essence.[15]

Reply to 1: The phrase "a thing that has nothing added to it" can be used in two ways.[16] In one way, it may be the case that its definition *precludes* any addition—thus, for example, the definition of an irrational animal is "that which is *without* reason." In another way, we may understand a thing to have nothing added to it, inasmuch as its definition does not require that anything should be added to it—thus "animal," in a general sense, does not include reason, because "to have reason" is not part of the general definition of "animal"; but neither is "to lack reason" part of the definition.[17] And so "existence without addition" in the first sense is the divine existence, whereas in the second sense "existence without addition" is existence-in-general [*esse commune*].

Reply to 2: "To be" [*esse*] can be used in two ways. In the first way, it means the act of existence [*actum essendi*];[18] in the second way it means the composition of a proposition, which the mind devises by joining a predicate to a subject. Taking "to be" in the first sense, we can understand neither God's existence nor his essence. In the second sense, however, we know that this proposition that we form about God when we say "God is," is true; and this we know from his effects, as was said above (1.2.2).

11. Thomas is drawing an analogy between existence and essence and actuality and potentiality (see 1.2, note 32). Existence actualizes a thing's potential to be an actually existing thing.

12. If God is the total cause of there being something rather than nothing, then it follows that God's own existence is not in need of actualization by anything. This fact makes God's existence radically free from all possibility of becoming. Or, as Thomas is wont to put it, God is "pure act."

13. There is a difference between being fire itself and being "on fire." Using Thomas's vocabulary, we would say that something that is on fire is not fire itself, but fiery by "participation." Similarly, things that "have being" but are not being itself are beings by participation.

14. The Piana edition (1570) of the *Summa* reads simply, *Deus est* (God exists).

15. If God were a being by participation, then his existence would be derived from something else, which would involve us in yet another infinite regress.

16. Or we might say, "There are two senses in which a thing can be said not to have a distinguishing feature."

17. In other words, its definition may *exclude* distinguishing features, or it may simply *not include* them. Thus, "Yankee fan" excludes the specification "humble," whereas "baseball fan" simply does not include it, but also does not exclude it, since some baseball fans are humble. "God" excludes any further specification beyond "existence itself," while that totality of beings that constitutes the world simply does not include any further specification, though all creatures do in fact have some such distinguishing features. For more on this point, see the next article.

18. I have chosen to translate *actus essendi* as "act of existence" because it is the act of existence that "actualizes" essence (and in that way is the "act of essence").

KNOWLEDGE OF GOD

1.12.12

Whether God can be known in this life by natural reason?

It seems that by natural reason we cannot know God in this life.

1. Boethius says in *The Consolation of Philosophy* (bk. 5, chap. 4) that "reason does not grasp simple form." But God is a supremely simple form, as was shown earlier (1.3.7).[1] Therefore natural reason cannot attain knowledge of him.

2. The soul understands nothing by natural reason without the use of an image [*phantasmate*], as is said in *De anima* (bk. 3, chap. 7, 431ª). But we cannot have an image of God because he is incorporeal. Therefore we cannot know God by natural knowledge.

3. Knowledge that is through natural reason belongs to both the good and the evil, since they have a common nature. But the knowledge of God

---

1. In speaking of "simple form," Aquinas presumes the view that things generally have a "composite" existence made up of "matter" and "form." Roughly speaking, the form is the structure of the thing that allows us to identify it as what it is (when we see a cow, we can know it as a cow because it has the "form" of a cow), whereas the matter is what differentiates *this* thing from *that* thing (The cow Bossy is different from the cow Belle because they are made up of different matter). God is not material (i.e., he is "incorporeal") and therefore has an existence that is "simple" rather than composite (i.e., composed of matter and form). The next objection develops this further and states that natural human reason is incapable of grasping form unless it encounters it in a particular material thing (we can only know "cowness" by encountering an actual cow). See 1.45, note 16. God is *supremely* simple because not only is God not composed of matter and form, but, further, in God essence and existence are identical. See 1.3, note 1.

belongs only to the good; for Augustine says in *De Trinitate* (bk. 1, chap. 2, no. 4), "The weak eye of the human mind is not fixed on that excellent light unless purified by the justice of faith." Therefore God cannot be known by natural reason.

On the contrary: It is written in Romans 1:19, "That which is known of God," namely, what can be known of God by natural reason, "is manifest in them."

I answer: Our natural knowledge begins from the senses.[2] Therefore our natural knowledge can go as far as it can be led by perceptible things. But our mind cannot be led by perceptible things so far as to see the essence of God, because perceptible creatures do not equal the power of God as their cause. Therefore from the knowledge of perceptible things the whole power of God cannot be known, and neither, consequently, can his essence be seen.[3] But because they are his effects and depend on their cause, we can be led from them so far as to know of God "whether he exists," and to know of him what must necessarily belong to him as the first cause of all things, exceeding all things caused by him.[4]

Therefore we know of his relationship with creatures, that he is cause of them all; also that creatures differ from him, namely, that he is not in any way part of what is caused by him; and that being uncaused is attributed to him not on account of any defect on his part, but because he exceeds all things.[5]

Reply to 1: Reason cannot grasp simple form so as to know "what it is" [*quid est*]; but it can know "whether it is" [*an est*].

Reply to 2: God is known by natural knowledge through the images of his effects.

---

2. See 1.1, note 33.

3. Up to this point Aquinas is basically agreeing with the objections. Given that our minds know by means of observing material things, they are unsuited to knowing God, who is immaterial.

4. Here Thomas disagrees with the objections, or rather he introduces a distinction that clarifies the objections. He distinguishes between knowing *that* something is [*an est*] and knowing *what* something is [*quid est*] (cf. 1.2, note 13). Since the world is caused by God it can yield the kind of knowledge of God that an effect can give us about its cause. We say "where there's smoke there's fire," but we probably should not say "where there's smoke there's a fire caused by burning coal." Smoke is an effect of fire, so smoke allows us to say *that* a fire exists as the cause of the smoke, but it does not allow us to say *what* the fire is: how the fire start started; what kind of fuel is burning; how long it has been burning; and, above all, what fire itself is. In other words, an effect cannot provide us with a definition of its cause. Were we to draw our definition of fire from smoke we would define it as a "smoke-producing thing." This is clearly not an adequate definition of fire, omitting as it does the fact that fire is hot, it consumes combustible material, and so on. Similarly, the world allows us to say *that* God is but not *what* God is.

5. The world is capable of telling us: (1) the kind of relationship that God has with it—that of a cause to its effect; (2) that, as the world's cause, God is not himself a part of the world (since nothing causes itself); and (3) that God's not being part of the world is not a defect in him but rather a sign of his perfection and transcendence. This is not *much* knowledge of God, but Aquinas wants to maintain that it is *genuine* knowledge of God.

Reply to 3: The knowledge of God's essence, because it is by grace, belongs only to the good;[6] but the knowledge of him that is through natural reason can belong to both good and bad. Therefore in his book of *Retractions* (bk. 1, chap. 4), Augustine says, "I do not approve what I said in prayer, 'God who wills that only the pure should know truth.' For it can be answered that many who are not pure can know many truths"—that is, by natural reason.

1.12.13

Whether a higher knowledge of God can be obtained by grace than by natural reason?

It seems that a higher knowledge of God is not obtained by grace than by natural reason.

1. Dionysius says in his *Mystical Theology* (chap. 1) that whoever is more closely united to God in this life is united to him as to something entirely unknown. He says this even of Moses, who nevertheless obtained a certain excellence in the knowledge conferred by grace. But to be united to God while not knowing "what he is" [*quid est*] also comes about through natural reason. Therefore God is not known to us more fully by grace than by natural reason.

2. We can acquire knowledge of divine matters through natural reason only by sense images [*phantasmata*]; and the same applies to the knowledge given by grace. Dionysius says in the *Celestial Hierarchy* (chap. 1, no.2) that "it is impossible for the divine ray to shine upon us except as screened round about by a variety of sacred veils." Therefore we cannot know God more fully by grace than by natural reason.

3. Our intellect clings to God by the grace of faith. But faith does not seem to be knowledge; for Gregory says that "things not seen are the objects of faith, and not of knowledge" (*Homilies on the Gospels,* sermon 26). Therefore a more excellent knowledge of God is not given to us by grace.

On the contrary: The Apostle says in 1 Corinthians 2:10, "God has revealed to us his Spirit," which "none of the princes of this world knew," namely, the philosophers, as the gloss explains.[7]

---

6. It is important to remember that for Aquinas we are good because God gives us grace, not that God gives us grace because we are good. Thus Thomas's point here is *not* that knowledge of God's essence—that is, the knowledge of *what* God is that the saints have in heaven—is a reward bestowed upon the good, but rather that it is a gift of grace.

7. When Thomas refers to the "gloss" he is speaking of explanatory notes on scriptural texts that were originally written either between the lines or in the margins of Scripture. These notes began as simple one-word definitions of unfamiliar terms, but grew into more elaborate commentaries that sought to explain the literal sense of the text. These commentaries were sometimes separated from the scriptural text and became books in their own rights. The most common of these glosses was that which was known as the *Glossa ordinaria*. Tradition ascribed the compilation of this text to Walafrid of Strabo (849), though most modern scholars doubt

I answer: We have a more perfect knowledge of God by grace than by natural reason. This is clear from the following: the knowledge that we have by natural reason contains two things, that is, images [*phantasmata*] derived from perceptible objects, and a natural intellectual light [*lumen naturale intelligible*], by virtue of which we abstract intellectual conceptions [*intelligibles conceptiones*] from them.[8]

In both of these, human knowledge is assisted by the revelation of grace, for the intellect's natural light is strengthened by the infusion of gratuitous light. Also, as in the case of prophetic visions, images are sometimes divinely formed in the human imagination, so as to express divine things better than do those images that we receive from perceptible objects. And sometimes perceptible things, or even voices, are divinely formed to express some divine meaning, as in the baptism [of Christ], the Holy Spirit was seen in the shape of a dove, and the voice of the Father was heard: "This is my beloved Son" (Matthew 3:17).[9]

Reply to 1: Although by the revelation of grace we cannot in this life know of God "what he is" [*quid est*], and thus are united to him as to one unknown, we nevertheless know him more fully to the degree that more and greater effects of his are demonstrated to us, and to the degree that we attribute to him some things known by divine revelation, to which natural reason cannot reach, such as, for instance, that God is three and one.[10]

---

his authorship and see the *Glossa* as accumulating over several centuries, beginning in the ninth century and culminating in the twelfth.

8. Two points to note here. First, here and elsewhere, I translate *intelligible* as "intellectual" rather than as "intelligible," which is used in many translations of Aquinas. I have made this choice primarily because in modern usage the word "intelligible" is normally contrasted with "unintelligible" and could mean either readily grasped by the mind or capable of being grasped through the senses—as in a transcription of a recording that reads [unintelligible] in those places where the transcriber could not make out what the speaker was saying. This latter sense in particular is not what Aquinas means by a thing being intelligible. For him, "intelligible" is associated exclusively with intellectual processes, thus my translation of *intelligible* as "intellectual," even though this word is also used to translate *intellectualis*.

Second, in understanding Thomas here it is helpful to have some idea of how he thinks we normally know things. To greatly simplify: The senses receive images of things [i.e., *phantasmata*]. From these images, reason (or "intellect's natural light") separates (or "abstracts") that structure of things that Aquinas (following Aristotle) calls the "form" (see note 1, above). Here Thomas calls this structure an "intellectual conception"; more commonly, he calls it the "intellectual species." This intellectual species is then imprinted or "impressed" on what Thomas calls the "passive intellect," which is the mind's potential for knowing.

9. God gives us a knowledge that exceeds our normal knowledge in three ways: (1) sometimes he strengthens reason's natural capacity (as in the case of the saints who see God in heaven, but also in certain special cases in this life); (2) sometimes he forms sense images (*phantasmata*) in our minds (as when a prophet is given knowledge of some distant or future event); and (3) sometimes he makes things themselves convey divine knowledge to us, through miraculous oracles. An example of the latter might be Numbers 22, when God causes Balaam's donkey to speak.

10. In this life, even with the aid of revelation, we cannot have knowledge of *what* God is, but Aquinas maintains that revelation still gives us a greater knowledge of God because we have a greater knowledge of his effects—specifically, those effects that constitute revelation.

Reply to 2: The stronger the intellectual light is in human beings, the much more excellent the intellectual knowledge that is had, whether from images received from the senses in the natural order, or divinely formed in the imagination. Thus through the revelation given by images a fuller knowledge is received by the infusion of divine light.

Reply to 3: Faith is a kind of knowledge, since the intellect is directed by faith to some knowable object. But this direction to one object does not proceed from the vision of the one who believes, but from the vision of the one who is believed. Thus to the degree that faith falls short of vision, it falls short of the knowledge that belongs to *scientia,* for *scientia* directs the intellect to one object by the vision and understanding of first principles.[11]

---

11. For Thomas, faith is something like "opinion," inasmuch as its object remains unseen, at least by us. But it is also like *scientia* in the certainty with which we hold to that unseen object of knowledge. One believes or has faith in a situation in which one cannot "see" the truth between two alternatives. As Thomas says in *De veritate* 14.1, "In this situation our understanding is determined by the will, which chooses to assent to one side definitively and precisely because of something which is enough to move the will, though not enough to move the understanding, namely, since it seems good or fitting to assent to this side. And this is the state of one who believes." Faith, contrasted with opinion, in when that which moves the will is God's grace.

Thus, faith is inferior to natural "vision" (in the sense of the knowledge derived from the process described in note 8, above) if we approach it from the perspective of *the one who knows.* It is clearly better to know about cows from having actually encountered cows than it is to know about them from a trustworthy authority. However, if we approach faith from the perspective of *what is known,* then it is superior to the kind of vision we have in this life, since our natural vision can know only natural things, whereas faith can know God. It is better to know God through faith than to know a cow through vision. The saints in heaven, of course, have it best of all, since they know God through "vision."

THE NAMES OF GOD

1.13.3

Whether any word can be applied to God in its literal sense?

It seems that no word is applied literally to God.[1]

1. All words that we apply to God are taken from creatures, as was explained earlier (1.13.1). But the names of creatures are applied to God metaphorically, as when we say that "God is a rock," or "a lion," or something similar. Therefore names are applied to God in a metaphorical sense.[2]

2. No word can be said literally of something if it is more truly denied of it than predicated of it.[3] But all such words as "good," "wise," and the like are more truly denied of God than predicated of him, as is clear from what Dionysius says in *The Celestial Hierarchy*, (chap. 2, no.3). Therefore none of these names belong to God in their literal sense.

3. Bodily names are applied to God in a metaphorical sense only, since he is incorporeal. But all such names imply some kind of bodily condition, for their meaning is bound up with time and composition and similar bodily conditions. Therefore all these names are applied to God in a metaphorical sense.

1. Though *nomen* means "name," I sometimes translate it in this article as "word," since Thomas is here clearly thinking not only of proper nouns, but of any word used to describe or identify God.

2. For Aquinas on the metaphors of Scripture, see above, 1.1.9.

3. On predication, see 1.3, note 2.

On the contrary: Ambrose says in *On the Catholic Faith* (bk. 2, prologue), "There are some words that express evidently the property of the divinity, and some that express the clear truth of the divine majesty, but there are others that are said of God metaphorically, by way of likeness." Therefore not all words are spoken of God metaphorically, but there are some that are spoken literally.

I answer: According to the preceding article (1.13.2), our knowledge of God is derived from the perfections that flow from him to creatures—perfections that are in God in a more eminent way than in creatures.[4] However, our intellect grasps them as they are in creatures, and signifies them by words in a way that accords with how it grasps them.[5] Therefore, as to the names we apply to God, there are two things to be considered, namely, the perfections that they signify [*perfectiones ipsas significatas*]—such as goodness, life, and such things—and their way of signifying [*modum significandi*].[6] With regard to what is signified by these names, they belong properly to God—more properly than they belong to creatures—and are spoken primarily of him. But with regard to their way of signifying, they are not properly said of God, for they have a way of signifying that belongs to creatures.[7]

Reply to 1: There are some words that signify these perfections flowing from God to creatures in such a way that the imperfect manner in which creatures participate in the divine perfection is part of the very meaning of the word itself—as "stone" signifies a material being—and words of this kind can be applied to God only in a metaphorical sense. Other words, however, express these perfections absolutely, without this sort of participation being part of their meaning, for example, "being," "good," "living," and the like. Such words can be said literally of God.[8]

4. By "more eminent" Aquinas means "more perfect."

5. In other words, we learn to use our repertoire of "perfection terms"—terms such as "good," "living," and so on—in our everyday encounters with good things and living things.

6. Here Thomas notes a distinction between *what* our words signify (the *res significata*) and *how* our words signify (the *modus significandi*). Verb tenses provide a clear example. In the statements "he ran," "he runs," and "he will run" the same thing (*res*) is spoken of—the act of running—but it is spoken of in three different ways (*modi*): as something past, as something present, and as something future. Likewise with nouns and adjectives: whether we say "he is good" or "he possesses goodness" we are speaking about the same thing, but in the first instance it appears as a quality ("good") and in the second instance it appears as a thing ("goodness").

7. Terms we apply literally to God refer truly to God as *res significata*, but according to the *modus significandi* of creatures. Thus a statement such as "God is good" is quite literally true; however, in this statement the word "good" signifies in the same way it does when we use it of creatures, since we acquire our repertoire of perfection terms in *this* world, which is a created world. Note, however, that Aquinas also says that even though we acquire our repertoire of perfection terms from our interaction with creatures, those creatures themselves derive their perfections (i.e., their goodness, their life. etc.) from God, and therefore our perfection terms are *more* truly applied to God than they are to creatures.

8. Here Thomas shows how to distinguish metaphorical language about God from literal language about God. Although a statement like "God is my rock and my redeemer" clearly says

Reply to 2: Such names as these, as Dionysius shows, are denied of God for the reason that what the name signifies is not fitting to him in the way that it signifies it, but in a more excellent way. Therefore Dionysius also says that God is "above all substance and all life"(*The Celestial Hierarchy*, chap. 2, no. 3).

Reply to 3: These names that are spoken literally of God imply bodily conditions not in the thing signified by the word, but as regards their way of signification. But those that are applied to God metaphorically imply and mean a bodily condition in the thing signified.[9]

1.13.5[10]

Whether what is said of God and of creatures is said of them univocally.

It seems that the things attributed to God and creatures are univocal.[11]

1. Every equivocal term is traced back to a univocal one, just as the many are traced back to the one;[12] for if the name "dog" is said equivocally of the

---

something positive about God, it cannot be a literal statement because, although a rock shares in the perfection of existence that flows from God to creatures, it shares in it in an imperfect way (i.e., in a way that falls short of God's existence). However, in a statement such as "God is good" the word "good" does not itself imply any creaturely imperfection—even though we acquire the term from imperfect creatures—and it therefore is used literally and not metaphorically.

9. A metaphorical statement about God speaks of God as if God were a creature (usually by implying materiality), whereas a literal statement about God speaks of God in a way derived from created things.

10. This is one of the most poured-over articles in the *Summa*. Many people see it as a (if not *the*) linchpin in Aquinas's thought, wherein he establishes his "doctrine of analogy." My own inclination is to say that the importance of analogy for Aquinas should not be *under*stressed, but neither should it be *over*stressed. The notion of analogical uses of *language*, as well as the notion of *causes* that are analogically related to their effects, are important to Thomas in trying to articulate how it is possible to say true things about a God who exceeds our capacity for comprehension. In creation, God imparts to us an existence that *shares* in God's own existence, while also being fundamentally *different* from God's existence (since our existence has a source outside of us, whereas God's does not). Thus although our language about God is manifestly inadequate to the task we give it, it is at the same time not entirely false, because it is a language that can speak truthfully about a world that shares in some way in God's own existence.

In this article, as so often in the *Summa*, Thomas is concerned with that we can *say*—with what true statements we can make. True statements are made by joining a subject with an appropriate predicate, which is what Aquinas calls "predication" (*praedicatio*). But the truth of statements is inseperable from the truth of things, so when we judge a statement to be true, we are not simply saying something about language, but about things. The peculiar thing about our statements about God is that we can know that our statements are true, without knowing, in a comprehensive sense, the thing about which we are speaking.

11. A term is used univocally when it has the same precise meaning in reference to different things. Thus, in saying "Fido barks" and "Spot barks" the word "bark" means one thing—the sound made by a dog.

12. A term is used equivocally when is has an entirely different meaning when used in reference to different things. Thus, in saying "Fido has a bark" and "the tree has bark" the word "bark" has two different meanings.

barking dog and of the dogfish, it must be said of something univocally—that is, of all barking dogs; otherwise we go on infinitely. There are some agents that are univocal and agree with their effects in both name and definition, as a human being generates a human being. There are some agents that are equivocal, such as the sun, which causes heat even though the sun is hot only in an equivocal sense. Therefore it seems that the first agent, to which all other agents are traced back, is an univocal agent. And thus what is said of God and creatures is predicated univocally.[13]

2. There is no likeness among equivocal things. Therefore it seems that something can be said of God and creatures univocally—since according to Genesis 1:26 creatures have a certain likeness to God ("Let us make the human being to our image and likeness").

3. As is said in the *Metaphysics* (bk. 10, chap. 1, 1053^a), a measure is homogeneous with the thing measured. But God is the first measure of all beings. Therefore God is homogeneous with creatures; and thus something can be said univocally of God and creatures.

On the contrary:[14] Whatever is predicated of various things under the same name but not in the same sense is predicated equivocally. But no name belongs to God in the same sense that it belongs to creatures. For instance, in creatures "wisdom" is a quality, but not in God.[15] Varying the genus changes the idea of something, since the genus is part of the definition. And the same reasoning applies to other terms.[16] Therefore, whatever is said of God and of creatures is predicated equivocally.

Further, God is more distant from creatures than any creatures are from each other. But the distance of some creatures makes any univocal predication of them impossible, as in the case of those things that are not in the same genus.

---

13. This objection finds its basis in the practice of speaking of agents (i.e., causes) as "univocal" and "equivocal." A univocal agent is one that produces something essentially like itself: in the example given here, a human being produces a human being. An equivocal agent is one that produces something different (in various respects) from itself: in the example given here, the sun produces heat. The objection argues that if God is, as Augustine put it, "the Cause of all causes" (*De civitate Dei,* bk. 5, chap. 8), then God is an agent that produces something essentially like itself, and therefore we speak of God univocally.

Note that the term "analogy," which Thomas will introduce in his response, is itself used analogously of both language and causes.

On the meaning of "predicated," see 1.3, note 2.

14. In this article the *sed contra* breaks with Aquinas's usual practice in the *Summa theologiae* of offering only one counterobjection. As becomes apparent in the rest of the article, this is because Aquinas is inclined to agree *neither* with the objections (which argue that our language about God is univocal) *nor* with the *sed contra* (which argues that our language about God is equivocal).

15. See 1.3, note 1.

16. In other words, if you have two different kinds of things, the same word must be used equivocally when applied to both. Thus we use the word "bright" equivocally in the sentence, "The bright student wore bright clothes."

Therefore it is even less the case that anything can be predicated univocally of God and creatures; rather, everything is predicated equivocally.

I answer: It is impossible for something to be predicated univocally of God and creatures. The reason for this is that every effect that is not an adequate result of the power of the efficient cause receives the likeness of the agent, not in its full degree, but in a measure that falls short. Thus, what is divided and multiplied in the effects is in the agent simply and in a unified manner; for example, the sun, by exercise of its one power, produces multiple and various forms in all inferior things.[17] In the same way, as said in the preceding article, all perfections existing in creatures in a divided and multiple manner, preexist in God in a united manner.

Thus when any term expressing perfection is applied to a creature, it signifies that perfection as something with a meaning distinct from other perfections. For instance, by the term "wise" applied to a human being, we signify some perfection distinct from a human being's essence, and distinct from his power and existence, and from all similar things; whereas when we apply to it God, we do not mean to signify anything distinct from his essence, or power, or existence.[18] Thus also this term "wise," applied to a person, in some degree circumscribes and encompasses the thing signified. This is not the case, however, when it is applied to God; in this case it leaves the thing signified as unencompassed, and as exceeding the signification of the name.[19] Therefore it is evident that this term "wise" is not applied in the same way to God and to a human being. And the same reasoning applies to other terms. Therefore no name is predicated univocally of God and of creatures.

Neither, on the other hand, are such names applied to God and creatures in a purely equivocal sense, as some have said.[20] Because if that were so, it follows that nothing at all could be known or demonstrated about God from creatures, for the reasoning would always be exposed to the fallacy of equivocation. Such a view is against the philosophers,[21] who prove many things about God, and also against what the Apostle says: "The invisible things of God are clearly seen by being understood through the things that are made" (Romans 1:20). Therefore it must be said that these names are said of God and creatures in an analogous sense, that is to say, according to proportion.[22]

17. In other words, the sun, which is both bright and hot, makes some things bright and other things hot.

18. Thus far, Thomas's argument agrees with that of the first *sed contra*.

19. This second argument against univocity bears some resemblance to the second *sed contra*, though here Aquinas's emphasis is on God's excess, rather than God's distance. This will be important when he argues for the possibility of analogical speech about God.

20. For example, the Jewish philosopher Moses Maimonides.

21. See 1.1, note 29.

22. As becomes apparent in the remainder of this article, it is misleading to take "proportion" as a strict definition of "analogy" (though in fact the Greek word "analogy" does mean "proportion"). The general form that analogies take is something like "A is to B as C is to D," and mathematical proportions can certainly be fit into this general analogical form, for example,

Names are used analogically in two ways: either because many things have a proportion to one thing (thus, for example, "healthy" is predicated of medicine and urine in relation and in proportion to health of a body, with one being a cause and the other a sign),[23] or because one thing has a proportion to another (thus "healthy" is said of medicine and an animal, since medicine is the cause of health in the animal body).[24] And in this second way some things are said of God and creatures analogically, and not in a purely equivocal nor in a purely univocal sense. For we can name God only from creatures, as was said earlier (1.13.1).[25] Thus whatever is said of God and creatures is said according to the relation of a creature to God as its principle and cause, in which the perfections of all things preexist in the most excellent way.[26]

This way of sharing meanings lies between pure equivocation and simple univocity. For in analogies the meaning is not, as it is in univocals, one and the same; yet it is not totally different, as in equivocals. Rather, a term that is said in multiple ways signifies various proportions to some one thing. Thus "healthy" applied to urine signifies the sign of animal health, and applied to medicine signifies the cause of the same health.

Reply to 1: Although in predications the equivocal must be traced back to the univocal, in actions the nonunivocal agent must precede the univocal agent.[27]

"2 is to 4 as 3 is to 9." However, it is clear that not everything that Aquinas means by analogy is encompassed in proportion. In fact, the case of analogy that he is concerned with here, the analogical application of human language to God, is one in which, strictly speaking, there can be no proportion, because God is infinite and there can be no proportion between finite and infinite. So here we might simply take "proportion" to mean that there is some ordered relationship that makes analogy possible, not that that relationship can be expressed in an algorithm.

23. That is to say, medicine and urine are both described as "healthy" because they are both related to the health of the body: medicine as a cause of it and urine as a sign of it. This is a case where the analogical use of the term "healthy" for both medicine and urine is made possible by their relationship to a third thing, the body, from which the primary meaning of "health" is drawn.

24. Whereas the first type of analogy involves the relationship of two uses of a term by virtue of their relationship to some third thing, in this second type we simply have two uses of a term related by virtue of the relationship of one thing to another.

25. What Aquinas seems to be saying here is that the analogies involved in using human language to speak of God are of the second type, because there is no third thing apart from God and creatures that relates the two. He returns, however, to the "medicine–urine" example (i.e., the first kind of analogy) at the end of his response, to illustrate the different *modi significandi* involved in analogy.

26. God is the cause of creatures; therefore, language about creatures can be applied to God. But when we use those terms that imply perfection (e.g., "one," "good," "true," etc.) we use them more properly in speaking of God than we do in speaking of creatures, since God is the source of those perfections as we find them in creatures.

27. Here Thomas distinguishes between the relationship of the univocal and the non-univocal (i.e., the equivocal or analogical) with regard to language ("predications") and with regard to causes ("actions"). Thus although it is true (as objection 1 states) that in the case of language the non-univocal use must be traced back to a univocal use (otherwise it would be impossible to say what a word means), this is not true in the case of causes.

For a non-univocal agent is the universal cause of the whole species, as in the case of the sun being the cause of the generation of all people.[28] But a univocal agent is not the universal efficient cause of the whole species (otherwise it would be the cause of itself, since it is contained in the species), but is a particular cause of this individual, which it constitutes as a member of the species.[29] Therefore the universal cause of an entire species is not a univocal agent; and the universal cause comes before the particular cause.[30] But this universal agent, while it is not univocal, nevertheless is not altogether equivocal, otherwise it could not produce its own likeness. Rather it can be called an analogical agent, in the same way that in predication all univocal predications are traced back to one first non-univocal analogical predication, which is being.[31]

Reply to 2: The likeness of the creature to God is imperfect, for, as said earlier (1.4.3), it does not represent God as a member of a common genus.[32]

Reply to 3: God is not a measure that is proportioned to things measured. Therefore it is not necessary that God and creatures should be in the same genus.

The arguments to the contrary prove that these names are not predicated univocally of God and creatures, but not that they are predicated equivocally.

It is important to remember that, for Aquinas, all effects are in *some* sense like their causes. The contrast drawn in the objection is between univocal and equivocal causes, but for Aquinas there can be no *purely* equivocal cause. In the case of the example given in the objection, the sun is not something entirely different from heat, since the sun is, in fact, hot. So when Aquinas is speaking of a non-univocal agent in this reply he is not speaking of a purely equivocal one, but of an analogical one.

28. The example Aquinas uses here is confusing, since we do not normally think of the sun as a "cause" of the human race. But one must certainly agree that without the sun there would be no human race.

29. Univocal agents can cause only this or that particular thing belonging to the same class as themselves; they cannot cause whole classes of things because they would then be their own cause. Thus a human being can be the univocal cause of another human being, but not of the category "human being."

30. Because a species is logically prior to its individual members, and because only a non-univocal agent can be the cause of a species, non-univocal agents are logically prior to univocal agents.

31. Aquinas returns here to the analogy between causes and language. Whatever we affirm in our language involves a logically prior affirmation of some sort of being. For example, consider the statements "The president *is* in the White House" and "The president *is* a human being." But note that Aquinas says this most basic use of language is itself analogical, since it is not exactly the same thing to be a human being and to be in a particular location. Presumably, I could change my location without ceasing to be me, whereas I could not cease to be a human being without ceasing to be me.

Thinking of the link between being and language in terms of God as the analogical cause of creaturely existence, we can say that although God's existence and our existence are not entirely dissimilar, they are no more similar than the use of "is" in the statements "The president is in the White House" and "The president is a human being."

32. That is, God and creatures do not share a category, not even that of "things that exist," since God is the *analogical* cause of the existence of creatures (see the previous note).

QUESTION 27

THE PROCESSION
OF THE DIVINE PERSONS

1.27.1

Whether there is procession in God?

It would seem that there cannot be any procession in God.[1]

1. Procession signifies outward movement. But in God there is nothing moveable, nor anything external. Therefore neither is there procession in God.

2. Everything that proceeds differs from that from which it proceeds. But in God there is no opposition [*diversitas*], but supreme simplicity.[2] Therefore in God there is no procession.

3. To proceed from another seems to be against the idea of a first principle. But God is the first principle, as shown above (1.2.3). Therefore procession has no place in God.

On the contrary: Our Lord says in John's Gospel (8:42), "From God I proceeded."

---

1. "Procession" (*processio*) should be taken to mean a "coming-forth," whether it be a person coming forth from her house or a thought coming forth from one's mind. *Processio* also has connotations of the English word "process," meaning an activity that issues in a result, which is not unrelated to the idea of "coming-forth," since the result "comes forth" from the person or thing engaged in the activity.

2. On "simplicity," see 1.3, note 1. The Latin word *diversitas* does not, like the modern English word "diversity," imply a benign or even harmonious multiplicity; rather, it implies a kind of contradiction.

I answer: Divine Scripture uses names that signify procession in relation to God.[3] This procession, however, has been understood in different ways. Some have understood it in the sense of an effect, proceeding from its cause. This is how Arius took it, saying that the Son proceeds from the Father as his first creature, and that the Holy Spirit proceeds from the Father and the Son as the creature of both. In this sense neither the Son nor the Holy Spirit would be true God. This is contrary to what is said of the Son in 1 John 5:20, "That . . . we may be in his true Son; this is true God." Of the Holy Spirit it is also said in 1 Corinthians 6:19, "Do you not know that your members are the temple of the Holy Spirit?" But it is God alone who has a temple.

Others take this procession to mean a cause proceeding to an effect, to the degree that it moves it or imprints its own likeness on it. This is how Sabellius took it,[4] who said that God the Father is called "Son" inasmuch as he takes on flesh from the Virgin, and the Father is likewise called "Holy Spirit" inasmuch as he sanctifies the rational creature and moves it to life. The words of our Lord, however, contradict such a meaning, when he speaks of himself in John 5:19: "The Son cannot of himself do anything"; and many other passages, in which it is shown that the Father himself is not the Son.

Careful examination shows that both of these opinions take "procession" as meaning movement toward something external, and therefore neither of them affirms procession as existing in God himself. But procession always supposes action, and thus just as there is an outward procession corresponding to the action directed toward external matter, so there must be an inward procession corresponding to the act remaining within the agent.[5] This applies most con-

---

3. Specifically, "Son" (i.e., one who "comes forth" from his parents) and "Spirit" (i.e., the Latin *spiritus,* which means "air" or "breath" that "comes forth" from the lungs).

4. In Aquinas's writings, the names of Arius and Sabellius are often paired in order to illustrate the two principle errors one can make regarding the Trinity: either overstressing (Arius) or understressing (Sabellius) the difference between the Persons. Aquinas offers similar pairings of heretics for other doctrinal issues: for example, Nestorius and Eutyches on the hypostatic union (i.e., the union of divinity and humanity in Christ—see 3.2, note 1). Aquinas is not interested in the details of the views associated with these names; rather, they are markers along what we might call a doctrinal *via negativa.* In his work *De rationibus fidei* (1264), chap. 9, Thomas writes: "The holy, catholic, and apostolic church proceeds carefully between contrary errors. It distinguishes the Persons in the Trinity against Sabellius, yet without falling into the error of Arius, but rather professes only one essence of the three Persons; in the mystery of the incarnation, on the other hand, it distinguishes the two natures against Eutyches, but does not separate the persons in the manner of Nestorius." In other words, pairs of heretical positions serve to indicate what is *not* meant by doctrines like the Trinity or the hypostatic union, without overdefining something that is ultimately rooted in the mystery of God.

5. Aquinas is searching for a suitable analogy by which he can speak of an action of "coming-forth" that does not imply that what comes forth is different in being from that which it comes forth from. The errors of Arius and Sabellius both stem from their inability to conceive of a genuine coming-forth that does not entail such a difference. Sabellius, to maintain the unity of God, denies that the coming-forth of the Son and Spirit is anything more than simply a way of expressing different modes of God's action in the world, whereas Arius, to maintain the

spicuously to the intellect, the action of which—that is, the act of understanding—remains within the one who understands. For whenever we understand,
by the very fact of understanding something comes forth within us [*procedit
aliquid intra ipsum*], which is a conception of the object understood, a conception issuing from our intellectual power and proceeding from our knowledge
of that object.[6] This conception is signified by the spoken word; and it is called
the "word of the heart" [*verbum cordis*], signified by the word of the voice.[7]

Since God is above all things, we should not understand what is said of God
according to the mode of the lowest creatures, namely bodies, but according
to the likenesses of the highest creatures, the intellectual substances, though
even the likenesses derived from these fall short in the representation of divine
things.[8] Procession, therefore, is not to be understood from what it is in bodies,
either according to movement from one place to another or by way of a cause
proceeding forth to its exterior effect, the way, for instance, the heat from a
hot thing makes something else hot. Rather it is to be understood along the
lines of an emanation in the mind, namely, as a mental word proceeds from
the speaker yet remains in him. It is in this sense that the catholic faith posits
procession in God.[9]

---

genuineness of the coming-forth, says that the Son (and, by implication, the Spirit) is different
in being from the Father.

   One way of thinking about what Aquinas means by "the act remaining within the agent" is to
think in terms of transitive and intransitive verbs. A transitive verb has an object that "receives"
its action ("The man hit *the dog*"), whereas an intransitive verb does not ("The man sinned").
Both kinds of verb involve action, but the action of the intransitive verb remains "within" the
one acting (event if it involves an external, physical action, as sinning often, but not always,
does). Thus we would not say, "The man sinned the dog by hitting it." For this analogy with
transitive and intransitive verbs, I am indebted to Herbert McCabe's essay "Aquinas on the
Trinity," *New Blackfriars* 80, no. 940 (June 1999), 276.

   6. The analogy that Thomas finds most appropriate is one that he takes from St. Augustine:
"And so you have a certain image of the trinity, the mind itself and its knowledge, which is its
offspring and its word about itself, and love as the third element" (*De Trinitate*, bk. 9, chap. 12,
no. 18). Aquinas's emphasis on a coming-forth that remains in the agent, however, is somewhat
different from Augustine's interest in how the analogy reconciles threeness and oneness.

   7. Aquinas's use of the term *verbum cordis* (word of the heart) can help us see that for Aquinas
thinking is structured in a way analogous to language. To know something is to have a concept
of it, which is something like having a word for it. Further, it is *only* by means of its concept
that we know something, even though it is the thing itself that we know, and not simply our
conception of it.

   8. We should always speak of God in analogies drawn from the highest creatures, while still
recognizing that God infinitely surpasses even the most exalted of creatures. Thus we should
draw our understanding of "coming-forth" not from biological generation, but from the spiritual
generation that occurs in the soul when a concept ("the word of the heart") is formed. But at the
same time we have to recognize that God's eternal generation of the Word infinitely surpasses
even the mind's generation of a concept.

   9. At first glance, it might appear that here Aquinas is elevating his particular way of understanding the "coming-forth" of the eternal Word—as analogous to the formation of a "mental
word" or concept—to the status of dogma (i.e., something that the church has said *must* be
believed by the faithful). But in fact, Aquinas is not saying this. Rather, he thinks that the

Reply to 1: This objection comes from the idea of procession in the sense of movement from one place to another, or of an action directed toward external matter or an exterior effect; but this kind of procession does not exist in God, as we have explained.

Reply to 2: Whatever proceeds by way of outward procession is necessarily different [*diversum*] from the source from which it proceeds. But whatever proceeds interiorly by means of an intellectual process is not necessarily different; indeed, the more perfectly it proceeds, the more closely it is one with the source from which it proceeds. For it is clear that the more a thing is understood, the more the intellectual conception is intimately joined to the one who understands, and the more they are one, since by the act of understanding itself the intellect is made one with the object understood.[10] Thus, as the divine intelligence is the very supreme perfection of God, as said above (1.14.2), the divine Word is necessarily perfectly one with the source from which he proceeds, without any kind of opposition [*diversitate*].

Reply to 3: To proceed from a principle, so as to be something outside and different from that principle, is contrary to the idea of a first principle; however, a procession by means of an act of intellect that is intimate and without opposition is included in the idea of a first principle. For when we say that the architect is the "principle" of a house,[11] we include in this idea of "principle" the architect's concept of what he is going to make. And if the architect were the *first* principle of the house, his conception of what he is going to make would likewise be included in the idea of the *first* principle.[12] God, who is the first principle of all things, may be compared to things created as the architect is to things designed.[13]

---

analogy between eternal Word and mental concept is simply one possible way (perhaps even the *best* possible way) of understanding what *is* a dogma of the church (defined at the Council of Nicea in AD 325), namely, that the Father brings forth the Son in such a way that the Son, while being distinct from the Father, shares fully in the Father's divinity.

10. Here Aquinas is displaying the particular aptness of intellectual processes as an analogy for understanding the processions in God. Thus he notes that although the coming-forth of one material thing from another necessarily implies a distinctness of being (e.g., a woman producing a child is giving birth to someone distinct in being from herself), this is not the case in the coming-forth of a concept from the mind. In fact, the more perfect the intellectual process is, the more closely the concept will resemble what it is that the mind knows. Thus in knowing a cow, the mind receives the "intellectual species" of the cow and thus takes on the form of the cow without actually becoming a cow. In bringing forth the concept of the cow, the more closely that concept resembles the intellectual species that the mind has taken on, the more perfect this process of concept generation is. See 1.12, note 8.

11. "Principle" is used here in the sense of "source" or "starting point" or "originator."

12. This is a loose translation of the sentence. The original Latin reads, *"Cum enim dicimus aedificatorem principium domus, in ratione huius principii includitur conceptio suae artis: et includeretur in ratione primi principii, si aedificator esset primum principium."* A more literal translation would be, "For when we say the builder is the principle of a house, in the meaning of this principle is included the conception of his art; and included in the meaning of the first principle, if the builder were to be the first principle."

13. The force of the objection is that first principles are not derived from anything else; if the Son proceeds from the Father, then he cannot be the first principle of creatures; but if he is

1.27.3

Whether any other procession exists in God besides that of the Word?[14]

It would seem that no other procession exists in God besides the generation of the Word.

1. For whatever reason we admit another procession, we should be led to admit yet another, and so on to infinity, which is unfitting. Therefore we must stop with the first and hold that there exists only one procession in God.

2. Every nature possesses only one way of communicating its nature, because operations derive unity and diversity from their results.[15] But procession in God is only by way of communication of the divine nature. Therefore, as there is only one divine nature, as was shown earlier (1.11.4), it follows that only one procession exists in God.[16]

3. If any procession other than the intellectual procession of the Word existed in God, it could only be the procession of love, which is by the operation of the will. But such a procession can be nothing other than the intellectual procession of reason, because in God his will is the same as his intellect, as was shown earlier (1.19.1).[17] Therefore in God there is no procession other than the procession of the Word.

On the contrary: The Holy Spirit proceeds from the Father, as is said in John 15:26; and he is distinct from the Son, according to the words of John 14:16, "I will ask my Father, and he will give you another Paraclete."[18] Therefore, there is another procession in God besides the procession of the Word.

---

not the first principle of creatures, then he is not God. In replying to this objection, Aquinas holds to his analogy of intellectual procession. When an architect conceives of a house, we can properly speak of the house as deriving from the architect's conception of it, because the architect's conception is not something external to the architect's identity.

14. Here Thomas is pursuing the analogy of human intellect in attempting to understand the Trinity. Now the question concerns whether this analogy can provide us with a way of thinking about a *second* "coming-forth" that remains within the agent, one that is distinct from the intellect's production of the concept?

15. The objection is that we judge two processes ("operations") to be the same if they issue in the same results. If we are talking about the process of a nature sharing or communicating itself, there can be only one such process because there is only one result. Thus when fire shares its nature with water (i.e., by heating it up), we have the single process called "heating." Any instance of fire communicating its nature is called "heating."

16. The only way there could be more than one process of self-communication of God's nature (i.e., more than one procession in God) would be if there were more than one divine nature, which would entail there being more than one God, since God *is* his nature.

17. This objection is, in essence, the same as the second objection in 1.27.1, namely, how can the multiplicity of procession in God be reconciled with the idea that God is radically simple?

18. For "Paraclete" read "Advocate" or "Comforter," which is a name the Gospel of John gives to the Spirit."

I answer: There are two processions in God: the procession of the Word, and another. To understand this clearly, we must bear in mind that procession exists in God only according to an action that is not directed to anything external, but remains in the agent itself. In an intellectual nature such action is the action of the intellect and the action of the will. The procession of the Word is perceived as an action of the intellect. The operation of the will within ourselves involves also another procession, that of love, by which the object loved is in the lover, in the same way that, by the conception of the word, the object spoken of or understood is in the one who understands it.[19] Therefore, besides the procession of the Word there is posited another procession in God, which is the procession of love.

Reply to 1: There is no need to go on to infinity in the divine processions, for the procession that is within the agent in an intellectual nature terminates in the procession of the will.[20]

19. In other words, the intellect has two operations of "coming-forth": knowing, which is an act of the intellect; and loving, which is an act of the will. But there seems to be a difficulty with this second kind of coming-forth, since we generally think of love involving something external to our will, something outside of us that draws our will to itself. Thus love does not seem to be a coming-forth that remains within God. However, we might note (as Aquinas does here) that just as through knowing something we virtually "become" what we know (see note 10, above), so in loving we virtually "become" what we love. Thus in loving, we love the object as we apprehend it, that is, as it is *in* us. This would seem to account for how the operation of love in God can be a coming-forth that remains within God. But there is still a problem. Although we know something by having a conception of it within our mind, we generally think that something has gone wrong if we love our idea of something rather than the thing itself. Indeed, Aquinas does not think that our becoming what we love involves the generation of a "thing" in us at all (or at least nothing beyond the conception of it we have formed); rather it is what he calls "an impulse and movement toward an object" (1.27.4). In discussing this question in his *Compendium theologiae*, Aquinas says, "The act of loving reaches its perfection not in a likeness of the beloved (in the way that an act of understanding reaches perfection in a likeness of the object understood); rather the act of love reaches its perfection in a drawing of the lover to the beloved person" (1.46).

The solution to this difficulty for Aquinas is that the operation (or "breathing forth") of love in God is not a matter of God's love being drawn by something "external"; rather, it is the love of the Father (who is God) for the Son (who is God). The generation of the Son is the Father's knowing of his own divine nature, and the breathing forth of the Spirit is the impulse of love that comes forth from the Father and the Son in that act of knowing.

20. This rather curt reply anticipates what Aquinas will say shortly in 1.27.5. It is important to remember that Aquinas does not think that by analyzing human reason he can prove that there is procession in God. Even if one accepts that both God and humans are intellectual beings, it does not follow that God's activity of knowing is anything like the human activity of knowing. We have no reason to think that God needs to generate a concept in order to know. What Aquinas is trying to do is simply to find an analogy that can help us understand what we already accept on the basis of revelation, namely, that God has from the beginning a Word that is with God and that is God, and that God also has a Spirit that descended upon the Word-made-flesh and now makes the saints holy. So if the objector *could* somehow demonstrate that human intellectual operations involve more than two "comings-forth," this would in no way disprove the Trinity; it would simply indicate that the analogy of human intellectual processes limps even worse than was originally thought.

Reply to 2: All that exists in God, is God, as was said above (1.3.4), which is not the case with others. Therefore the divine nature is communicated by whatever procession is not external, but this does not apply to other natures.[21]

Reply to 3: Though will and intellect are not different in God, nevertheless the nature of will and intellect requires that the processions belonging to each of them exist in a certain ordered relationship. For the procession of love occurs in due order as regards the procession of the Word, since nothing can be loved by the will unless it is conceived in the intellect. So we perceive a certain ordered relationship of the Word to the principle from which it proceeds, even though in God the substance of the intellect is the same as the concept of the intellect; so too, even though will and intellect are the same in God, nevertheless, because the idea of love is that it comes forth [*procedat*] only from the conception of the intellect, there is still a distinction of order between the procession of love and the procession of the Word in God.[22]

21. This response is perhaps somewhat less than satisfactory. Thomas does not really answer the objection's claim that one nature equals one process of self-communication; he simply refers back to the claim that anything "in" God *is* God, that is, shares the divine nature. Thus he seems entirely to beg the question (i.e., presumes what he sets out to prove) of whether there is a second procession in God. However, to understand what he is doing here, we should note two characteristics of Aquinas's trinitarian theology that are implicit in this response.

First, Thomas *never* tries to prove that God is triune (see article 1.32.1, below); this is something that he accepts on the basis of faith. Such an assumed starting point is not, however, question-begging, since Thomas is not trying to "prove" anything. Further, Thomas's response questions the objection's assumption that the analogy of a nature communicating itself can serve as a source of information about the number of processions in God. It cannot; only Scripture can give us that information.

Second, like the previous response, this response underscores the point that we should not push our analogies too far in speaking and thinking about God's nature. As much as the processions of the Word and Spirit are like a created being communicating its nature to something else (e.g., fire heating water), we cannot require that these processions conform to the communication of a created nature in every way. As the Fourth Lateran Council (1215) stated, "No likeness can be expressed between creator and creature without implying a greater unlikeness" (chap. 2).

22. The Latin word *ordo* can have the sense of "relation"—placing things in a certain order is a matter of giving them a particular set of relations to one another. What Aquinas seems to be saying in this response is that he is willing to grant that because of divine simplicity (see 1.3, note 1) God's intellect and will are not things distinct from God's existence (in doctrinal terms, the Son and Spirit are both *homoousious* or of "one substance" with the Father). However, God's thinking and willing *do* have a certain relationship to each other that allows them to be distinguished from each other. Thus, when Aquinas says that "there is a distinction of order between the procession of love and the procession of the Word in God," we could paraphrase him as saying that the procession of the Son and the Spirit are different because they are related in different ways to their origin: the Son proceeds from the Father as his image (just as the concept arises from the intellect's knowledge of itself), and the Spirit proceeds from the Father and (or through) the Son (just as will must be moved by the concept of what attracts it). So the two cases of coming-forth (Son and Spirit) and that from which they come forth (Father) are all the same "substance" (i.e., God), but they differ as the different terms of their different relations. See note 1.36, note 10.

THE DIVINE PERSONS

1.29.4

Whether this word "person" signifies relation?

It would seem that this word "person," as applied to God, does not signify relation, but substance.[1]

1. Aquinas asks this question because the traditional teaching of the church (in Greek) that God is one *ousia* and three *hypostases* came to be translated in the Latin West as one *substantia* and three *personae*. In this article, Aquinas is trying to relate what he has said in question 1.27 and 1.28 about Father, Son, and Spirit as "relations" with the more traditional theological vocabulary of the Western Church, where they are called "Persons." As we shall see, the language of three "Persons" raises some significant theological difficulties, yet Thomas is unwilling to abandon the language, hallowed as it is by centuries of use. However, he will clarify that, when used in the case of the Father, Son, and Holy Spirit, "person" means "relation."

This is an extremely complex article, but the problem it addresses is not all that esoteric. Christians generally say that they believe in a "personal God," by which they mean a divine being that is distinct from the world and to which they can relate in an interpersonal way. God is not simply an "impersonal" force. At the same time, the Christian tradition has used the word "person" as a way of expressing the distinction and relatedness between the Father and the Son and the Holy Spirit—the three "Persons" of the Trinity. But this seems to be a confused (and confusing) use of language: Is God a "person" or is God three "Persons"? Here Aquinas is trying to sort this out.

All of the objections really turn on the same issue: if the Father, Son, and Spirit are to be distinct "Persons," does this not entail their being three distinct substances (that is, three distinct "somethings"), and not simply relations? A complicating factor in this question is that the Latin word used for the unity of God—*substantia*—translates into Greek as *hypostasis,* the word

1. Augustine says in *De Trinitate* (bk. 7, chap. 6, no. 11), "When we speak of the person of the Father, we mean nothing else but the substance of the Father, for 'person' is said with reference to himself, and not with reference to the Son."

2. The question "What?" refers to essence.[2] But, as Augustine says in the same place (*De Trinitate*, bk. 7, chap. 4, no. 7; cf. bk. 5, chap. 9, no. 10), when we say "there are three who bear witness in heaven, the Father, the Word, and the Holy Spirit,"[3] and it is asked, "Three what?" the answer is, "Three Persons." Therefore "person" signifies essence.

3. According to the Philosopher in the *Metaphysics* (bk. 4, chap. 7, 1012ª), that which is signified by a word is its definition. But the definition of "person" is "the individual substance of the rational nature," as stated earlier (1.29.1).[4] Therefore "person" signifies substance.

4. "Person," in the case of human beings and angels, does not signify a relation, but rather something absolute.[5] Therefore, if in God it signified a relation, it would be said equivocally of God and of human beings and angels.

On the contrary: Boethius says in his *De Trinitate* (chap. 6) that every word that refers to the Persons signifies relation. But no word belongs to the Persons more strictly than this word "person" itself. Therefore this word "person" signifies relation.

I answer: A difficulty arises concerning the meaning of this word "person" in God because, in contrast to the nature of the names belonging to the essence,

---

used in the East for the distinctness of Father, Son, and Spirit. Both words literally mean "that which stands under." So when Greek-speaking Christians heard Latin-speaking Christians say that God was one *substantia,* they heard this as a denial that Father, Son, and Spirit were really distinct; in other words, they heard echoes of the Sabellian heresy (see 1.27, notes 4 and 5, as well as the entry for Sabellius in the glossary of names). This (mistaken) impression could be exacerbated by Aquinas's claim that the Persons of the Trinity were "merely" relations of origin.

The notion of "relation" itself presents a further difficulty. Thomas conceives of a relation not as something "between" two entities, but at least in the case of a "real" relation (see 3.1, note 7), as something that an entity possesses. In other words, "relation" is a property that inheres in things, and not something that arises between them. In this understanding, Thomas follows Aristotle, for whom "relation" was one of the ten "categories" (see 1.3, note 2). The difficulty is that "relation" is normally an accidental property of things, which cannot be the case with God, who is supremely simple and therefore has no accidents (see 1.3, note 1).

2. See 1.12, note 4.

3. This is the so-called "Johannine comma," which in the West during the Middle Ages was taken as an authentic part of the first letter of John (coming at 5:7). It is now apparent that this verse, which appears nowhere in Greek manuscripts, was a gloss on the text (see 1.12, note 7) that found its way into the text itself. One should also note that Augustine's remarks from *De Trinitate* about "Three what?" make no reference to the Johannine comma, though Thomas makes it sound as though they do.

4. This definition of "person," taken from Boethius (*De duabus naturis,* chap. 3), was a standard one in the Middle Ages. In the course of this article, Aquinas takes this standard definition and modifies it significantly.

5. For "something absolute" read "a substance."

it is predicated plurally of the three;[6] also it does not in itself refer to another, as do the words that signify relation.[7]

Therefore some have thought that "person," by virtue of its basic meaning, signifies the divine essence, as is the case with the words "God" and "wise." In order to meet heretical objections, however, a council decreed that it was to be taken in a relative sense,[8] and especially when used in the plural (as when we say, "three Persons") or when used with the addition of a distinguishing adjective (as when we say, "one is the person of the Father, another of the Son," and so on). However, used in the singular, it may be either absolute or relative.

But this does not seem to be a satisfactory explanation, because if "person," by virtue of its proper meaning, expresses the divine essence only, it follows that when we speak of "three Persons," the heretics would not have been silenced, but would have had still more reason to argue.[9]

For this reason, others maintained that "person" signifies in God both the essence and the relation. Some of these said that it signifies the essence directly [in recto] and relation indirectly [in obliquo], since "person" means something like "in itself one" [per se una], and oneness pertains to the essence.[10] To say that something is "in itself" [per se] implies relation indirectly; indeed, the Father is understood to exist "in himself," as relatively distinct from the Son.[11] Others, however, said, on the contrary, that it signifies relation directly and essence indirectly,[12] since in the definition

6. The "names belonging to the essence" would be such terms as "goodness" or "wisdom" or "power." We do not say that God is "three goodnesses," even though the Father, Son, and Spirit are all in fact good. We do, however, say that God is "three Persons." On "predicated," see 1.3, note 2.

7. In other words, the Son can be "the Son" only because of his relation to the Father, which is implied in the word "Son" itself. But the word "person" has no such implication.

8. In discussing this issue in De potentia 9.4, Aquinas specifies that the council he is referring to is the Council of Nicea, though it is difficult to find a place in the documents of Nicea that corresponds to the view described here. In this same discussion, he also identifies one of the unnamed quibusdam (some) of the previous sentence ("some have thought") as Peter Lombard.

9. In other words, some have said that the Council of Nicea decreed that "person" be used in a peculiar way when speaking of the Persons of the Trinity, in order to respond to the threat of Arianism. Aquinas says that such a peculiar use of language, imposed by a conciliar fiat, would not have been an effective answer to the heretics. Thomas recognizes that when we speak of God we must use our ordinary way of speaking in peculiar ways, but apparently if a particular use of language is too peculiar (so as to be entirely equivocal) it causes confusion among the faithful and ridicule from unbelievers. What Aquinas wants to show is that the Council of Nicea is not simply inventing a new use of the word "person" (i.e., "hypostasis") but is discovering a meaning of "person" that was implicit all along.

10. Various figures have been suggested as among those Thomas is thinking about here: Gilbert of Porrée (twelfth century), Alan of Lille (twelfth century), and Alexander of Hales (thirteenth century).

11. In other words, if one takes unity to be the key to the meaning of the word "person," then it is clear that the divine nature is "a person," since God is one. At the same time, the Father, Son, and Spirit can by implication be called "persons" since they are distinct from each other.

12. Simon of Tournai (twelfth century) and William of Auxerre (thirteenth century) are sometimes suggested as holders of this view.

of "person" the term "nature" is mentioned indirectly.[13] This latter view came nearer to the truth.

To resolve the question, we must consider that something may be included in the meaning of a narrower term that is not included in the broader term, the way "rational" is included in the meaning of "human being," and not in the meaning of "animal."[14] So it is one thing to ask the meaning of the word "animal," and another to ask its meaning when the animal in question is a human being. Similarly, it is one thing to ask the meaning of this word "person" in general, and another to ask the meaning of "person" as applied to God.[15] For "person" in general signifies the individual substance of a rational nature. An individual is that which in itself is undivided, and is distinct from others. Therefore, in any nature, "person" signifies what is distinct in that nature. Thus in human nature it signifies *this* flesh, *these* bones, and *this* soul, which are the sources of human individuality, and which, though not belonging to the meaning of "person" in general, nevertheless do belong to the meaning of a particular human person.[16]

Distinction in God, however, is only by relation of origin, as stated earlier (1.28.3).[17] Relation in God is not as an accident in a subject, but is the divine

13. Thomas is referring to the Boethian definition of "person" as "the individual substance of the rational nature" (and he is using "nature" and "essence" interchangeably). He is pointing out that the definition does not speak of the nature itself, but of something belonging to the nature. Therefore "person" applies to a nature only indirectly, while it applies to what shares in the nature (i.e., the relations) directly. As Aquinas notes, he thinks this view is closer to the truth.

14. Aquinas here presumes the definition of human beings as "rational animals," so the category "human beings" is a narrower subcategory of the broader category of animals-in-general. What makes the subcategory narrower is that it includes more in its definition; in this case, it includes the attribute "rational."

15. Just as there is a difference between asking what an animal-in-general is and asking what a human animal is, so too there is a difference between asking what a person-in-general is and asking what a divine Person is.

16. Included in the general meaning of the term "person" are those things that distinguish a person from other members of its class. In the case of human beings, for example, what makes one human person distinct from another is that he or she consists of this *particular* flesh, these *particular* bones, this *particular* soul, and so on; no other human person shares these particulars. Just as the qualifier "rational" is part of the definition of human beings but is not part of the definition of the broader category "animals," so too being constituted by these particulars is part of what it means to be this *particular* human being, but it is not part of what it means to be a human being in general.

The larger point here is that "human nature" is not a person; only particular instances of human nature are persons. Thus "person" means this or that particular person, distinguished from other persons by being made of particular bones and flesh and soul. So although the particulars that make me who I am are not part of the definition of "person," since one can be a person without having *my* particular bones and flesh and soul, the definition of "person" does require that one have *some* particular bones and flesh and soul, otherwise he or she would not be distinct.

17. See 1.27, note 22. The Persons in God, unlike human persons, are not distinguished by bones and flesh. They are distinguished by their relations of origin.

essence itself; thus it is subsistent, for the divine essence subsists. Therefore, just as "godhood" [*deitas*] *is* God, so too the divine "fatherhood" [*paternitas*] *is* God the Father, who is a divine person.[18] Therefore "divine person" signifies a relation as subsisting. And this is to signify relation as a substance, and such a relation is a hypostasis subsisting in the divine nature,[19] although in truth that which subsists in the divine nature *is* the divine nature itself.[20]

Thus it is true to say that the word "person" signifies the relation directly, and the essence indirectly—but it does not signify the relation inasmuch as it is a relation, but inasmuch as it is signified in the manner of a hypostasis.[21] So, likewise, it signifies the essence directly and the relation indirectly, since the essence is the same as the hypostasis. In God, "hypostasis" signifies what is distinct by virtue of a relation, and thus relation, as such, enters into the notion of the person indirectly.

We can therefore say that this signification of the word "person" was not clearly perceived before it was attacked by heretics. Therefore, this word "person" was used just like any other absolute term. But afterwards it was applied to express relation, because it lent itself to that signification. So this word "person"

18. I hope readers will forgive the barbarism of "godhood," but I wanted to find a way of rendering *deitas* that would show its parallel with *paternitas*. Here it is important to follow Thomas's thinking carefully. Although the relations are something distinct from each other, they are not distinct from all that it means to be God (i.e., "the divine essence"); therefore, what is true of the divine essence is true of them as well. One of the things that is true of God is that God is "simple" (see 1.3, note 1), so just as *deitas* is not distinct from God, *paternitas* is not distinct from the person of the Father. Thus the person of the Father *is* the relationship of fatherhood.

19. On "hypostasis," see note 1, above.

20. Once again, since the relations are distinct from each other but not from the divine essence, they share fully is everything that the divine essence is. One of the things that the divine essence is, is "subsisting." Thus the divine Persons are what Aquinas terms "subsistent relations"—things constituted by and existing as their mutual relations. Just as "human person" means "human nature subsisting as particular bones, flesh, and soul" so "divine Person" means "the divine nature subsisting as a relation." And just as a human person is distinct insofar as he or she subsists in the particulars of this flesh, these bones, and this soul, so too are the divine Persons distinct insofar as they subsist in the particular relations of Father, Son, and Spirit.

It might also help to note that here Thomas is employing his distinction (see 1.13, note 6) between *what* is signified (*res significata*) and the *way* it is signified (*modus significandi*). Though the Persons are not distinct from the divine nature, because God is supremely simple, we speak of them as if they were accidents, because our way of speaking about relations is taken from creatures, in which relations are accidental.

21. We cannot apply the word "person" to just any relationship, but only to those relationships of origin that are the Father, Son, and Spirit, because only those relations, by virtue of their identity with the divine essence, are subsistent. For example, if I am next to a tree, I have the relationship of being alongside the tree. But that "alongsideness" is not identical with my essence; if I move away from the tree, the "alongsideness" ceases to exist without changing who I am. In the case of God, however, the relations *are* hypostases that are identical with God's essence.

means relation not only by use and custom, according to the first opinion, but also by force of its own proper signification.[22]

Reply to 1: This word "person" is said regarding the thing itself and not another, because it signifies a relation, not in a relation-like way, but in the manner of a substance that is a hypostasis. In that sense Augustine says that it signifies the essence, since in God essence is the same as the hypostasis, because in God "what he is" and "that whereby he is" are the same.[23]

Reply to 2: "What" sometimes asks about the nature expressed by the definition, as when we say, "What is a human being?" and we answer, "A mortal rational animal." Sometimes it asks about the *suppositum,* as when we ask, "What swims in the sea?" and answer, "A fish." So to those who say, "Three what?" we answer, "Three Persons."[24]

Reply to 3: In God, the individual—that is, distinct and incommunicable substance—includes the idea of relation, as explained above.

Reply to 4: The different sense of the less common term does not produce equivocation in the more common. Although a horse and an ass have their own proper definitions, nevertheless they are spoken of univocally in the word "animal," because the common definition of "animal" applies to both. So although relation is contained in the signification of "divine person," but not in that of "angelic person" or of "human person," it does not follow that the word "person" is used in an equivocal sense. But neither is it applied univocally, since nothing can be said univocally of God and creatures (1.13.5).[25]

22. Here Aquinas is trying to account for how the meaning of "person" as "that which makes a distinct instance of a nature" was overlooked for so long. The oversight was the result of the emphasis on the element of subsistence (i.e., independent existence) rather than on distinctness. But once we use the word "person" to mean divine "Person" we see that it can mean a relationship, so long as that relationship is not simply an attribute of something distinct (as "alongsideness" can be an attribute of mine so long as I am alongside the tree) but is itself something distinct.

23. In a human person, what I am—that is, a specific human being—is something distinct from that which makes me human—that is, human nature. In the case of the divine Persons, on the other hand, what they are—Father, Son, and Holy Spirit—is identical with what makes them divine—that is, the divine nature or essence.

24. Thomas's examples may be a bit confusing. His point is simply that when we ask "What?" we are asking sometimes about the nature (definition) of a thing (e.g., "What is a barbell?") and sometimes about a particular thing (e.g., "What just fell on my foot?").

25. Once again, language used about both God and creatures is analogical. Here the meaning of "person" in both cases fits the Boethian definition, "the individual substance of the rational nature," but in the case of creatures, persons are individuated by matter (human beings) or species (angels), whereas in the case of God, the Persons are distinguished by their relations.

KNOWLEDGE OF THE TRINITY

1.32.1

Whether the Trinity of the divine Persons can be known by natural reason?

It would seem that the Trinity of the divine Persons can be known by natural reason.[1]

1. Philosophers came to the knowledge of God only by natural reason, and yet we find that they said many things about the Trinity of Persons. Indeed, Aristotle says in *On the Heavens and the Earth* (bk. 1, chap.1, 268ᵃ), "Through this number"—namely, three—"we bring ourselves to acknowledge the greatness of one God, surpassing all things created."[2] And Augustine says in his *Confessions* (bk. 7, chap. 9, no. 13), "There"—that is, in the Platonic books—"I read, not in fact in these words, but with the same meaning and enforced by many and various reasons, that 'in the beginning was the Word, and the Word was with God, and the Word was God.'" And so on, in such

1. The first objection offers examples of pagan thinkers who write things that sound as if they have knowledge of the Trinity. The point is that if these pagans knew of the Trinity, they must have done so by the exercise of their natural reason, since the Trinity was not revealed to them.

2. The objection quotes the version of Gerard of Cremona (1114–1187), who was translating from Arabic and did not accurately represent what Aristotle wrote (i.e., "We make further use of the number three in the worship of the gods"). This article was probably written at some point prior to the fall of 1268. William of Moerbeke's far more accurate translation of *On the Heavens and the Earth* did not appear until 1271.

words the distinction of Persons is taught. We read, moreover, in a gloss on Romans 1 and Exodus 8, that the magicians of Pharaoh failed in the third sign (that is, as regards knowledge of a third person—i.e., of the Holy Spirit), and thus it is clear that they knew at least two Persons.[3] Likewise Trismegistus says, "The monad begot a monad, and reflected upon itself its own heat."[4] By these words the generation of the Son and procession of the Holy Spirit seem to be indicated. Therefore knowledge of the divine Persons can be obtained by natural reason.

2. Richard of St. Victor says in the book *De Trinitate* (bk. 1, chap. 4), "I believe without doubt that probable and even necessary arguments can be found for any explanation of the truth."[5] So even to prove the Trinity of Per-

3. On the "gloss," see 1.12, note 7.

4. "Hermes Trismegistus" was supposedly the author of the third-century "hermetic books," which represented a fusion of Platonism, Stoicism, and eastern religions.

5. The second objection offers examples of Christian thinkers who tried to show the necessity of God's triunity through the use of natural reason. On the whole, medieval theologians, with the possible exception of Peter Abelard, did not try to "prove" the Trinity in such a way as to convince those who did not already believe in it. Rather, beginning from faith in the Trinity, they tried to discover "necessary reasons" why God *must* be triune. As we shall see, for Aquinas, even this task causes reason to step beyond its proper limits. The first such example the objection offers is Richard of St. Victor (d. 1173). In book 3 of his work *De Trinitate*, Richard argued roughly thus, in four steps:

1. God is, by definition, the highest good (*Summum Bonum*). As St. Anselm (who lived roughly two generations before Richard) said in his work the *Proslogion,* God is that than which no greater can be conceived. Therefore, if God is good, God must be the highest good. Now what *is* this highest good? Love. Richard does not try and justify his claim that love is the highest good; he seems to assume that it is obvious, which, of course, fits with 1 John 4:8: "God is love."

2. Now if God is the *Summum Bonum,* and that *Summum Bonum* is love, it follows that God must not simply be love, but the highest form of love. And this highest form of love is called *caritas.* Richard says that for love to truly be *caritas,* it must be interpersonal love—love that is shared between two persons. Where there is only one person, *caritas* cannot exist (*De Trinitate*, bk. 3, chap. 2). Therefore if God is to be the highest good, there must be an "other" toward whom God's love is directed.

3. Since *caritas* is interpersonal, it must not simply be given, but also received. God's love is infinite love, since God is infinite. Therefore the other whom God loves must be a *divine* other, because a mere creature, being finite, could not receive infinite divine love. Thus there must be two divine Persons *within the Godhead*. Also, for love to be perfect (as God's love must be) it must be reciprocal (we all know that unrequited love is something less than perfect). Yet for the "other" to perfectly respond to God's love, that other must also be God.

4. Thus in order for God to be the most perfect, infinite love, there must be two divine Persons within the reality of the one God. Yet, Richard argues, this is not yet the highest form of love. With love that remains merely the love between two persons, there is still the possibility that it can remain self-absorbed and narcissistic (if you have ever had a roommate who has fallen in love, you know what I mean). For Richard, the highest form of love is the love shared by two for a third: "There is shared love when two persons love a third in a harmony of affection and a community of love, and when the loves of the two converge in the single flame of love they have for the third" (*De Trinitate*,

sons some have brought forward an argument based on the infinite goodness of God, who communicates himself infinitely in the procession of the divine Persons; while some are moved by the consideration that "no good thing can be joyfully possessed without partnership."[6] Augustine proceeds to prove the Trinity of Persons by the procession of the word and of love in our own mind, and we have followed him in this (1.27.1 and 3).[7] Therefore the Trinity of Persons can be known by natural reason.

3. It seems to be superfluous to hand on to human beings that which cannot be known by human reason. But it should not be said that the divine handing on of knowledge of the Trinity is superfluous. Therefore the Trinity of Persons can be known by human reason.

On the contrary: Hilary says in *On the Trinity* (bk. 2, no. 9), "Let no person think to reach the sacred mystery of generation by his own mind." And Ambrose says (*On the Catholic Faith*, bk. 1, chap. 10), "It is impossible to know the secret of generation. The mind fails, the voice is silent." But the Trinity of divine Persons is distinguished by origin of generation and procession, as is clear from what is said earlier (1.30.2). Therefore, since a person cannot know and grasp by understanding that for which no necessary reason can be given, it follows that the Trinity of Persons cannot be known by reason.

I answer: It is impossible to arrive at knowledge of the Trinity by natural reason. For, as explained above (1.12.4, 11, 12), human beings cannot obtain knowledge of God by natural reason except from creatures. But creatures lead us to the knowledge of God in the way that effects lead to their cause. Accordingly, by natural reason we can know of God only that which necessarily belongs to him as the source of things, and we have cited this fundamental principle in discussing God earlier (1.12.12). Now, the creative power of God is common to the whole Trinity, and therefore it belongs to the unity of the essence, and not to the distinction of the Persons.[8] Therefore, by natural reason

---

bk. 3, chap. 19). Thus, in order for God's love to be the most perfect possible, there must be a third divine person within the reality of God.

A similar sort of argument can be found in St. Bonaventure's *Itinerarium* 6.2.

6. In *De veritate* 10.13, obj. 6, Thomas identifies Boethius as the source of this quotation, though it in fact comes from Seneca's sixth epistle.

7. The reference is to Augustine's use of an analogy between the human mind and the Trinity in his attempt to understand and explain how the Trinity can be both one and three. Just as the human mind can be constituted by the distinct faculties of memory, reason, and will without becoming schizophrenic, so too God can exist as Father, Son, and Spirit without being three gods. As the objection points out, Aquinas himself uses this analogy to explore the Persons of the Trinity (see articles 1.27.1 and 2, above). What the objection seems to presume is that, beginning from our knowledge of our faculties of memory, reason, and will, we can argue that God is necessarily three in one.

8. Here Aquinas invokes the theological principle that with regard to the world the Trinity always works as a unity; it is the *Trinity* that creates the world, not one of the Persons of the Trinity. Behind this principle is the notion that the Persons of the Trinity are not simply three "functions" of God (e.g., creating, redeeming, and sustaining), nor are they a divine "division of labor"; rather, they are a communion of love that acts as a unity in our world.

we can know what belongs to the unity of the essence, but not what belongs to the distinction of the Persons.[9]

Whoever, then, tries to prove the Trinity of Persons by natural reason takes away from faith in two ways. First, with respect to the dignity of faith itself, which consists in its being concerned with invisible things that exceed human reason. Therefore the Apostle says in Hebrews 11:1 that "faith is of things that appear not." The Apostle also says in 1 Corinthians 2:6–7, "We speak wisdom among the perfect, but not the wisdom of this world, nor of the princes of this world; but we speak the wisdom of God in a mystery that is hidden." Second, with respect to the usefulness of drawing others to the faith; for when anyone, trying to prove the faith, brings forward arguments that are not cogent, he falls under the ridicule of the unbelievers, since they suppose that we stand upon such arguments, and that we believe on such grounds.[10]

Therefore, we must not attempt to prove what belongs to faith, except by authority alone, to those who receive the authority. As regards others, it suffices to prove that what faith teaches is not impossible.[11] Therefore Dionysius says in *On the Divine Names* (chap. 2, no. 2), "If someone wholly resists Scripture he is far off from our philosophy. . . . If, however, he has care for the truth of the writings"—that is, Holy Scripture—"we too follow this rule."

Reply to 1: The philosophers did not know the mystery of the Trinity of the divine Persons by its proper attributes, such as paternity, sonship, and procession,[12] for according to the Apostle's words in 1 Corinthians 2:6, "We speak the wisdom of God, which none of the princes of the world"—that is, the philosophers—"knew." Nevertheless, they knew some of the essential attributes appropriated to the Persons, such as power to the Father, wisdom to the Son, goodness to the Holy Spirit; as will later on appear (1.39.7–8).[13]

---

9. Natural reason knows God by arguing from the effect to the cause, and the effects of God in the world are brought about by the Persons of the Trinity acting as one; therefore all we can know about God from the world is that God is a unity, not that God is triune. Knowledge of the Trinity must come to us through God's self-revelation in Jesus Christ.

10. In other words, if you use reason to prove something that cannot be proved by reason, you end up looking stupid.

11. As we saw earlier (see 1.1, notes 23 and 26), you can prove things to those who grant your first principles but not to those who do not. Thomas does think, however, that you can show people who do not grant your first principles that your views are not impossible. This is what Thomas does with the Christian doctrine of the Trinity: he shows that it is not an unreasonable belief, even if it is a belief at which one cannot arrive through reason alone.

12. See 1.36, note 10.

13. Despite things that sound like Christian trinitarian belief in their writings, pagan philosophers did not know about the Trinity itself. Thus, for example, although they knew that God possessed power, wisdom, and goodness, they did not associate ("appropriate") these attributes with three Persons in God.

The language of "appropriation" is typical in Western theology of the Trinity and is often associated with Augustine. As Aquinas defines it, appropriation is "the showing-forth (*manifestatio*) of the Persons through the essential attributes" (1.39.7). In other words, there are certain properties that we attribute to God by virtue of God being God (i.e., "essential attributes"),

So, when Aristotle said, "By this number," and so on, we must not understand this to mean that he applied a threefold number to God, but that he wished to say that the ancients used the threefold number in their sacrifices and prayers on account of some perfection residing in the number three.

In the Platonic books also we find "In the beginning was the word," not meaning the person begotten in God, but meaning the ideal pattern (*ratio idealis*) by which God made all things, and which is appropriated to the Son.[14] And even if the Platonists knew things appropriated to the three Persons, they are said to have failed in the third sign—that is, in the knowledge of the third person—because they deviated from the goodness appropriated to the Holy Spirit, in that knowing God "they did not glorify him as God," as said in Romans 1:21. Further, because the Platonists asserted the existence of one primal being, whom they also declared to be the father of the universe, they consequently asserted the existence of another substance beneath him, which

---

including such things as eternity, beauty, enjoyment, power, wisdom, unity, and so forth. We do not need to know that God is triune in order to know that God is eternal, beautiful, and so forth; these are things we can know from God's act of creating. And yet, in order to have a better grasp of the divine Persons, we can associate these essential attributes with particular Persons on the basis of the scriptural language of Father, Son/Word, and Spirit.

Thus Thomas argues in 1.39.8 that, for example, the Son and Spirit are no less powerful than the Father, but "power" is appropriated to the Father because power "has the meaning of 'source' [*habet rationem principii*]," and the Father "is the source of all divinity." In the same way, the Father and Spirit are no less wise than the Son, yet "wisdom" is appropriated to the Son/Word because a word is "nothing other than a concept of wisdom." Similarly, the Father and Son are no less good than the Spirit; however, "goodness" is appropriated to the Spirit because goodness is "the meaning and goal of 'love' [*ratio et objectum amoris*] and "Love" is the proper name of the Spirit" (cf. 1.37).

This association of essential properties with specific Persons through "appropriation" has been criticized by a number of modern theologians, most notably Karl Rahner (1904–1984) and, following upon his work, Catherine Mowry LaCugna (1953–1997). The essence of the criticism is that the "theory" or "doctrine" of appropriation is a kind of rescue operation necessitated by an approach to the Trinity that diminishes the distinctiveness of the Persons, such that Father, Son, and Spirit are not really distinct from each other, but only distinct in our understanding of them. In this view, Augustine and Aquinas resort to appropriations in an (inadequate) attempt to maintain the distinctness of the Persons. Such criticisms seem to me to miss the mark entirely. Appropriation is neither a theory nor a doctrine, but a practice of speaking whereby we associate things that are true of all three Persons in a particular way with one of them. Thomas's reflections on this association of essential properties with particular Persons are not intended to establish the distinctness of the Persons; the relations of origin do that (i.e., the Son is distinct from the Father because the Son comes forth from the Father; the Father does not come forth from the Son). Rather, his reflections are intended to illuminate how language that names the attributes of creatures ("power," "wisdom," "goodness") can be borrowed and applied to God so as to illuminate (i.e., *manifestare*) the distinctiveness of the Persons. As Jean-Pierre Torrell puts it, appropriated terms offer "one of our rare chances to mumble something about the unsayable"; see Jean-Pierre Torrell, *Saint Thomas Aquinas: Spiritual Master,* trans. Robert Royal (Washington, D.C.: The Catholic University of America Press, 2003), 158.

14. The Platonists knew that God had reason ("word"), but they did not conceive of this as a distinct person within the godhead.

they called "mind" or the "paternal intellect," containing the idea of all things, as Macrobius relates in his *Commentary on the Dream of Scipio* (bk. 1, chap. 2).[15] The Platonists did not, however, assert the existence of a third separate substance that might correspond to the Holy Spirit. But we do not assert that the Father and the Son differ in substance, which was the error of Origen and Arius, who in this followed the Platonists.

When Trismegistus says, "Monad begot monad," and so on, this does not refer to the generation of the Son, or to the procession of the Holy Spirit, but to the production of the world. For one God produced one world on account of his love for himself.

Reply to 2: Argumentation may be employed in two ways to establish a point. In one way, it is used for the purpose of furnishing sufficient proof of some fundamental premise, as in natural *scientia,* where reasons are brought forth that are sufficient to show that the movement of the heavens is always of uniform velocity. In the other way, reasons are brought forth, not as furnishing a sufficient proof of a fundamental premise, but as confirming an already established premise by showing the congruity of its results, as the theory of eccentrics and epicycles is considered as established in astronomy, because thereby the visible appearances of the heavenly movements can be explained. But it is not as if this reasoning were sufficient, since some other theory might explain them.[16]

In the first way, we can prove that God is one, and similar matters. In the second way, reasoning serves to manifest the Trinity: that is, assuming the Trinity to be true, it is shown to be congruent with reason. We must not, however, think that the Trinity of Persons is adequately proved by such reasoning.[17]

This becomes evident when we consider each point. The infinite goodness of God is manifested also in creation, because to produce from nothing is an act of infinite power. For if God communicates himself by his infinite goodness, it is not necessary that an infinite effect should proceed from God, but simply that according to its own mode and capacity it should receive the divine goodness.[18] Likewise, when it is said that "joyous possession of good

15. Macrobius was a Latin Neoplatonist writer of the fifth century.

16. Thomas makes his point with yet another distinction: reason can be used to prove a fact, or reason can be used to show that a fact we have accepted on some other basis can be made to fit with what we know through reason. The astronomical specifics of "eccentrics" and "epicycles" (circles that have their center on the circumference of other circles), by which ancient astronomers such as Ptolemy attempted to explain what they observed in the heavens, are not particularly significant to the point he is making.

17. Reason can "manifest" the harmony or congruence of Christian trinitarian faith with what reason can tell us about God, but it cannot *prove* that faith. Put another way, reason cannot discover the land of trinitarian faith, but it can help us explore that land once it is discovered. This is the kind of use to which reason is put in arguments from *convenientia* (see 3.1, note 1).

18. Against Richard of St. Victor's proof, Aquinas claims that creation would be a sufficient sharing of God's goodness, so that one need not posit "otherness" in God. However, there is no reason why Aquinas could not find value in Richard's argument as a "manifestation" of the Trin-

requires partnership," this holds in the case of one person not having perfect goodness, who therefore needs to share some other's good in order to have the goodness of complete happiness. Nor is the image in our mind an adequate proof in the case of God, since intellect is not found univocally in God and ourselves. Therefore, Augustine says in his commentary on John (*Homilies on the Gospel of John*, sermon 27, no. 7) that by faith we arrive at knowledge, and not the other way around.[19]

Reply to 3: There are two reasons why the knowledge of the divine Persons was necessary for us. In one way, it was necessary for the right idea of creation. By saying that God made all things by his Word, we exclude the error of those who say that God produced things by necessity. When we say that in him there is a procession of love, we show that God produced creatures not because he needed them, nor because of any other extrinsic cause, but on account of the love of his own goodness. So Moses, when he had said, "In the beginning God created heaven and earth" (Genesis 1:1), added, "God said, 'Let there be light'" (Genesis 1:3), to manifest the divine Word, and then said, "God saw that the light was good" (Genesis 1:4), to show proof of the divine love. The same is also found in the other works of creation, in another way, and chiefly, that we may think rightly concerning the salvation of the human race, accomplished by the incarnate Son, and by the gift of the Holy Spirit.[20]

---

ity. In particular, it can show us how creation need not be necessary in order for divine goodness to be shared. But the non-necessity of God's act of creation is not in itself a part of the idea of God, so one cannot claim that it provides a necessary reason for positing the Trinity.

19. In other words, the objection has misread Augustine's intent in offering an analogy for the Trinity drawn from the human mind.

20. Aquinas thinks we need to know about the Trinity for two reasons: (1) It shows us that God was in no way compelled to create the world—God was not "lonely" and in need of something to love—rather the world is an overflow of the love shared by Father, Son, and Spirit. (2) It shows us that in our salvation through Christ and the Holy Spirit it is truly God himself who saves us. Here Thomas indicates why the doctrine of the Trinity is not some esoteric bit of information about the inner life of God; rather, it is a necessary backdrop to a proper understanding of God's two great acts on our behalf: our creation and our recreation through Christ and the Spirit.

QUESTION 36

THE PERSON
OF THE HOLY SPIRIT

1.36.2

Whether the Holy Spirit proceeds from the Son?[1]

It would seem that the Holy Spirit does not proceed from the Son.

1. The point at issue here is one that has contributed to the split between the Eastern and Western churches. On this question, the creed promulgated by the Council of Constantinople in 381 (commonly called the "Nicene Creed") reads, "We believe in the Holy Spirit, the Lord, the giver of life, who proceeds from the Father, who with the Father and the Son is worshiped and glorified." At a local council in Toledo, Spain, in 589, the word *Filioque* ("and the Son") was first added to the phrase "proceeds from the Father." Over the course of the Middle Ages this usage spread throughout the Western church and was adopted in Rome (which was originally not inclined to accept it) around the year 1000. The *Filioque* became a point of theological controversy between East and West in 867 when Photius, the Patriarch of Constantinople, accused the Western church of unwarranted innovation leading to a host of theological difficulties. Photius argued that the claim that the Father and Son together were the source of the Spirit was equivalent to saying that the divine essence, which the Father and Son share, was the source of the Spirit. But, since the Spirit shares the divine essence no less than the Son and the Father, this would mean that the Spirit was the source of his own procession (*Mystagogy on the Holy Spirit*, no. 6). Further, Photius saw the *Filioque* as a denigration of the Spirit, writing in a letter to the bishops of the Eastern church, "By the *Filioque* teaching, the Holy Spirit is two degrees or steps removed from the Father, and thus has a much lower rank than the Son." In his view, the *Filioque* was not simply bad theology, it was heresy. Also, as much at issue as the question of the *Filioque* itself was the question of the authority of the Western church to make an addition to the creed without consent of the Eastern church. This issue is raised in the second objection.

1. As Dionysius says (*On the Divine Names,* chap. 1), "We must not dare to say anything concerning the substantial divinity except what has been divinely expressed to us by the Holy Scripture." But in the Holy Scripture we are not told that the Holy Spirit proceeds from the Son, but only that he proceeds from the Father, as is clear from John 15:26: "The Spirit of truth, who proceeds from the Father." Therefore the Holy Spirit does not proceed from the Son.

2. In the creed of the Council of Constantinople we read, "We believe in the Holy Spirit, the Lord and giver of life, who proceeds from the Father; with the Father and the Son to be adored and glorified." Therefore it should not be added in our creed that the Holy Spirit proceeds from the Son, and those who added such a thing appear to be worthy of anathema.[2]

3. John of Damascus says (*On the Orthodox Faith,* bk. 1, chap. 8), "We say that the Holy Spirit is from the Father, and we name him the Spirit of the Father; we do not say that the Holy Spirit is from the Son, yet we name him the Spirit of the Son." Therefore the Holy Spirit does not proceed from the Son.

4. Nothing proceeds from that in which it rests.[3] But the Holy Spirit rests in the Son; for it is said in the legend of Blessed Andrew, "Peace to you and to all who believe in the one God the Father, and in his only Son our Lord Jesus Christ, and in the one Holy Spirit proceeding from the Father, and abiding in the Son."[4] Therefore the Holy Spirit does not proceed from the Son.

5. The Son proceeds as the Word. But, in ourselves, our breath [*spiritus*] does not seem to proceed from our word.[5] Therefore neither does the Holy Spirit proceed from the Son.

6. The Holy Spirit proceeds perfectly from the Father. Therefore it is superfluous to say that he proceeds from the Son.

Thomas's most extensive discussion of this issue is found in *Against the Errors of the Greeks,* which he wrote circa 1264 at the request of Pope Urban IV as a kind of "expert opinion" on a collection of Greek patristic texts compiled by Nicholas of Durazzo and entitled *Libellus de processione Spiritus Sancti et de fide trinitatis contra errores Graecorum.* The second part of this text by Aquinas is taken up mainly with a defense of the *Filioque,* based on the texts in Nicholas's *Libellus.* Unfortunately, many of the texts in this collection—and particularly those that supported the *Filioque*—were spurious, or had been altered with interpretive glosses by Nicholas to support the Western view, making Thomas's work much less useful than it might be. Still, *Against the Errors of the Greeks* indicates Thomas's fundamental conviction that one should always seek to resolve disputed questions with arguments based on the authorities shared by the disputants. See his discussion in 1.1.8, above.

2. The objection quotes the Nicene-Constantinopolitan Creed (381) in its original form, and notes the anathemas (i.e., condemnations) leveled against those who would add to it.

3. In other words, "coming-forth" and "remaining" appear to be contradictory.

4. The legend of Blessed Andrew is found in Migne's *Patrologia Graeca* (Paris, 1857-1866), vol. 2, col. 1217.

5. The objection is drawing on the fact that in Latin (as also in Greek and Hebrew) the same word means both "spirit" and "breath." Therefore, the point is that just as our breath *accompanies* our words and does not *originate* in them, so too the Spirit *accompanies* the Son (i.e., the Word) but does not *originate* in him.

7. It is said in Aristotle's *Physics* (bk. 3, chap. 4, 203^b) that "to exist [*esse*] and to be possible [*posse*] do not differ in things that are perpetual," and much less so in God. But it is possible for the Holy Spirit to be distinguished from the Son, even if he did not proceed from him;[6] for Anselm says in his *On the Procession of the Holy Spirit* (chap. 1), "Of course the Son and the Holy Spirit have their existence from the Father; but in different ways: one by birth, the other by procession, so that they are thus distinct from one another." And a little further on he says, "For even if for no other reason were the Son and the Holy Spirit distinct, this alone would suffice." Therefore the Holy Spirit is distinct from the Son, without existing from him.

On the contrary: Athanasius says, "The Holy Spirit is from the Father and the Son; not made, nor created, nor begotten, but proceeding."[7]

I answer: It must be said that the Holy Spirit is from the Son, since if he were not from him, he could in no way be personally distinguished from him, as appears from what has been said earlier (1.28.3; 1.30.2). It cannot be said that the divine Persons are distinguished from each other in any absolute sense, because it would follow that there would not be one essence of the three Persons, since everything that is spoken of God in an absolute sense belongs to the unity of essence. Therefore it must be said that the divine Persons are distinguished from each other only by the relations.[8] But the relations can distinguish the Persons only insofar as they are opposed relations. This is clear from the fact that the Father has two relations: one by which he is referred back to the Son, and the other to the Holy Spirit. But these are not opposed relations, and therefore they do not make two Persons, but belong only to the one Person of the Father. If therefore in the Son and the Holy Spirit there were only the two relations by which each of them were related to the Father, these relations would not be opposed to each other, as neither would be the two relations whereby the Father is related to them. Therefore, as the person of the Father is one, it would follow that the person of the Son and of the Holy Spirit would be one, having two relations opposed to the two relations of the Father.[9] But this is

6. The objection argues that since God is pure act (see 1.3, note 12), if it is possible for something to be true of God, then it must be actually true; and since the distinct coming-forth of the Spirit is *possible* without the Spirit coming forth from the Son, then this distinct coming-forth must be *actually* the case.

7. Here Thomas quotes not Athanasius but the so-called Athanasian Creed, which is a Latin composition that dates from a time later than Athanasius, probably the fifth century.

8. As mentioned before (1.29, note 1), Eastern Christians have tended to read statements such as "It cannot be said that the divine Persons are distinguished from each other in any absolute sense" and "The divine Persons are distinguished from each other only by the relations" as implying that the Father, Son, and Spirit are not *really* distinct and that the Persons are *merely* relations. This, however, is a misreading. Aquinas's point is that the Father, Son, and Spirit are constituted as distinct precisely *through* their relatedness, not *in spite of* it.

9. Here Thomas is addressing the issue raised in the seventh objection, in which the claim is made that the Son and Spirit have different ways of coming-forth from God, the former by being begotten or born and the latter by being breathed-forth or proceeding. Thomas's point,

heretical since it destroys faith in the Trinity. Therefore the Son and the Holy Spirit must be related to each other by opposite relations. But in God there cannot be any opposing relations, except relations of origin, as proved earlier (1.28.4). And opposing relations of origin are to be understood in the sense of a "source," [*principium*] and of that "which is from the source" [*quod est a principio*]. Therefore we must conclude that it is necessary to say that either the Son is from the Holy Spirit, which no one says, or that the Holy Spirit is from the Son, as we confess.[10]

Furthermore, the order of the procession of each one agrees with this conclusion. For it was said earlier (1.27.2, 4; 1.28.4) that the Son proceeds by the way of the intellect as Word, and the Holy Spirit by way of the will as Love. Now love must proceed from a word, for we do not love anything unless we apprehend it by a mental conception. Therefore also in this way it is manifest that the Holy Spirit proceeds from the Son.

---

however, is that these two ways of coming-forth are insufficient to establish the distinction between the Son and Spirit; rather, these two ways of coming-forth are sufficient to establish only the distinction of Son and Spirit from the Father, because these ways say nothing of the relation of origin that the Son and Spirit have with regard to *each other*, but only of their relation to the Father. If the Son and the Spirit are indistinguishable, then we have at best some sort of quasi modalism, in which the Son and Spirit differ in name only (see 1.27, notes 4 and 5, as well as the entry "Sabellius" in the glossary of names).

10. Thomas is referring back to an earlier discussion (1.32.2, 3) in which he discusses the five *notiones* or abstract concepts by which we know the relations that are the Persons of the Trinity. He describes these "notions" as follows: "The divine essence is signified as *what;* and the person as *who;* and the property as *whereby*" (1.32.2); so the subsistent relations are "whos," and the abstract concepts are those things "by which" the subsistent relations are conceived of as distinct. Thus the Father is known by the three notions of *innascibilitas* (the inability to be "begotten" or "produced"), *paternitas* (fatherhood or the capacity to bring forth a "likeness") and *spiratio* ("breathing-forth" or producing a spirit); the Son is known by the notion of *filiatio* (sonship, or having been "begotten" or "produced" as son or likeness); and the Sprit is known by the notion of *processio* (having "come forth"). Notice that all of these notions except *innascibilitas* refer to origination, either as the one who produces or the one who is produced. And this relatedness in terms of origination must be expressed in terms of mutually exclusive notions.

So the relationship between the Father and the Son is known by two opposed notions: *paternitas* and *filiatio*—within the same relationship, one cannot be both father and son (though, of course, someone's son could in turn become someone else's father). Likewise, the relationship between the Father and the Spirit is known by two opposed notions: *spiratio* and *processio*—one cannot be both the breather and the breath that comes forth. It is these oppositions that enable the Persons to be known as distinct.

Aquinas's specific point here is that the notions *filiatio* and *spiratio,* while indeed *different* notions, are not *opposed* notions, because they do not describe a "producer" but two things that are produced. So if the Son and Spirit are to be known as distinct from each other, then there must be a notion by which one can be known as the producer of the other. Aquinas's solution is to say that the Father and the Son are both known by the notion *spiratio* or, more properly, *spiratio communis* (shared breathing-forth). The Spirit proceeds from the Father *and* the Son—as the creed declares once *Filioque* has been added to it—and so Son and Spirit are distinct from each other as "producer" and "produced."

He notes that the difficulty could also be solved if the Spirit were understood as the producer of the Son. But, he goes on to say, there is no precedent for this notion in Scripture or tradition.

We derive a knowledge of the same truth from the very order of nature itself;[11] for nowhere do we find that several things proceed from one thing without relation [*ordine*], except in those that differ only by their matter, as is the case when one knife maker produces many knives distinct from each other materially, with no relation [*ordinem*] to each other.[12] In things in which there is not simply a material distinction, however, we always find that some relation [*ordo*] exists in the many things produced. Thus it is that the beauty of the divine wisdom is displayed in the order of creatures produced. So if from the one Person of the Father, two Persons proceed, the Son and the Holy Spirit, there must be some relationship [*ordinem*] between them; and no other relationship can be ascribed to them except the order of their nature, by which one is from the other. Therefore it cannot be said that the Son and the Holy Spirit proceed from the Father in such a way that neither of them proceeds from the other, unless we posit a material distinction in them, which is impossible.[13]

Therefore the Greeks themselves recognize that the procession of the Holy Spirit has some relation [*ordinem*] to the Son; for they grant that the Holy Spirit is the Spirit "of the Son," and that he is from the Father "through the Son." Some of them are said also to concede that "he is from the Son," or that "he flows from the Son," but not that he proceeds. This refusal seems to come from ignorance or obstinacy. A just consideration of the truth will convince anyone that the word "procession" is the one most commonly applied to all that denotes origin of any kind; for we use the term to describe any kind of origin, as when we say that a line proceeds from a point, a ray from the sun, a

11. In this paragraph and the following one I translate the various forms of *ordo* sometimes as "order" and sometimes as "relation" (see 1.27, note 22). In the latter case, I have put the Latin in parenthesis.

12. Material things that come from the same producer are distinguished by being made up of different matter. So even if the knife maker could produce two knives that were identical, they would be different inasmuch as they would be made out of different matter and therefore could not occupy the same place at the same time.

13. Material things can be distinguished by their matter; nonmaterial things, such as angels and God, must be distinguished from each other by the order or relationship [*ordo*] that they have with each other. In the case of the angels' relationship to each other, or the angels' relationship to God, this order can be one of greater and lesser perfection. As Thomas puts it in his *De potentia* (10.5), "In nonmaterial things, which cannot be multiplied through material differences, it is impossible for there to be plurality except through some kind of order. Thus in nonmaterial created substances there is an order of more-and-less-perfect, by which one angel is more perfect in nature than another."

But this obviously cannot be the case with the Persons of the Trinity, since no one Person shares more perfectly in the divine nature than another. In this article of the *Summa*, Thomas leaves this loose end untied, but in *De potentia* he continues, "Since it is impossible for there to be an order of [greater and less] perfection in God (as the Arians proposed, saying that the Father is greater than the Son, and both are greater than the Holy Spirit), we must conclude that a plurality of divine Persons can be understood only according to the relationships of origin, that is to say, the Son being from the Father and the Holy Spirit from the Son." The order is not one of greater or lesser perfection, but of origin.

stream from a source, and likewise in everything else. Therefore, granted that the Holy Spirit originates in *any* way from the Son, we can conclude that the Holy Spirit *proceeds* from the Son.[14]

Reply to 1: We should not say anything about God that is not found in Holy Scripture either explicitly or implicitly. Although we do not find it verbally expressed [*per verba*] in Holy Scripture that the Holy Spirit proceeds from the Son, still we do find it in the meaning [*quantum ad sensum*] of Scripture, especially where the Son, speaking of the Holy Spirit, says in John 16:14, "He will glorify me, because he shall receive from what is mine [*de meo*]."[15] It is also a rule of Holy Scripture that whatever is said of the Father applies to the Son, even if an exclusive term be added,[16] except in cases in which the Father and the Son are distinguished from each other by opposite relations. Thus when our Lord says in Matthew 11:27, "No one knows the Son, but the Father," the idea of the Son knowing himself is not excluded. Therefore when we say that the Holy Spirit proceeds from the Father, even if it is added that he proceeds from the Father alone, the Son would not be at all excluded by this, because the Father and the Son are not opposed to each other in being the principle of the Holy Spirit, but only in the fact that one is the Father and the other is the Son.

---

14. Aquinas accuses his opponents of verbal quibbling, noting that they grant that the Spirit somehow originates from the Son, yet they balk at the word "proceeds." His point is that "originate" and "proceed" are, in everyday usage (i.e., in geometry, etc.), synonyms. Thus although Thomas is willing to make a distinction between the ways in which the Sprit proceeds from the Father and from the Son—the Spirit proceeds from the Father *through* the Son (1.36.3)—he maintains that this distinction does not deny that the Spirit proceeds from Father and Son together, as *unum principium* (1.36.4).

Thomas is perhaps being a bit unfair to his opponents. What he dismisses as mere verbal quibbling in fact reflects a real difference between Greek and Latin. Medieval theologians in both East and West had an insufficient understanding of the semantic difference between the Greek *ekporeuesthai* (meaning specifically "to issue forth as from an origin") and the Latin *procedere* (meaning more generically "to move forward" or "to come forth"), which is more akin to the Greek *proienai*. In recent ecumenical dialogues between Catholic and Orthodox theologians, it has been argued, to my mind plausibly, that both the Orthodox condemnation of the *Filioque* and the Roman countercondemnation were based on a failure to recognize that the Latin tradition used one word (*procedere*) where the Greek tradition used two (*ekporeuesthai,* for the Spirit's coming forth from the Father; and *proienai,* for the Spirit's coming forth from the Son).

15. It may not be immediately apparent how this verse supports the *Filioque*. In his commentary on John's Gospel (chap. 16, lecture 4, §2115), Thomas clarifies his point somewhat, noting that the preposition *de* "expresses consubstantiality along with a relation of origin." So when Christ says that the Spirit receives "from" [*de*] what is his, and then says that what is his is "all that the Father has" (16:15), he is saying implicitly (*quantum ad sensum*) that he, along with the Father, is the source of the Spirit's divine essence.

16. In other words, even if "alone" or "only" is added. In interpreting a passage such as John 17:3—in which Christ prays to the Father, "That they may know you, the only true God"—Thomas says that "such a way of speaking is not to be taken too literally, but it should be piously expounded, whenever we find it in an authentic work" (1.31.4).

Reply to 2: In every council of the church a creed has been drawn up to meet some prevalent error condemned in the council at that time. Therefore subsequent councils are not to be described as making a new creed but as explaining, by some addition directed against heresies that were arising, what was implicitly contained in the first creed. Therefore in the decision of the Council of Chalcedon, it is declared that those who were gathered together in the Council of Constantinople handed down teaching concerning the Holy Spirit, without implying that there was anything wanting in the teaching of their predecessors who had gathered together at Nicea, but clarifying against heretics what those predecessors had meant.[17] Therefore, because at the time of the ancient councils the error of those who said that the Holy Spirit did not proceed from the Son had not arisen, it was not necessary to make any explicit declaration on that point. But later on, when certain errors arose, in another council assembled in the West, the matter was explicitly defined by the authority of the Roman pontiff, by whose authority also the ancient councils were summoned and confirmed.[18] Nevertheless, the truth was contained implicitly in the belief that the Holy Spirit proceeds from the Father.

Reply to 3: The Nestorians were the first to introduce the error that the Holy Spirit did not proceed from the Son, as appears in a Nestorian creed condemned in the Council of Ephesus. This error was embraced by Theodoret the Nestorian,[19] and several others after him, among them John of Damascus. Therefore, on that point his opinion is not to be held. Alternatively, it has been said by some that although John of Damascus did not confess that the Holy Spirit was from the Son, those words do not expressly deny it.

Reply to 4: When the Holy Spirit is said to rest or abide in the Son, it does not mean that he does not proceed from him, for the Son also is said to abide in the Father, even though he proceeds from the Father. Also, the Holy Spirit is said to rest in the Son, either as the love of the lover abides in the beloved, or in reference to the human nature of Christ, because of what is written in

17. The original creed of the Council of Nicea (325) ended abruptly with "And [we believe] in the Holy Spirit." The Council of Constantinople (381) added the familiar final lines of the so-called Nicene Creed: "The Lord and giver of life, who proceeds . . ." Aquinas's point is that the bishops gathered at Constantinople were in no way repudiating Nicea but were clarifying the implicit claim of the Spirit's divinity in response to new heresies that had arisen since the formulation of the creed of Nicea.

18. The reference here is possibly to the so-called *Fides Damasi*, a creedal formula originating in southern Gaul, probably at the end of the fifth century, but attributed to St. Damasus, who was pope in the latter half of the fourth century. This document probably did not itself contain the *Filioque* in its original form; rather, it was added later, just as it was to the Nicene Creed. These historical matters aside, Thomas's point is that the church can modify authoritative creedal statements in order to address new errors that arise, without this constituting any sort of repudiation of prior creedal forms.

19. Theodoret of Cyrus, who in the fifth century accused Cyril of Alexandria of erroneously holding that the Spirit proceeded from the Son.

John 1:33, "On whom you shall see the Spirit descending and remaining upon him, he it is who baptizes."[20]

Reply to 5: "Word" in God is not understood according the likeness of the vocal word, from which the breath [*spiritus*] does not proceed; for it would then be only metaphorical.[21] Rather, it is understood according to the likeness of the mental word, from which love proceeds.

Reply to 6: Because the Holy Spirit proceeds from the Father perfectly, not only is it not superfluous to say he proceeds from the Son, but it is absolutely necessary because one power belongs to the Father and the Son, and because whatever is from the Father must be from the Son, unless it is opposed to the property of sonship [*filiationis*]. For the Son is not from himself, although he is from the Father.[22]

Reply to 7: The Holy Spirit, as a Person, is distinguished from the Son because the origin of one is distinguished from the origin of the other. But the difference of origin itself comes from the fact that the Son is only from the Father, whereas the Holy Spirit is from the Father and the Son. Otherwise the processions would not be distinguished from each other, as explained above.

20. To say that the Spirit "rests" in the Son is not to deny that the Spirit comes forth from the Son. Note that in arguing this point, Aquinas gives two possible explanations without feeling a need to choose between them.

21. Metaphors are comparisons with material things (see 1.1, note 34). Therefore if "spirit" were a reference to our breath it would be a metaphor, and the statement "God is spirit" could not be literally true.

22. If the Trinity is truly "one God," then this God must exercise his power as a unity in all things; the only exception is that the Persons of the Son and Spirit do not originate themselves.

QUESTION 45

THE WAY IN WHICH THINGS COME FORTH FROM THE FIRST PRINCIPLE

1.45.5

Whether it belongs to God alone to create?

It would seem that it does not belong to God alone to create.

1. According to the Philosopher (Aristotle, *De anima*, bk. 2, chap. 4, 415ª), the perfect is that which can make its own likeness. But immaterial creatures are more perfect than material creatures, which nevertheless can make their own likeness, for fire generates fire, and a human being begets a human being. Therefore an immaterial substance can make a substance similar to itself. But immaterial substance can be made only by creation, since it has no matter from which to be made. Therefore a creature can create.[1]

2. The greater the resistance is on the part of the thing made, the greater the power that is required in the maker. But a "contrary" is more resistant

---

1. Aquinas has already specified that he is using "creation" to indicate not simply the giving of a new structure to matter, but giving something its entire existence. The way theologians put this is to say that creation is *ex nihilo* (from nothing). Carving a statue is not, properly speaking, an act of creation since it is involves giving matter (rock or wood) a new form (that of a person or cow). However, if a nonmaterial being (e.g., an angel) could engender another nonmaterial being, then this *would* be an act of creation, since it would not be simply the imparting of form to matter.

than "nothing." Therefore it requires more power to make something from its contrary—which, nevertheless, a creature can do—than to make a thing from nothing. Much more therefore can a creature do this.[2]

3. The power of the maker is measured by what is made. But created being is finite, as we proved earlier when discussing the infinity of God (1.7.2–4). Therefore only a finite power is needed to create something created. But to have a finite power is not contrary to the idea of a creature. Therefore it is not impossible for a creature to create.

On the contrary: Augustine says in *De Trinitate* (bk. 3, chap. 8, no. 13) that neither good nor bad angels can create anything. Much less therefore can any other creatures.

I answer: At first glance, according to what precedes (1.45.1), it is evident enough that creation can be only the action of God alone;[3] for more universal effects must be traced back to more universal and prior causes. Now among all effects the most universal is existence itself; and therefore it must be the proper effect of the first and most universal cause, and that is God.[4] Therefore also it is said in the *Book of Causes* (proposition 3) that neither an intelligence nor a noble soul gives existence, except inasmuch as it works by divine operation.[5] But to produce existence absolutely, not as this or that being, is part of the meaning of "creation." Therefore it is manifest that creation is the particular act of God alone.

---

2. If an agent (i.e., a "doer") does something, it follows that it can also do a lesser thing; in other words, if I can jump three feet, it follows that I can also jump two feet. The objection says that it is a greater thing to make something from preexisting matter than to make something from nothing, since the matter offers resistance to the activity of the maker. Therefore, since creatures can make things out of matter (e.g., statues, houses, boats, etc.) they certainly can do the lesser thing of making something from nothing.

3. Here Aquinas is referring back to the first article in the question (1.45.1), where he has argued that "creation" means to make something from nothing.

4. The most fundamental (or "most universal") activity of anything is the very activity of existing. Whatever causes that activity must therefore be the most fundamental cause. As Aquinas argued in the first three of the five ways (see 1.2.3, above), this is what people call "God."

5. The *Liber de causis* (*Book of Causes*) is the work of an unknown author, who was probably Muslim or Jewish, writing at some point prior to the twelfth century. In Thomas's day it was commonly thought to be a work by Aristotle, even though it clearly reflects a much more Platonist viewpoint. In fact, much of it is taken from the *Elements of Theology* by the fifth-century pagan Neoplatonist Proclus, though the author has subtly altered Proclus's thought to accommodate a view of the universe as the intentional creation of God, rather than a necessary emanation. In his earlier writings, Thomas seemed unsure of Aristotle's authorship of this work. When William of Moerbeke's translation of Proclus's *Elements* appeared in 1268, Thomas quickly realized that this was the ultimate source of the *Liber de causis*. He was apparently the first to make this identification, and in his own commentary on the *Liber de causis* (1272) he made use of Proclus's work to interpret it.

In the *Liber de causis,* the author posits—in addition to the first cause that is "higher than eternity and before it"—causes that he calls "intelligences" (identified by Thomas with angels), as well as "souls." In Thomas's interpretation of the *Liber de causes*, both intelligences and souls can be causes by virtue of their sharing in the first cause, which is God.

It happens, however, that something shares the action properly belonging to something else,[6] not by its own power, but instrumentally, since it acts by the power of another, in the way that air, by the power of fire, can heat and ignite. Therefore some have supposed that even though creation is the proper act of the universal cause, some lesser cause acting by the power of the first cause can still create.[7] Avicenna thus asserted that the first separate substance created by God then created another after itself, along with the substance of the world and its soul, and that the substance of the world creates the matter of inferior bodies.[8] In the same way the Master says,[9] in his book of *Sentences* (bk. 4, distinction 5), that God can communicate to a creature the power of creating, so that it creates ministerially, not by its own power.[10]

But this cannot be, because the secondary instrumental cause does not share in the action of the superior cause, except inasmuch as it acts, by virtue of something proper to itself, to prepare for the effect of the principal agent. Therefore if it has no effect on the basis of what is proper to itself, it is used to no purpose. Nor would there be any need of particular instruments to carry out particular actions. Thus we see that a saw, in cutting wood, which it does as something belonging to its own form, produces the form of a bench, which is the effect properly belonging to the principal agent.[11] Now the proper effect of God creating is what is presupposed by all other effects—that is to say, existence in the absolute sense [*esse absolute*]. Therefore, nothing else can act as a preparation and instrument for this effect, since creation is not from anything presupposed that could be prepared by the action of the instrumental agent.[12]

6. "Shares" is a translation of the Latin *participare*, which means both "imparting" and "sharing in," not unlike our word "share." If I say to you that "I want to share your power," it could mean that I want some of it simply for myself, or it could mean that I want to share it with others.

7. Here Aquinas is introducing something like an objection into the body of his argument. He sketches an opinion that he will go on in the next paragraph to refute.

8. "Avicenna" is the Latin name for the Muslim philosopher and physician Ibn-Sina (980–1037).

9. Peter Lombard.

10. To use the example Aquinas uses in the next paragraph, we say "A carpenter cuts a piece of wood," and we say "A saw cuts a piece of wood." Both statements can be true at the same time. Therefore (so this argument goes) a creature could be used by God in the act of creation in such a way that we could truly say the creature creates. Thomas, however, rejects this analogy.

11. In other words, a tool shares in the action of the one who wields it by making a unique contribution to the wielder's purpose. This contribution is "dispositive," meaning that it prepares for what the tool wielder wants to do (e.g., the carpenter wants to build a bench, and the saw prepares the wood for this purpose).

12. "Creation" names that relation by virtue of which something exists. Because creation is ex nihilo, prior to creation there is nothing to be prepared by a tool; there is simply nothing. We might say that instrumental causality presumes a context, whereas creation brings the context into existence.

Therefore it is impossible for any creature to create, either by its own power, or instrumentally, or ministerially.[13]

It is particularly unfitting to say that it is something bodily that creates, since no body acts except by touching or moving, thus requiring in its action some preexisting thing that can be touched or moved, which is contrary to the very idea of creation.

Reply to 1: A perfect thing imparting [*participans*] a nature makes a likeness of itself,[14] not by producing that nature in an absolute sense, but by applying it to something else; for an individual human being cannot be the cause of human nature absolutely, because he would then be the cause of himself. Rather, he is the cause by which human nature is in the person who is begotten;[15] thus he presupposes in his action particular matter, by which this particular human being exists.[16] But just as an individual human being shares in human nature, so every created being shares, so to speak, in the nature of existing [*naturam essendi*]; for only God is his own existence, as we have said earlier (1.7.1, 2).[17] Therefore no created being can produce a being absolutely, except in the sense that it causes existence to be "in this particular thing." So the action by which something makes its own likeness necessarily presupposes that material by

---

13. Timothy McDermott translates (paraphrases, really) this paragraph as follows: "But this only happens when the tool has something of its own to contribute, preparing the main effect; the tool would otherwise be useless, and specific jobs would not require specific tools. Thus a saw by cutting wood, its own specialty, shapes a bench, the carpenter's specialty. But God's proper effect in creating is what every other effect presupposes, namely existence itself. Nothing can act as a tool and contribute to that effect, for creation presupposes nothing that the operation of a tool could prepare. So it is altogether impossible for creatures to create, either by their own power or as tools and intermediaries"; see *Summa Theologiae: A Concise Translation*, ed. and trans. Timothy McDermott (Allen, Tex.: Christian Classics, 1989), 86.

14. Thomas means "perfect" in the sense of a thing having actualized its potential. Thus any actual human person is in this sense a "perfect" human nature, as any fire is a "perfect" fiery nature. Also, note that for Aquinas things are what they are because they share or "participate" in a particular nature. Thus Denis and Sophie are human beings because they share in human nature. In this view of things, Thomas follows both Plato and Aristotle, though they disagreed with each other on the exact nature of this participation.

15. When humans reproduce, they do not produce "human nature" but a particular instance of human nature. If human nature did not already exist, then there would be no humans to engage in reproduction.

16. Aquinas holds the view that what differentiates the human nature of Sophie and the human nature of Denis is that in these two different cases human nature structures different bits of matter. So Sophie's nature makes her a *human being*, but her matter makes her *this* human being. To fully appreciate Aquinas's position, it helps to remember that "material," as Aquinas understands it, occupies a certain segment of space and time. Thus Sophie's possession of "matter" amounts to her having lived out her humanity in a particular time and place—that is, to her having a particular history—and this is what differentiates her from all other human beings.

17. To say that human beings share in human nature is to say that they *have* human nature; it is not to say that they *are* human nature. Likewise, every created thing that exists participates in the act of existing but is not itself that act of existing; we say it *has* existence, not that it *is* existence. Even though existence is "proper" to (i.e., truly belongs to) existing things, only God *is* his own act of existing; everything else must have its existence imparted to it by God.

which a thing is "this particular thing."[18] But in an immaterial substance it is not possible to presuppose any material by which it is "this particular thing." Since it is a subsisting form, it is what it is by its form, by which it has existence. Therefore an immaterial substance cannot produce another immaterial substance like itself in regard to its existence, but only in regard to some added perfection, as when we say, following Dionysius (*The Celestial Hierarchy*, chap. 8, no.2), that a superior angel illuminates an inferior one.[19] In this way, even in heaven there is fatherhood, as the words of the Apostle in Ephesians 3:15 make clear, "From whom all fatherhood in heaven and on earth is named." From this it appears evident that no created being can cause anything, unless something is presupposed, which is against the very idea of creation.

Reply to 2: A thing is made from its contrary coincidentally [*per accidens*], as is said in the *Physics* (bk. 1, chap. 7, 190^b), but something is made directly [*per se*] from the subject that is in potentiality.[20] And so the contrary resists the agent to the degree that it prevents the potentiality from attaining the actualization that the agent intends to bring about. For example, fire seeks to bring the matter of water to an actualization like itself, but it is blocked by the form and contrary dispositions [of water], which prevent the potentiality from being brought to actualization.[21] The more the potentiality is restrained, the more power is required in the agent to bring about its actualization of the matter.[22] Therefore, much greater power is required in an agent when no potentiality preexists.[23] For this reason it is apparent that it is an act of much greater power to make a thing from nothing than from its contrary.

Reply to 3: The power of one who makes something is reckoned not only from the substance of the thing made, but also from the way it is made: a greater heat not only heats more, but heats more quickly. Therefore, although creating some finite effect does not show an infinite power, creating it from nothing *does* show an infinite power, as is clear from what has been said (reply to objection 2). For if a greater power is required in an agent in proportion to the distance of the potentiality from actuality, it follows that the power of that which produces something from no presupposed potentiality is infinite,

18. A creature can make *this* or *that* being, but cannot make *being* itself, for, in the case of material beings, its making presupposes what differentiates *this* from *that*—namely, matter.

19. With regard to immaterial beings (e.g., angels), no matter can be presupposed; what is presupposed is the very existence of the other immaterial being that is acted upon.

20. We make fire from wood because the matter *per se* is apt for that purpose (wood burns well); if the wood is coincidentally ("accidentally") wet, it is opposed to burning. Wet wood can eventually be made to burn, given a hot enough fire, because it can lose the accidental property (wetness) that is contrary to its burning.

21. On "act" (or "actualization") and "potency," see 1.2, note 32.

22. That is, what we might call "contrariness" works by making the matter less apt to receive a particular structure ("form"). Thus, being wet impedes wood's potential to be fire, and you need a hotter fire to make it burn.

23. In creation from nothing, there is not simply a "blocked" potential but no potential whatsoever.

because there is no proportion between "no potentiality" and "some potentiality," which the power of a natural agent presupposes, just as there is no proportion between "nonbeing" and "being."[24] And because no creature has an absolutely infinite power, any more than it has an infinite being, as was proved earlier (1.7.2), it follows that no creature can create.

24. We should not think that we can create a continuum, with "existence" at one end and "nonexistence" at the other, not least because there are no intermediary stages between existing and not existing: you either are or you are not. To bring something into existence where once there was nothing is an act so radical that only infinite power (i.e., God's) can bring it about.

THE
FIRST
HALF
OF THE
SECOND
PART

WHAT IS HAPPINESS?

1–2.3.8

Whether perfect human happiness consists in the vision of the divine essence?

It would seem that perfect human happiness [*beatitudo*] does not consist in the vision of the divine essence.[1]

1. Dionysius says in the *Mystical Theology* (chap. 1.3) that a human being is united to God by that which is highest in the intellect as to something completely unknown. But that which is seen in its essence is not altogether unknown. Therefore the final perfection of the intellect,[2] namely, happiness, does not consist in God being seen through his essence.

2. The higher the nature, the higher its perfection. But to see his own essence is the perfection proper to the divine intellect. Therefore the final perfection of the human intellect does not reach to this height, but consists in something less.

1. One might also translate *beatitudo* as "blessedness." In any case, it is important to see that Aquinas is not referring to a feeling or emotion, but to a state of fulfillment, which I shall occasionally express with the translation "perfect human happiness." Also, with regard to "vision," remember that for Aquinas "vision" equals "knowledge," and the "essence" of something is its distinctive nature—that which makes it *this* kind of thing rather than *that* kind of thing. We might say that to have vision of a thing's essence is to have a definition for it.

2. Earlier (1–2.3.5) Aquinas argued that because it is our intellect (our capacity to know) that makes us distinctive as human animals, our ultimate happiness or fulfillment as human beings must be one that engages this distinctiveness, that is, our capacity to know.

On the contrary: It is written in 1 John 3:2, "When he shall appear, we shall be like him; and we shall see him as he is."[3]

I answer: Final and perfect happiness cannot consist in anything other than the vision of the divine essence. To make this clear, two points must be observed. First, a human being is not perfectly happy as long as something remains for him to desire and seek. Second, the perfection of any power is judged according to its object. Now the object of the intellect is *what a thing is* [*quod quid est*], that is, the essence of a thing, as said in *De anima* (bk. 3, chap. 6, 430[b]);[4] for this reason the intellect attains perfection insofar as it knows the essence of a thing.[5] If therefore an intellect knows the essence of some effect, by which it is not possible to know the essence of the cause (i.e., to know of the cause *what it is*), that intellect cannot be said to reach that cause in an absolute sense, although it may be able to gather from the effect the knowledge *that* the cause is [*an sit*].[6] Consequently, in knowing an effect, and knowing that it has a cause, there naturally remains in a human being the desire to know about the cause *what it is*. This desire is one of wonder and causes inquiry, as is stated in the beginning of the *Metaphysics* (bk. 1, chap. 2, 982[a]).[7] For instance, if someone, knowing the eclipse of the sun, considers that it comes from some cause and does not know what that cause is, he wonders about it, and from wondering proceeds to inquire. Nor does this inquiry cease until he arrives at a knowledge of the essence of the cause.

If therefore the human intellect, knowing the essence of some created effect, knows no more of God than *that he is;* the perfection of that intellect does not yet reach the first cause in an absolute way, but there remains in it the

3. Thomas could not read Greek or Hebrew and therefore depended on St. Jerome's Latin translation of the Bible, commonly called the Vulgate. However, when writing and teaching he often quoted Scripture from memory, and sometimes his version of a passage does not correspond to the Vulgate. This may be a result of faulty memory or a slip of the tongue; or, in a few cases, he may be quoting an alternative translation. Most of these differences are not significant. In this case, the Vulgate reads "*because* we shall see him" rather than "*and* we shall see him."

4. The intellect is fulfilled—reaches its goal—when it possesses the definition of a thing; in other words, when it can answer the question *quid est?* (What is it?). One might say that Aquinas envisions human beings as animals who are different from other animals in that they constantly ask *quid est?*

5. The language of the intellect attaining perfection sounds to us more exalted than Aquinas intends it to be. To attain perfection in this sense is not to become omniscient. In fact, our intellects attain a certain kind of perfection all the time; for example, when we look at a four-legged beast that gives milk and say "that's a cow."

6. This is our situation in this life with regard to God. We can know the essence of the effect (i.e., the world as a whole), but we cannot know the essence of the cause. All we can know of the cause is *that* it is, not *what* it is.

7. As with "perfection," so too "wonder" (*admiratio*) should not be given an overly exalted interpretation: here "wonder" seems simply to mean being puzzled. Given that human beings are fulfilled by knowing what something is, so long as we do not know what something is we are puzzled and keep inquiring. Our intellects are "perfected" with regard to something when we cease being puzzled and stop our inquiry because we know what the thing is.

natural desire to seek the cause. For this reason it is not yet perfectly happy. Consequently, for perfect happiness the intellect needs to reach the very essence of the first cause.[8] Thus it will have its perfection through union with God as with that object in which alone perfect human happiness consists,[9] as stated earlier (1–2.1.7; 1–2.2.8).

Reply to 1: Dionysius speaks of the knowledge of those who are on the road [*in via*], journeying toward happiness.[10]

Reply to 2: As stated earlier (1–2.1.8), "end" can be taken in two ways. In one way, it can be taken with regard to the thing itself that is desired, and in this way the same thing is the end of the higher and lower natures, and indeed of all things, as stated earlier. In the other way, it can be taken with regard to the attainment of this thing, and thus the end of the higher nature is different from that of the lower, according to their respective relationships to that thing. So the happiness of God—who, in understanding his essence, comprehends it—is higher than that of a human being or an angel, who sees it but does not comprehend.[11]

8. Here Aquinas's topic does become exalted: the "perfect happiness" or ultimate fulfillment (i.e., *beatitudo*) of human beings occurs when we cease being puzzled about and inquiring after the cause of *everything*, not simply of this or that thing. In other words, our intellects are ultimately perfected when we can answer the question *quid est?* with regard to God.

9. For Aquinas "vision of the divine essence" is not simply having a bit of information about God; rather, it actually brings us into *union* with God. In 1.12.5 Aquinas says that the "light of glory" (see 1–2.5, note 9) makes those who see God "*deiform*—that is, like to God." This description fits with Aquinas's general views on how we know things (see 1.12, note 8). One way to put it is that "knowing" something amounts to possessing that thing's "form" without actually *being* that thing. When I know that Bossy is a cow I am in possession of the "form" of "cowness" through the intelligible species of the cow being imprinted on my mind. In the case of the vision of God, the "light of glory" fulfills the function in the mind that the intelligible species fulfills in knowing created things.

10. Dionysius is referring to human beings in this life. Aquinas, like Augustine, sees human life as a journey or pilgrimage toward God.

11. Aquinas says that human beings (and angels) can "see" God's essence but cannot "comprehend" it. This is an important, though somewhat obscure, point. We might say that there are three kinds of knowledge of God: (1) that of "wayfarers," who can know *that* God is but not *what* God is (see 1.12, note 4); (2) that of the angels and the saints in heaven, who can know *what* God is but cannot have an exhaustive knowledge of God; and (3) God's own knowledge of himself.

THOSE THINGS
THAT ARE REQUIRED FOR HAPPINESS

1–2.4.6

Whether perfection of the body is necessary for perfect human happiness?

It would seem that perfection of the body is not necessary for perfect human happiness.[1]

1. As a Christian, Thomas believes not simply in the immortality of the soul but also, as the Apostles' Creed puts it, "in the resurrection of the body and the life everlasting." This conviction is rooted both in the Christian tradition and in Thomas's Aristotelian conviction that human beings are not souls that occupy bodies but a unity of body and soul; therefore, if a human being is to have hope, it must be hope for the whole person, body *and* soul. Like other Christians, Thomas holds that the resurrection of the body will occur at the second coming of Christ. But some problems arise.

First, if it is the whole person who is fulfilled by the vision of God, as Thomas has argued, would not it make more sense to say that the vision of God awaits the reunion of body and soul at the second coming, and that prior to this the soul exists in some sort of interim state that does not involved either reward or punishment? This is a view that Thomas, in various places (e.g., *Summa contra Gentiles* 4.91; *De rationibus fidei* 1), associates with some "Greeks" (i.e., Eastern Orthodox Christians) and that he argues against on the basis of various scriptural passages, such as Luke 23:43, where Christ tells the good thief, "Today you will be with me in paradise." What, Aquinas argues, could paradise be but the proper reward of the self—the vision of God. Thomas also argues that since the soul is capable of being rewarded or punished as soon as it is separated from the body, it is fitting that its reward or punishment not be delayed.

1. Perfection of the body is a bodily good. But it has been shown earlier (1–2.4.2) that happiness does not consist in bodily goods. Therefore the perfect condition of the body is not necessary for human happiness.

2. Perfect human happiness consists in the vision of the divine essence, as shown above (1–2.3.8). But the body has no role in this operation, as was also shown earlier (1–2.4.5). Therefore no particular bodily condition is necessary for perfect happiness.

3. The more the intellect is abstracted from the body, the more perfectly it understands.[2] But happiness consists in the most perfect operation of the intellect.[3] Therefore the soul should be abstracted from the body in every way. Therefore, perfect happiness in no way depends on a particular condition of the body.[4]

On the contrary: Perfect happiness is the reward of virtue; therefore it is written in John 13:17, "You shall be blessed, if you do them." But the reward promised to the saints is not only that they shall see and enjoy God,

---

Second, even if the vision of God is possessed by the souls of the saints prior to the reunion of body and soul at the second coming, does this reunion somehow enhance their enjoyment of God? Having defined perfect human fulfillment (*beatitudo*) in 1–2.3.8 as the vision of God's essence, which is an activity of the mind, Aquinas is left with the question: Are the currently disembodied souls of the saints somehow less happy now than they will be when they are reunited with their bodies? Are they "distracted" from their enjoyment of God by a desire for their bodies? In his *Sentences,* Peter Lombard had, in essence, answered affirmatively: the happiness of the souls of the blessed is increased by their reunion with their bodies. But this would seem to mean that the vision of God is somehow insufficient for human fulfillment, and that human beings require the addition of some created thing—the body—for complete happiness, in which case final human happiness would depend, at least in part, on a creature. But in 1–2.2.8, Thomas argues the general point that ultimate happiness cannot depend on a creature; and in 1–2.4.5 he argues the specific point that the union of body and soul cannot be an essential requirement for seeing God, since we do not see God through sense-images, though it might still have a role to play in the "well-being" (*bene esse*) of our seeing God.

All of this is an important backdrop for Thomas's discussion in this article, which deals not simply with the soul's union with the body, but also with the perfection or fulfillment of that body. (In thinking about the perfection of the body, it is good to keep in mind the sense of "perfection" as actualization or completion; see 1.45, note 14). In a sense, Thomas is not simply asking whether the body is some sort of external aid to the soul's fulfillment (as if the soul alone constituted the "self"), but rather whether the body itself is "saved" by having some sort of share in the vision of God.

2. For Aquinas's account of knowledge, see 1.12, note 8. In this case, the objection focuses on how our knowledge of what something is depends on "abstracting" (or setting to the side) the particularity of what we perceive through our senses. Thus when I know the animal in front of me to be a dog, it is by setting aside the material particularity of the animal so as to see what it has in common with all other animals called "dogs."

3. On the perfection of the intellect, see 1–2.3, note 5.

4. The first two objections argue for the nonnecessity of the perfection of the body for human happiness. This objection raises the stakes, arguing that since knowledge involves a process of "abstraction" or separation of the mind from the body, the perfect knowledge that is involved in the vision of God would require a correspondingly perfect separation of mind and body; thus the union of body and soul actually *hinders* the perfect happiness of the soul.

but also that their bodies shall be well-disposed; for it is written in Isaiah 66:14, "You shall see and your heart shall rejoice, and your bones shall flourish like the grass." Therefore a good condition of the body is necessary for happiness.

I answer: If we speak of the kind of happiness that a person can have in this life, it is evident that a good bodily condition is necessarily required for it, for this happiness consists, according to the Philosopher (*Ethics,* bk. 1, chap. 13, 1102ª), in "an operation according to perfect virtue," and it is clear that a person can be hindered from every operation of virtue by physical disability.[5]

But speaking of perfect happiness [*beatitudine perfecta*],[6] some have maintained that happiness requires no particular condition of body—indeed, it requires that the soul be entirely separated from the body. Therefore Augustine, in *The City of God* (bk. 22, chap. 26), quotes the words of Porphyry, who said that "for the soul to be happy, it must be severed from everything physical." But this is unfitting, for it is natural to the soul to be united to the body; therefore it is not possible for the perfection of the soul to exclude the body's natural perfection.[7]

Consequently, we must say that the perfect condition of the body is required for happiness that is in every way perfect, and this is the case both as a condition for and as a result of happiness.[8]

It is a *condition* for perfect happiness because, as Augustine says in his *Literal Commentary on Genesis* (bk. 12, chap. 35), "if a body is such that it is difficult and burdensome to govern, like the flesh that is corruptible and weighs upon the soul, the mind is turned away from that vision of the highest heaven." From this he concludes that "when this body will no longer be 'animal,' but 'spiritual,' then it will be made equal to the angels, and that which formerly was its burden will be its glory."[9]

5. Thomas does not mean, of course, that a physically disabled person cannot be moral. Rather, like Aristotle, he holds that our attainment of complete human excellence (which is another way of translating the Greek word *arete,* normally translated as "virtue") involves excellence of body as well as of soul, since human beings are unities of body and soul.

6. That is, the happiness that follows this life.

7. This argument, of course, presumes that the union of body and soul is "natural." Here we run up against a point of fundamental philosophical disagreement between Thomas and those whose views he would oppose. Thomas is well aware of the argument that the union of body and soul—or, perhaps, the "imprisonment" of the soul in the body—is something profoundly *un*natural. In his day, a mild form of this view was held by certain Christian Platonists; a more virulent form was held by those Christian heretics known as Albigensians or Cathars, who argued that matter was evil and that the soul was a divine spark held captive in the body. To a Cathar, it would be all too obvious that *only* the separation of body and soul could lead to blessedness.

8. Or, as a more literal translation of Aquinas would have it, it is necessary "both antecedently and consequently." In other words, perfection of the body comes (logically speaking) both "before" (as a condition for its possibility) and "after" (as a result of its attainment) the final perfection of the soul.

9. In common with the whole Christian tradition, Thomas holds that the resurrected bodies of the just, like Christ's resurrected body, will not simply be reanimated (i.e., reunited with

It is a *result* of perfect happiness because there will be an overflow from the happiness of the soul into the body, so that this, too, will attain its perfection. Therefore Augustine says in the letter to Dioscorus (epistle 118, chap. 3) that "God gave the soul such a powerful nature that from its exceeding fullness of happiness the strength of incorruption overflows into the lower nature."[10]

Reply to 1: Happiness does not consist in bodily good as its object, but bodily good can add a certain beauty [*decorem*] and perfection to happiness.[11]

Reply to 2: Although the body contributes nothing to that function of the intellect by which the essence of God is seen, nevertheless it might prove a hindrance. Consequently, perfection of the body is required so that it does not hinder the lifting up of the mind.

Reply to 3: The perfect operation of the intellect indeed requires that the intellect be abstracted from this corruptible body that weighs upon the soul, but not from a spiritual body, which will be completely subject to the spirit. This shall be discussed in the third part of this work.[12]

---

the soul) but will be fundamentally transformed. In the Middle Ages qualities such as "clarity," "invulnerability," "subtlety," and "agility" were typically ascribed to such transformed bodies. The key point, however, is that the transformed human body is no longer a burden that hinders the soul's enjoyment but is the perfect medium through which the soul's glory is manifested. Note, however, that it does not seem to be a medium for knowledge, as it is currently, since God will be known directly through the light of divine glory (see 1–2.5, note 9).

10. Thomas habitually speaks of the perfection of the body as something that is a kind of "excess" or "overflow" from the perfection of the soul. Here he is clear that the perfection of the soul, absolutely speaking, has priority over the perfection of the body.

11. *Decorem* implies a kind of ornamentation or adornment. Thomas's use of this term suggests a way out of what can seem to be the circular claim that the perfection of the body both is prior to and follows upon the perfection of the soul. The perfection of the body is not of the essence of human fulfillment, because this fulfillment is nothing other than knowing or "seeing" God, which is done through the soul and in which all human desire is satisfied. However, the full glorification of the soul involves the glorification of the body to which it is naturally united, and thus, in a qualified sense, the soul still desires to be united with its body. As Thomas puts it in 1–2.4.5 *ad* 5, in the vision of God the soul already possesses the highest good that can be desired, but it does not possess it in every possible way, since it does not possess it through bodily perfection: "After the body is taken up again, perfect happiness does not become more intensive, but more extensive."

12. The discussion in question can be found in the so-called *Supplementum,* questions 82 and following. Thomas never finished writing the *Summa,* breaking off a few months before his death, while in the midst of treating the sacrament of penance. Thus he never wrote the sections dealing with the sacraments of anointing of the sick, marriage, and ordination—nor the sections that would have treated the "Four Last Things"—death, judgment, heaven, and hell. Thomas's followers put together the *Supplementum* out of his early commentary on Peter Lombard's *Sentences,* in order to round out the original plan of the *Summa.* The *Supplementum* is usually considered to be of somewhat mixed value in understanding Thomas's mature views, since it is based on material written twenty years prior to the *Summa.*

Question 5

THE ATTAINMENT OF HAPPINESS

1–2.5.1

Whether human beings can attain happiness?

It would seem that human beings cannot attain happiness.

1. Just as the rational nature is above the sensual nature, so the intellectual nature is above the rational, as Dionysius declares in several passages of *On the Divine Names* (chaps. 4, 6, 7).[1] But irrational animals, which have the sensual nature only,[2] cannot attain the goal of the rational nature. Therefore neither can a human being, who is of rational nature, attain the goal of the intellectual nature, which is perfect happiness.

2. True happiness consists in seeing God, who is pure truth. But by nature a human being discerns truth in material things. For this reason "he understands

---

1. Rational nature (e.g., human beings) knows things through a process of reasoning. Intellectual nature (e.g., angels) knows without having to go through a reasoning process. We might call this a knowledge by direct intuition; intellect, like sense experience, is a kind of immediate "seeing." Thus when an angel knows that all men are mortal and that Socrates is a man, it knows at the same time that Socrates is mortal; it does not need to go through the process of drawing this conclusion from the premises. However, Socrates himself can know of his own mortality only by a process of reasoning.

2. To say that animals without reason have only a "sensual nature" is to say that they can have a *kind* of knowledge, but it is knowledge that remains at the level of sense impression; they are not capable of abstract or conceptual reasoning. A lioness can see an antelope and hunt it down, but she cannot form the concept "antelope."

the intellectual species in the sense image [*phantasma*],"³ as *De anima* (bk. 3, chap. 7, 431ᵇ) says. Therefore he cannot attain perfect happiness.⁴

3. Happiness consists in attaining the highest good. But one cannot arrive at the top without rising above [*transcendat*] the middle. Midway between God and human nature is the angelic nature, which human beings cannot rise above; it therefore seems that it is not possible to attain happiness.

On the contrary: It is written in Psalm 94:12, "Blessed is the person whom you shall instruct, O Lord."

I answer: Complete happiness means the attainment of the perfect good. Therefore, whoever is capable [*capax*] of the perfect good can attain happiness.⁵ That a human being is capable of the perfect good is apparent, both because his intellect can apprehend the universal and perfect good, and because his will can desire it.⁶ Therefore a human being can attain complete happiness. Further proof follows from the fact that human beings are capable of seeing God, as stated in 1.12.1, and perfect human happiness consists in this vision, as we stated (1–2.3.8).

Reply to 1: The rational nature exceeds the sensual differently than the intellectual surpasses the rational; for the rational nature exceeds the sensual with regard to the object of its knowledge, because the senses are in no way able to have knowledge of the universal, of which reason does have knowledge. But the intellectual nature surpasses the rational as to the mode of knowing the same intellectual truth; for the intellectual nature grasps instantly the truth that the rational nature reaches by the inquiry of reason, as was made clear in the first part (1.58.3 and 1.79.8).⁷ Therefore reason arrives by a kind of movement at that which the intellect grasps in an instant. Consequently a rational nature can attain perfect happiness, which is the perfection of the intellectual nature, but in a way different from the angels; for the angels attained it instantly after

---

3. See 1.1, note 33, and 1.12, note 8.

4. The logic of the objection seems unassailable: Happiness is seeing God. Human beings see only by means of sense images. Sense images are of material things. God is not material. Therefore human beings cannot see God. Therefore human beings cannot attain happiness.

5. *Capax* means "to have a capacity for."

6. Three points to note: (1) Thomas is not talking about our knowledge of God in this life but about the knowledge of the saints in heaven. (2) Our intellect can "apprehend" God, but this does not mean that we can "comprehend" God (see 1–2.3, note 11). In 1.12.7 *ad* 2 Aquinas writes: "God is called incomprehensible not because anything of him is not seen; but because he is not seen as perfectly as he is capable of being seen." (3) For Aquinas, our ability to desire something is a "capacity" for that thing; we could not desire something unless it were possible to attain it. However, in the case of our desire for God, our "capacity" must be created in us by grace. Thomas will speak of a "natural desire" for the vision of God, not because we have that desire apart from grace, but because our very nature remains unfulfilled apart from the fulfillment of that desire.

7. Rational knowledge surpasses sense knowledge with regard to *what* it knows, whereas intellect surpasses reason with regard to *how* it knows.

the beginning of their creation, whereas human beings attain it after a time. But there is no way for a sensual nature to attain this goal.[8]

Reply to 2: To human beings in the present state of life the natural way of knowing intellectual truth is by means of sense images. But after this state of life, they have another natural way, as was stated in the first part (1.84.7 and 1.89.1).[9]

Reply to 3: A human being cannot rise above the angels in the degree of nature, so as to be by nature above them. But one can rise above them by an act of the intellect, in understanding that there is above the angels something that makes human beings happy. Having attained this, one will be perfectly happy.

8. Aquinas did not think that there could be nonrational animals in heaven since they could not partake of the vision of God, and heaven is in a sense nothing but the vision of God.

9. In 1.89.1 Aquinas argues that while soul and body are united it is natural for the soul to understand by means of sense images of material things. However, the situation is different for the soul after death, when it is separated from the body (until, that is, the resurrection of the body at the second coming). In this situation, the mind understands in a way analogous to the angels: God directly "informs" the mind. For humans, this is an *un*natural or, more accurately, *super*natural way of knowing (in the sense that it goes beyond the nature of a human being as a "rational animal"), and so the mind must be illuminated by God's gift of what Aquinas calls "the light of glory" (*lumen gloriae*). Philosophers who do not share Aquinas's theological presuppositions find him extremely unconvincing on this point, since they are unwilling to grant the existence of disembodied intelligence or the existence of a God who could impart the "light of glory" to such a disembodied intelligence. See, for example, Anthony Kenny, *Aquinas on Mind* (London: Routledge, 1993), 126–27. Aquinas's response to the objection does seem to be more an assertion than an argument.

Aquinas also fails to address the question of how the resurrected body will see God. Unfortunately, Aquinas ceased writing the *Summa theologiae* before he reached this topic. We do, however, have some idea of his views on this subject. In 1.12.4 *ad* 2 Aquinas adopts St. Augustine's view that the eyes of our risen bodies shall "see" God by seeing God's activity perfectly manifest in God's creatures; God is the "indirect" object of our glorified senses.

THE VARIOUS KINDS OF LAW

1–2.91.4

Whether there was any need for a divine law?

It would seem that there was no need for a divine law.

1. As stated earlier (1–2.91.2), the natural law is a kind of sharing in us of the eternal law. But the eternal law is a divine law, as stated earlier (1–2.91.1). Therefore there was no need for a divine law in addition to the natural law and the human laws derived from it.[1]

2. It is written in Sirach 15:14 that "God left the human race in the hand of its own deliberation." But deliberation [*consilium*] is an act of reason, as

---

1. Aquinas distinguishes several kinds of "law"—by which he means the plan or pattern by which God orders and guides the universe. The most fundamental form of law is God himself, whose wisdom orders all things. This is what Aquinas calls "eternal law." "Natural law," as Thomas uses it, should not be confused with the modern idea of a "law of nature." For Aquinas, natural law is the eternal law as we can know it from our own natures. In particular, we can know from observing our own natures what Aquinas calls the "first principle of practical reason," which is "do good and avoid evil." From natural law, the particular laws of human societies are derived.

Aquinas also speaks here of "divine law." In some sense, as the objection points out, *all* true law is divine law, since it derives from God's own wisdom. What the article asks, however, is whether God's ordering wisdom is sufficiently discovered in the natural law, making any other knowledge of God's law unnecessary. As we shall see, Aquinas's view is that natural law is *not* sufficient, and we need further revelation of God's wisdom, above all through the covenant of the Old Testament and the gift of the Holy Spirit, who orders or guides the hearts of believers—not simply telling us what to do but helping us to do it (see 1–2.106.1).

stated earlier (1–2.14.1). Therefore human beings were left to the direction of their reason. But a dictate of human reason is a human law, as stated earlier (1–2.91.3). Therefore there is no need for human beings to be governed by a divine law as well.

3. Human nature is more self-sufficient than nonrational creatures. But nonrational creatures have no divine law beyond the natural inclination placed within them. Therefore, it is even less the case that the rational creature should have a divine law beyond the natural law.

On the contrary: David asked God to set his law before him, saying (Psalm 119:33), "Set a law before me, Lord, on the path of your justifications."

I answer: Beyond natural and human law, it was necessary to have a divine law for directing human conduct. There are four reasons for this.

First, because law directs human beings toward proper action in relation to their ultimate purpose. And indeed if human beings were oriented only toward a purpose that was proportionate to their natural ability, there would be no need for them to have any further direction with regard to their reason, beyond the natural law and human law that is derived from it. But human beings are oriented toward the goal of eternal happiness, which is disproportionate to their natural ability, as stated earlier (1–2.5.5); therefore, it was necessary that, above and beyond natural and human law, human beings should be directed to their goal by a law given by God.[2]

Second, because—on account of the uncertainty of human judgment, especially in contingent and particular matters—different people form different judgments on human acts, and from this opposed and contrary laws result.[3] Therefore, in order that human beings may know without any doubt what they should do and what they should avoid, it was necessary for them to be directed in their proper acts by a law given by God, for it is certain that such a law cannot be in error.

Third, because human beings can make laws in those matters of which they are competent to judge, but human beings are not competent to judge interior movements, which are hidden, but only exterior actions, which are manifest. Yet the perfection of virtue requires human beings to conduct themselves correctly in both kinds of acts. Consequently, human law could not sufficiently inhibit and direct interior acts; rather, for this it was necessary that a divine law should be added.[4]

2. Note that Aquinas's argument here is quite similar to what he says in 1.1.1 about the need for *sacra doctrina*.

3. Aquinas is aware that different times and places hold different ethical values; he simply does not take this statement of fact to indicate that morality is relative. He also notes that on the whole there is more agreement on general principles (you should not murder) and less on particular cases (is it murder to kill a thief stealing your golf clubs from your garage?).

4. Like Jesus and the prophets of the Old Testament, Aquinas thinks that our goodness is more a matter of our inner disposition than our outer behaviors (though he does not think that

Fourth, because, as Augustine says in *On Free Will* (bk. 1, chap. 5), human law cannot punish or forbid all evil deeds, because while aiming at doing away with all evils, it would also do away with many good things, and would hinder the advance of the common good, which is necessary for human interaction. Therefore, in order that no evil might remain unforbidden and unpunished, it was necessary for the divine law to be added, by which all sins are forbidden.

And these four causes are touched upon in Psalm 19:8, where it is said, "The law of the Lord is unspotted" (i.e., it allows no foulness of sin), "converting souls," because it directs not only exterior, but also interior acts; "the testimony of the Lord is faithful," because of the certainty of what is true and right, "giving wisdom to little ones," by directing human beings to a supernatural and divine goal.

Reply to 1: Through natural law, human nature shares in the eternal law in proportion to its capacity. But human beings need to be led to their supernatural goal in a way that is yet higher. Therefore the law given by God is added, by which human beings share in the eternal law in a higher way.[5]

Reply to 2: Deliberation is a kind of inquiry; therefore it must proceed from some premises. But it is not enough for it to proceed from premises imparted by nature, which are the precepts of the natural law, for the reasons given above;[6] rather, there is need for certain additional premises, namely, the precepts of the divine law.

Reply to 3: Irrational creatures are not intended for an end higher than that which is in proportion to their natural powers; consequently, we cannot think about them in the same way.

---

outer behaviors are unimportant). And since human law can judge only outward behavior, there is need of a divine law by which our hearts are judged. For Aquinas this is above all the law of the gospel, which is equivalent to the gift of the Holy Spirit.

5. Just as grace is needed to bring human nature to its proper perfection, so too the divine law is needed to transform natural law.

6. The reference is to the reasons given already in the body of this article.

QUESTION 109

THE NECESSITY OF GRACE

1–2.109.2

Whether human beings can wish and do good without grace?

It would seem that human beings can wish and do good without grace.[1]

1. Something is in one's power if one is lord of it. But human beings are lords of their acts, and especially of their willing, as stated earlier (1–2.1.1, 1–2.13.6). Therefore, human beings, left to themselves and without the help of grace, can wish and do good.

1. For Thomas, "grace" is an analogical concept—that is, the term has a variety of related but not identical meanings. Most fundamentally, the word "grace" (*gratia*) finds its place in a picture of the world in which God shows favor to human beings by giving them what they need in order to attain fulfillment through eternal life with God. Thus, it can refer either to God's favorable disposition toward humanity (what later theologians called "uncreated grace") or to those gifts that God gives so that we may attain eternal life (what later theologians called "created grace").

Although Thomas distances himself from some of the rhetorical excesses committed by Augustine in the midst of the Pelagian controversy, his teaching on the need for grace remains profoundly indebted to Augustine. This indebtedness is not always obvious to readers who focus on Aquinas's fundamentally "optimistic" account of human nature (i.e., sin does not destroy the goodness of our nature) and who therefore do not see the rather strict limits Thomas places on the good we can accomplish without a special divine assistance that goes beyond what God as first mover imparts to human nature. What becomes clear in this article is that Thomas sees human beings as incapable of doing anything to earn salvation or even to *will* to do good, apart from God's gift of grace. At the same time, he thinks there is a meaningful sense in which we can speak of human beings "meriting" salvation by their good actions.

This article is particularly relevant to the question of the relationship between nature and grace (see 1.1, note 28) and to the related question of whether there is a purely natural human perfection or fulfillment (see 1.1, note 7).

2. One has more power over what is in accordance with one's nature than over what is beyond one's nature. But sin is against a human being's nature, as John of Damascus says (*On the Orthodox Faith*, bk. 2, chap. 30), whereas deeds of virtue are in accordance with that nature, as stated earlier (1–2.71.1). Therefore since one can sin from one's own power, it appears to be even more the case that one can likewise wish and do good.

3. Truth is the good of the intellect, as the Philosopher says in the *Ethics* (bk. 6, chap. 2, 1139^b). But the intellect can know truth by itself, just as every other thing can do its own natural activity by itself. Therefore, it is even more the case that human beings can, left to themselves, do and wish good.[2]

On the contrary: The Apostle says in Romans 9:16, "It is not of him who wills," namely, to will, "nor of him who runs," namely, to run, "but of God who shows mercy." And Augustine says in *On Rebuke and Grace* (chap. 2, no. 3) that "without grace human beings do nothing truly good, whether thinking, or wishing and loving, or acting."

I answer: Human nature may be looked at in two ways: first, in its integrity, as it was in our first parent before sin; second, as it is corrupted in us after the sin of our first parent.[3] Now in both states human nature needs

2. All three of the objections share the presumption that an action in accord with a rational being's nature is somehow "possessed" by that being. There is certainly truth in this presumption, since it makes sense to speak of "my" actions only if they in some sense belong to me. The second objection also makes the valid point that if I am to be blamed for my sins, it is only right that I be praised for my good actions, which is possible only if they are in a real sense "mine." The objections also share the presumption that in order for these actions to be *mine,* I must be capable of doing them apart from divine grace.

3. For Thomas, human nature in its "integrity" is what he calls the state of "original justice," in which the intellect (or higher powers of the soul) submits to God; the lower powers of the soul (those oriented toward the senses) submit to the intellect; and the body submits to the soul. This was the state in which God created the first humans, and from which they fell into sin, which is the "state of corruption." The state of original justice is a condition of "integrity" because it is a state in which the various aspects of the human person—intellect, senses, and body—are harmoniously integrated with each other on account of the harmonious relation of the human person as a whole to God. Sin destroys this harmonious relationship, which results in a corruption or dis-integration of intellect, senses, and body; the result of this corruption is human mortality. Human beings are now born into this situation of disintegration, which we call the state of "original sin," and the chief sign of this condition is the fact that we die.

Note that Thomas understands Adam and Eve to be historical individuals. However, his understanding of human nature's states of integrity and corruption does not depend on the historicity of Adam and Eve. The most important point is that human nature is not inherently sinful (thus we may speak of its state of integrity), but in actual fact no human is born without the wound of sin (the state of corruption). These claims can be maintained without appeal to Adam and Eve as historical figures. The difficult question is whether these claims can be maintained without appealing to the "state of integrity" as a historical period (even if it is only a moment in duration) at the beginning of human history when an individual group of human beings were in fact without sin, or is it sufficient to maintain that this is simply a logical possibility that was never realized historically. Because Thomas presumes Adam and Eve as historical figures, he never considers the second possibility, and consequently neither accepts nor rejects it.

the help of God as first mover, to do or wish any good whatsoever, as stated earlier (1–2.109.1). But in the state of integrity, in terms of the sufficiency of the power of acting, human beings by their natural endowments could wish and do the good that was in proportion to human nature, such as the good of acquired virtue, though they could do no good that surpassed human nature, such as the good of infused virtue.[4] In the state of corrupt nature, however, human beings fall short of what is in accordance with human nature, so that they are unable to fulfill it by their own natural powers.[5] Yet because human nature is not completely corrupted by sin, so as to be deprived of every natural good, even in the state of corrupted nature it can, by virtue of its natural endowments, work some particular good, such as building dwellings, planting vineyards, and other such things. Yet it cannot do all the good natural to it, so that it falls short in nothing. It is like a sick person who can make some movements by himself, yet cannot move fully like the movements of a healthy person, unless cured by the help of medicine.[6]

4. Here Thomas distinguishes two ways in which human beings need God's assistance in order to do or wish any good. First, all action must ultimately be traced back to God as the first mover; thus, even prior to the fall of humanity, Adam and Eve needed this sort of general divine assistance to do any good—although they needed nothing beyond God's ever-present activity as the source of creation in order to do "the good that was in proportion to human nature." Second, human beings need a special and additional divine assistance ("infused grace") because they have been called by God to a destiny that exceeds what human nature can do. Even in the state of original justice, human beings required this special assistance; indeed, the state of original justice was itself a special gift of divine grace and not a natural endowment of human nature, since it involved submission of the intellect to God, which is a good that exceeds human nature.

What exactly Aquinas means by "the good that was in proportion to human nature" is somewhat obscure. Apparently this good does not include the submission of the intellect to God, since Aquinas denies this in 1.100.1, where he says that original justice was not something that flowed from human nature itself, but was "a gift conferred by God on the entire human nature." Therefore, the good Thomas has in mind must entail something more modest, such as an ad hoc ability to follow God's law.

5. Whereas prior to the fall human beings were able to do "the good that was in proportion to human nature" with only the general assistance of God as the first mover, the disintegration brought about by sin makes it impossible to live and act in a fully human manner apart from the special assistance of God's grace.

6. The difficulties of the position Aquinas is attempting to map out on the human need for grace are manifest in these last two sentences. Thomas is unwilling to say that human beings cannot do *any* good apart from grace, since there are certain undeniably good things that human beings, even sinful human beings, accomplish without any special divine assistance. It does seem absurd, for example, to think that a special act on God's part is required every time a person succeeds in building a house or raising a crop. Such a view would seem to imply that God's creation has been so thwarted by sin that it has virtually ceased to function.

At the same time, one should attend to the modesty of the kinds of things Aquinas lists as possible for fallen human beings without grace: building and planting, neither of which implies a moral good, but only a sort of technical accomplishment. The picture becomes a bit muddier in the fifth article of this same question, where (quoting a spurious work attributed to Augustine) Thomas offers a similar list of "works conducive to a good that is natural to

And thus in the state of nature in its integrity, one needs a strength from grace that is added to natural strength for one reason, namely, in order to do and wish supernatural good. But in the state of corrupted nature one needs this grace for two reasons: in order to be healed and, beyond this, in order to carry out works of supernatural virtue, which are meritorious.[7] Furthermore, in both states human beings need divine help in order to be moved to act well.

Reply to 1: Human beings are in control of their actions, and of their willing or not willing, because of the deliberation of reason, which can be bent to one side or the other. But if they are in control of their deliberating or not deliberating, this can be only by virtue of a previous deliberation. And since

---

human beings" and includes "having friends" among them. This muddies the picture because friendship among human beings, unlike building and planting, *is* a moral achievement; indeed, there is a sense in which it is for Aquinas the penultimate moral achievement, exceeded only by friendship with God.

We might sort out this matter by observing that Aquinas describes the things that human beings can do apart from grace as "particular" things, and not as the complete good of which human nature is capable in the state of integrity. Taking the difficult case of friendship, we might say that for fallen human nature it is possible to have friendships, but that apart from grace such friendships cannot characterize our lives in their totality. Sin has fragmented our lives in such a way that, apart from grace, the goods we can accomplish can never make us a good person.

7. Because the language of "merit" has been controversial, particularly between Catholics and Protestants, it is worth saying briefly what Thomas means by it. To say that an action "merits" a reward is to say that the reward is a fitting response to that act; to say that someone merits salvation is to say that their use of their freedom, as expressed in their actions, is such that salvation is a fitting response on God's part. In discussing merit, Thomas makes a distinction between meriting something according to a strict measure of justice, such that a denial of the reward would be unjust (i.e., meriting something *de condigno*), and meriting something in the sense that it is fitting that a reward be given, but the denial of the reward would not in itself be unjust (i.e., meriting something *de congruo*). We might think of this as the difference between paying your bill and leaving a tip (provided the tip is not, as it is in the United States, something that is de facto payment for the waiter). The tip is not something justice requires, but neither is it *un*just, since it is a fitting response to the service given. But whether we are speaking of merit *de condigno* or merit *de congruo*, we should note certain peculiarities that indicate the caution we must use in speaking of merit.

Thomas himself notes in 1–2.114.1 that we use the word analogically when we speak of God "rewarding" human action, since we can act in the first place only because God has given us the capacity to act: "a human being obtains from God, as a reward for his doing, what God gave that person the power to do in the first place." Further, even when Thomas speaks of Christ as a human being meriting on our behalf, it is in the context of speaking of the grace that was bestowed on Christ as the head of the church, and which Christ shares with us. In other words, merit always, even in the case of Christ, presumes the gift of God's grace. We might say that merit is a matter of *convenientia* (see 3.1, note 1): although God is never compelled to reward human action, it is "fitting" all the same that God respond to certain actions is certain ways; thus we can say that those actions merit their reward. In the case of Christ, however, Thomas pushes this point further. Because the grace by which Christ merits salvation for himself and others is not simply the grace of "adoption" but that of "union" (i.e., he is not simply an adopted son of God, but God the Son, the second Person of the Trinity) Thomas says in 1–2.114.3 that the reward God's gives Christ is not simply "fitting" (*de congruo*) but a matter of justice (*de condigno*).

this cannot go on to infinity, we must finally arrive at this conclusion: that the free will of human beings is moved by an external principle that is above the human mind, that is, by God, as the Philosopher proves in the chapter "On Good Fortune" (*Eudemian Ethics,* bk. 7, chap. 14, 1248ª). Therefore, even when it was unweakened by sin, the human mind was not master of its activity to such a degree that it did not need to be moved by God;[8] this is even more the case with the free will of human beings weakened by sin, since by sin's corruption of its nature it is hindered from willing good.

Reply to 2: To sin is nothing else than to fail in the good that belongs to any being according to its nature.[9] Now just as every created thing has its existence from another and is nothing considered in itself, so too it needs to be preserved by another in the good that pertains to its nature; for left to itself it can fail in good, just as left to itself it can fall into nonexistence, unless it is upheld by God.[10]

Reply to 3: Human beings cannot even know truth without divine help, as was stated earlier (1–2.109.1).[11] And yet human nature is more corrupted by sin with regard to the desire for good, than with regard to the knowledge of truth.

1–2.109.6

Whether human beings, left alone and without the external aid of grace, can prepare themselves for grace?

It would seem that human beings, left to themselves and without the external aid of grace, can prepare themselves for grace.[12]

8. To extend the analogy between existing and doing good (which pertains also in the reply to objection 2), we might say that just as genuine existence does not imply that our existence is somehow independent from God, so too genuine human willing and acting does not imply that either our will or action is accomplished without divine assistance. My action, no less than my existence, is "mine" even if it has God as its source.

9. This is a clear statement of Thomas's fundamental understanding of human sin: it is a failure to live in accord with our human nature (cf. 3.46, note 48). This understanding might be contrasted with other approaches, such as those that see sin primarily as a violation of God's law. However, the contrast should not be made too strongly, since Aquinas conceives of human nature as itself a kind of sharing in the divine law.

10. Thomas's point is not entirely clear. The kind of divine assistance—being "upheld by God"—that he refers to here seems to be not the general action of God as first mover, by which things are held in existence, but the supernatural gift of grace. Again, we see the paradoxes of human nature: we can live as fully human only by virtue of a gift that exceeds our humanity.

11. This "help" referred to here is not to the gift of grace but the action of God as first mover, at least as regards those things that are within human beings' natural capacity to know.

12. Given Thomas's view that grace perfects nature (see 1.1, note 28), it is tempting to think of human nature as forming a kind of foundation upon which the superstructure of grace is built. This is not, however, how Thomas understands the relationship between the two. His usual formulation is that grace *perfects* nature, meaning that it does not simply add something

1. Nothing impossible is laid upon human beings, as stated earlier (1–2.109.4 *ad* 1). But it is written in Zechariah 1:3, "Turn to me . . . and I will turn to you." But to prepare for grace is nothing more than to turn to God. Therefore it seems that human beings, left to themselves and without the external aid of grace, can prepare themselves for grace.

2. One prepares oneself for grace by doing what lies within oneself to do, since if human beings do what is in them to do, God will not deny them grace;[13] for it is written in Matthew 7:11 that God gives his good Spirit "to those who ask him." But something is said to be in us if it lies within our power. Therefore it seems to lie within our power to prepare ourselves for grace.

3. If a person needs grace in order to prepare for grace, that person will likewise need grace to prepare for the first grace, and so on to infinity, which is impossible. Therefore it seems that we must not go beyond what was said first, that is, that human beings, left to themselves and without grace, can prepare themselves for grace.

4. Proverbs 16:1 says, "It belongs to a human being to prepare the soul." But something is said to belong to a human being when one can do it by oneself. Therefore it seems that human beings, left to themselves, can prepare themselves for grace.

On the contrary: It is written in John. 6:44, "No one can come to me unless the Father, who has sent me, draws him." But if human beings could prepare themselves, they would not need to be drawn by another. Therefore human beings cannot prepare themselves without the help of grace.

I answer: The preparation of the human will for the good is twofold. First it is prepared to operate well and to enjoy God, and such preparation of the will cannot take place without the gift of grace as a lasting disposition [*gratia habituale*],[14] from which flows works worthy of reward, as stated earlier

---

on to human nature but transforms it so as to fulfill it. So one cannot distill a purely natural basis upon which grace builds, since with the gift of grace human nature is, as it were, renovated. This issue manifests itself here in the context of asking whether human beings can, by their own natural powers, do things that prepare themselves to receive grace.

13. The idea that "to do that which lies within oneself" (*facere quod in se est*) is sufficient preparation for grace can be traced back to the anonymous fourth-century writer known as Ambrosiaster. In the medieval period the idea was defended by Alexander of Hales, and it is a principle that would become extremely important for theologians later in the Middle Ages, such as William of Ockham and Gabriel Biel.

14. What Thomas means by "grace as a lasting disposition" or "habitual grace" (on "habits," see 2–2.2, note 11) is perhaps most evident in the various contrasts according to which medieval theologians spoke about grace. The most important of these contrasts for Aquinas (which he discusses in 1–2.111) are:

    1. Gratuitous grace (*gratia gratis data*) versus sanctifying grace (*gratia gratum faciens*), which is further subdivided into (a) habitual grace and (b) actual grace. Sanctifying grace is the act of God that makes us holy by (a) giving us a capacity to act lovingly (habitual grace) and (b) moving us to act lovingly (actual grace). Gratuitous grace refers to those gifts that God gives us not for the sake of our own holiness but for the good of others. In his commentary on Paul's First Letter to the Corinthians, Aquinas identifies

(1–2.109.5). In a second way, it is possible to think that the human will is prepared for the gift of the lasting disposition of grace. In order to prepare oneself to receive this gift, it is not necessary to presuppose the gift of any further lasting disposition of the soul, otherwise we should go on to infinity. Rather, we must presuppose some gratuitous help from God, moving the soul from within, or inspiring the good we propose to do,[15] for we need divine assistance in these two ways, as stated earlier (1–2.109.2, 3).

It is clear that we need the help of God to move us; for since everything that acts does so in order to attain a goal, every cause must direct its effect toward its goal, and since the order of doers or movers corresponds to the order of the goals, human beings must therefore be directed to their ultimate goal by the motion of the first mover, and to their immediate goal by the motion of any of the subordinate movers.[16] This is like the way in which the spirit of a soldier is bent toward seeking victory by the motion of the leader of the army, and toward following the regimental flag by the motion of the flag bearer. And thus since God is, absolutely speaking, the first mover, it is by his motion of directing everything in the general tendency toward goodness that everything seeks to be made like God in its own way. Therefore Dionysius says in the

---

these with the charismatic gifts Paul discusses in 1 Corinthians 12, and he makes the point that these gifts are given for the building up of the church.

2. Operating grace (*gratia operans*) versus co-operating grace (*gratia co-operans*). Operating grace is the first movement of grace, in which God works within us to heal our souls so that we both are disposed to act in a good way and will to act in that way. This grace in no sense involves an action on our part; as Thomas puts it, "our mind is moved and does not move" (1–2.111.2). Co-operating grace, on the other hand, follows upon operating grace and does involve actions that flow forth from the soul that has been healed. But even in the case of co-operating grace, the soul does not act as if it were an independent source of action, working alongside God's action; its action is always dependent upon the co-operating movement of grace. Co-operating grace is the action of grace on those occasions when, Thomas says, "our mind both moves and is moved" (1–2.111.2).

3. Prevenient grace (*gratia praeveniens*) versus subsequent grace (*gratia subsequens*). Because grace brings about a change in human beings, it operates within history and the flow of time. In other words, it first brings about one effect and then another. In 1–2.111.3 Thomas lists five effects of grace, each one leading to the other: (1) the healing of the soul; (2) the desiring of good; (3) the doing of good; (4) perseverance in doing good; and (5) attaining glory. When we speak of one of these effects as preceding the other, we speak of prevenient (i.e., "coming before") grace; when we speak of one of these effects as following upon the other, we speak of subsequent or consequent (i.e., "following upon") grace. Thus, the action of grace causing the soul to desire good is prevenient with regard to our doing the good, and the action of grace causing us to do the good is consequent upon our desiring the good.

15. That is, we must presuppose some actual grace.

16. Timothy McDermott's free translation of this sentence perhaps makes Aquinas's point a bit clearer: "For when agents are acting in subordination to one another, their goals are correspondingly subordinated, the initial agent acting toward the ultimate goal and the secondary agents to the nearer goals"; see Timothy McDermott, *Summa Theologiae: A Concise Translation* (Allen, Tex.: Christian Classics, 1989), 310.

book *On the Divine Names* (chap. 4) that "God turns all to himself."[17] But he directs righteous people to himself as a particular goal that they seek, and to which they wish to cling, according to Psalm 73:28, "It is good for me to cling to my God." And the fact that they are turned to God can spring only from God's having turned them. But to prepare oneself for grace is, as it were, to be turned to God, just as one who has his eyes turned away from the light of the sun prepares himself to receive the sun's light by turning his eyes toward the sun. Therefore it is clear that human beings cannot prepare themselves to receive the light of grace except by the gratuitous help of God moving them inwardly.[18]

Reply 1: A person's turning to God is by free will, and for this reason one is commanded to turn oneself to God. But free will cannot be turned to God unless God himself turns it, according to Jeremiah 31:18, "Turn me and I shall be turned, for you are the Lord, my God," and Lamentations 5:21, "O Lord, turn us to you, and we shall be turned."[19]

Reply to 2: A person can do nothing unless moved by God, according to John 15:5, "Without me, you can do nothing." Therefore when one is said to do what lies within oneself to do, this is said to be in that person's power inasmuch as he or she is moved by God.

Reply to 3: This objection holds true for grace as a lasting disposition, for which some preparation is required, since every form requires a suitableness in that which is to be its subject. But no additional motion need be presupposed for a human being to be moved by God, since God is the first mover.[20] Therefore we need not go to infinity.

Reply to 4: It belongs to human beings to prepare their souls, since they do this by their free will. And yet they do not do this without the help of God moving them and drawing them to himself, as was said above.

17. To this point in this paragraph Thomas is not speaking of grace but of God's providence, by which God guides and governs the world.

18. The logic of Thomas's point may not be immediately apparent. He is positioning grace as a special instance of God's providence. In the general case of God's providence, nothing moves without being moved by God—so too in the case of grace. If preparation for grace involves a "movement," then, like all movement, it cannot be done independently of God's action. Aquinas goes on to make the point that the preparation of the soul for grace *is* in fact a kind of movement—one that Scripture describes as "turning." Thus such preparation cannot be done apart from God's gracious action.

Here we can see clearly the influence of St. Augustine on Thomas, for it was Augustine's position in his dispute with the followers of Pelagius that no action on the part of human beings could prepare them to receive grace. Even when we do that which is within us (see objection 2 and Thomas's reply), we do it under the action of grace.

19. This reply might seem baffling unless one realizes that for Thomas freedom is not defined by our independence from divine action; rather, our actions are free when God wills them to be such.

20. No infinite regress is involved if we understand the turning of the will to be a matter of actual grace and not habitual grace (see note 14, above).

THE SECOND HALF OF THE SECOND PART

QUESTION 2

THE ACT OF FAITH

2-2.2.3

Whether it is necessary for salvation to believe anything above natural reason?

It would seem unnecessary for salvation to believe anything above natural reason.

1. The salvation and perfection of a thing seem to be sufficiently insured by its natural endowments.[1] But matters of faith surpass natural human reason, since they are things unseen, as was said earlier (2–2.1.4). Therefore believing seems unnecessary for salvation.

2. It is dangerous for a person to assent to matters in which he is unable to judge whether what is proposed to him is true or false; according to Job 12:11, "Does not the ear discern words?" But human beings cannot make this kind of judgment in matters of faith, since we cannot trace them back to first principles, by which all our judgments are guided. Hence it is dangerous to believe in such matters.[2] Therefore believing is not necessary for salvation.

3. Humanity's salvation rests on God, according to Psalm 37:39, "But the salvation of the just is from the Lord." According to Romans 1:20, "the invisible things of God. . . are clearly seen, being understood by the things that are

---

1. The objection's presupposition (borrowed from Aristotle) is that the goal of a thing (that which fulfills its nature) must be within the grasp of its nature.

2. In matters of faith we "borrow" our first principles from God's own self-knowledge (see 1.1, note 17). The objection seems to be saying that this is a shaky basis for knowledge.

made, even his eternal power and divinity." Those things that are clearly seen by the understanding, however, are not an object of belief.[3] Therefore it is not necessary for salvation that one should believe certain things.

On the contrary: It is written in Hebrews 11:6, "Without faith it is impossible to please God."

I answer: Wherever one nature is subordinate to another, we find that two things concur toward the perfection of the lower nature: one of these is according to that nature's proper movement, while the other is according to the movement of the higher nature. Thus water by its proper movement moves toward the center [of the earth], whereas according to the movement of the moon, it moves around the center according to its ebb and flow.[4] Similarly, the planets have their proper movements from west to east, whereas in accordance with the movement of the first heaven, they have a movement from east to west.[5] Now only the created rational nature is immediately subordinate to God. This is because other creatures do not attain to something universal, but only to something particular, sharing in the divine goodness either only by existing (as in the case of inanimate things), or also by living (as in the case of plants), or by knowing individual things (as in the case of animals).[6] However, a rational nature, inasmuch as it knows the universal meaning of "good" and "being," is immediately related to the universal principle of existence.[7]

Consequently the perfection of a rational creature consists not only in what belongs to it according to its nature, but also in what is attributed to it on account of a supernatural sharing in divine goodness.[8] Therefore it was said above (1–2.3.8) that ultimate human happiness consists in a supernatural vision of God. A human being cannot attain this vision unless taught by God, according to John 6:45, "Every one that has heard from the Father and has learned comes to me." However, a person does not acquire a share of this learn-

---

3. This objection makes roughly the same point found in 1–2.91.4, obj. 1, above.

4. Aquinas's example here presumes that water has a built-in direction of movement: downward. Remember that this is before Sir Isaac Newton came up with laws of gravity. Despite the obsolete physics of his example, Aquinas's point remains fairly clear: when one thing is under the sway of another (i.e., "subordinate" to it) you must take two things into account in order to understand its movement: both the natural inclination of the thing, and the influence of that which is acting upon it. Thus the weight of water explains why the ocean stays on the earth, but you cannot explain tides unless you take into account the moon (of course, after Newton we know that both occurrences are in fact the result of gravity).

5. The cosmology of this example is even less useful than the previous one.

6. Inanimate things have being; in addition, plants have life (or a "vegetative soul") and animals have knowledge of particular things (or a "sensitive soul").

7. Only rational creatures (humans and angels) have an immediate relation to God, because their reason allows them to apprehend or "grasp" abstractions ("good-in-general," "existence-in-general") and thus to grasp God as the universal cause of existence.

8. Humans are under the sway of God in something like the way the ocean is under the sway of the moon. The moon gives the ocean a capacity (and thus a purpose) that it otherwise would not have. Thus in talking about human purpose, we must take into account not simply what human beings can do, but also what God can do.

ing instantly, but little by little, according to the ways of human nature. And everyone who learns in this way needs to believe in order to come to perfect knowledge [*scientia*]. In this way, the Philosopher as well remarks that "a learner ought to believe" (*On Sophistical Refutations,* chap. 2, 165[b]).

Therefore in order to come to a perfect vision of heavenly happiness, one must first of all believe God, as a disciple believes the master who is teaching him.[9]

Reply to 1: Since human nature is dependent on a higher nature, natural knowledge does not suffice for its perfection, and some supernatural knowledge is necessary, as stated above.[10]

Reply to 2: Just as a person assents to first principles by the natural light of the intellect, so too a virtuous person has, by the habit of a virtue, right judgment concerning things that are fitting to that virtue. In this same way, a person assents to the things of faith, and rejects what is contrary to faith, by the light of faith that God bestows. Therefore, there is no danger or "condemnation to those who are in Christ Jesus" (Romans 8:1) and whom he has enlightened by faith.[11]

---

9. Because it is through our intellects that we are directly under God's sway, Aquinas uses the analogy of a teacher to explore how God's influence over us is exercised. He makes the point that at the outset of the student–teacher relationship the teacher sees more of the educational goal than does the student, and therefore the student must take much on trust. In 1–2.2.2, Aquinas distinguishes this sort of loving trust in God from a mere belief in things about God by using a distinction borrowed from St. Augustine (found in, e.g., *Homilies on the Gospel of John,* sermon 29, no. 6). One might "believe in God" (*credere Deum*), in the sense of believing that God exists or that certain things are true about God. Or one might "believe God" (*credere Deo*), in the sense of trusting in God. The distinction is fairly obvious: it is the distinction between believing, for example, that the president of the United States exists, and believing that what the president of the United States tells you is true. One can certainly do the former without the latter. Augustine and Thomas also distinguish a third form of belief—*credere in Deum*—which we might (awkwardly) translate as "believing toward God," which is to say that we make God the end or goal of our faith, and consequently the object of our love.

In his commentary on John (chap. 6, lecture 3, §901), Thomas notes that according to the first two understandings of "belief" we can believe in a creature: I can believe that the president exists, and I can trust in what he says. But in the third sense, only God can properly be the object of my belief, because it is only by being united to God through love that I find the perfect happiness that Thomas calls *beatitudo.* Thus, Thomas says, "to believe in God as our goal belongs to faith that is given shape by charity [*credere in Deum ut in finem, est proprium fidei formatae per caritatem*]."

10. That is, in the body of the article.

11. In his response, Aquinas draws an analogy between faith and moral virtue, inasmuch as each is a *habitus*—that is, a disposition that is not given with human nature but that functions as something like a "second nature." For Thomas, a *habitus* is not a habit in the way that chewing your nails is; rather, it is more like the ability to speak French. A *habitus* is an acquired quality or disposition that makes it possible to act in a particular way—even inclines one to act in that way. So someone who has the "habit" of French is someone who has learned to speak the language and thereby acquired the ability to act in a certain way (i.e., in a French-speaking way).

The analogy makes the point that just because something is not given with human nature, it is not for this reason "unreliable." Indeed, virtues, far from being unreliable, are necessary

Reply to 3: In many respects, faith perceives the invisible things of God in a higher way than natural reason does, in proceeding from creatures to God.[12] Therefore it is written in Sirach 3:25, "Many things are shown to you above human understandings."

2–2.2.7

Whether it is necessary for salvation to believe explicitly in the mystery of Christ?

It would seem that it is not necessary for the salvation of all that they should believe explicitly in the mystery of Christ.

1. A human being is not bound to believe explicitly in that about which the angels are ignorant, since the unfolding of faith is through divine revelation, which reaches human beings by means of the angels,[13] as stated earlier (2–2.2.6; 1.111.1). But even the angels were ignorant of the mystery of the incarnation, and thus, according to the commentary of Dionysius (*The Celestial Hierarchy,* chap. 7.3), it is they who ask in Psalm 24:8, "Who is this king of glory?" and in Isaiah 63:1, "Who is this that comes from Edom?" Therefore human beings were not required to believe explicitly in the mystery of Christ's incarnation.

2. It is evident that blessed John the Baptist was one of the great ones [*maioribus*] and nearest to Christ,[14] who said of him in Matthew 11:11 that "among those who are born of women, there has not arisen one greater." But John the Baptist does not appear to have known the mystery of Christ explicitly, since he asked Christ, "Are you he that is to come, or should we look for another?" as it is put in Matthew 11:3. Therefore even the greatest were not required to have explicit faith in Christ.

3. Many Gentiles obtained salvation through the ministry of the angels, as Dionysius states (*The Celestial Hierarchy,* chap. 9, no.3). It would seem, however, that the Gentiles had neither explicit nor implicit faith in Christ, since

---

for us to act morally. So too, faith is not unreliable, but necessary for us to know the truth about God.

12. Although there can be a "natural" knowledge of God, this knowledge is both quantitatively and qualitatively different from the knowledge that comes through faith. Quantitatively, there are some things that can be known through faith (e.g., the doctrine of the Trinity) that cannot be known through reason. Qualitatively, the things we know about God through natural reason are known *better* through supernatural faith.

13. Drawing on Christian Neoplatonic writers like Dionysius, as well as on the role angels play in the stories of the Bible, Aquinas believes that angels have an important role in mediating revelation.

14. The description of John as one of the *maiores,* as well as the distinction in the body of the article between *maiores* and *minores,* carries the implication of wisdom and learning, perhaps as we might use the term "elder" to speak of the leaders in certain cultures. The term *minores,* which I translate as "lowly," carries the implication of intellectual unsophistication, though it also has the implication of low social status.

no revelation was made to them. Therefore it seems that it was not necessary for the salvation of all to believe explicitly in the mystery of Christ.[15]

On the contrary: Augustine says in *On Rebuke and Grace,* "Our faith is sound if we believe that no one, whether old or young, is delivered from the contagion of death and the bonds of sin, except by the one mediator of God and human beings, Jesus Christ."[16]

I answer: As stated earlier (2–2.2.5; 2–2.1.8), that through which human beings obtain perfect happiness belongs, strictly speaking and in itself, to the object of faith.[17] But the mystery of Christ's incarnation and passion is the way by which people come to perfect happiness, for it is written in Acts 4:12 that there is no other name "given to human beings by which we must be saved." Therefore belief of some kind in the mystery of Christ's incarnation was necessary at all times and for all persons, but this belief differed according to differences of times and persons.[18]

Before the state of sin the [first] man believed explicitly in Christ's incarnation insofar as it was intended for the consummation of glory, but not as it was intended to free us from sin by the passion and resurrection, since the man had no foreknowledge of his future sin.[19] Apparently he did, however,

15. Here Thomas is asking what might seem like a very modern question: how can knowledge of Christ be necessary for salvation if those who have never heard of Christ are to have any chance of being saved?

16. Though the view expressed can be found in chapter 7 of Augustine's *De correptione et gratia,* the actual quotation comes, more or less, from Augustine's letter to the bishop Optatus (epistle 190, chap. 2, no. 5).

17. Put differently, *what* we believe in when we have faith (i.e., the object of our faith) is that thing by which we gain eternal happiness (*beatitudo*).

18. The reference to belief of "some kind" means either explicit belief or implicit belief. Aquinas says (2–2.1.7) that "all the articles of faith are contained implicitly in certain primary matters of faith, such as God's existence, and his providence over the salvation of humanity." So the explicit belief that God provides for the salvation of human beings contains the implicit belief in salvation through Christ—provided, of course, that one does not explicitly reject salvation through Christ. In 2–2.2.5 Thomas says that to believe certain things implicitly is "to be ready to believe them."

With regard to "times," Aquinas proposes a three-fold division: before sin, after sin, and after grace (i.e., the incarnation). One might compare this with the historical scheme Thomas uses in his remarks on the human need for grace in 1–2.109.2, above, as well as his discussion of the degrees of prophecy in 1–2.174.6, below. With regard to "persons," Aquinas distinguishes between what the "great ones" or learned [*maiores*] should know and what the "lowly" or uneducated people [*minores*] should know. On the whole, much more explicit belief is expected of the learned.

19. When he says "before the state of sin," Aquinas is not speaking of individuals (since the doctrine of original sin teaches that all are born in a state of sin) but of Adam and Eve before the fall (see 1–2.109, note 3).

The point here is that in becoming flesh Christ in some way "completes" God's work of creation (i.e., it is related to "the consummation of glory"); it does not simply repair the damage wrought by sin. Therefore Adam believed in Christ's incarnation as the consummation of God's work, but not as the remedy for sin. Note that Aquinas says that Adam believed *explicitly* in Christ's becoming flesh; thus his belief in the incarnation was not simply implicit in his explicit

have foreknowledge of the incarnation of Christ, from the fact that he said in Genesis 2:24, "For this reason a man shall leave father and mother, and shall cleave to his wife." Of this passage, the Apostle says in Ephesians 5:32 that this "is a great sacrament . . . in Christ and the church," and it is not believable that the first man was ignorant about this sacrament.

After sin, however, the mystery of Christ was believed in explicitly, not only with regard to the incarnation, but also as to the passion and resurrection, by which the human race is freed from sin and death. Otherwise they would not have foreshadowed Christ's passion by certain sacrifices both before and under the Law.[20] The meaning of these sacrifices was known explicitly by the great ones [maiores], while the lowly [minores], under the veil of those sacrifices, believed them to be intended by God in reference to Christ's coming, and thus their knowledge was in a way "veiled."[21] And, as stated earlier (2–2.1.7), the nearer they were to Christ, the more distinct was their knowledge of Christ's mysteries.

Since grace has been revealed, however, both the great ones and the lowly are required to have explicit faith in the mysteries of Christ, particularly those that the whole church celebrates and publicly proclaims, such as the articles that refer to the incarnation, of which we have spoken earlier (2–2.1.8). But regarding other subtle considerations referring to the articles about the incarnation, people are bound to believe them more and less explicitly, according to what is fitting to one's state and office.[22]

Reply to 1: The mystery of the Kingdom of God was not entirely hidden from the angels, as Augustine observes in the *Literal Commentary on Genesis* (bk. 5, chap. 19), yet certain aspects of it were more fully known to them when Christ revealed these things.

Reply to 2: It was not out of ignorance that John the Baptist inquired about Christ's coming in the flesh, since he had clearly professed his belief in [the incarnation], saying in John 1:34, "I saw, and I gave testimony, that this is the Son of God." Therefore he did not say, "Are you he that has come?" but "Are you he that is to come?" asking about the future, not about the past. Likewise one should not believe that he was ignorant of Christ's future suffering, both

---

belief in God's providence; rather, it was a divinely given foreknowledge that God would become flesh (on explicit versus implicit belief, see the previous note). This might seem at first (and perhaps even second) glance to run counter to what Aquinas says in 3.1.3, below.

20. That is, both prior to and following the giving of God's Law to Moses on Mt. Sinai.

21. The animal sacrifices of the Old Testament are a typological foreshadowing of the death of Jesus on the cross (on the notion of "typology," see 1.1, note 39). According to Aquinas, the "great ones"—such as the prophets—had explicit knowledge that these sacrifices pointed toward the death and resurrection of Christ as the source of our salvation, whereas the "lowly" held this belief as an implication of their explicit belief that the sacrifices were provided by God as a means of forgiving sins.

22. That is to say, who you are and what your job is in the church determines how explicitly you must believe the finer points of doctrine. It is no great matter if a butcher holds that Christ would have become incarnate even if humans had not sinned (see 3.1.3, below); but it does matter if a teacher of theology holds the same belief.

because he had already said, "Behold the Lamb of God, who takes away the sins of the world" (John 1:39),[23] foretelling his future sacrificial offering, and because other prophets had foretold it, as may be seen especially in Isaiah 53. We may therefore say with Gregory (*Homilies on the Gospels,* sermon 6) that he asked this question because he did not know whether Christ would descend into hell in his own person. He knew that the power of Christ's passion would be extended to those who were detained in limbo—according to Zechariah 9:11, "You also, by the blood of your testament, have sent forth . . . prisoners out of the pit, in which there is no water"[24]—but he was not bound to believe explicitly, before its fulfillment, that Christ was to descend there himself.

It may also be said, as Ambrose observes in his commentary on Luke 7:19, that he did not make this inquiry from doubt or ignorance, but from devotion. Or one can say, with Chrysostom (*Homilies on Matthew,* sermon 36), that he did not inquire as though he himself were ignorant, but so that his disciples would be satisfied on that point by Christ. Therefore Christ directed his answer to the disciples, pointing to the signs of his works.[25]

Reply to 3: Many Gentiles received revelations of Christ, as is clear from their predictions. Thus we read in Job 19:25, "I know that my Redeemer lives."[26] The Sibyl, too, foretold certain things about Christ, as Augustine states in *Against Faustus the Manichean* (bk. 13, no. 15).[27] Moreover, we read in the history of the Romans that,[28] at the time of Constantine Augustus and his mother Irene, a tomb was discovered in which a man lay on whose breast was a golden plate with the inscription, "Christ shall be born of a virgin, and in him, I believe. O sun, during the lifetime of Irene and Constantine, you shall see me again."[29]

If, however, some were saved without receiving any revelation, they were not saved without faith in a mediator. Though they did not have faith explicitly, they nevertheless had implicit faith in divine providence, believing God to be

23. The Vulgate has the singular "sin of the world." See 1–2.3, note 3.

24. See 3.65, note 21.

25. As he does in a number of places, Aquinas considers many possible literal meanings of a difficult text without feeling compelled to settle on one. In this case the difficult text is a story from Matthew's Gospel: John the Baptist, who is in prison, sends a messenger to Jesus to inquire if he is the expected Messiah. The difficulty arises because other texts, particularly in the Gospel of John, indicate that John knows who Jesus is. Thus in John 1:29–30, we read that John the Baptist sees Jesus and says, "Here is the Lamb of God who takes away the sin of the world! This is he of whom I said, 'After me comes a man who ranks ahead of me because he was before me.'" Aquinas presents several attempts by previous writers to deal with this difficulty without giving *the* definitive solution.

26. Though Job appears in the Old Testament, he is nowhere identified as an Israelite.

27. Sibyls were prophetesses in pagan Greek literature.

28. This story is found in the *Chronographia* of the ninth-century Byzantine historian Theophanes the Confessor.

29. To this point in his reply, Thomas is presuming that various pre-Christian pagans *did,* in fact, receive revelation, so as to believe *explicitly* in Christ.

the liberator of humanity, in whatever way was pleasing to him, and according to the revelation of the Spirit to those who knew the truth, as stated in Job 35:11, "Who teaches us more than the beasts of the earth."[30]

2-2.2.8

Whether it is necessary for salvation to believe explicitly in the Trinity?

It would seem that it was not necessary for salvation to believe explicitly in the Trinity.

1. The Apostle says in Hebrews 11:6, "He who comes to God must believe that he exists and that he rewards those who seek him." But one can believe this without faith in the Trinity. Therefore it was not necessary to believe explicitly in the Trinity.

2. Our Lord said in John 17:6, "Father, I have manifested your name to people," which Augustine interprets as follows: "Not the name by which you are called God, but the name by which you are called my Father." And further on he adds, "In that he made this world, God is known to all nations; in that he is not to be worshiped together with false gods, 'God is known in Judea'; but, in that he is the Father of this Christ, through whom he takes away the sin of the world, this name of his, previously hidden, he now makes known to them" (*Homilies on the Gospel of John*, sermon 106, no. 4). Therefore before the coming of Christ it was not known that fatherhood and sonship were in the Godhead. Therefore, the Trinity was not explicitly believed.

3. That which we are bound to believe explicitly about God is the object of perfect happiness. But the object of perfect happiness is the highest good, which can be understood to be in God apart from any distinction of Persons. Therefore it was not necessary to believe explicitly in the Trinity.

On the contrary: In the Old Testament the Trinity of Persons is expressed in many ways. Thus at the very outset of Genesis it is written, in order to express the Trinity, "Let us make the human being to our image and likeness" (Genesis 1:26).[31] Therefore from the beginning it was necessary for salvation to believe in the Trinity.

---

30. See note 17, above. Aquinas says that one cannot be saved without belief in Christ, but this may be an implicit belief rooted in the explicit belief that God in his goodness would provide the means for human salvation. So Aquinas's ultimate answer to this question depends on a number of distinctions: the need for explicit faith is not absolute, but depends on circumstances. In some circumstances—where Gods' revelation has not been given (pagans) or where it has been given under a "veil" that cannot be penetrated by the unlearned (the simple folk of the Old Testament)—implicit faith suffices. However, now that grace has appeared in Christ, all who have access to the truth of the incarnation are bound to believe it explicitly, whether they be simple or learned.

31. The *sed contra* here employs a standard medieval explanation for the use of the plural: "Let *us* make the human being to *our* image and likeness." It is the three Persons of the Trinity who are speaking.

I answer: It is impossible to believe explicitly in the mystery of Christ without faith in the Trinity. For the mystery of Christ includes this: that the Son of God took flesh, that he renewed the world through the grace of the Holy Spirit, and further that he was conceived by the Holy Spirit.[32] And therefore, just as the mystery of Christ was believed explicitly before Christ by the great ones, but implicitly and under a veil, so to speak, by the lowly, so too was it with the mystery of the Trinity. Consequently, once grace had been revealed all were bound to explicit belief in the mystery of the Trinity. And all who are born again in Christ have this bestowed on them by the invocation of the Trinity, according to Matthew 28:19, "Go therefore and teach all nations, baptizing them in the name of the Father, and of the Son, and of the Holy Spirit."

Reply to 1: Explicit faith in those two things was necessary at all times and for all people, but it was not sufficient at all times and for all people.[33]

Reply to 2: Before Christ's coming, faith in the Trinity lay hidden in the faith of the great ones, but by Christ it was shown to the world through the apostles.

Reply to 3: The great goodness of God, as we understand it now through its effects, can be understood apart from the Trinity of Persons. But as it is in itself, the way it is seen by the blessed, it cannot be understood without the Trinity of Persons.[34] Further, the sending [*missio*] of the divine Persons leads us into perfect happiness.[35]

2–2.2.10

Whether reasons in support of what we believe lessen the merit of faith?

It would seem that reasons in support of what we believe lessen the merit of faith.[36]

32. Although Thomas believes that Christ explicitly taught his disciples about the Trinity (e.g., in Matthew 28:19), here he seems to be saying that the Trinity is first and foremost revealed in Christ's life itself: in his coming as the Son from the Father through the work of the Holy Spirit. Thus the Trinity is not simply an interesting fact about God; rather it is the understanding of God that one must have in order to make proper sense out of the life, death, and resurrection of Jesus, which is why Thomas says that one cannot have explicit faith in Christ without faith in the Trinity.

33. In other words, belief in God's existence and goodness is a necessary but not sufficient (at least in some circumstances) condition for salvation.

34. The goodness of God that we know through his effects is what one might call an "undifferentiated" goodness; however, the goodness of God as it is known by the saints (and as that knowledge is shared with us through *sacra doctrina*) is the goodness of the love shared by the Father, Son, and Spirit.

35. The sending or "mission" of the divine Persons refers to the incarnation of Christ and the giving of the Spirit on Pentecost. Some manuscripts of the *Summa* read *visio* here, and thus, "the vision of the divine Persons leads us into perfect happiness." Either reading is possible.

36. For Thomas, something is meritorious inasmuch as it is deserving of reward. See 1–2.109, note 7.

1. Gregory says (*Homilies on the Gospels,* sermon 26) that "there is no merit in believing what is shown by reason." If, therefore, human reason provides sufficient proof, the merit of faith is altogether taken away. Therefore it seems that any kind of human reasoning in support of matters of faith diminishes the merit of believing.

2. Whatever diminishes the amount of virtue, diminishes the amount of merit, since "happiness is the reward of virtue," as the Philosopher states in the *Ethics* (bk. 1, chap. 9, 1099^b). But human reasoning seems to diminish the amount of the virtue of faith, since it is essential to faith to be about the unseen, as stated earlier (2–2.1.4, 5).[37] But the more a thing is supported by reasons the less is it unseen. Therefore human reason in support of matters of faith diminishes the merit of faith.

3. Contrary things have contrary causes. Now an incentive contrary to faith increases the merit of faith, whether it be persecution pushing one to renounce the faith, or an argument persuading one to do so. Therefore reason in support of faith diminishes the merit of faith.[38]

On the contrary: It is written in 1 Peter 3:15, "Always be prepared to satisfy every one that asks you a reason for that faith and hope that is in you."[39] But the Apostle would not give this advice if the merit of faith were diminished by it.[40] Therefore reason does not diminish the merit of faith.

I answer: As stated earlier (2–2.2.9 *ad* 2), the act of faith can be meritorious to the extent that it is subject to the will, not only regarding use, but also regarding assent.[41]

Human reason in support of what we believe can be related to the will of the believer in two ways. First, as preceding the act of the will—for instance, when one would not have the will to believe, or to believe readily, unless moved by human reason. In this way human reason diminishes the merit of faith, in the same way that, as was said earlier regarding moral virtues (1–2.24.3 *ad* 1;

---

37. Faith results when the will moves reason to assent with certainty to a truth it *cannot see:* I assent to (i.e., hold as true) the Pythagorean theorem because Socrates tells it to me, and I know him to be a trustworthy and intelligent person. Knowledge, on the other hand, occurs when reason, moved by what it "sees," assents with certainty to a truth: I assent to the Pythagorean theorem because I understand the proof.

38. The objection draws an analogy between the persecution of a martyr and the "intellectual persecution" one undergoes when an unbeliever tries to argue you out of your faith. Drawing out the analogy one might say that, for the objection, using reason in the latter case would be like the martyr taking a sword into the arena to fight off the lions.

39. The Vulgate reads simply, "of that hope that is in you." See 1–2.3, note 3.

40. Normally "the Apostle" refers to Paul, but here it refers to Peter.

41. Something is deserving of reward only if it is what Aquinas calls a "human act"—that is, an act of will in which we do something freely and consciously. In the case of knowing something through reason, our assent to a truth cannot be meritorious because our reason is "compelled" by the evidence, though there *can* be merit in the use to which we put our knowledge. In the case of faith, however, the actual assent to truth is an act of the *will* (moved by God's grace in such a way as not to compromise its freedom) and so can be deserving of reward (see note 37, above).

1–2.77.6 *ad* 2), an emotion [*passio*] that precedes choice makes the virtuous act less praiseworthy.[42] For just as a person should perform acts of moral virtue on account of the judgment of reason, and not on account of emotion, so a person should believe matters of faith on account of the divine authority, and not on account of human reason.[43]

Second, human reason can be consequent to the will of the believer; for when a person has a will that believes readily, he loves the truth he believes, and he ponders and embraces whatever reasons he can find in support for it.[44] In this sense, human reason does not exclude the merit of faith but is a sign of greater merit. Again, it is like the case of moral virtues, in which a consequent emotion is the sign of a will that is more ready to act, as stated earlier (1–2.24.3 *ad* 1).[45] This is the meaning of John 4:42, where the Samaritans say to the woman [at the well], who symbolically represents human reason, "now we believe, not on account of your words."

Reply to 1: Gregory is speaking of the case of a person who has no will to believe unless prompted by reason. But when one has the will to believe things that are of the faith, solely on the authority of God, the merit of faith is not lost or diminished, even if one has demonstrative reasons for some of them (e.g., the existence of God).

Reply to 2: Reasons in support of the authority of faith are not demonstrations that can bring intellectual vision to the human intellect.[46] For this reason matters of faith do not cease to be unseen. But reasons do remove obstacles to faith, by showing that what faith proposes is not impossible.[47] Therefore, such reasons do not diminish the merit or the amount of faith. But in the case not of the articles of faith but of the preambles to the articles—even though demonstrative reasons in support of them take away from the nature of faith,

42. For example, a teenage girl who simply *likes* Disney movies is less deserving of reward for having seen *Snow White* twenty-five times with her little sister than she would have been had she performed this feat because reason told her it was a good thing to do in order to attain the goal of loving her little sister as a creature of God.

43. Many of us would hold that it is better to believe something because we have thought it out for ourselves than to believe it on the authority of someone else. In the case of divine truths, however, Aquinas thinks it is better to believe them on God's authority than it is to believe them on the authority of our own reason, both because God's reason far surpasses our reason and because such belief testifies that we love and trust in God.

44. One might call this the "exploratory" use of reason: we not only use reason to "prove" things about God but also to explore those things that we already believe about God (see 3.1, note 1 on *convenientia*). This is what St. Anselm means by his famous phrase *fide quaerens intellectus* (faith seeking understanding).

45. Thomas thinks the emotions have a genuine place in the moral life; indeed, although we should not do virtuous things simply because we associate them with pleasant emotions, a person for whom virtuous action brings with it no joy is less virtuous than a person who enjoys being good. Likewise, a person who is prompted by faith to try to understand what he or she believes has attained a more worthy faith than one who *simply* accepts things on authority.

46. In other words, such reasons are not proofs.

47. See 1.1, note 23, regarding the ad hoc strategy of answering objections.

because they make apparent that which is proposed—nevertheless such reasons do not take away from the nature of charity, which makes the will ready to believe them even if they are unseen, and so the measure of merit is not diminished.[48]

Reply to 3: Whatever is in opposition to faith, whether it consist in a person's thoughts or in outward persecution, increases the merit of faith, insofar as the will is shown to be readier and more firm in believing. Therefore the martyrs had more merit of faith for not renouncing faith on account of persecution, and even the wise have greater merit of faith for not renouncing their faith on account of the reasons brought forward by philosophers or heretics in opposition to faith. On the other hand, things that are favorable to faith do not always diminish the readiness of the will to believe, and therefore they do not always take away from the merit of faith.[49]

48. The "preambles to faith" are those things that reason can grasp about God without divine aid (see Thomas's reply to the first objection in 1.2.2, above). They should not, however, be thought of as preliminary steps of pure reason that one *must* take before one can believe. One may well hold the preambles on the basis of faith rather than reason. For example, one does not need to be able to use reason to prove God's existence before one can accept the rest of the Christian faith. Indeed, *most* Christians hold to the preambles on the basis of faith rather than reason. But even if one does hold a preamble of faith based on a proof, one deserves a reward for faith so long as one's belief would not cease in the absence of this proof.

49. In the end, Aquinas's basic view on this question seems to be that reason does not diminish the merit of faith, so long as one would believe the matter even if one could not reason one's way to it. And in the case of the "exploratory" use of reason (see note 44, above), it can *increase* the merit of faith.

Hope

2–2.17.2

Whether eternal happiness is the proper object of hope?[1]

It would seem that eternal happiness is not the proper object of hope.[2]

1. A person does not hope for that which surpasses every movement of the soul, since the act of hope is a kind of movement of the soul. But eternal happiness surpasses every movement of the human soul, for the Apostle says in 1 Corinthians 2:9 that it has not "entered into the human heart." Therefore perfect happiness is not the proper object of hope.

2. Prayer is an expression of hope, for it is written in Psalm 37:5, "Commit your way to the Lord and trust in him, and he will do it." Now human beings legitimately pray to God not only for eternal happiness, but also for the goods,

---

1. In reading this article it is helpful to bear in mind that for Aquinas something we hope for must be a future good that is difficult yet possible to obtain. Thus the object of hope has four distinguishing features: it is *good*, not evil (distinguishing hope from fear); *future*, not present (distinguishing hope from enjoyment); *difficult*, not easy (also distinguishing hope from enjoyment); and *possible*, not impossible (distinguishing hope from despair). Aquinas defines hope in this way in 1–2.40.1.

2. When Aquinas speaks of the "proper object" of an action it is helpful to think in terms of the direct object of a verb—in other words, that which receives the action. Thus in the action "Thomas hit the ball" the object of the action is, of course, the ball. Aquinas is inquiring into the *proper* object (i.e., appropriate recipient) of the action of hoping. "Ball" is the proper object of "hit," whereas "his mother" is not. So the question concerns the appropriate recipient of the activity of hoping.

both temporal and spiritual, of the present life,[3] and also to be delivered from the evils that will no longer be in eternal happiness, as is clear from the Lord's Prayer. Therefore eternal happiness is not the proper object of hope.

3. The object of hope is something difficult. But in relation to human beings, many other things besides eternal happiness are difficult. Therefore eternal happiness is not the proper object of hope.

On the contrary: The Apostle says in Hebrews 6:19 that we have hope "that enters in," that is, makes us to enter "within the veil," namely, into the happiness of heaven, according to the interpretation of a gloss on these words.[4] Therefore the object of hope is eternal happiness.

I answer: As stated earlier (2–2.17.1), the hope of which we speak now reaches out to God by leaning on his help in order to obtain the hoped for good.[5] But an effect must be proportioned to its cause, and therefore the good that we should properly and principally hope for from God is the infinite good, which is in proportion to the power of our divine helper, since it belongs to an infinite power to lead to an infinite good. Such a good is eternal life, which consists in the enjoyment of God himself;[6] for from him we should hope for nothing less than himself, since his goodness, by which he imparts good things to a creature, is no less than his essence.[7] Therefore the proper and principal object of hope is eternal happiness.

Reply to 1: Eternal happiness does not enter into the human heart perfectly, that is to say, so that it would be possible for a wayfarer to know what it is and

---

3. The objection is simply pointing out that we ask for many things from God apart from eternal happiness. On the whole we see nothing wrong with saying things such as "I hope I get that job" or "I hope my mother gets better."

4. On the "gloss," see 1.12, note 7.

5. In 1–2.40 Aquinas has already spoken about hope as a *passio* or "feeling" (one that, according to 1–2.40.6, abounds in young men and drunkards). But the hope Aquinas speaks of here is not simply a feeling but what the Christian tradition calls (along with faith and charity) a "theological virtue." A virtue is an abiding disposition that enables us to engage in some activity. Thomas says in 1–2.62.1 that the theological virtues are called "theological" for three reasons: (1) they have God as their object; (2) they are "infused" (or instilled) in us by God; and (3) and they are revealed by God in Scripture.

So theological virtues are the dispositions that God gives us that allow us to attain the ultimate goal of our existence. They are capacities that are, as it were, added to our natural capacity so as to enable us to reach that which we ultimately desire—God.

6. Since hope as a theological virtue is something that is instilled in us by God, it must reflect the infinite power of its cause. Therefore hope's proper object must be something infinite—namely, God himself.

7. In speaking of the feeling of hope, we can normally discern two "objects." For example, if I hope that you will give me twenty dollars, then my hope might be articulated in two ways: (1) I hope to have twenty dollars (*what* I hope for); and (2) I am placing my hope in you (*in whom* I hope). Now in the case of the theological virtue of hope, these two merge into one, since *what* I hope for (eternal life—i.e., a sharing in God's own nature) is identical with the one *in whom* I hope (God). This is why hope is a *theological* virtue, because God is its object.

how it is constituted.[8] Yet according to a general idea—namely, "the perfect good"—it is possible for it to be apprehended by a human being. This is the way that the movement of hope toward it arises. Therefore the Apostle says pointedly in Hebrews 6:19 that hope enters in, "even within the veil," because that which we hope for is as yet veiled to us.

Reply to 2: We should not pray to God for any other goods unless they are directed toward eternal happiness. Therefore hope chiefly regards eternal happiness; the other things for which we pray to God, it regards secondarily and as oriented toward eternal happiness. In the same way, faith regards God principally, and, secondarily, those things that are oriented toward God, as stated earlier (2–2.1.1).[9]

Reply to 3: To one that longs for something great, all lesser things seem small. For this reason, to one that hopes for eternal happiness, nothing else appears difficult compared with that hope. But with regard to the ability of the one who hopes, other things in addition may be difficult for him, so that he may have hope for such things in relation to hope's principal object.

8. A "wayfarer" is someone in this life, as opposed to those in heaven (the blessed) and those in hell (the damned).

9. We may hope for many things, but we exercise the virtue of hope only when we hope for something as leading us toward our ultimate goal: eternal life with God. Thus I may hope to meet someone and fall in love and marry because I would find this personally fulfilling. But such hope is only a feeling, not the theological virtue. On the other hand, I may hope to find a spouse who will help me to love God and thus to obtain eternal life. This would be the theological virtue of hope, not merely the feeling of hope.

Q U E S T I O N 19

THE GIFT OF FEAR

2-2.19.11

Whether fear remains in the heavenly homeland?

It would seem that fear does not remain in the heavenly homeland [*in patria*].[1]

1. It is written in Proverbs 1:33, "He shall enjoy abundance, without fear of evils," which is to be understood as referring to those who already enjoy wisdom in eternal happiness. But every fear is about some evil, since evil is the object of fear, as stated earlier (1–2.42.1).[2] Therefore there will be no fear in the heavenly homeland.

---

1. In speaking of heaven as our *patria* or "homeland," Aquinas is invoking the Augustinian image of God as our true homeland and God incarnate in Christ as the way to that homeland. Thus in *De doctrina Christiana* (bk. 1, chap. 11), Augustine writes, *cum ergo ipsa sit patria, viam se quoque nobis fecit ad patriam* (although God himself is our homeland, he also made himself the way to that homeland). Human beings are wayfarers (or, as both he and Aquinas put it, *viatores*: those on the road) in exile from our true home because of sin, and we seek to return. During our time of exile, we experience the "restlessness" or *inquietudo* of which Augustine wrote in his *Confessions* (bk. 1, chap. 1): *fecisti nos ad te et inquietum est cor nostrum donec requiescat in te* (you have made us for yourself, and our heart is restless until it rests in you). It is because we are in exile that we suffer such things as fear: it is part of the restlessness or disturbance from which we will be freed when we rest in God. In using the term *patria* in this article, Thomas is alluding to Augustine's understanding of this promised rest, and he is asking if there is any sense in which fear of God, which is spoken of positively in Scripture, can be a part of that rest.

2. Just as hope has some future good as its object, so fear has some future evil as its object.

148

2. Human beings will be conformed to God in the heavenly homeland, according to 1 John 3:2, "When he shall appear, we shall be like him." But God fears nothing. Therefore human beings in the heavenly homeland will have no fear.

3. Hope is more perfect than fear, since hope looks to the good and fear looks to evil. But there will be no hope in the heavenly homeland. Therefore there will not be fear there either.

On the contrary: It is written in Psalm 19:9, "The fear of the Lord is holy, enduring forever."

I answer: Servile fear, or fear of punishment,[3] will be in no way present in the heavenly homeland, since such a fear is excluded by the security that is essential to eternal happiness, as stated earlier (1–2.5.4).[4] But with regard to filial fear, just as it grows as charity grows,[5] so too is it perfected when charity is made perfect. Therefore, in the heavenly homeland it will not have quite the same act as it has now.[6]

In order to make this clear, it is necessary to understand that the proper object of fear is a possible evil, just as the proper object of hope is a possible good. Since the movement of fear is like fleeing, fear implies fleeing from a possible difficult evil; indeed, small evils inspire no fear. Now just as a thing's good consists in retaining its proper place in the order of things, so too a thing's evil consists in forsaking its proper place. But the proper place of a rational

3. In 2–2.19.2 Aquinas distinguishes four kinds of fear: worldly, servile, initial, and filial. Aquinas calls fear that turns us *away* from God "worldly fear" (*timor mundanus*). On the other hand, fear may turn us toward God in several ways. We may turn toward God out of fear of punishment, and this is what Aquinas calls "servile fear" (*timor servilis*). Or we may turn toward God out of fear of offending God's goodness, much as we may fear hurting the feelings of someone we love; Aquinas calls this "filial fear" (*timor filialis*) or, when quoting Augustine in this article, "chaste fear." Aquinas also recognizes that we may have a mixed motivation for our fear: Maria may fear failing her introductory theology course both because she does not want to disappoint her parents (not to mention her teacher) and because she does not want to lose her scholarship. This is what Aquinas calls "initial fear" (*timor initialis*), which is located between servile and filial fear. "Initial fear" is characteristic of those who are just beginning to love God. As such, it is closer to filial fear than it is to servile fear.

4. The blessed in heaven have no fear of punishment. Indeed, freedom from such fear is essential to the joy of heaven.

5. The more we love someone, the more we wish to avoid hurting or offending them.

6. "Quite the same act as it has now" translates Aquinas's Latin accurately, but it does not help us understand what he is saying, in part because of the flexibility of the term *actus*. The term can mean "action," but it can also mean a perfected state of existence, as in the case of *actually* being something rather than *potentially* being something (see 1.2, note 32). Here Aquinas seems to be saying simply that "fear" in heaven will be a fundamentally different kind of thing than "fear" in this life. As the rest of the article shows, he seems to have some doubts whether there is really any point in even using the word "fear" to describe those in heaven. But since Scripture speaks of "fear of God" as "everlasting" (see the text cited in the *sed contra*), Aquinas has a stake in arguing that although it might be *misleading* in some cases to speak of the fear that remains in the blessed, it is not *improper* to do so (since Scripture never speaks improperly).

creature is that it should be under God and above other creatures.[7] Therefore, just as it is an evil for a rational creature to submit to a lower creature through love, so too is it an evil for it not to submit to God but to presumptuously revolt against him or treat him with contempt. This evil is possible to a rational creature considered according to its nature, on account of the natural flexibility of the free-will. But in the blessed it becomes impossible, on account of the perfection of glory.[8] Therefore avoiding the evil of not being subject to God will exist in the heavenly homeland as something possible to [human] nature, although impossible in the state of bliss. But on our journey [to that homeland] this evil is avoided as something altogether possible.[9]

Therefore Gregory—interpreting Job 26:11, "The pillars of heaven tremble and quake at his command"—says in the *Moralia in Job* (bk. 17, chap. 29), "The very powers of heaven that gaze on him without ceasing, tremble while contemplating. But this awe, far from being a punishment, is not from fear but from wonder," because, that is to say, they are in wonder at God's transcendent existence and incomprehensibility. Augustine, in *The City of God* (bk. 14, chap. 9), also admits fear in heaven in this sense, although he leaves the question doubtful. "If," he says, "this chaste fear that endures for ever and ever is to be in the future life, it will not be a fear that is afraid of an evil that might possibly occur, but a fear that holds fast to a good that we cannot lose. For when we love the good that we have acquired with an unchangeable love, without doubt our fear is secure, if one may put it this way, in avoiding evil. 'Chaste fear' signifies the will that cannot consent to sin and by which we avoid sin, not with concern for our weakness, for fear that we might sin strongly, but with the tranquillity born of charity. But if no sort of fear at all is possible there. . . perhaps fear is said to endure for ever and ever because that to which fear leads us is everlasting."

Reply to 1: The passage quoted excludes from the blessed the fear that denotes concern and anxiety about evil, but not the fear that is accompanied by security, as Augustine said.

---

7. Note Aquinas's hierarchical conception of existence. Evil is a matter of the hierarchy being *dis*ordered. Thus in the case of created beings with minds, two forms of disorder are possible: (1) they might place created beings without minds above themselves (as when one becomes enslaved to material goods), or (2) they might place themselves—mere creatures—above God, who is the uncreated source of creation.

8. Aquinas believes that part of the perfection of the blessed is their inability to sin. He sees this inability as the perfection of their free will, not as something that compromises their freedom (see 1–2.109, note 19).

9. This is a difficult sentence to follow (and to translate). Aquinas is saying that if we take avoidance of evil as the key element in fear, then we *can* say that the blessed have fear, in that they avoid evil. However, this is a peculiar kind of avoidance. In the state of bliss, humans remain human, and thus by nature subject to sin, yet de facto it has become impossible for them to be evil because they are so enraptured by God's glory. So we might say that whereas the fear of wayfarers is with regard to a possible future evil, the fear of the blessed is with regard to a de facto *im*possible future evil.

Reply to 2: As Dionysius says in his *On the Divine Names* (chap. 9), "the same things are both similar and dissimilar to God. They are similar on account of a contingent imitation of what cannot be imitated"—that is, inasmuch as they imitate, so far as they can, God, who cannot be imitated perfectly—"and they are dissimilar because they are the effects of a cause of whom they fall infinitely and immeasurably short." Therefore, if there can be no fear in God, since there is none above him to whom he may be subject, it does not follow that there is none in the blessed, whose happiness consists in perfect subjection to God.[10]

Reply to 3: Hope implies a kind of defect—namely, that happiness lies in the future—that is removed when happiness is present. But fear implies a natural defect in a creature, according to which it is infinitely distant from God, and this defect will remain even in the heavenly homeland. Therefore fear will not be cast out altogether.[11]

10. Here fear is linked to subjection—that is, a kind of filial fear.

11. Although reference to the future is an essential part of the definition of hope, it is not an essential part of the definition of fear. Thus something called "fear" can remain in heaven. See note 9, above.

QUESTION 23

CHARITY

2–2.23.1

Whether charity is friendship?

It would seem that charity is not friendship.[1]

1. It is the special feature of friendship to live together with friends, as the Philosopher says in the *Ethics* (bk. 8, chap. 5, 1157[b]).[2] But human beings have charity toward God and the angels, "whose fellowship [*conversatio*] is not with mortals," as Daniel 2:11 says.[3] Therefore charity is not friendship.

1. The Latin tradition translates the Greek word *agape* as *caritas*. One might simply translate *caritas* as "love," but Aquinas uses other words (*dilectio, amor*) that could also be translated in this way. Moreover, *caritas* is not simply synonymous with these other terms. Like the Latin tradition as a whole, Thomas uses *caritas* to name our love of God and neighbor, a love that is possible only because of God's prior gift of love. To mark Thomas's use of this term, therefore, I have used the somewhat obsolete word "charity."

2. One point to note in this article is Aquinas's constant dialogue with Aristotle on the subject of friendship. Thomas draws on Aristotle's *Nichomachean Ethics* as a rigorous analysis of human friendship that can help us clarify what it means to speak of "friendship with God." However, as becomes obvious, Thomas does not simply adopt Aristotle's views on friendship and apply them to God. Rather, Thomas argues that all true human friendships are grounded in friendship with God, an argument that leads to some rather dramatic revisions of what "friendship" means—revisions that would probably have baffled Aristotle (e.g., the notion of loving one's enemies).

3. The citation is from Daniel, but the objection is essentially Aristotelian. In the *Nichomachean Ethics* (bk. 8, chap. 7, 1158[b]-1159[a]), Aristotle says that if two parties are greatly unequal in terms of virtue or wealth or anything else, "then they are no longer friends, and do not even

2. There is no friendship without reciprocal love, as it says in the *Ethics* (bk. 8, chap. 2, 1155[b]). But charity extends even to one's enemies, according to Matthew 5:44, "Love your enemies." Therefore charity is not friendship.

3. According to the Philosopher in the *Ethics* (bk. 8, chap. 3, 1156[a]), there are three kinds of friendship, directed respectively toward the pleasurable, the useful, and the honorable.[4] But charity is not friendship for usefulness or pleasure, for Jerome says in his letter to Paulinus, which is to be found at the beginning of the Bible (epistle 53),[5] "True friendship cemented by Christ depends not on household interests, nor on mere bodily presence, nor on crafty and cajoling flattery, but is when people are drawn together by the fear of God and the study of the divine Scriptures." Neither is it the friendship of the honorable, since by charity we love even sinners, whereas the friendship of the honorable is only for the virtuous, as it says in the *Ethics* (bk. 8, chap. 4, 1157[a]). Therefore charity is not friendship.

On the contrary: It is said in John 15:15, "Now I will not call you servants . . . but my friends." But this was not said to them except on account of charity. Therefore charity is friendship.

I answer: According to the Philosopher in the *Ethics* (bk. 8, chap. 2, 1155[b]), not every love has the nature of friendship, but only that love that is accompanied by wishing someone well—that is, when we love someone in such a way as to wish good to them. If, however, we do not wish good to what we love, but wish its good for ourselves (this is what we mean when we say that we love wine, or a horse, or something similar), it is not the love of friendship, but a kind of desire; for it would be absurd to speak of being friends with wine or with a horse.[6]

---

expect to be so." He continues, "And this is most manifest in the case of the gods; for they surpass us most decisively in all good things. . . . Much can be taken away and friendship remain, but when one party is removed at a great distance, as is God, the possibility of friendship ceases." In Thomas's commentary on this section of the *Nichomachean Ethics*, he identifies the "gods" as "separated substances"—namely, angels—thus accounting for the objection's reference to God *and* angels.

4. Aristotle says that in useful friendship (*amicitia utilis*) and pleasurable friendship (*amacitia delectabilis*), the friend is not loved for his or her own sake, but because they can provide us with some thing we need or simply because we find that person's presence enjoyable (e.g., because they are funny or beautiful). In honorable friendship (*amicitia honesti*), on the other hand, the friend is loved for his or her own sake—that is, because of the virtues (which are more than simply pleasing qualities, such as beauty or wit) he or she possesses. As Aristotle puts it, "Perfect friendship is the friendship of men who are good, and alike in virtue; for these wish well alike to each other *qua* good, and they are good in themselves" (*Nichomachean Ethics*, bk. 8, ch.3, 1156[b]). So these friendships are "honorable" in that both parties are virtuous, and what they desire and rejoice in is the friend's virtue.

5. The reference is to Jerome's letter as forming a sort of preface to the Vulgate.

6. Here Aquinas acknowledges that simply because charity is a type of love, this does not mean that it is friendship, because not all love involves friendship. Although we might say that we "love" a particular food, that food does not thereby become our friend, in part because we do not desire that the food be good—in other words, we do not have "benevolence" toward it.

But well-wishing does not suffice for friendship, for a certain mutual love is required, since a friend is a friend to a friend,[7] and such well-wishing is founded on a certain communion [*communicatione*].[8]

Accordingly, because there is communion between humanity and God inasmuch as he communicates his perfect happiness to us, some kind of friendship must be based on this same communication. Regarding this communion, 1 Corinthians 1:9 says, "God is faithful, by whom you are called into the fellowship of his Son."[9] The love based on this communion is charity; therefore it is evident that charity is the friendship of human beings toward God.[10]

Reply to 1: The life of human beings is twofold. On the one hand, there is the outward life of the senses and the body, and with regard to this life there is no communion or fellowship between us and God or the angels. On the other, there is the spiritual life of human beings according to the mind. And with regard to this life there is fellowship between us and both God and the angels,[11]

Rather, the goodness of the food incites our desire, which is not the same thing as benevolence, since we might seek to fulfill that desire by consuming the food and thereby destroying it. So if charity is to be friendship, it must fulfill certain other criteria: in this case, it must involve well-wishing. Thomas's introduction of the example of the horse seems to muddy his point, for it seems that we *can* desire that a horse be good, because horses, as animate creatures, grow and develop.

   Thomas's discussion raises a difficult point. How can a creature have benevolence toward God? How can a creature wish that God be good, or that good things accrue to God? In 2–2.28.1, Thomas speaks of "the love of benevolence, by which someone rejoices on account of the friend's prospering." This is certainly a kind of "benevolence" that humans could exercise toward God: to rejoice in God's goodness.

   7. Beyond well-wishing, friendship also involves mutuality: you cannot be friends with someone who does not consider herself your friend. This is another reason that one cannot be friends with an inanimate object: it cannot consider you its friend. In the case of other people, mutuality is possible, but not inevitable, and friendship that is not mutual is called stalking.

   8. On *communicare*, see 3.1, note 5. Because of the flexibility of the terms *communicatio*, which Thomas trades on in his response here, I have translated it sometimes as "communion" and sometimes as "communication." To say that friendship depends on *communicatio* covers two points that Aristotle makes about friendship: it must be based on a something shared in common (whether this be a matter of usefulness, pleasure, or goodness), and the parties must actually be in communication with one another (see *Nichomachean Ethics*, bk. 8, chap. 2, 1155[b]).

   9. Aquinas's quotation of this verse from 1 Corinthians is an indication of his fundamental departure from Aristotle: because God becomes incarnate in Christ, there is communion/communication between God and humanity (see 3.1.1, below), and therefore friendship is possible between God and humanity.

   10. Here it should be underscored that the charity Aquinas is speaking of is a theological virtue (see 1–2.17, note 5), which means that it is instilled in us by God. As 1 John 4:19 says, "We love because he first loved us." The initiative is always on God's part. Nothing we do wins God's friendship; it is a gift freely bestowed. As Thomas says in his commentary on John's Gospel (chap. 15, lecture 3, §2012), "keeping the commandments is not the cause of divine friendship but the sign, the sign both that God loves us and that we love God."

   11. Even apart from our communion with God in Christ, through the simple fact of our creation as rational beings we share something with God. This sharing is, as Thomas goes on to note, incomplete in this life but will be perfected in the next life, through the grace of Christ.

which is, indeed, incomplete in this present state of life. Therefore it is written in Philippians 3:20, "Our common life is in heaven." But this common life will be completed in our heavenly homeland, when "God's servants shall serve him, and they shall see his face" as it says in Revelation 22:3–4.[12] Therefore charity is incomplete here, but will be completed in heaven.

Reply to 2: Friendship extends to someone in two ways. First, with regard to the specific person, and in this way friendship extends only to one's friends. Second, it extends to someone with regard to someone else, as in the case when someone is friends with a certain person, and for his sake loves everyone with some connection to him, whether they are children, or servants, or related in any way whatsoever. Indeed so much do we love our friends that for their sake we love all who belong to them, even if they hurt or hate us. In this way, the friendship of charity extends even to our enemies, whom we love because of charity toward God, to whom the friendship of charity is chiefly directed.[13]

Reply to 3: The friendship of the honorable is directed only to one who is virtuous as the principal person, but for that person's sake we love those who belong to him, even if they are not virtuous. In this way charity, which above all is the friendship of the honorable, is extended to sinners, whom we love out of charity for God's sake.

12. The quotation from Philippians, with its reference to our "common life" (in Latin, *conversatio;* in Greek, *politeuma*), indicates another way in which Thomas departs from Aristotle in his account of friendship. For both Thomas and Aristotle, friendship is essentially "political," inasmuch as it depends on friends sharing a common life. For Aristotle, the common life upon which friendship is based is that of the *polis* or city-state: it would be unthinkable for a citizen of Athens to be friends with a citizen of Sparta, because it is in the life of the *polis* that the diverse interests of individuals are coordinated so as to form a common good. Of course, even within the *polis* the possibility of friendship is limited; those who do not share fully in the "common life" of the city—women, slaves, children, foreigners—cannot be friends in the fullest sense of the term.

For Thomas, however, the common life of Christians is not that of some earthly city-state, with its attendant limitations; it is rather the common life of the heavenly Jerusalem, in which all those who are chosen for salvation share without regard to status. Thus friendship is possible across boundaries that seemed unbreakable in the ancient world—ultimately even across the boundary that separates the divine and the human.

13. If we love someone, we love all those who are connected with them. But because all creatures exist only by virtue of their relatedness to God, in loving God we are called to love all creatures. This does not, however, lessen the paradox of having charity toward our enemies, such that our enemies are our friends. A similar argument is used in the reply to the next objection.

DIFFERENT KINDS OF PROPHECY

2–2.174.6

Whether the degrees of prophecy change as time goes on?

It would seem that the degrees of prophecy change as time goes on.[1]

1. Prophecy is intended for knowledge of divine matters, as stated earlier (2–2.174.2). But according to Gregory (*Homilies on Ezekiel,* sermon 16), "knowledge of God went on increasing as time went on." Therefore degrees of prophecy should be distinguished according to the passing of time.

2. Prophetic revelation is made by way of God speaking to human beings; the prophets, however, declared the things revealed to them in both words and writing. Now it is written in 1 Kings 3:1 that before the time of Samuel "the word of the Lord was precious," that is, rare, and yet afterwards it was delivered to many. Similarly, the books of the prophets do not appear to have been written before the time of Isaiah, to whom it was said (Isaiah 8:1), "Take

---

1. Earlier (2–2.171.1) Aquinas discussed the nature of prophecy, describing it as an enlightening of the prophet's intellect with knowledge that surpasses what is naturally possible for human beings. But prophecy is also given for the purpose of being communicated; therefore the prophet must speak on behalf of God and communicate this enlightened knowledge to other people. Aquinas also says that since the knowledge revealed through prophecy surpasses human reason, prophecy is at times accompanied by miracles that confirm what the prophet says.

Here Aquinas is asking whether we can discern a historical pattern to God's revelatory activity. What we get in the body of this article is a kind of scheme of how God acts in time and space to bring humanity into communion with himself.

a great book and write in it with a human pen," after which many prophets wrote their prophecies. Therefore it would seem that with the passing of time the degree of prophecy progressed.

3. Our Lord said in Matthew 11:13, "The prophets and the law prophesied until John." Afterwards, however, the gift of prophecy was in Christ's disciples in a much more excellent manner than in the ancient prophets, according to Ephesians 3:5, "In other generations" the mystery of Christ "was not known to the sons of humanity, as it is now revealed to his holy apostles and prophets in the Spirit." Therefore it would seem that degrees of prophecy should be separated according to the passing of time.

On the contrary: As stated earlier (2–2.174.4), Moses was the greatest of the prophets, and yet he preceded the other prophets. Therefore the degree of prophecy did not increase according to the passage of time.

I answer: As stated earlier (2–2.174.2), prophecy is intended for knowledge of divine truth. By contemplating divine truth we are not only instructed in faith but also guided in our actions, according to Psalm 43:3, "Send forth your light and your truth; they have guided me." Now our faith consists chiefly in two things. First, in the true knowledge of God, according to Hebrews 11:6, "He that comes to God must believe that he is." Second, in the mystery of Christ's incarnation, according to John 14:1, "You believe in God; believe also in me."[2]

If, therefore, prophecy is spoken of in relation to faith in the Godhead as its goal, it progressed according to three divisions of time—namely: before the Law, under the Law, and under grace.[3] For before the Law, Abraham and the other patriarchs were prophetically taught things that pertain to faith in the Godhead. Therefore they are called prophets, according to Psalm 105:15, "Do no evil to my prophets," which is said especially on account of Abraham and Isaac. Under the Law, however, the prophetic revelation of things pertinent to faith in the Godhead occurred in a way that was still more excellent than before, because at that time not only special persons or certain families, but the whole people had to be instructed in these matters. Therefore the Lord said to Moses in Exodus 6:2–3, "I am the Lord, who appeared to Abraham, to Isaac, and to Jacob, by the name of God Almighty, and my name *Adonai* I did not show to them." Thus

2. Thomas says in 1.1.4 that theology or holy teaching is both "practical" and "speculative," that is, it is concerned with both knowledge of the truth and right human action. It follows from this division that prophecy, by which God teaches humanity, has both an ethical and an intellectual dimension: prophets tell people how to reform their lives, and they tell them the truth about God. The intellectual dimension of prophecy is two-fold: it concerns (1) the truth about God's nature and (2) the truth about God's becoming flesh in Christ. Note that these are the two truths that, according to Aquinas, one must believe at least implicitly in order to be saved (see 2–2.2.7–8, above).

3. Here Thomas gives us a three-fold division of the history of prophecy: from Abraham to Moses (before the Law); from Moses to Jesus (under the Law); and from Jesus to today (under grace). This is somewhat different from the division of history made in 2–2.2.7, above.

previously the patriarchs had been taught to believe in a general way about the unity and omnipotence of God, but Moses was more fully instructed in the simplicity of the divine essence, when it was said to him in Exodus 3:14, "I am who am."[4] This name is signified by Jews in the word *Adonai* on account of their veneration for that unspeakable name.[5] Afterward, in the time of grace, the mystery of the Trinity was revealed by the Son of God himself, according to Matthew 28:19, "Go . . . teach all nations, baptizing them in the name of the Father, and of the Son, and of the Holy Spirit."[6]

Within each time period, however, the most excellent revelation was that which was given first. The first revelation before the Law was given to Abraham, for it was at that time that people began to stray from faith in one God by turning away toward idolatry, whereas no such revelation was necessary earlier while all persisted in the worship of one God. A lesser revelation was made to Isaac, being founded on the revelation made to Abraham. For this reason it was said to him in Genesis 26:24, "I am the God of Abraham your father," and similarly to Jacob in Genesis 28:13, "I am the God of Abraham your father, and the God of Isaac." Likewise also in the state of the Law, the first revelation that was given to Moses was more excellent, and on this revelation all the other revelations to the prophets were founded. And so too in the time of grace, the entire faith of the church is founded on the revelation made to the apostles concerning the faith in one God and three Persons; as it is said in Matthew 16:18, "On this rock," that is, of your confession, "I will build my church."[7]

With regard to faith in Christ's incarnation, it is evident that the nearer prophets were to Christ, whether before or after him, the more fully, for the

4. Aquinas takes the revelation of God's name to Moses at the burning bush—"I am who am"—as a revelation of the radical simplicity of God's nature (see 1.3, note 1); it reveals God as one whose definition is the act of existence. Therefore, *what* God is is not different from the fact *that* God is.

5. Aquinas is referring here to the Jewish practice of substituting the word *Adonai* (Lord) wherever the name of God (written "YHWH") appears in Scripture. Jews consider the actual name of God too holy to be spoken by human beings.

6. Looked at from the perspective of the three time periods, we can discern a progressive revelation of the divine nature: first God's omnipotence and unity are revealed to Abraham and to those living prior to the Law; then God's simplicity is revealed to Moses and to those living under the Law; and finally God's triune nature is revealed through Christ to the apostles and to those living under grace.

7. Although the three periods themselves represent a progressive deepening of the knowledge we have of God's nature, *within* each of the periods the revelation of God's nature is, as it were, kicked-off by a revelation that is normative for the rest of the historical period.

In this article, contrary to his usual practice in the *Summa*, Thomas seems more inclined to agree with the objections than with the *sed contra*. As time has passed, the human race has on the whole had more of God's truth revealed to it. At the same time, there is no *simple* historical progression of revelation; just because one lives later in time is no guarantee that one knows the truth about God better. Thus, for example, Thomas presumes that the divine revelation made to the apostles is superior to any subsequent revelation.

most part, they were instructed on this point. Yet after him they were instructed more fully than before, as the Apostle declares in Ephesians 3:5.[8]

As regards the guidance of human actions, the prophetic revelation is differentiated not according to the passage of time but according to what the circumstances are. As it is written in Proverbs 29:18, "When prophecy shall fail, the people shall be scattered abroad." For this reason, whatever the time, people were divinely instructed about what they were to do, according to what was advantageous for the salvation of God's chosen ones.

Reply to 1: The saying of Gregory is to be understood as referring to the time before Christ's incarnation, with regard the knowledge of this mystery.[9]

Reply to 2: As Augustine says in *The City of God* (bk. 18, chap. 27), "just as in the early days of the Assyrian kingdom promises were made most explicitly to Abraham, so too at the outset of the western Babylon," which is Rome, "under whose government Christ was to come, in whom these promises," namely, the promises made to Abraham, "were to be fulfilled, the oracles of the prophets were given not only in spoken but in written words, testifying to the great event to come. For while prophets were scarcely ever lacking to the people of Israel from the time that they began to have kings, it was exclusively for their benefit, not for that of the nations. But when those prophetic writings were being established with greater publicity, which at some future time were to benefit the nations, it was fitting to begin when this city," namely, Rome, "was being built, which was to govern the nations."

It is above all in the time of the kings that the prophets were numerous in the people of Israel, because then the people were not oppressed by other nations, but had their own king; and for this reason it was fitting for them, having liberty, to be taught by the prophets what to do.

Reply to 3: The prophets who foretold the coming of Christ could not continue past John the Baptist, who with his finger pointed to Christ as actually present. Nevertheless, as Jerome says on this passage, "This does not mean that there were no prophets after John; for we read in the Acts of the Apostles that Agabus and the four maidens, daughters of Philip, prophesied."[10] In addition, John the Evangelist wrote a prophetic book about the end of the church. And at all times those with the spirit of prophecy have not been lacking, not for bringing forward any new teaching of the faith, but for directing human actions.[11]

8. Things are different with regard to the revelation of Christ's incarnation. Here the three periods are not important; rather, Christ forms a central point that divides history into before and after. The closer one is to Christ in time—whether before or after—the better knowledge one has, and one has better knowledge after than before. Thus David, coming later, had a fuller revelation of Christ than did Moses (2–2.174.4 *ad* 1).

9. In other words, Gregory presumes not a three-fold division of history but the two-fold division of before and after Christ.

10. The passage in question is John 1:29ff. Jerome's comment is found in his *Commentary on Matthew*.

11. Aquinas holds that the ethical dimension of prophecy has continued, presumably up into his own day. However, the intellectual dimension of prophecy—prophecy as revealing truths

Thus Augustine says in *The City of God* (bk. 5, chap. 26) that the emperor Theodosius "sent a message to John, who lived in the Egyptian desert, and whom he knew by his ever-increasing fame to be endowed with the prophetic spirit, and from him he received a message assuring him of victory."[12]

about God—ceases with the New Testament. Thus the prophetic revelation of doctrine has ended, but prophecy that draws out of the implications of what is already believed has not.

12. Whether by accident or design, Thomas has chosen three different men named "John"— John the Baptist, John the Evangelist, and John the Egyptian monk—to make his point here.

THE
THIRD
PART

QUESTION 1

THE FITTINGNESS
OF THE INCARNATION

3.1.1

Whether it was fitting that God should become incarnate?

It would seem that it was not fitting [*conveniens*] for God to become incarnate.[1]

1. Since God from all eternity is the very essence of goodness, it was best for him to be as he had been from all eternity. But from all eternity he had

---

1. In the first sentence of the first article of the third part of the *Summa* we encounter the extremely important term *conveniens*. In this translation it is generally rendered as "fitting" or "suitable." In using this term Aquinas is indicating a particular kind of reasoning that one employs in *sacra doctrina*. For example, Aquinas sees the incarnation of God in Jesus Christ as a truth given to us in revelation. It is not something that we can "prove" through the use of reason, not least because it regards a contingent fact of history (see 1.1, note 18). However, there is still a role for reason here, not in proving the incarnation, but in manifesting how it fits together (*convenire* means literally "to come together") with other things that Christians hold true about God. This term is especially prominent in the third part of the *Summa,* which deals with Christ. In this part, Aquinas repeatedly inquires after the *convenientia* of various things that Christians hold to be revealed truth. We should note that the use of this term, and the kind of reasoning behind it, is hardly unique to Thomas. It plays a major role in the writings of Anselm, for whom it is linked with the notion of *rectitudo* or "rightness," and in Thomas's contemporary Bonaventure.

been without flesh. Therefore it was most fitting for him not to unite himself to flesh. Therefore it was not fitting for God to become incarnate.[2]

2. It is not fitting to unite things that are infinitely apart, just as it would not be a fitting union if one were to paint a figure in which "the neck of a horse was joined to the head of a man" [Horace, *Ars. poetica,* line 1]. But God and flesh are infinitely apart, since God is most simple and flesh is most composite—especially human flesh.[3] Therefore it was not fitting that God should be united to human flesh.

3. A body is as distant from the highest spirit as evil is from the highest good. But it would be completely unfitting that God, who is the highest good, should assume evil. Therefore it is not fitting that the highest uncreated spirit should take on a body.

4. It is not fitting that he who surpassed the greatest things should be contained in the least, and that he who has charge of great things should leave them for lesser things. But God, who takes care of the whole world, cannot be contained by the whole universe. Therefore it would seem unfitting that "within the small body of a squalling infant should lie hidden he, in comparison with whom the whole universe is accounted as little; . . . and that this Ruler should leave his throne for so long, and transfer the government of the whole world to so frail a body," as Volusianus writes to Augustine.[4]

On the contrary: It would seem to be most fitting that the invisible things of God should be made known by visible things, since it was for this purpose that the whole world was made, as is clear from the word of the Apostle in Romans 1:20, "The invisible things of God . . . are clearly seen, being understood by the things that are made." But, as John of Damascus says (*On the Orthodox Faith,* bk. 3, chap. 1), by the mystery of incarnation "God's goodness, wisdom, justice, and power"—or virtue—"are made known simultaneously: his goodness, for he did not despise the weakness of his own handiwork; . . . his justice, because . . . he did not snatch humanity forcibly from death, but caused the tyrant to be defeated by no other; . . . his wisdom, for he found a suitable solution for a most difficult problem;" his power or virtue, "for there is nothing greater than for God to become a human being."

I answer: A thing is "fitting" [*conveniens*] if it belongs to something because of its very nature; thus, for human beings it is fitting to reason, since this befits them inasmuch as it is their nature to be rational. But God's very nature is goodness, as is clear from Dionysius in *On the Divine Names* (chap. 1, no. 5). Therefore, whatever pertains to the idea of goodness befits God.

2. If God is unchanging (as Aquinas believes), how can we speak of God becoming human without admitting that God has changed? In terms of the notion of *convenientia* (see previous note), how can these two beliefs—(1) that God is unchanging and (2) that God became incarnate—"come together" in a coherent way?

3. See 1.12, note 1.

4. Numbered as epistle 135 among Augustine's letters.

But it pertains to the idea of goodness to communicate itself to others, as is plain from Dionysius (*On the Divine Names,* chap. 4, no. 1).[5] Therefore it pertains to the idea of the highest good to communicate itself in the highest manner to the creature, which is brought about chiefly by "his so joining created nature to himself that one person is made up of these three—the Word, a soul, and flesh," as Augustine says in *De Trinitate* (bk. 13, chap. 17). Therefore it is manifest that it was fitting that God should become incarnate.[6]

Reply to 1: The mystery of the incarnation was not brought about through God being changed in any way from the state in which he had been from eternity, but through his having united himself in a new way to creation or, rather, through having united it to himself.[7] It is fitting that creation, which is by its very definition mutable, should not always be in one way. Therefore, just as creation began to be even though it had not been before, so likewise it is fitting that creation, not having been previously united to God, was later united to him.[8]

Reply to 2: To be united to God in unity of person was not fitting to human flesh according to its natural endowments, since it was above its dignity. Nevertheless, it was fitting that God, by reason of his infinite goodness, should unite it to himself for the salvation of humanity.

Reply to 3: Every condition by which any creature whatsoever differs from the creator has been established by God's wisdom for the purpose of God's goodness; for God—who is uncreated, immutable, and incorporeal—produced mutable and corporeal creatures because of his own goodness. And so also the

---

5. Aquinas is exploiting the dual meaning of *communicare,* which can mean both to pass along information (what we usually mean by "to communicate") and to "share." So when Aquinas speaks of the good as "communicating" itself, this means not so much that it makes itself known as that goodness shares itself. In the specific case of God, God is that existence who shares the goodness of his existence with us by creating us.

6. Here Thomas explains the incarnation in terms of God's desire to "share" himself with us, and since God is the highest goodness, it is only fitting that God would share himself in the highest way possible—by actually becoming one of us. Note how this argument *ex convenientia* (see note 1, above) works: Aquinas does not think he is proving that God *had* to become incarnate, but rather showing that the incarnation fits with our understanding of God as the highest goodness.

7. Here Aquinas employs a distinction that he made earlier (1.13.7) between a "logical" (or "notional") relation and a "real" relation. Suffice it to say that for Aquinas the incarnation does not involve a change in God because God's relation to creatures is a logical one. To use a rough analogy, if I teach you to speak French, *you* will have changed (you can now speak French), but *I* will remain unchanged (I could speak French before, and I can speak French now), even though now you can say something about me that you could not say before (i.e., "You taught me French"). To use another analogy, if you are standing on my right and then move around to my left, your position relative to me has changed, but I have not undergone any change, even though you can say something about me that you could not say before (i.e., "You are standing on my right"). Becoming human is a similar kind of thing on God's part; it involves a change in creatures (in the case of the incarnation, the human nature of Jesus) but not in God.

8. The incarnation *would* be *inconveniens* (unfitting) if it involved a change on God's part, but it is entirely fitting for creatures to change.

evil of penalty was established by God's justice for God's glory.[9] But evil of fault is committed by withdrawing from the plan of the divine wisdom and from the order of the divine goodness.[10] And therefore it is fitting that God could have assumed a created, mutable, and corporeal nature subject to penalty; but it was not fitting that he assume the evil of fault.[11]

Reply to 4: As Augustine replies in the letter to Volusian (epistle 137, chap. 2), "The Christian teaching nowhere holds that God was so poured into human flesh as either to desert or lose—or to transfer and, as it were, compress within this frail body—the care of governing the universe. This is the thought of people unable to conceive of anything but bodily things . . . God is great not in bulk, but in might. Therefore the greatness of his might feels no confinement in narrow surroundings. If the passing word of a person is heard simultaneously by many, and completely by each of them, then it is not incredible that the abiding Word of God should be everywhere at once." Therefore nothing unfitting arises from God becoming incarnate.

3.1.2

Whether it was necessary for the restoration of the human race that the Word of God should become incarnate?

It would seem that it was not necessary for the restoration of the human race that the Word of God should become incarnate.

9. The "evil of penalty" refers to the occurrence of bad things, such as illness, which for Aquinas are a result of sin's entry into the world, and yet are somehow (perhaps in ways not obvious to us) a part of the way in which God provides for creatures. Were God somehow to forestall the evil consequences that flow naturally from sin, we might fail to understand our proper relationship as creatures to God our creator. The "evil of penalty" shows that turning away from God, who is the source of our existence, results in a diminishment of that existence. The evils we suffer give us knowledge of ourselves, so that, as Catherine of Sienna (1347–1380) wrote: "We see our own nothingness, that our very existence is ours by grace and not because we have a right to it, and every grace beyond our existence as well—it is all given to us with boundless love. Then we discover so much of God's goodness poured out on us that words cannot describe it" (Letter 73, in *The Letters of St. Catherine of Sienna,* vol. 1, trans. Suzanne Noffke, O.P. [Binghamton, N.Y.: Medieval and Renaissance Texts and Studies, 1988]). On "penalty" or *poena* in general, see 3.46, note 48.

10. The "evil of fault" refers to the willing of evil, which for Aquinas is something that God is not responsible for and that people do by turning away from God's will. On the difference between *poena* and *culpa,* see 3.65, note 4.

11. Thomas's point is that, in a sense, it is not as good to be bodily as it is to be pure spirit, and it is even less good to be embodied in fallen flesh that is subject to sickness and death. But this deficiency of goodness can be willed by God as part of a greater overarching good—that is, the self-communication of God and the salvation of humanity. However, there is another sort of deficiency of goodness—that is, the evil of fault—that cannot be willed by God in view of a greater good because it involves the will itself being evil, which is contrary to God's nature.

1. Since the Word of God is perfect God, as has been said in the first part (1.27.2 *ad* 2; cf. 1.4.1, 2), no power was added to him by taking on flesh. Therefore, if the incarnate Word of God restored [human] nature, he could also have restored it without taking on flesh.

2. Further, for the restoration of human nature, which had fallen through sin, nothing more would seem to be required than that humanity should repay for sin. Because God cannot require from human beings more than they can do, and because he is more inclined to be merciful than to punish, it seems that just as God ascribes the act of sin to humanity, he should likewise ascribe to it the opposite act of destroying sin. Therefore it was not necessary for the restoration of human nature that the Word of God should become incarnate.

3. Further, it pertains especially to the salvation of humanity that God be revered. Thus it is written in Malachi 1:6, "If I am Lord, where is my fear? If Father, where is my honor?" But people revere God more by considering him raised above everything and far removed from the senses. Thus in Psalm 113:4, it is said, "The Lord is high above all nations, and his glory above the heavens," and farther on, "Who is like the Lord our God?" (v. 5), which pertains to reverence. Therefore, it would seem unfitting to human salvation that God should become like us by assuming flesh.

On the contrary: What frees the human race from destruction is necessary for human salvation. But such is the mystery of the incarnation, according to John 3:16, "God so loved the world that he gave his only-begotten Son, that whoever believes in him may not perish, but have life everlasting." Therefore it was necessary for human salvation that God should become incarnate.

I answer: Something is said to be necessary to some purpose in two ways. First, when something cannot be without it, in the way that food is necessary for the preservation of human life. Second, when a goal is achieved in a better and more fitting [*convenientius*] manner, in the way that a horse is necessary for a journey. In the first way, the incarnation of God was not necessary for the restoration of human nature, for God with his omnipotent power could have restored human nature in many other ways. In the second way, however, the incarnation of God *was* necessary for the restoration of human nature. Hence Augustine says in *De Trinitate* (bk. 13, chap. 10), "We shall also show that other ways were not lacking to God, to whose power all things are equally subject; but that there was not a more fitting way of healing our misery."[12]

12. Here Thomas distinguishes two ways in which a "means" might be thought of as necessary to a given "end." In the first way, the means is a sine qua non with regard to the end: you must have food in order to live. In the second way, the means is the most "fitting" one for obtaining the end, either because it allows the end to be obtained more easily, or because the means brings along with it a variety of other goods in addition to the specific purpose sought. Thomas argues that the first sort of necessity does not apply to the incarnation, because of God's omnipotence: God is free from any absolute necessity, except that which attaches to the divine nature itself (i.e., God is not free to make divinity something less than divine; therefore, for example, God cannot will to be evil).

The incarnation may be considered with regard to our furtherance in good.[13] First, with regard to faith, which is made more certain by believing God himself who speaks. Thus Augustine says in *The City of God* (bk. 11, chap. 2) that, in order that humanity "might journey more trustfully toward the truth, the Truth itself, the Son of God, having assumed human nature . . . , established and founded faith." Second, with regard to hope, which is thereby greatly strengthened. Thus Augustine says in *De Trinitate* (bk. 13, chap. 10), "Nothing was so necessary for raising our hope as to show us how much God loved us. And what could afford us a stronger proof of this than that the Son of God should deign to be a sharer in our nature?" Third, with regard to charity, which is greatly enkindled by this. Thus Augustine says in *On the Instruction of Beginners* (chap. 4), "What greater cause is there of the Lord's coming than to show God's love for us?" And afterward he adds, "If we have been slow to love, at least let us not be slow to love in return."[14] Fourth, with regard to right action, in which he set us an example. Thus Augustine says in a sermon on the Lord's birth (sermon 371), "A human being, who *could* be seen, was *not* to be followed; God, who could *not* be seen, *was* to be followed. And therefore, so that we might be shown one who could be both seen and followed by human beings, God was made a human being." Fifth, with regard to the full sharing in divinity, which is true human blessedness and the goal of human life. This is bestowed upon us by Christ's humanity, for Augustine says in a Christmas sermon, "God became a human being, that human beings might become God."[15]

13. Here Aquinas begins introducing what, in his mature theology, serves as a key structuring device for his discussions of human salvation: our salvation involves both our "furtherance in good" and our "removal from evil." As one contemporary theologian puts it, salvation for Thomas is fundamentally a matter of our possession of the image of God, which, after the fall, involves both "image perfection" and "image-restoration"; see Romanus Cessario, O.P., *The Godly Image: Christ and Salvation in Catholic Thought from Anselm to Aquinas* (Petersham, Mass.: St. Bede's Publications, 1990), 128. In other words, salvation is not simply a matter of God forgiving human sin, but is a more comprehensive process of our being drawn beyond our natures so as to become "sharers of the divine nature" (2 Peter 1:4).

This understanding of salvation is worth underscoring because of the common claim that theologians in the medieval West focused almost exclusively on the crucifixion and the forgiveness of sin in their discussion of human salvation. At least in the case of Aquinas, this is manifestly not the case; see, for example, 3.53.1, below, where Aquinas describes Christ's resurrection as a *cause* of our salvation. Salvation does involve the lifting of the burden of sin, but it also involves the lifting up of human nature through participation in divine goodness.

14. Note that in these first three reasons we find the triad of faith, hope, and charity—the theological virtues, which are the key to human participation in divine goodness (see 1–2.15, note 5).

15. The phrase Thomas quotes is not found in the authentic sermons of Augustine, though it is found in sermon 128 in the *Patrologia Latina* (Paris, 1844–1855), vol. 39, among the sermons that have in the past been ascribed to Augustine, but that are now thought not to be authentic. The phrase is more commonly associated with Eastern Christian thought and is first found in Athanasius's *On the Incarnation*, chap. 54. The fact that Aquinas would accept its attribution to Augustine indicates that in his eyes the theological gulf between Eastern and Western forms of Christianity was not as wide as some today would make it out to be.

The incarnation was also useful for our withdrawal from evil. First, because one is taught by it not to prefer the devil to oneself, nor to honor him who is the author of sin. Thus Augustine says in *De Trinitate* (bk. 13, chap. 17), "Since human nature is united to God so as to become one person, do not let these proud spirits dare to prefer themselves to human beings simply because they have no bodies."[16] Second, because we are taught by this the greatness of human dignity, so that we should not defile it with sin. Thus Augustine says in the book *On True Religion* (chap. 16), "God has proved to us how high a place human nature holds among creatures, inasmuch as he appeared to us as a true human being." And Pope Leo says in a sermon on the nativity (sermon 21, no. 3), "O Christian, acknowledge your worth. Having been made a partner of the divine nature, refuse to return to your former worthlessness through evil deeds."[17] Third, because in order to take away human presumption, "the grace of God is shown to us in the man Christ, though no merits went before," as Augustine says in *De Trinitate* (bk. 13, chap. 17). Fourth, because "human pride, which is the greatest stumbling-block to our clinging to God, can be refuted and cured by such humility on the part of God," as Augustine says in the same place. Fifth, in order to free humanity from the slavery. Indeed, as Augustine says in *De Trinitate* (bk. 13, chap. 13), this "should be done in such a way that the devil should be overcome by the justice of a human being, Jesus Christ," and this was done by Christ making repayment for us. But a mere man could not have made repayment for the whole human race, and God was not bound to repay. Thus it was proper for Jesus Christ to be both God and a human being. For this reason Pope Leo says in the same sermon on the nativity (sermon 21, no. 2), "Weakness is received by strength, lowliness by majesty, mortality by eternity, in order that one and the same mediator of God and humanity might die in one and rise in the other—for this was our fitting remedy. Unless he was God, he would not have brought a remedy; and unless he was human, he would not have set an example."[18]

16. That is, the incarnation shows us that immaterial beings are not inherently "higher" than human beings by virtue of their immateriality. Thus, humans should not subject themselves to demonic forces simply because of their immateriality.

17. We can once again note the fundamentally positive account that Aquinas gives of human salvation. In these first two points, even when discussing salvation under the heading of our removal from evil, Thomas focuses on how the incarnation shows us the dignity and worth of human nature. It is only after addressing the false "humility" that leads us to undervalue ourselves, and so subject ourselves to sin, that Thomas turns to the pride that leads us to overvalue ourselves. Of course, Thomas does see human pride as a major source of sin, but not as the *only* source.

18. It is in this fifth point that Aquinas introduces the notion of "repayment" or "satisfaction" (*satisfactio*), which he will develop at greater length in 3.48.2. Here we might note that *satisfactio* is the key image by which Thomas understands the significance of Christ's suffering and death, but it by no means exhausts the significance of his death for human salvation. Even here, this image seems to blend with another interpretation of Christ's death that is also characteristic of Thomas: that of Christ as the example for human beings to imitate.

And there are very many other advantages that followed, beyond human apprehension.

Reply to 1: This reason follows from the first kind of necessity, without which we cannot reach the end.

Reply to 2: Repayment can be said to be sufficient in two ways.[19] In one way, perfectly, inasmuch as it is condign, that is, compensation equal to the fault committed. In this way repayment sufficient for sin cannot be made by one who is merely human because the whole of human nature was corrupted by sin, so that neither the goodness of any person, nor even many people, could make up adequately for the harm done to the whole of the nature. Further, a sin committed against God has a kind of infinity, derived from the infinity of the divine majesty; for the greater the person we offend, the more grievous the offense. Thus for equivalent repayment [*condignam satisfactionem*] it was necessary that the act of the one repaying should have an infinite efficacy—namely, the act of one who is both God and a human being.

In the other way, repayment may be termed sufficient even though it is imperfect—that is, the one accepting it may be content with it, even though it is not compensation equal to the fault committed. In this way the repayment of one who is purely human is sufficient. And because every imperfect thing presupposes something perfect by which it is sustained, the repayment of everyone who is merely human has its efficacy from the repayment of Christ.[20]

Reply to 3: God did not lessen his majesty by taking flesh, and consequently he did not lessen the reason for revering him, which is increased by the increase of knowledge of him. On the contrary, inasmuch as he wished to draw near to us by taking flesh, he drew us to know him better.[21]

---

19. In speaking of merit, Thomas distinguishes between a reward that one is owed in justice (meriting *de condigno*) and a reward that is fitting but not owed in justice (meriting *de congruo*); see 1–2.109, note 7. In this response, Thomas makes a similar distinction with regard to repayment—between one that is equivalent to what is owed (*condigna*) and one that is imperfect yet sufficient (*satisfactio sufficiens imperfecte*) because it is graciously accepted by the one to whom recompense is due. These two distinctions are related because on the cross Christ merits *de condigno* because he makes equivalent repayment (*satisfactio condigno*).

20. Here again Aquinas's discussion of repayment connects to his discussion of merit. On the cross Christ makes an equivalent repayment for human fault and therefore receives merit in strict justice. This perfect repayment and reward forms the basis upon which human beings receive reward *de congruo* for the imperfect repayment they make through acts of love toward God and their neighbors. To adapt the analogy of the bill and the tip I used earlier to talk about merit (1–2.109, note 7), we might say that it is only because Christ has satisfied justice by paying the bill (that is, making adequate repayment to God) that the tip we leave (that is, our good deeds) constitutes something deserving of reward. One hardly expects a reward if one leaves a tip but walks away from the check.

21. In the case of God, familiarity does not breed contempt.

3.1.3

Whether, if humanity had not sinned, God would have become incarnate?[22]

It would seem that if humanity had not sinned, God would still have become incarnate.

1. As long as a cause remains, the effect also remains. But as Augustine says in *De Trinitate* (bk. 13, chap. 17), "Many other things are to be considered in the incarnation of Christ" besides absolution from sin, and these were discussed earlier (3.1.2).[23] Therefore if humanity had not sinned, God would have become incarnate.

2. It belongs to the omnipotence of the divine power to perfect his works, and to manifest himself by some infinite effect. But no mere creature can be called an infinite effect, since it is finite by its very essence. It seems that only in the work of incarnation is an infinite effect of the divine power manifested in a special manner, by things infinitely distant being joined, since it has been brought about that a human being is God. And in this work especially the universe would seem to be perfected, since the last creature—namely, humanity—is united to the first principle—namely, God. Therefore, even if humanity had not sinned, God would have become incarnate.

3. Sin has not made human nature more capable of grace.[24] But after sin it is capable of the grace of union, which is the greatest grace. Therefore, if humanity had not sinned, human nature would have been capable of this grace, and God would not have withheld from human nature any good it was capable of.[25] Therefore, if humanity had not sinned, God would have become incarnate.

22. This article might be read fruitfully in conjunction with 2–2.2.7, above. Aquinas's answer to this question is often contrasted with that of John Duns Scotus (ca. 1266–1308), a Franciscan friar who has come to be known as "the subtle doctor" because of the difficulty and complexity of his thought. Despite this complexity, in the late Middle Ages he had arguably greater influence than Aquinas did. On this question, Scotus argued (in a way not found in any of the objections in this article) that the motive for the incarnation was not first and foremost the salvation of fallen humanity, but the glorification of Christ's human soul through its sharing in the beatific vision (i.e., "the vision of the divine essence," see 1–2.3.8). Therefore, Christ would have become incarnate even if there had been no need to save humanity.

23. Aquinas says that Christ came both to withdraw us from evil and to advance us in the good (see note 13, above). Christ advances us in the good in a variety of ways, for example, by strengthening faith, hope, and charity; by giving us an example of doing good; and by bestowing upon us a full participation in divinity.

24. The unstated authority here is Paul in his Letter to the Romans, who asks rhetorically, "What then are we to say? Should we continue in sin in order that grace may abound?" and answers with an emphatic, "By no means!" (Romans 6:1–2).

25. The argument of this objection is as follows: (1) Human nature can be joined with divine nature; (2) sin cannot bring about anything good; (3) sin is not responsible for the capacity of

4. God's predestination is eternal. But it is said in Romans 1:4 that Christ "was predestined the Son of God in power." Therefore, even before sin, it was necessary that the Son of God should become incarnate, in order to fulfill God's predestination.

5. The mystery of the incarnation was revealed to the first man, as is clear from what he says in Genesis 2:23, "This now is bone of my bones," and so on. The Apostle says this is "a great sacrament . . . in Christ and in the church," as is plain from Ephesians 5:32.[26] But a human being could not be conscious of his fall before it happened, for the same reason that the angels could not, as Augustine proves in his *Literal Commentary on Genesis* (bk. 11, chap. 18). Therefore, even if humanity had not sinned, God would have become incarnate.

On the contrary: Expounding what is set down in Luke 19:10, "For the Son of Man has come to seek and to save that which was lost," Augustine says in *De verbis Domini*,[27] "If humanity had not sinned, the Son of Man would not have come." And regarding 1 Timothy 1:15, "Christ Jesus came into this world to save sinners," a gloss says,[28] "There was no cause of Christ's coming into the world, except to save sinners. Take away diseases, take away wounds, and there is no need of medicine."

I answer: There are different opinions about this question. Some say that even if humanity had not sinned, the Son of God would have become incarnate.[29] Others assert the contrary, and it seems that our assent should be given to this view; for the things that spring solely from God's will, beyond all that is owed to the creature, can be made known to us only through being revealed in the Holy Scripture, in which the divine will is made known to us. Therefore, since everywhere in the Holy Scripture the sin of the first human being is assigned as the reason of incarnation, it is more fitting to say [*convenientius dicitur*] that the work of incarnation was intended by God as a remedy for sin,[30] so that if sin had not existed the incarnation would not have been. And yet the

---

human nature to be joined with divine nature; (4) this capacity would exist apart from sin; (5) God would not leave a human capacity unfulfilled; (6) therefore Christ would have become incarnate to join human and divine nature, even apart from sin. This argument raises an issue (i.e., no. 5) that would become important later in Catholic theology: the question of whether God is obliged to give human beings the beatific vision (i.e., "the vision of the divine essence," see 1–2.3.8) for the completion of their natures. See Aquinas's response to this objection below.

26. In Ephesians, Paul speaks of the union of husband and wife as a "mystery" (in the Vulgate, *sacramentum*) of the union of Christ and the church.

27. This text is found in modern editions of Augustine's sermons as number 174, chap. 2. Thomas quotes Augustine as saying *Si homo non peccasset, Filius non venisset,* but what Augustine wrote was a bit more poetic: *Si homo non perisset, Filius hominis non venisset* (If humanity had not been lost, the Son of Man would not have come).

28. On the "gloss," see 1.12, note 7.

29. One of the people who said this was Thomas's teacher Albert the Great, in his commentary on Lombard's *Sentences.*

30. On *convenientia*, see note 1, above.

power of God is not limited to this; even had sin not existed, God could have become incarnate.[31]

Reply to 1: All the other causes that are assigned in the preceding article have to do with a remedy for sin;[32] for if human beings had not sinned, they would have been endowed with the light of divine wisdom, and would have been perfected by God with the righteousness of justice in order to know and carry out everything necessary. But because human beings, upon deserting God, fell to the level of bodily things, it was necessary that God should take flesh and, by means of bodily things, should provide them with the remedy of salvation.[33] Therefore, regarding John 1:14, "And the Word was made flesh," St. Augustine says (*Homilies on the Gospel of John,* sermon 2, no. 16), "Flesh had blinded you; flesh heals you; for Christ came and overthrew the vices of the flesh."

Reply to 2: The way things are produced from nothing shows in itself the infinity of divine power.[34] Furthermore, for the perfection of the universe it is sufficient that the creature be ordered in a natural manner to God as to its goal. But it exceeds the limits of the perfection of nature that a creature should be united to God in a person.[35]

31. Thomas is stating his view with considerable care here. He is not saying, as is sometimes thought, that God would not have become incarnate if humans had not sinned. What he is saying is that this question is rooted in the mystery of the divine will and goes beyond the natural scope of human knowledge. The only basis we have for addressing such questions is divine revelation, as recorded in Scripture, and if we look at Scripture we see that "Christ Jesus came into the world to save sinners" (1 Timothy 1:15). Of course, Thomas is not basing his answer on a single verse; the entire story of God incarnate in Christ has the particular shape that it does because it is the story of incarnation as a remedy for sin. To ponder what the story would have been if humans had never sinned is simply to indulge in idle speculation. It is worth remembering, however, that those who say that God would *not* have become incarnate if humans had not sinned are also indulging in idle speculation that goes beyond what God has revealed.

What Thomas is establishing in this article is an approach to the incarnation that will shape his whole discussion. He begins with what God has *in fact* done in Christ, not with what God *might* have done; he is concerned about our actual history with God, not some possible alternative history. This is an approach that might be called "reasoning *from* revelation"—in other words, given what God has in fact done, how does this fit with other things that we hold to be true about God. So Thomas will not ask, "Should Christ have been born in Bethlehem?" (much less "Was Christ *really* born in Bethlehem?"), but rather, "Why was it fitting for Christ to be born in Bethlehem?"

32. Thomas seems to be saying that both the "removal from evil" and the "advancement in good" occur because of the need to remedy human sin.

33. Apart from human sin, God could have simply advanced human beings in good through the infusion of the light of divine wisdom. But sin involves a turning from spiritual things to material things (literally, "collapsing into" them), therefore because of sin it is fitting for God to advance human beings in good by material means.

34. Though creation is a finite effect of God's infinite power, the act of bringing forth creation from nothing is something no finite power could do; therefore creation is an adequate manifestation of God's infinite power.

35. It is difficult to know what Aquinas means when he speaks of human beings having God as their goal or purpose "in a natural manner," since he also says that union with God exceeds the capacities of human nature (1.1.1). What he seems to be saying is that human nature is "naturally"

Reply to 3: A double capacity can be seen in human nature. One is in the order of natural power, and this is always fulfilled by God, who fulfills everything according to its natural capability. The other is in the order of the divine power, which all creatures obey instantly, and the capacity we speak of pertains to this. But God does not fulfill all such capacities of nature; otherwise God could do in creatures only what he has in fact done, and this is false, as stated in the first part (1.105.6).[36]

But nothing would prohibit human nature from being been raised to something greater after sin; for God allows evils to happen in order to bring from them something greater. Therefore it is written in Romans 5:20, "Where sin abounded, grace did more abound." Therefore, too, in the blessing of the Paschal candle, we say, "O happy fault, that merited such and so great a redeemer!"[37]

Reply to 4: Predestination presupposes the foreknowledge of future things. Therefore, just as God predestines that a person will be saved by the prayers of others, so also he predestined the work of incarnation to be the remedy of human sin.[38]

---

perfected (i.e., human beings are fulfilled as humans) only through a union with God that goes beyond the natural capacities of human nature (see 1.1, note 7). But, he goes on to say, this perfection of human nature does not require the kind of union of humanity and divinity that occurs in Christ, which he will later characterize as a "hypostatic" or "personal" union (see 3.2.2).

36. Here Thomas is raising an issue that would be much debated both in the late sixteenth century (in the controversy over the teachings of Michel Baius) and in the twentieth century (in the controversy between traditional Thomists and the so-called *Nouvelle Theologie*). As noted earlier (see the previous note), one can argue that for Aquinas there is no purely "natural" fulfillment for human beings; human existence is in some sense thwarted, apart from its supernatural fulfillment. Thomas maintains repeatedly that fulfillment is impossible apart from God's grace. But the question is whether God is somehow "obligated" to give grace to human beings, since he has created them such that they cannot be fulfilled without it. If God is obligated, then in what sense is grace a "gift" (which is the meaning of the word "grace")? Thomas's answer is clear: God is in no sense obligated to fulfill the human capacity for supernatural fulfillment. Here Thomas describes this supernatural capacity as the ability to "obey instantly" or, put in a different way, the ability to respond to God's gracious initiative. This capacity is something that goes beyond what human nature requires, though apart from exercising this capacity, humans in fact do not reach their fulfillment.

With regard to the specific issue at hand, Thomas takes it as a given that God could act in human history in ways different from the ways God has in fact acted, but Thomas is unwilling to speculate about such matters, beyond stating this very general principle.

37. The phrase "happy fault" or *felix culpa* comes from the text of the *Exultet*, the chant sung by the deacon at the beginning of the Vigil of Easter. This notion of *felix culpa* is sometimes used to argue that God's fulfillment of human nature *requires* the fall of humanity. Aquinas, however, would not subscribe to this interpretation of *felix culpa*. As we have seen, Thomas is unwilling to speculate about what might have been, and therefore unwilling to say whether human evil was somehow necessary to God's plan of bringing human beings into union with him (though he does seem to exclude any intrinsic necessity of the fall). What we see from the history of God's dealings with humanity is not the necessity of evil, but rather God's ability to bring good out of evil.

38. Without delving into the mystery of divine predestination, Thomas simply notes that just as Christ's incarnation is foreknown by God, so too the fact that "Christ Jesus came into

Reply to 5: Nothing prevents an effect from being revealed to someone to whom the cause is not revealed. Therefore the mystery of incarnation could be revealed to the first human being without his being conscious of his fall ahead of time; for not everyone who knows the effect knows the cause.[39]

---

the world to save sinners" was also foreknown by God. Indeed, since *everything* is foreknown by God, it is impossible to distinguish on *this* basis between one thing being necessary and another thing being contingent. Such distinctions must be based on *how* something is foreknown by God. The things God knows do invariably occur, but if God knows them as occurring freely, then their invariable occurrence will still be free occurrence. If God knows them as occurring necessarily, then their occurrence will be necessary. This strikes many people as extremely counterintuitive, though it may help to keep in mind that God is outside the flow of time, so that divine "foreknowledge" is no different from any other sort of divine knowledge. What God knows is in the future for us, but it is in the eternal present for God.

39. The logic of the objection is that since marriage is a sign of the union of Christ and the church, and since Adam knew this sign, he therefore had faith in the incarnation. Aquinas does not dispute this point. After all, since the incarnation is foreknown by God, God could certainly share this knowledge with Adam. The objection takes a further step, arguing that Adam could not have foreknowledge of his sin, and therefore foreknowledge of the incarnation is something distinct from foreknowledge of sin. Again, Aquinas agrees, but adds that the distinction is that of cause and effect. Just as we can know an effect without knowing the cause (we can recognize a fire without knowing who lit it), so too Adam could know of the incarnation without knowing that it was occasioned by sin.

QUESTION 2

THE MODE OF UNION OF THE WORD INCARNATE

3.2.2

Whether the union of the incarnate Word took place in the person?[1]

It would seem that the union of the incarnate Word did not take place in the person.

1. This article is one of many in which Thomas reflects on how we might best speak about the union of humanity and divinity in Christ. Thomas takes as his starting point the definition of the Council of Chalcedon (AD 451): Jesus Christ is "one and the same Christ, Son, Lord, Only-begotten, recognized in *two natures, without confusion,* without change, without division, without separation; the distinction of natures being in no way annulled by the union, but rather the characteristics of each nature being preserved and *coming together to form one person* and subsistence, not as parted or separated into two persons, but one and the same Son and Only-begotten God the Word, Lord Jesus Christ" (emphasis added). Thomas is not trying to prove this definition but to make sense of it, to suggest why it is important, and to indicate what it allows us to say about God incarnate.

In the council's definition and in this section of the *Summa,* the key terms are "nature" (the *particular kind* of thing something is) and "person" (the *thing* that is of some particular kind). In brief, we can understand "nature" and "person" as corresponding to two different questions: "*What* is it?" (the nature) and "*Who* is it?" (the person). The question of the proper use of these terms was the source of much uninspiring rancor over the course of the fourth and fifth centuries. On one side of the dispute were those who said that because Jesus was one "who" (a divine person) he could be only one "what" (i.e., his nature was solely divine). These folks came to be called "monophysites" (i.e., one-nature), and in Aquinas they are usually represented by

176

1. The person of God is not other than his nature, as we said earlier (1.39.1). If, therefore, the union did not take place in the nature, it follows that it did not take place in the person.[2]

2. Christ's human nature has no less dignity than ours. But personhood is related to dignity, as was stated earlier.[3] Therefore, since our human nature has its own personhood, even more so should Christ's have its own personhood.

3. Boethius says in *On the Two Natures* (chap. 3) that a person is an individual substance of a rational nature.[4] But the Word of God took on an individual human nature, for "universal human nature does not exist of itself, but is the object of pure thought," as John of Damascus says (*On the Orthodox Faith*, bk. 3, chap. 11). Therefore human nature has its own personhood. Therefore it does not seem that the union took place in the person.[5]

---

the Egyptian monk Eutyches. On the other side were those who said that since Jesus was two "whats" (divine and human) he must in some sense be two "whos" (a divine being and a human being) that are somehow conjoined. In Aquinas, this view is usually represented by Nestorius.

The claim of Chalcedon, which Thomas will attempt to explain and explore, is that God incarnate is only one "who" (a divine person) but two "whats" (two natures: human and divine). This particular article explores the claim that "one" should go with "person" rather than "nature," while at the same time maintaining that the unity of Christ's person does not entail that he have only one nature. Part of what makes this terminology confusing is that "person" and "nature" are also employed in the theology of the Trinity (see 1.29, note 1), in which it is said that God has "one nature" (divinity) existing as "three Persons" (Father, Son, and Spirit). So in the case of the Trinity, plurality is ascribed to the Persons and unity to the nature, whereas in the case of Christ, plurality is ascribed to the natures and unity is ascribed to the person. Aquinas wants to show that this may indeed be confusing, but not because the terminology itself is confused; rather, confusion arises because we do not always adequately grasp the proper use of the terminology.

2. This objection identifies a key problem in the claim that Jesus Christ is one person with two natures: granted that God is "simple" (see 1.3, note 1), God's nature (*what* God is) is not a different thing from God's person (*who* God is). Therefore, it is nonsensical to claim that Christ, who is God, could have two natures but only one person. However, the claim is, from a logical perspective, nonsensical only if "nature" and "person" not only refer to the same reality (that is, have the same *res significata*), but also function in the same way (that is, have the same *modus significandi*) in the statement "Christ is two natures and one person." For a fuller discussion, see notes 7–12, below.

3. See 1.29.3 *ad* 2, where Aquinas says: "Although this name 'person' may not belong to God as regards the origin of the term, nevertheless it excellently belongs to God in its objective meaning; for as famous men were represented in comedies and tragedies, the name 'person' was given to signify those who held high dignity. Therefore, those who held high rank in the church came to be called 'persons.' For this reason the definition of 'person' is given by some as 'hypostasis distinct by reason of dignity.' And because subsistence in a rational nature is of high dignity, every individual of the rational nature is called a 'person.'"

4. See 1.29, note 4.

5. The objection makes the point that God became incarnate not by taking on or "assuming" human nature in the abstract, but by taking on a particular, individual human nature—the human nature of Jesus of Nazareth. What normally makes a human nature particular or, as Boethius puts it, "an individual substance" is personhood. Therefore Jesus's human nature must have its own personhood, so that his human and divine natures could not be united in a single person.

On the contrary: We read in the Council of Chalcedon, "We confess that our Lord Jesus Christ is not partitioned or divided into two persons, but is one and the same only-begotten Son and Word of God."[6] Therefore the union of the Word is made in the person.

I answer: "Person" has a different meaning from "nature," namely, "nature" designates the essence of the species, which is signified by the definition. And if nothing was found to be added to what pertains to the concept of the species, there would be no need to distinguish the nature itself from the individual subsisting in this nature (i.e., the *suppositum* of the nature), because every individual subsisting in a nature would be completely identical with its nature.[7] Now in certain subsisting things, we happen to find things that do not belong to the concept of the species, that is, accidents and individuating principles, which appear chiefly in those things that are composed of matter and form. Therefore, in these things the nature and the *suppositum* really differ, not as if they were wholly separate, but because the *suppositum* itself includes the nature of the species, and in addition certain other things besides the concept

6. One of the things that distinguishes Aquinas's theology of the incarnation from that of other medieval theologians is his careful rereading of the documents of the early Christian councils that forged the mainstream Christian articulation of the relationship of humanity and divinity in Christ. Aquinas is in fact the first medieval theologian in the West to quote directly from the Council of Chalcedon.

7. It will be helpful at this point to clarify the relation of the terms *suppositum*, "person," and "nature." Roughly speaking, for Aquinas a *suppositum* (or the equivalent Greek term, *hypostasis*) is the individual entity about which a statement is made. Thus in the proposition "Socrates is a human being," the *suppositum* is Socrates. A "nature" (which is the same thing as "the concept of the species") indicates that which makes a thing the kind of thing it is. In the proposition "Socrates is a human being," the term "human being" designates the "nature" of Socrates, a nature that corresponds to the definition "rational animal." The term "person" simply indicates a *suppositum* that possesses a rational nature.

This distinction between *suppositum* and "nature" helps us understand why a statement such as "The husband of Xanthippe is the teacher of Plato" is true. A seemingly similar true statement, "All bachelors are unmarried men," is true because "bachelor" and "unmarried" have the same meaning (or, in technical terms, "signification"); put differently, "bachelors" and "unmarried men" indicate the same nature. But this is clearly not the case with "The husband of Xanthippe is the teacher of Plato." One cannot be an unmarried man without being a bachelor (presuming that "widower" is simply a kind of bachelor), but one can certainly be the teacher of Plato without being the husband of Xanthippe. Rather, "The husband of Xanthippe is the teacher of Plato" is true because the phrases "husband of Xanthippe" and "teacher of Plato" refer to the same *suppositum*—Socrates.

Aquinas says that if an individual entity were nothing but its nature, then there would be no distinction between *suppositum* and nature. In the case of Socrates, however, this is not the case, since in addition to being a rational animal, he is also the husband of Xanthippe and the teacher of Plato, and many other things besides. Aquinas will go on to argue that a distinction between *suppositum* and nature characterizes *any* material being, since in addition to its nature it has its particular matter (see 1.12, note 1). Indeed, this distinction applies even to nonmaterial creatures (such as angels), since in addition to their natures they possess something else: the fact of having been created (see 1.3, note 1).

of the species.[8] Therefore the term *suppositum* indicates a whole that has a nature as its "formal" and perfecting part.[9] Consequently, in things that are composed of matter and form the nature is not predicated of the *suppositum*, for we do not say "this human being is his humanity."[10] But if there is a thing in which there is nothing outside the species or its nature, as in the case of God, the *suppositum* and the nature are not really distinct in it, but only in our way of thinking. Then it is called "nature" inasmuch as it is an essence, and a *suppositum* inasmuch as it is subsisting.[11] And what is said of a *suppositum* is understood to be applied to a person in the case of rational or intellectual creatures, for a person is nothing else than "an individual substance of rational nature," according to Boethius.

Therefore, whatever is in any person is united to him in person, whether it belongs to his nature or not.[12] And so, if the human nature is not united to God

8. Aquinas argues that in material creatures there is a real difference between *suppositum* and nature, but there is not a separation. At least in the case of material beings, Thomas bases his argument on Aristotle's view that natures exist only as adhering in some subject or *suppositum*. Just as one never finds matter without it being some specific *kind* of matter, so too one never finds an identity without it being some particular *instance* of that identity.

9. On "form," which is here identical with "nature," see 1.12, note 1. The form is "perfecting" because it makes a thing what it is.

10. What Thomas says here is initially a bit puzzling since in the proposition "Socrates is a human being," it certainly seems to be the case that a nature ("human being") is being predicated of a *suppositum* ("Socrates"). Aquinas's concern is that we not let grammatical predication in a proposition (on predication, see 1.3, note 2) lead us to think of a person as an empty point of reference to which a nature can be attached. I am not an "x" that possesses human nature; I just simply *am* that totality that we call a human person. There is no Socrates apart from his possession of a human nature. Socrates is a human in a different way than he is a husband to Xanthippe or a teacher to Plato. Presumably we could imagine that were Socrates a single student instead of a married teacher he would nonetheless still be Socrates; but we cannot imagine that were Socrates to possesses the nature of a cow he would be the same *suppositum*. The upshot of this discussion is that, as noted before, nature and person are distinguishable, but not separable: a human nature is always found only in a particular person.

11. If we should be wary of separating nature and person in the case of human beings, we should be even more wary in the case of God, since God's simplicity (see 1.3, note 1) requires that the words "divinity" and "God" signify the same thing (the same *res significata*), though they do so in different ways (according to a two-fold *modus significandi*). Thus "divinity" signifies as if it were an essential quality belonging to God, and "God" signifies as if it were that to which the essential quality of "divinity" belongs. The reason for this dual way of signifying is the problem that is inherent in *all* theological language: we want to speak about the uncreated existence of God, but our language and conceptual apparatus is designed to speak about created existences (see 1.13, note 6). Aquinas consistently attempts to find the least inadequate use of the human way of speaking, so that human speech can point to the mystery of God.

12. At this point, it is helpful to step back an see where Aquinas has led us. The basic problem is how to reconcile the notion of divine simplicity with the single *suppositum* and the dual natures of Christ. Aquinas does not want to retreat from his strong affirmation of the identity of God's essence (nature) and existence (*suppositum*). At the same time, he wants to say something about Christ's *suppositum* (namely, that it is one) that he does not want to say about his nature. For Aquinas, this difficulty hardly comes as a surprise, since our creaturely language is woefully inadequate to the theological task. On the other hand, it is the only language we have

the Word in person, it is not united to him in *any* way, and thus belief in the incarnation is altogether done away with, which subverts the entire Christian faith.[13] Therefore, since the Word has united a human nature to himself—which does not, however, belong to his divine nature—it follows that the union took place in the person of the Word, and not in the nature.

Reply to 1: Although in God nature and person are not really different, the words still differ in their ways of signifying God, as was said above, since "person" signifies him in the manner of something that subsists. And because human nature is united to the Word in such a way that the Word subsists in it,[14] but not in such a way that anything is added to the definition of his [divine] nature, nor in such a way that his nature would be changed into something else, it follows that the union of human nature to the Word of God took place in the person and not in the nature.

Reply to 2: Personhood is necessarily related to the dignity and perfection of a thing, insofar as it is part of the dignity and perfection of that thing to exist by itself (which is understood by the word "person"). But it is a greater dignity to exist in something nobler than oneself than to exist by oneself. Therefore the human nature of Christ has a greater dignity than ours, because in us human nature, being existent by itself, has its own personhood, but in Christ it exists in the person of the Word.[15] In the same way, it belongs to the dignity of a form

---

available. So when speaking of God we must attend carefully to the *way* in which our language embodies meaning (the *modus significandi*), while realizing that our language never adequately says *what* we mean (the *res significata*).

When we attend to the way in which our language embodies meaning, we see that "person" or *suppositum* is the subject of which things are predicated. If we conceive of this as a grammatical rule, what Thomas wants to alert us to how in our ordinary speech it is the subject (or person) that unites different predicates; for example, "Socrates" unites "the husband of Xanthippe" and "the teacher of Plato." When we say "Jesus Christ is divine and human," we predicate two distinct predicates ("divine" and "human") of the same *suppositum*. For more on the logic of the statement "God is a human being," see 3.16.1, below.

13. This might seem a rather dire statement to make about rather technical theological terms, but it indicates that for Aquinas the technicalities of the incarnation are crucial; indeed, it is the unity of the *suppositum* or person that allows us to ascribe to God certain things concerning the human nature of Jesus Christ. Thus we can say "God was born of the Virgin Mary" and "God died on the cross." In Aquinas's view, the truth of such statements is the whole point of the incarnation. See my annotations to 3.16.1 for further discussion of this point.

14. *Verbum in ea subsistat:* this wording seems at first as if it must be a mistake on Aquinas's part, since it sounds as if the human nature is the subject or *suppositum* in which the Word is found. However, everything else Thomas has said indicates the opposite: the Word, and not the human nature, is a subsisting thing; it is in this way that Thomas makes "the Word" the subject of the verb *subsistere*. To make Thomas's point clearer, we might translate this clause as, "human nature is united to the Word in such a way that the Word subsists as human."

15. Following the teaching of the Council of Chalcedon, Aquinas does not conceive of the person that unites humanity and divinity as some neutral *suppositum;* rather, it is the second person of the Trinity, the divine Word. Thus, although Christ has a genuine human nature, this nature exists in the divine *suppositum* of the Word. Strictly speaking, therefore, although Christ has a human nature, he is not a human "person." However, we must remember that

to fulfill a species, yet the capacity for sensation in human beings, because of its union with the nobler form that perfects it, is more noble in humans than in nonrational animals, where it is itself the form that perfects.[16]

Reply to 3: As John of Damascus says (*On the Orthodox Faith,* bk. 3, chap. 11), "the Word of God . . . did not assume human nature in general, but in particular [*in atomo*]"—that is, in an individual—otherwise every human being would be the Word of God, just as Christ was. Yet we must bear in mind that not every individual in the genus "substance" is a person, even in the case of rational natures. Rather, this is the case only with that which exists by itself, and not that which exists in some more perfect thing.[17] Therefore the hand of Socrates, although it is a kind of individual, is not a person, because it does not exist by itself, but in something more perfect, that is, in the whole. The same thing is signified by the designation of a person as "an individual substance," for the hand is not a complete substance, but part of a substance. Therefore, although the human nature is a kind of individual in the genus of substance, it does not have its own personhood, because it does not exist separately but in something more perfect, namely, in the person of the Word. Therefore the union took place in the person.

---

for Thomas "person" means the subject to which things are attributed; it does not carry our modern notion of "personality." Thomas does maintain in 3.5.3 that Christ has a fully human psychology, because he possesses a fully human soul (in Greek, *psyche*). See also 3.9.4, below.

16. Both human beings and other animals have the capacity for sensation; in animals this capacity comes from the "sensitive soul," which is their substantial form (i.e., that which makes them what they are), whereas in humans this capacity comes from the "rational soul." Thus in human beings the capacity for sensation has greater "nobility" than it does in animals, because it is the capacity of a more noble substantial form.

Thomas alludes in passing here to what was, in his day, one of his most controversial teachings: the unity of substantial form in human beings. Many of Thomas's contemporaries, like Bonaventure, held that human beings possessed three souls (and therefore three substantial forms) corresponding to the three levels of life: the capacity for life and generation (as with plants); the capacity for sensation (as with nonrational animals); and the capacity for thought (as with human beings and angels). Thomas, in contrast, held that in order for a human being to be one thing, he or she could have only one substantial form, and this was the rational soul. It is perhaps difficult for people today to fully appreciate the heat generated by this debate.

17. In other words, not every thing (or "substance") is an individual entity in the same sense that a "person" is. Some things exist as parts of larger wholes. The analogy Aquinas goes on to use is in some ways unfitting, since Jesus's humanity is not a "part" of him in the same way that Socrates' hand is a part of him. In particular, Aquinas wants to speak of Christ's humanity as "a kind of individual in the genus of substance," but he has already denied that Socrates' hand is an individual substance (it is, rather, a part of a substance). Thomas is aware of how feeble his analogy is; so, as with all analogies, we have to recognize both how it is fitting and how it is unfitting for what he wants to say. Christ's humanity is like a part of an individual inasmuch as it receives its existence from that to which it is joined (i.e., the divine person of the Word). However, it is unlike a part of a whole inasmuch as it is a kind of individual substance.

QUESTION 8

THE GRACE OF CHRIST, AS HE IS THE HEAD OF THE CHURCH

3.8.1

Whether Christ, inasmuch as he is human, is the head of the church?[1]

1. Modern readers are sometimes puzzled by the fact that Aquinas has no extended treatment of the church in the *Summa,* or anywhere else, for that matter. Rather, his views on what theologians today would call "ecclesiology" are scattered throughout the *Summa;* they can be found in such places as his discussion of "states of life" in the second part and his discussion of the sacraments in the third part. This scattering of his comments on the church should not be taken as an indication that Thomas thought the church was theologically unimportant. It is possible that he did not offer a "treatise" on the church because he lived in a time when circumstances did not call for much in the way of explicit reflection on the nature of the Christian community. In particular, there were no major schisms in the Western church, as there had been in fourth-century North Africa and as there would be in fourteenth- and sixteenth-century Europe. In the absence of such circumstances, Thomas could presume that his readers pretty much agreed on the nature of the church.

At the same time, the church and its practices form a kind of deep background against which Thomas displays his theology. Despite the lack of an "ecclesiology," Thomas's theology is a thoroughly "ecclesial" one; he seeks to "think with the church," as Ignatius of Loyola would put it some three hundred years later. In the *Summa,* he always and everywhere refers to the church's Scriptures and laws and practices. He presumes that theology is a communal enterprise and that the community of the church has a divinely willed order. But he also thinks that the proper order for reflecting on the church is to begin with the mysteries of faith and not with

It would seem that it does not belong to Christ, inasmuch as he is human,[2] to be the head of the church.

1. The head imparts sense and motion to the limbs. But spiritual sense and motion, which are by grace, are not imparted to us by the human Christ because, as Augustine says in *De Trinitate* (bk. 15, chap. 26), not even Christ, as human, but only as God, bestows the Holy Spirit. Therefore it does not belong to him, inasmuch as he is human, to be the head of the church.[3]

2. A head would not seem to have another head. But God is the head of Christ, inasmuch as he is human, according to 1 Corinthians 11:3, "The head of Christ is God." Therefore Christ himself is not a head.

3. The head of a person is a particular bodily member, receiving influence from the heart. But Christ is the universal principle of the whole church. Therefore he is not the head of the church.[4]

On the contrary: It is written in Ephesians 1:22, "And he . . . has made him head over all the church."

I answer: Just as the whole church is called one mystical body because of its likeness to the natural body of a person, which has different acts according to its different members—as the Apostle teaches in Romans 12:4–5 and 1 Corinthians 12:12—so likewise Christ is called the head of the church because of a likeness with the human head.[5]

In this we may consider three things: order, perfection, and power. Order: for the head is the first part of a human being, beginning from the top. And this is why every principle is usually called a "head," according to Ezekiel

---

the church itself. In other words, if you properly understand the mysteries of God and Christ and the sacraments, then you will have a proper understanding of the church.

This article, for example, occurs as part of a larger discussion (two questions, consisting of twenty-one articles) on the grace of Christ. In this discussion, Aquinas considers the sense in which Christ, as human, was a recipient of grace and how he, as the "head" of the church, transmits the grace he receives to the members of the church. Here Aquinas is drawing on Paul's image of the church as the body of Christ (e.g., 1 Corinthians 12:12–27), as well as on the Letter to the Ephesians' elaboration of Christ as head of the body. Aquinas takes this to be an example of metaphorical speech (on metaphor, see 1.1.9, above), but it is a singularly powerful metaphor inasmuch as it is a description of the real relationship of Christians (and indeed of all humanity, since all living people are potentially Christians) to Christ.

2. Note that the objection concerns the specific question of whether Christ, *as human,* is head of the church, and not the question of whether Christ as the Son of God or as the second Person of the Trinity is the head of the church. In other words, does Christ's humanity have a role to play in the communication of grace to the church?

3. The objection makes the point that what it means to be the "head" of the church is to give the gift of the Holy Spirit, which only God can do; therefore Christ bestows the Spirit inasmuch as he is divine, but not inasmuch as he is human.

4. The implication is that "heart" would be a more appropriate metaphor.

5. As mentioned, Aquinas seems to be asking about the aptness of a particular metaphor—that of Christ as "head"—but we shall see that in arguing for the metaphor's aptness he is at the same time arguing for a particular understanding of the role of Christ's humanity in human salvation.

16:25, "At every head of the way, you have set up a sign of your prostitution."[6] Perfection: since all the senses, both interior and exterior, dwell in the head, whereas in the other members there is only touch; and therefore it is said in Isaiah 9:15, "The aged and honorable, he is the head."[7] Power: for the power and movement of the other members, and the guiding of them in their actions, is from the head, because of the power of sensation and motion that rules there. Therefore the ruler is called the head of a people, according to 1 Kings 15:17, "When you were a little one in your own eyes, were you not made the head of the tribes of Israel?"

These three things belong spiritually to Christ.[8] First, because of his nearness [*propinquitatem*] to God his grace is the highest and primary (though not actually first in time),[9] since all have received grace on account of his grace, according to Romans 8:29, "For those whom he foreknew, he also predestined to be made conformable to the image of his Son, that he might be the first-born among many brothers." Second, he had perfection with respect to the fullness of all graces, according to John 1:14, "We saw him . . . full of grace and truth,"[10] as was shown.[11] Third, he had the power of bestowing grace on all the members of the church, according to John 1:16, "Of his fullness we have all received."[12] And thus it is plain that Christ is fittingly called the head of the church.

6. If you start at the top of a human being, the first thing you encounter is the head. That is why we use the metaphor of "head" when we are talking about the *principium* or "starting point" of anything.

7. "Perfection" here has the sense of "complete": because the head possesses the complete set of five senses, it is "perfect." For similar uses of "perfect" see 1.45, note 14, and 1–2.3, note 5.

8. That is, these things belong to Christ by virtue of his human nature, not simply by virtue of his divine nature.

9. Christ's humanity is "closest" or "most nearly related" to God; *propinquitatem* can have both meanings. It therefore is the *principium* of all humans who shall be saved. Aquinas notes, however, that Christ's primacy is not temporal. Aquinas believed that some people who lived prior to the birth of Christ, such as Moses and Abraham, could be saved through faith in God's promise to send a redeemer. Thus their reception of grace was temporally prior to the existence of Christ's human nature. However, Christ *is* first in the sense of being the "source" that allows human beings to draw near to God, including those who lived before him in time but had faith in him as the coming redeemer.

10. The Vulgate reads, "We saw *his glory.*" See 1–2.3, note 5.

11. See 3.7.9: "Christ has the fullness of grace. First, since he has grace in its highest degree, in the most perfect way it can be had. And this appears, first, from the nearness of Christ's soul to the cause of grace; for it was said earlier that the nearer a recipient is to the inflowing cause, the more it receives. Therefore the soul of Christ, which is more closely united to God than all other rational creatures, receives the greatest outpouring of his grace. Second, in his relation to the effect; for the soul of Christ so received grace that, in a manner, it is poured out from his soul upon others. And therefore it was proper [*oportuit*] for him to have the greatest grace, just as fire, which is the cause of heat in other hot things, is of all things the hottest."

12. Note that in talking about Christ's "power" or his status a "ruler," Thomas speaks in terms of Christ's capacity to bestow grace. Christ rules his members not by external command but by moving them inwardly through grace, just as the head moves the body "from within."

Reply to 1: To give grace or the Holy Spirit authoritatively [*auctoritative*] is fitting for Christ inasmuch as he is God;[13] but to give it instrumentally is also fitting for him as human, since his humanity is "the instrument of his divinity."[14] And therefore by the power of the divinity his actions were beneficial, that is, by causing grace in us, both by meriting it and by bringing it about. Augustine, however, is denying that Christ as human gives the Holy Spirit with authority. Even other saints are said to give the Holy Spirit instrumentally or ministerially, according to Galatians 3:5, "He . . . who gives to you the Spirit."[15]

Reply to 2: In metaphorical speech we must not expect a likeness in all respects, for in that case there would not be a likeness but the real thing itself. Accordingly, a natural head does not have another head because one human body is not part of another; but a metaphorical body, that is, an ordered multitude, is part of another multitude, as the household is part of the city. Therefore, the father who is head of the household has a head above him, namely, the civil ruler. And therefore there is no reason why God should not be the head of Christ, even though Christ himself is head of the church.[16]

Reply to 3: The head has a visible prominence over the other exterior members, but the heart has a certain hidden influence. And therefore the

13. The English word "authoritatively" means "done with power" or "done by someone whose opinion is to be credited." In addition to these meanings, the Latin word *auctoritative* means "done in the manner of a first principle or a principle cause." Thus, as God, Christ gives grace simply because God is the source of all grace.

14. Thomas is possibly quoting John of Damascus, *On the Orthodox Faith,* bk. 3, chap. 15. John is certainly an important source for Aquinas's notion of Christ's humanity as an "instrument" of his divinity (on instrumental causality in general, see 1.45, note 10). This notion is one that Thomas discovered in his reading of the Greek fathers, and it is one of the distinctive features of his Christology. It is significant because an instrument actually contributes something of its own distinctive form to the task for which it is used, which is why a piece of wood cut by an ax is different from a piece of wood cut by a saw, even if the same artisan wields the two different tools. Thomas's understanding of the instrumental causality of Christ's humanity gives his theology of grace a distinctively Christian cast. Grace is not simply some sort of generic divine gift; rather, it is a gift that is determinatively shaped by the instrument through which it is given: the humanity of God incarnate. This notion is also significant because Thomas uses this same language of "instrument" when talking about the sacraments (see 3.62, note 10). We might say, therefore, that Christ's humanity is the primary "sacrament" by which God bestows grace upon human beings.

15. Aquinas seems to be saying that in terms of his humanity taken in itself Christ "gives" the Holy Spirit in a way that is not essentially different from the way in which any holy person might give the Holy Spirit: that is, as an instrument. So we should say that in terms of his humanity Jesus was a "saint"—in other words, he was one whose humanity was perfected by God's grace. Of course, Christ differs from other saints inasmuch as he is holy through the grace of the hypostatic union, whereas saints are holy through the grace of adoption in Christ (see 3.16, note 9).

16. Here Aquinas shows his typical concern that we know what kind of language we are using when speaking about God. We should not confuse the literal naming of something as a "head" with a metaphorical naming. Although it would be grotesque for a physical head to have another head placed on top of it, we commonly describe someone metaphorically as the "head" of a group even though he may have someone in authority over him.

Holy Spirit is compared to the heart, since he invisibly gives life and unity to the church, whereas Christ, in his visible nature, is compared to the head, as when one person is set over another person.[17]

17. Although Aquinas is concerned that we not confuse metaphorical language with literal language, he is also aware that metaphors are not "false," and indeed can make the truths of faith more vivid and living for us. Therefore he is willing to exploit the metaphors of "head" and "heart" to make a point about the relationship of Christ and the Spirit to the church: Christ as the visible authority, the Spirit as the hidden influence that unifies and gives life.

CHRIST'S KNOWLEDGE IN GENERAL

3.9.4

Whether Christ had any knowledge acquired through experience?[1]

1. Question 3.9 sketches the different kinds of knowledge that Christ possessed. Thomas presumes in this question that as the second Person of the Trinity Christ had "divine" knowledge—that is, all the knowledge that properly belongs to God, possessed in the way that God possesses it. Thomas does not try to explain what the experience of having "divine knowledge" would be, though it would seem to include omniscience, which is a form of knowledge that is beyond the capacity of our imagination. He then goes on to sketch out three kinds of human knowledge that Christ had: (1) Beatific knowledge: knowledge that the blessed in heaven have of God. Aquinas says that if Christ is to be the cause of this knowledge in us, then it must be something that he himself possesses. (2) Infused knowledge: knowledge directly imprinted on the passive intellect by God—the sort of knowing-by-divine-gift that the angels possess. (3) Acquired knowledge: knowledge obtained in the ordinary human way, through sense experience. In this article Aquinas argues for Christ's possession of this last form of human knowledge, and in doing so departs from the typical view of medieval theology, and indeed from his own earlier view (see note 5, below).

It is worth noting that Aquinas is not particularly concerned with what we would call the "psychology" of Jesus. He never tries to depict what it would be like for one human being to possess these three forms of knowledge—what the "experience" of God incarnate would have been like. It is not clear to me that Thomas would have even understood such questions. Rather, he is concerned with showing what must be affirmed of Christ's human knowledge if Christ is to be both truly human and truly divine. The modern psychological question may be a good one, but it is not the question that provoked the answers Aquinas gives here, or anywhere.

Before reading the rest of this article, it is important to understand Aquinas's views on the normal apparatus of human knowledge. See 1.12, note 8, and 1.27, note 10.

187

It would seem that in Christ there was no knowledge acquired through experience.

1. Whatever was fitting for Christ, he had most perfectly. But Christ did not possess acquired knowledge most perfectly, since he did not devote himself to the study of letters, by which knowledge is acquired in its perfection; for it is said in John 7:15, "The Jews wondered, saying, 'How does this man know letters, having never learned?'" Therefore it seems that in Christ there was no acquired knowledge.[2]

2. Nothing can be added to what is full. But the potential of Christ's soul was filled with intellectual species divinely infused, as was said earlier (3.9.3).[3] Therefore no acquired species could be added to his soul.

3. One who already has the habit of knowledge acquires no new habit through what he receives from the senses,[4] otherwise two forms of the same species would be in the same thing together. Instead, the habit that previously existed is strengthened and increased.[5] Therefore, since Christ had the habit of infused knowledge, it does not seem that he acquired a new knowledge through what he perceived by the senses.[6]

On the contrary: It is written in Hebrews 5:8, "Since he was the Son [of God], he learned obedience by the things that he suffered," that is, "experienced," says a gloss.[7] Therefore there was in the soul of Christ some knowledge from experience, which is acquired knowledge.

I answer: As is plain from what was said earlier, "nothing that God implanted in our nature was lacking" in the human nature assumed by

2. The objection presumes two things: (1) If Christ had acquired knowledge, it would be knowledge acquired in the most perfect way; and (2) formal instruction is the most perfect way of acquiring knowledge. However, Christ did not have formal instruction, therefore . . .

3. In the previous article, Thomas argues that the "passive" or "receptive" part of Christ's human intellect was actualized when God directly imprinted upon it ("infused") the intellectual conceptions by which he knows things. Put more plainly, but less precisely, Christ as a human being possessed by divine gift knowledge of all things. The objection argues that if this were the case, then there would be no need for Christ to gain knowledge of things in the ordinary human way—in other words, through experience.

4. On "habit" in Aquinas, see 2–2.2, note 11.

5. When I encounter a cow for the first time, I gain a new intellectual conception: "cowness." When I encounter a cow for the second or third or fourth time, I do not acquire a second or third or fourth conception of "cowness." Rather, my already existing conception of "cowness" is strengthened, perhaps because I now see that certain features that I thought were essential to being a cow (e.g., being brown) are in fact incidental.

The view that Christ's experientially acquired knowledge was simply an enhancement of knowledge already imprinted by God was the common view of Thomas's contemporaries. His teacher Albert the Great wrote in his commentary on Lombard's *Sentences* (bk. 3, distinction 13, a.10) that sense experience did not "create" (*faciens*) a *habitus* but only "stimulated" (*excitans*) one that already existed.

6. Since Christ already had a full set of intellectual conceptions by divine gift, he could not, strictly speaking, learn anything. When he encountered a cow for the first time he already possessed the concept "cow," so at no point in his human life did he ever learn what a cow was.

7. On the "gloss," see 1.12, note 7.

the Word of God.[8] But it is clear that God implanted in human nature not only a passive but an active intellect. Therefore one must necessarily say that in the soul of Christ there was not merely a passive intellect, but also an active intellect. But if in other things "God and nature make nothing superfluous," as the Philosopher says in *On the Heavens and the Earth* (bk. 1, chap. 4, 271ª), still less is there anything superfluous in the soul of Christ. Something that does not have its proper function is superfluous, since "all things exist for the sake of their functions," as is said in *On the Heavens and the Earth* (bk. 2, chap. 3, 286ª). Now the proper function of the active intellect is to make intellectual species actual by abstracting them from sense images; therefore, it is said in *De Anima* (bk. 3, chap. 5, 430ª) that the active intellect is that "by which [the soul] is made all things."[9] And thus it is necessary to say that in Christ there were intellectual species received into the passive intellect by the action of the active intellect. This means that there was acquired knowledge in him, which some call knowledge "from experience" [*experimentalem*].[10]

And therefore, although I wrote differently earlier,[11] it must be said that in Christ there was acquired knowledge, which is truly knowledge in a human fashion, not only as regards the subject receiving it but also as regards the active cause. For such knowledge springs from Christ's active intellect, which is

8. The specific reference is a bit unclear, but one might look, for example, at the fifth question of the third part. Thomas also appears to be silently quoting a phrase from John of Damascus (*On the Orthodox Faith,* bk. 3, chap. 6).

Along with the mainstream of the Christian tradition, Aquinas held that Christ was human in every normal sense of the term. Specifically, there was no power or faculty of human nature that was lacking in him, usurped, as it were, by a divine faculty or nature. So if human beings have a faculty for acquiring knowledge through sense experience, Christ, too, must possess that faculty, or else he would be something less than human. We might think of this aspect of Aquinas's theology of Christ as informed by his conviction that "grace perfects and does not destroy nature" (see 1.1, note 28). On the other hand, it is possible that this conviction is itself informed by the church's teaching on the integrity of Christ's humanity. In other words, because we see in Christ the perfection and not the destruction or supplanting of his humanity, we come to know this perfection of created natures as God's characteristic way of acting in the world.

9. In other words, the active intellect abstracts the form of the thing known from the sense image and imprints it on the soul (see 1.12, note 8); by taking on the form of the thing it knows, the rational soul becomes "virtually" that thing. Since the soul has the capacity to know anything knowable, it is (virtually) all things.

10. If Christ is to have a complete humanity, he must have both the capacity to receive conceptual knowledge (the passive intellect) and the capacity to derive concepts from sense experience (the active intellect). But there would be no point in having these capacities if he did not exercise them, because a capacity exists in order to carry out its "proper operation" or characteristic activity. Therefore, if Christ had an active intellect, then it must have engaged in its characteristic activity, which is to derive concepts from sense experience.

11. This is a question on which Aquinas, somewhat famously, changed his mind. Not surprisingly, in his early commentary on Lombard's *Sentences* (bk. 3, distinction 14, a. 3, subquestion 5 *ad* 3; distinction 18, a. 3 *ad* 5) he follows the view of his teacher Albert the Great.

natural to human nature.[12] Infused knowledge, on the other hand, is attributed to the soul on account of a light infused from on high, and this manner of knowing is suited to the angelic nature. But beatific knowledge, by which God's essence itself is seen, is proper and natural to God alone, as was said in the first part (1.12.4).

Reply to 1: Since there is a twofold way of acquiring knowledge—by discovery and by being taught—the way of discovery is the higher, and the way of being taught is secondary.[13] Therefore it is said in Aristotle's *Ethics* (bk. 1, chap. 4, 1095[b]), "He indeed is best who knows everything by himself; yet he is good who obeys him that speaks well." And therefore it was more fitting for Christ to possess a knowledge acquired by discovery than by being taught, especially since he was given by God to be the teacher of all, according to Joel 2:23, "Be joyful in the Lord your God, because he has given you a teacher of justice."

Reply to 2: The human mind has two relations. One is to higher things, and in this respect the soul of Christ was full of infused knowledge. The other relation is to lower things, that is, to sense images [*phantasmata*], which naturally move the human mind by virtue of the active intellect. Now it was necessary that even in this respect the soul of Christ should be filled with knowledge, not because the first fullness was not in itself sufficient for the human mind, but because it was proper for it to be also perfected with regard to sense images.[14]

Reply to 3: Acquired and infused habits are not to be classed together because the habit of knowledge is acquired by the relation of the human mind to sense images; therefore, another habit of the same kind cannot be acquired repeatedly. But the habit of infused knowledge is of a different nature, com-

---

12. This is Thomas's mature position: Christ possessed genuine knowledge acquired through experience. What was it that caused Thomas to change his view and take up a view that his contemporaries would have considered misguided, if not heretical? No doubt in part he saw this view as a fitting consequence of the affirmation of the full humanity of Christ. If, as the Letter to the Hebrews would have it, Christ "had to become like his brothers and sisters in every respect, so that he might be a merciful and faithful high priest in the service of God," then he must have acquired knowledge through experience.

13. Thomas simply denies the premise of the objection, namely, that formal instruction is the best way of acquiring knowledge. Indeed, Thomas later (3.12.3) goes on to deny that Jesus ever learned anything from anyone; rather he gained all his acquired knowledge on his own. This idea somewhat diminishes the sense that Jesus was "like his brothers and sisters in every respect." However, it is entirely consistent with Thomas's view that *scientia* is superior to faith as a way of knowing.

14. With respect to *what* Christ knows, infused knowledge is certainly sufficient and acquired knowledge can add nothing. But with respect to *how* Christ knows, acquired knowledge adds to infused knowledge the operation of the active intellect. However, this reply seems to skirt the issue of whether, to put is crudely, there is any "room" for experientially acquired concepts in an intellect that has been "filled" with divinely imparted concepts. In part, Aquinas's answer to this question is found in the reply to objection 3.

ing down to the soul from on high, without an relation to sense images. And therefore these habits are each defined differently.[15]

15. To address the question of how one can have the same knowledge from two different sources (e.g., knowledge of a cow through a divinely imprinted concept and knowledge of a cow through encountering a cow), Aquinas simply denies that these two bits of knowledge are the same *habitus,* since they come from different sources. However, Aquinas does not go on to spell out exactly how this distinction works. Indeed, his reply seems more an assertion than any sort of argument.

WHAT IS FITTINGLY SAID
OF CHRIST

3.16.1

Whether this is true: "God is a human being"?[1]

It would seem that this is false: "God is a human being."

1. This no doubt seems to us an odd question to ask, and Aquinas addresses it in a highly technical way that draws upon certain views on the logic of predication. But in terms of Aquinas's overall discussion of Jesus Christ the question actually makes a lot of sense. In the *Summa,* this article is framed within the larger question concerning what we can and cannot say about God, given the Christian belief that Jesus is God incarnate: one person (or, what is more important in this article, one *suppositum* or "logical subject") who possesses two natures, divine and human. Within the context of this larger question Thomas also has articles asking such things as whether one can truly say that "a human being is God" or that "Christ is a creature."

Aquinas's point here is that because Jesus was both divine and human—because two natures are united in one logical subject—we can make certain statements about God that we could not make otherwise, such as "God was born of the Virgin Mary" or "God died on the cross." Our ability to say such things about God stems from what is known as the *communicatio idiomatum* or "exchange of properties." In Jesus, God took on a human nature and thus identified himself with such humble human activities as birth and death.

Note that the claim Aquinas is inquiring about, *Deus est homo,* can be translated as either "God is human" or "God is a human being"; in the context of this question the second translation is likely the better one.

1. Every affirmative proposition of remote matter [*materia aliqua remota*] is false.[2] But this proposition, "God is a human being," is of remote matter, since the forms signified by the subject and predicate are as far apart as they can be. Therefore, since the proposition in question is affirmative, it would seem to be false.

2. The three divine Persons are in greater mutual agreement than the human nature and the divine. But in the mystery of the incarnation one Person is not predicated of another;[3] namely, we do not say that the Father is the Son, or vice versa. Therefore it seems that we should not predicate human nature of God by saying that God is a human being.

3. Athanasius says that "just as the soul and the flesh are one human being, so God and a human being are one Christ."[4] But this is false: "The soul is the body." Therefore this also is false: "God is a human being."

4. It was said in the first part (1.39.4) that what is predicated of God, not relatively but absolutely, befits the whole Trinity and each of the Persons. But this term "human being" is not relative, but absolute.[5] Therefore, if it is truly predicated of God, it would follow that the whole Trinity and each of the Persons is a human being, which is clearly false.

On the contrary: It is written in Philippians 2:6–7, "who, being in the form of God . . . emptied himself, taking the form of a servant, being made in human likeness and found in the human condition." Thus he who is in the form of God is a human being. But he who is in the form of God is God. Therefore God is a human being.

2. In this context, the term *materia* means the "subject matter" of the proposition—that is, the subject and predicate contained in the proposition. For Thomas, there are three possible relations of the subject and predicate: (1) if the predicate forms all or part of the definition of the subject, then the "matter" is said to be "necessary" or "natural" (e.g., "A human being is a rational animal"); (2) if the predicate is something that may or may not be true of the subject, then the "matter" is said to be "possible" or "contingent" (e.g., "The woman is laughing" or "The table is blue"); (3) if the predicate cannot be properly joined to the subject, then the "matter" is said to be "remote" (e.g., "The woman is a table" or "The table is laughing"). Statements of the last sort strike us not as wrong (the way "The woman is laughing" might be wrong if the woman is in fact crying) but as nonsensical. Similarly, the objection argues, the statement "God is a human being" seems nonsensical, along the lines of "black is white" or (with a nod to George Orwell) "war is peace."

3. In this context it is helpful to understand "predicated" (see 1.3, note 2) in its grammatical sense, that is, according to the function of a predicate in a sentence. So to say "God is a human being" is to "predicate" humanity of God (since "God" is the subject and "human being" is the predicate). The objection argues that even though the Father, Son, and Spirit share the same nature, we still do not say "the Father is the Son" or "the Son is the Spirit." Even less, then, should we be able to say "God is a human being," since we are in this case talking about two *different* natures.

4. The quotation is not from Athanasius but from the so-called Athanasian Creed (see 1.36, note 7).

5. The objection contrasts a term like "human being" with a term like "father." One can cease to be a father by ceasing to have a certain relationship to something else (i.e., a son), but one cannot cease to be a human being without simply ceasing to be.

I answer: This proposition "God is a human being" is admitted by all Christians, yet not all with the same meaning. Some grant the proposition, but not according to the proper understanding of the terms.[6] Thus the Manicheans say the Word of God is a human being, yet not truly human, but only apparently human, inasmuch as they say that the Son of God assumed an imaginary body. In this way, God is said to be a human being in the same way that a bronze figure is called a human being—because it has the appearance of a human being.[7] Similarly, those who held that Christ's body and soul were not united could not say that God is truly a human being; rather, he is figuratively called a human being by reason of the parts.[8] Both these opinions were disproved earlier (3.2.5–6; 3.5.1–2).

Some [Christians], on the contrary, maintain the reality on the human side but deny the reality on the side of God; for they say that Christ, who is the God-man [*qui est Deus homo*], is God not naturally but by participation, that is, by grace, in the same way as all other holy men are called gods—Christ being more excellently so than the rest, on account of his more abundant grace.[9] And thus, when it is said that "God is a human being," the word "God" does not stand for the true and natural God. This is the heresy of Photinus,[10] which was disproved earlier (3.2.10, 11).

But some [Christians] grant this proposition, together with the reality of both terms, holding that Christ is truly God and truly a human being,

6. According to Aquinas, anyone who would call themselves a Christian would be willing to say that "God is a human being." Differences arise either over how the terms "God" and "human being" are understood, or over the nature of the union described by the word "is."

7. The Manicheans were a quasi-Christian group in the third and fourth centuries who believed that material reality was inherently evil and who therefore believed that Jesus's material human body was simply an illusion.

8. In the twelfth century, Peter Abelard, wishing to maintain the reality of Christ's humanity, had argued that although there was only one person in Christ (as Chalcedon taught), the human and divine natures were distinct *hypostases*. This view, called the *homo-assumptus* view, was widely seen in the Middle Ages as a revival of Nestorianism (see 3.2, note 1), since most theologians saw *persona* and *hypostasis* as synonymous in this context (as Aquinas himself does). Followers of Abelard, attempting to avoid the charge of Nestorianism, modified this theory in order to explain how the human nature could be a distinct hypostasis while not being a "person." They argued that the body and soul were not united to each other, and so did not form a person, according to the Boethian definition of "person" as "an individual substance of rational nature"; rather, each was independently joined to the person of the Son of God. This latter view, known as the *habitus* theory of the incarnation, is the object of Thomas's criticism here. In Thomas's eyes, those who hold this view are not so much Nestorian (as was Abelard) as something worse: their position is equivalent to Manicheanism inasmuch as it makes the humanity of Christ only an apparent humanity.

9. Christian's believe that they are all "adopted" children of God through grace (which is why Christians can pray to God as "our Father"), but only Christ is God "by nature." The position Thomas is arguing against here is one that would deny this distinction and depict Jesus as simply a holy person. He would then be "divine" only in that sense and not in the sense that God the Father and the Holy Spirit are divine.

10. Photinus was a fourth-century heretic. Not much is known about his teachings, but he apparently denied that Jesus was truly divine.

but they do not preserve the truth of the predication;[11] for they say that "human being" is predicated of God on account of a some sort of conjunction, whether of dignity, authority, affection, or indwelling. It was in this way that Nestorius held God to be a human being: that this means nothing more than that God is joined to a human being by the sort of conjunction in which a human being is indwelled by God, and united to him by affection, and by a sharing in divine authority and honor. And those who suppose two *supposita* or hypostases in Christ fall into the same error,[12] since it is impossible to understand how, in the case of two things distinct in *suppositum* or hypostasis, one can be properly predicated of the other, unless it is merely by means of a figurative expression, inasmuch as they are united in something. It is as if we were to say that Peter is John because they are somehow mutually joined together.[13] And these opinions also were disproved earlier (3.2.3, 6).

Supposing, therefore, according to the truth of the Catholic faith,[14] that true divine nature is united with true human nature not only in the person but also in the *suppositum* or hypostasis, we say that this proposition is true and proper: "God is a human being"—not only according to the truth of its terms, that is, because Christ is truly God and truly human, but also according to the truth of the predication. For a word signifying the common nature in the concrete may stand for whatever is contained in the common nature, as this term "human" may stand for any individual human being. And thus this word "God," from the very way that it signifies, may stand for the person of the Son of God, as was said in the first part (1.39.4). Now we may truly and properly predicate of every *suppositum* of any nature a word signifying that nature in the concrete, as "human" may properly and truly be predicated of Socrates and Plato. Therefore, since the person of the Son of God, for whom this word "God" stands, is a *suppositum* of human nature, this word "human" may be truly and properly predicated of this word "God," on the ground that it stands for the person of the Son of God.[15]

11. In other words, they understand "God" and "human being" correctly but do not understand how these two things are joined.

12. Thomas is presumably speaking of Abelard and others who held the *homo-assumptus* view (see note 8, above). On the term *suppositum* (and the roughly equivalent Greek term *hypostasis*), see 3.2, note 7.

13. One might think of the way in which some couples who are expecting a baby will say, "We are pregnant." Such a claim is, of course, "merely . . . a figurative expression." The pregnancy cannot be properly predicated of the man, since the man and the woman remain distinct *supposita*. The fact that it is only the woman who is pregnant usually becomes quite clear at the onset of labor, if not earlier.

14. Here Thomas is not trying to prove that Jesus is fully divine and fully human and yet a single *suppositum;* he is, rather, presuming it. He is trying to show what can be said logically based on this belief.

15. Timothy McDermott paraphrases this passage as follows: "So we say that *God is a man* is a true literal proposition, both in the terms it uses and in the predication it makes. For any

Reply to 1: When different forms cannot come together [*convenire*] in one *suppositum*,[16] the proposition is necessarily in remote matter: the subject signifying one form and the predicate another. But when two forms *can* come together in one *suppositum*, the matter is not remote, but natural or contingent, as when I say, "Something white is musical."[17] But the divine and human natures, although as far apart as possible, nevertheless come together, by the mystery of incarnation, in one *suppositum*, in which neither exists accidentally but both essentially [*secundum se*].[18] Therefore this proposition is in neither remote nor contingent matter, but in natural matter. "Human being" is not

---

term that signifies a common nature concretely can be used to refer to any individual possessing the nature in question: *a man* can refer to any individual man, *God* to the person of the Son of God. Such terms can also be used as true and literal attributes of any individual subject possessing the nature: Socrates or Plato can literally and truly be said to *be a man,* and so therefore can the Son of God, referred to in this proposition as *God."* See Timothy McDermott, *Summa Theologiae: A Concise Translation* (Allen, Tex.: Christian Classics, 1989), 496.

This paraphrase helps some, but perhaps not enough. More light might be shed if we compare the statement "God is a human being" to "God is the rock of my salvation." For Aquinas these are two distinct kinds of statements: the first is *literally* true, whereas the second is metaphorically true, but literally false. "God" and "human being" are used literally, whereas "rock" is used metaphorically. This is what Thomas means by "the truth of its terms."

But "God is a human being" is also literally true because "is" is used in the way we use it when we make literal statements, which is what Thomas means by "the truth of the predication." So the term "human" can be used in the abstract to refer literally to any individual instance of human nature, and likewise "God" can be used to refer literally to any individual instance of divine nature. These abstract terms also can be applied literally to any concrete individual subject [*suppositum*] possessing that nature. So in the statement "God is a human being," the term "God" is applied literally to Jesus because his *suppositum* is divine, but the term "human" is applied literally to him because he has a human nature.

In the case of "God is the rock of my salvation," the *suppositum* indicated by the term "God" does not in fact possess a mineral nature, and therefore the statement cannot be true in a literal way.

16. Note here how the notion of *convenientia* is insinuated into the discussion (see 3.1, note 1). One might reword the objection to say that the proposition "God is a human being" is an "unfitting" one.

17. Some "natures" [*formae*] *can* be combined in an affirmative proposition, either because one of the natures is an accidental matter (i.e., a property of something that is changeable and does not enter into its definition) or because it is a necessary matter.

The example "something white is musical" seems bizarre, but Aquinas is thinking here of an example he will mention in the next question (3.17.2, below): Socrates, who is both white and musical. Though being white and being musical are "different forms," they are accidental, and thus can be combined in an affirmative proposition.

18. In saying that the divine and human natures are possessed by Jesus "essentially" and not "accidentally" Thomas is saying that Jesus is human in a different way than a chair is blue (which is a changeable property of the chair). Rather Jesus is human in the same way that a chair is something in which one sits (which is part of the definition of a chair, or what a chair is per se). The statement "God is a human being" is said of Jesus essentially because both "God" and "a human being" enter into the definition of who Jesus is (even though "human being" is not part of the definition of "God," nor "God" part of the definition of "human being").

predicated of God accidentally but essentially [*per se*], as of its own hypostasis,[19] not on account of the form signified by this word "God," but on account of the *suppositum,* which is the hypostasis of the human nature.[20]

Reply to 2: The three divine Persons come together in one nature, yet are distinguished in *suppositum,* and therefore they are not predicated one of another.[21] But in the mystery of the incarnation the natures, being distinct, are not predicated of one another when they are signified abstractly, for the divine nature is not human. But because they agree in *suppositum,* they are predicated of each other when signified concretely.[22]

Reply to 3: "Soul" [*anima*] and "flesh" are signified abstractly, in the same way as "divinity" and "humanity." Speaking concretely, we say "something alive" [*animatum*] and "something fleshly" or "something bodily," just as, in the latter case, we say "God" and "human being." Therefore in neither case is the abstract predicated of the abstract, but only the concrete of the concrete.[23]

Reply to 4: This term "human being" is predicated of God because of the union in the person, and this union implies a relation. Therefore it does not follow the rule of those terms that are predicated absolutely of God from eternity.[24]

---

19. That is, we say "God is a human being" because the second Person of the Trinity is the proper *suppositum* of Jesus's human nature.

20. As so often when speaking of divine things, Thomas finds that no single form of normal human discourse is suitable. Rather, we must speak "between," as it were, our normal ways of speaking. Thus when speaking of God, we must speak of God sometimes as if God were a "nature" (a general category of things) and sometimes as if God were a particular concrete instance of a nature. The same sort of speech applies to the incarnation: our language is somewhat like language about accidental properties and somewhat like language about essential natures, but not precisely like either. See 3.2, note 17, and 3.17, note 13.

Perhaps the most significant point Aquinas makes in this somewhat difficult reply is that humanity and divinity are not different forms (*formae diversae*). The statement "God is a human being" is not a contradiction like "black is white" because all differences must appear against some common background. "Black" and "white" are both colors—there is a common category of which they are distinct kinds. Cast against this common background, the statement "black is white" appears obviously nonsensical. "Divinity" and "humanity," however, do not share any such background because part of what Aquinas means by "divinity" is that which is not contained in *any* category. Thus when we encounter the claim of the Christian faith that "God is a human being," we may disbelieve it, but, according to Aquinas, we cannot accuse it of being nonsense.

21. On "predicated," see 1.3, note 2.

22. In other words, we can say "God is a human being" but we cannot say "divinity is humanity," nor can we say "Jesus is Socrates." In the latter case, we have (presumably) distinct *supposita,* as we do in the case of the Persons of the Trinity. In the former case, we have distinct natures.

23. Thus one could not say that "the soul is flesh" (*anima est caro*), but one *could* say "something alive is something fleshly" (*animatum est carneum*), since being alive and being fleshly are both properties of a single concrete "something."

24. To say that the second Person of the Trinity became incarnate is to speak of a particular relationship between the second Person of the Trinity and the human nature of Jesus. One might say that "incarnate" is a relational term, and as such is more like "begotten" than it is like "simple" or "eternal" or "wise." Just as only one Person of the Trinity is the relationship named by the term "begotten," so too only one Person of the Trinity has that relationship to humanity named by the term "incarnate." On the notion of the Persons of the Trinity as relations, see 1.29.4, above.

CHRIST'S UNITY WITH REGARD TO HIS EXISTENCE

3.17.2

Whether there is only one existence in Christ?[1]

1. This is thought by many to be a key article in Aquinas's theology of Christ, for several reasons. First, in this article Thomas employs a number of concepts that are distinctively (if not uniquely) his, most especially the notion of *esse*. It is as if in this article Thomas is trying to fuse his mastery of the classical theological vocabulary derived from the church councils of the first five centuries with his metaphysical language of existence.

Another reason this article has excited interest over the centuries is that in another work— *Quaestio disputata de unione Verbi incarnati,* article 4—Aquinas seems to contradict what he says here. When, in *De unione, Aquinas* confronts the question "Whether in Christ there is only one existence [*esse*]?" he says that although there is in Christ only a single existence in an absolute sense [*esse simpliciter*], there is, because of his human nature, another existence that is "secondary" [*secundarium*]. In the present article, and indeed in all of his other writings, Thomas nowhere mentions such a "secondary existence."

Some authors (e.g., Cajetan), seeing the differences between the two texts as dramatic, have argued that *De unione* must be either an early work by Thomas, or not by Thomas at all. More recently, some scholars have claimed that it was written at almost exactly the same time as this article of the *Summa* (the spring of 1272, in Paris). If so, then it would seem Thomas himself did not see any contradiction between the two texts. Indeed, some recent authors (e.g., the Benedictine theologian Herman-Michel Diepen, in the mid-twentieth century) have argued that *De unione* represents the "true" position of Aquinas.

It would seem that in Christ there is not only one existence *[esse]*, but two.[2]

1. John of Damascus says in his *On the Orthodox Faith* (bk. 3, chap. 13) that whatever is a consequence of a nature is doubled in Christ. But existence is a consequence of a nature, for existence is from the form.[3] Therefore in Christ there are two existences [*duo esse*].

2. The existence of the Son of God is the divine nature itself, and is eternal. However, the existence of the human being Christ is not the divine nature, but is an existence in time.[4] Therefore there is not only one existence in Christ.

3. Although there are three Persons in the Trinity, there is nevertheless only one existence because of the unity of nature. But in Christ there are two natures, although there is one person. Therefore in Christ there is not only one existence.[5]

4. In Christ the soul gives some existence to the body, since it is its form. But it does not give the divine existence, since this is uncreated. Therefore in Christ there is another existence besides the divine existence, and thus in Christ there is not only one existence.

On the contrary: A thing is said to be one to the degree that it is said to be a being [*ens*], for "one" and "being" [*ens*] are interchangeable. Therefore, if there were two existences [*duo esse*] in Christ, and not one only, Christ would be two, and not one.

I answer: Because in Christ there are two natures and one hypostasis,[6] it follows that things belonging to the nature in Christ must be two, and that those belonging to the hypostasis in Christ must be only one. But existence pertains both to the nature and to the hypostasis: to the hypostasis as "that which has

---

My own view is that *De unione* says substantially the same thing as Thomas's other writings: in all texts addressing this issue Thomas's main concern is to maintain that Christ has a single act of existence as a person (i.e., a single *esse*); Thomas nowhere envisions the unity of Christ's person as some sort of combination of two independent acts of existing. However, in all texts the human nature can be spoken of as having the sort of *esse* "by which" something exists as this or that sort of thing, and this is what *De unione* calls "secondary" *esse*.

2. For some general remarks on *esse*, see 1.3, note 1. It is important to remember that in this article Thomas is not asking whether there are two "beings" or "entities" in Christ, but whether Christ, by virtue of his human and divine natures, possesses two distinct activities of existing (*duo esse*).

3. That is, Socrates *is* a human being because Socrates possesses the form of humanity. The identification of "form" or "nature" as that which gives existence is also the basis for objections 3 and 4.

4. This objection makes two distinguishable points: (1) if Christ's human nature does not have its own independent act of existence, then it does not possess a created existence, and therefore is not a creature; and (2) if Christ's human nature is temporal and his divine nature is eternal, then *esse* cannot be predicated univocally of these two natures (see 1.13.5), and hence Christ must have two distinct acts of existence.

5. In the Trinity we have the principle of one nature—one *esse*. Therefore if the person of Christ has two natures, he must have two *esse*.

6. On "nature" and "hypostasis," see 1.29, note 1.

existence" and to the nature as "that by which something has existence."[7] For we speak of a nature in the way we speak of a form, which is said to be a being because something is "on account of" it: "on account of" whiteness a thing is white; and "on account of" human nature a thing is a human being.

It must be borne in mind that if something is a form or nature that does not pertain to the existence-as-a-person [*esse personale*] of a subsisting hypostasis,[8] this existence is said to belong to the person not simply, but in some particular respect.[9] Thus to be [*esse*] white is the existence [*esse*] of Socrates, not because he is Socrates, but because he is white. And there is no reason why one hypostasis or person should not have multiple instances of this sort of existence, for the existence on account of which Socrates is white is distinct from the existence on account of which he is a musician. But that existence that belongs to the hypostasis or person *as such* cannot possibly be multiplied in one hypostasis or person, since it is impossible that one thing should not have one existence.[10]

7. Here Aquinas begins by agreeing with John of Damascus, as cited in the first objection, that what belongs to the natures of Christ is two-fold. Thus, for example, Aquinas will argue in the following question (3.18) that Christ has two wills: divine and human. However, contrary to the first objection, Aquinas does not think that this "doubling" settles the question, since *esse* belongs to *both* the natures *and* the person/hypostasis (on "hypostasis," see 3.2, note 7), but in different ways. Aquinas characterizes this difference as that between the existence by which something is what it is, and the existence that is that thing's act of existing. We can see this difference in the way we use forms of the verb "to be": the difference, for example, between saying "I am happy" or "I am a human being" and saying simply "I am." In the first two statements, I am asserting something about myself, and thus the "am" is a consequence of my happy or human nature; in the third statement, I am simply asserting my existence, and the "am" is a consequence of my existing as this particular person. Statements like the first two can obviously be multiplied, since I can be both a happy being *and* a human being and much else besides. But the third statement cannot be multiplied, since the "I" that exists as a happy human is only one instance of existing.

8. What Aquinas means by *esse personale* is that by which a person exists at all, as opposed to that by which a person exists as this or that *kind* of person. Later in this article I translate *esse personale* as "personal existence" in order to make Aquinas's Latin resemble normal English, but the reader should be aware that I am translating the same Latin term.

9. This is the difference between "I am happy" and "I am a human being." I can cease to be happy, but I am still myself; if I cease to be a human being, I cease to be me and become something else—for example, a corpse. Thus being human is integral to my *esse personale*, whereas being happy is an "accident" or nonessential quality of my existence-as-a-person.

10. To schematize what Aquinas has said thus far:

1. There is the *esse* of a hypostasis or subject (the *esse personale* or "existence-as-a-person"), which is its act of existing, and which cannot be multiple.

2. There is the *esse* of a nature or predicate, which makes a thing exist in this or that particular way (as a human being, as something white, as something happy, as something musical); the *esse* of a nature can be either:

   a) the *esse* of an "accident" (such as being white, or musical, or happy, or a particular age, height, weight, etc.), of which one subject can possess many, or

   b) the *esse* that belongs to the subject "simply" and by which it is what it is. This *esse* seems closely related to the *esse* of the hypostasis, and like the *esse* of the hypostasis

If, therefore, the Son of God acquired a human nature, not hypostatically or personally, but accidentally, as some maintained, it would be necessary to assert two existences in Christ: one inasmuch as he is God, and the other inasmuch as he is a human being.[11] Thus in Socrates we indicate one existence inasmuch as he is white, and another inasmuch as he is a human being, since "being white" [*esse album*] does not pertain to the personal existence of Socrates. But being possessed of a head, being bodily, being alive—all these *do* pertain to the one person of Socrates, and therefore there arises from these things only the one existence of Socrates. And if it so happened that, after the person of Socrates was constituted, he acquired hands or feet or eyes (as happened to the man born blind),[12] no new existence would be added to Socrates by these things, but only a certain relation to them. That is, he would be said to exist not only with reference to what he had previously, but also with reference to what he later acquired.[13]

Thus, because the human nature is united to the Son of God hypostatically or personally and not accidentally, as was said earlier (3.2.5, 6), it follows

---

can be only singular. An example would be the being of a subject's nature as human or canine. One might be both musical *and* happy, but one cannot be both a human being and a dog.

11. This was in fact the view of most scholars in the thirteenth century (for example, William of Auxerre prior to Thomas and Duns Scotus after him), who held that the best analogy for thinking about the relationship between Christ's humanity and his divinity was to think about the way in which an accident or nonessential quality is related to the subject that has that quality. However, for Thomas this view smacked of the heresy of Nestorius. Also, an objection that he does not make here but that is undoubtedly in the back of his mind is that if the human nature of Christ were conceived as an "accident," then it would seem to be a quality that realizes a potential in God—that is, the potential to have a human nature—and this would seem to compromise divine simplicity and perfection (see 1.3, notes 1 and 12).

12. See chapter 9 of John's Gospel. Note that Thomas is not simply offering this Johannine text as a decorative proof-text for an essentially philosophical argument. The example of the man born blind is a particularly apt one because the question of whether he is the same person (i.e., has the same *esse personale*) after the healing as before is raised by the crowd (9:8–9).

13. The analogy between Christ's human nature and a part of a human being is one Aquinas has already used (see 3.2, note 17). Socrates' hand is what it is only because it is a part of the person Socrates. Similarly, Christ's humanity is what it is only because it is a part of the person of the Son of God. The key point in this analogy is that when something is a part of a whole, its act existence is the existence of that whole.

Aquinas's analogy has been much criticized, not least by Duns Scotus (see Scotus's *Ordinatio* 3.6.1 nn. 4–5). Scotus argued that a part shares in the existence of the whole only because it shares in the form or nature of the whole. But the human nature of Christ does not share the divine nature; this would be the opposite heresy from Nestorianism, namely, monophysitism (the view that Christ had only a divine nature, see 3.2, note 1). Therefore the part–whole analogy is, according to Scotus, simply misleading. In defense of Aquinas, one can say that he must be aware of the failings of this analogy, but he prefers to maintain it rather than take the path followed by most medievals, who said that Christ's human nature is an accretion to his divine person that possesses its own act of existence. One might say that Christology is always a balancing act between Nestorianism and monophysitism, and Thomas's own judgment in his context is that it is the former that is the greater danger.

that in acquiring a human nature he acquired no new personal existence [*esse personale*], but only a new relation of the already existing personal existence to human nature, in such a way that the person is said to subsist not only according to the divine, but also according to the human nature.[14]

Reply to 1: Existence is a consequence of nature, not as "that which has existence" [*habentem esse*], but as "that by which something is" [*qua aliquid est*]. However, it is a consequence of the person or hypostasis as "that which has existence." Therefore it has unity from the unity of hypostasis, rather than duality from the duality of the nature.[15]

Reply to 2: The eternal existence of the Son of God, which is the divine nature, becomes human existence inasmuch as the human nature is assumed by the Son of God in the unity of person.[16]

Reply to 3: As was said in the first part (1.3.3; 1.39.1), since the divine Person is the same as the nature, there is no distinction in the divine Persons between the existence of the Person and the existence of the nature, and, consequently, the three Persons have only one existence.[17] But they would have a

---

14. Despite the seeming complexity of this article, Aquinas's argument is in fact quite simple. The *esse* of Christ's humanity "belongs" to the hypostasis/*suppositum*/person of the Son of God, and therefore must be one, following the principle laid down at the beginning of the response: "things belonging to the nature in Christ must be two; and . . . those belonging to the hypostasis in Christ must be only one."

It is important to ask what is finally at stake for Aquinas in this article. Certainly he is concerned to maintain the unity of Christ against the various views that would lead to "Nestorianism," which he believes disallows such crucial claims as "God is a human being" (see 3.16, note 1). Salvation grows out of the fact that, in Christ, God's eternal act of existence becomes the act of existence of a human nature (see the reply to objection 2 in this article). This view becomes apparent in 3.42.4, below, where salvation turns on the unity of divine and human action in Christ's self-offering on the cross.

Also, Aquinas's desire to associate *esse* with hypostasis/*suppositum*/person reflects his firm metaphysical conviction that it is concrete things—matter shaped or "informed" by a nature—rather than "forms" or "natures" themselves, that are most real, that exist most intensely. Thus, in the case of rational beings, the question of existence is always primarily a question of "personal existence," and when we ask about the existence of Christ, we must speak first and foremost of the single, concrete person Jesus Christ, in whom are united divinity and humanity.

It is also important to remember that for Aquinas God's *esse*—God's eternal act of existence—is something ungraspable to human reason (see 1–2.3, note 11). As Henk Schoot argues, by positing in Christ a unity of *esse*, Aquinas locates the union of humanity and divinity in a realm that is irreducibly mysterious to the mind of creatures. All accounts of this union must "limp," because it is a union that reaches "all the way down" to the incomprehensible divine act of existence. See Henk Schoot, *Christ the "Name" of God: Thomas Aquinas on Naming Christ* (Leuven: Peeters, 1993).

15. See 3.16, note 1.

16. God's eternal act of existence is the act of existence of a human nature, not because that human nature is eternal or uncreated, but because at a particular moment in history that nature was "assumed" or "taken on" by the second Person of the Trinity. Thus, Thomas's view is not "monophysite."

17. Here Thomas invokes the principle of divine simplicity (see 1.3, note 1) to argue that God's nature and person are not distinguished from each other in terms of *esse*. However, he

three-fold existence if the existence of the Person were distinct in them from the existence of the nature.

Reply to 4: The soul in Christ gives existence to the body, insofar as it makes it actually alive, which is to give it the fulfillment of its nature and species. But if we take the body thus perfected by the soul and consider it apart from the hypostasis possessing them, then this whole composed of soul and body, which we call "humanity," does not signify "what is" [*quod est*] but "whereby it is" [*quo aliquid est*]. This is why existence itself belongs to the subsisting person, since it has a relation to such a nature, and the soul is the cause of this relation, since it perfects human nature by informing the body.[18]

---

still maintains that the three Persons of the Trinity are distinct, not because their existence as Persons is somehow different from the act of existence of their shared nature (as, for example, three instances of it, the way Peter, Paul, and Mary are three instances of human nature), but because they are distinct from each other by virtue of their relations of origin. Still, they share in the same act of existence, which is the divine nature. See 1.29.4, above.

It is not immediately apparent how this response answers the objection. Perhaps Aquinas's point is that the divine act of existence is not a "thing" that can be numbered alongside some other thing, and then added up to make two things. The unity of the divine act of existence is not like a "one" in a series of numbers; rather it is the unity of the utter uniqueness of God's act of existing. In this sense, just as the one divine nature cannot be added to the three Persons to make four things, so too the "one divine act of existence" cannot be added to the "one human act of existence" to arrive at two acts of existence.

18. With this reply we can return to the difficulty presented by the seeming contradiction between Aquinas's view presented here, which firmly maintains that Christ has but one *esse*, and the view presented in *Quaestio disputata de unione Verbi incarnati,* article 4, which says that Christ's human nature possesses an existence "that is not the principle *esse* of its suppositum, but secondary" (see note 1, above). This reply seems to indicate that even here Aquinas is willing to speak in a certain, qualified sense of the *esse* that the human nature possesses of itself, though this is *esse* only in the sense that it is by the human nature that Christ exists as a human being. What seems consistent between the two accounts is that the human nature in no way contributes to the "existence-as-a-person" (*esse personale*) of Christ, since Christ's personhood is the divine personhood of the second Person of the Trinity.

QUESTION 27

THE SANCTIFICATION
OF THE BLESSED VIRGIN

3.27.2

Whether the Blessed Virgin was sanctified before animation?[1]

1. This article is the subject of some controversy, not least because Thomas appears to deny here what would later (in 1854, with the Apostolic Constitution *Ineffabilis Deus*) become official Catholic dogma, namely, that Mary, from the moment of her conception, was preserved from the stain of original sin. This doctrine, the immaculate conception, is sometimes confused with the virgin birth, though its relation to Jesus's birth is a tangential one. Its specific concern is with what it means for Mary to be "fully of grace," and therefore a suitable mother for Christ.

Though a feast day for the conception of Mary dates back to the seventh century, the claim that she was conceived "immaculately" (i.e., without original sin) was rather late in developing, really gaining currency only with Duns Scotus. The views Aquinas expresses here were commonly held in his day (by, among others, Bernard of Clairvaux, Peter Lombard, Alexander of Hales, Bonaventure, and Albert the Great). Aquinas did hold that Mary was cleansed from original sin in the womb of her mother, but he argues here that this cleansing occurs at some point after her conception.

Some scholars have argued that there are shifts in Thomas's writings on this question. For example, in his earlier commentary on Lombard's *Sentences* he wrote that Mary "was made immune from original and actual sin" (bk. 1, distinction 44, q. 1, a. 3 *ad* 3). Scholars have argued that the language of Mary being made "immune" (*immunis*) to original sin approaches the doctrine of the immaculate conception. If so, then the position represented in this present article would indeed represent a shift in Thomas's position. It is possible, however, to read too much into his use of the word *immunis,* which can mean simply "free from" and does not nec-

204

It would seem that the Blessed Virgin was sanctified before animation.[2]

1. As we have stated (3.27.1), more grace was bestowed on the Virgin Mother of God than on any saint. But it seems some were granted sanctification before animation; for it is written in Jeremiah 1:5, "Before I formed you in the womb of your mother, I knew you," and the soul is not infused before the formation of the body. Likewise, Ambrose says of John the Baptist (*Commentary on Luke,* bk. 1, 1:15), "The spirit of life was not yet in him, and already he possessed the Spirit of grace." Therefore it is even more the case that the Blessed Virgin could be sanctified before animation.

2. As Anselm says in *On the Virginal Conception* (bk. 18), "It was fitting that this Virgin should shine with such a purity that none greater can be conceived, apart from God." For this reason it is written in Song of Songs 4:7, "You are all fair, O my love, and there is not a spot in you."[3] But the purity of

---

essarily imply some sort of divine preventative measure. Some have also argued that in the late *Expositio super saltuatione angelica* (Sermon on the Angelic Greeting) Thomas shows an acceptance of Mary's immunity from original sin. In most of the medieval copies of this text we find the claim that "the virgin incurred neither original nor mortal nor venial sin," but in a few of these copies "original sin" is omitted from this list. It is certainly possible that "original sin" was added in most copies in order to make Thomas conform to the growing theological consensus in favor of the immaculate conception. Such corruptions in the manuscript would explain the fact that in the same text Thomas says, "The blessed Virgin was conceived in original [sin], but not born [in original sin]." Since it is doubtful that Thomas contradicted himself within a few short paragraphs, it makes sense to assume that most of the manuscripts we have of the *Expositio super saltuatione angelica* were altered. On balance, then, it seems likely that Thomas did not change his views on this matter.

It should be noted, however, that in this article Aquinas is not addressing precisely the question of the immaculate conception. His question differs on at least two counts: (1) he is asking whether Mary was "sanctified," not whether she was "preserved" from sin; (2) he is asking whether this could happen before "animation," which is, for Aquinas, something different from "conception." As we shall see, he holds that conception (the beginning of the formation of the person) is prior to animation (the reception of the rational soul).

It should also be noted, at the outset, that Aquinas discusses Mary in the context of Christology. This is an approach that was somewhat eclipsed after the Reformation, when Mary tended to become, in her own right, a subject of theological reflection. Thomas, however, never forgets that Mary called herself *ancillia Dei* (the handmaid of God), and he treats her as an ancillary topic in his theology of Christ. Aquinas devotes four questions, consisting of sixteen articles, to "Mariology," which is quite austere by post-Reformation standards. Of course, he discusses Mary in other places in the *Summa,* but the fact that he is content to let his discussion of her be lodged in the midst of a variety of christological questions is itself instructive.

2. By "animation" Thomas means the infusion or imparting of the rational soul (*anima*) to the body. Following Aristotle, Aquinas held that the fetus became animated only at some period after conception—around forty days for males and fifty days for females—because the soul requires a "due quantity" of matter for its infusion. The one exception he makes is the case of Christ, who received his rational soul at the moment of his conception (see 3.33.2).

3. Advocates for the doctrine of the immaculate conception often point to Anselm's *De conceptu virginali et originali peccato* as the text that prepared the way for the later work of Duns Scotus. Regarding Mary's holiness, Anselm applies the same sort of logic he uses to prove God's existence in his *Proslogion* (see 1.2, note 2). Anselm's student and biographer, Eadmer, appears to have been the first Western theologian to propose that Mary's purity—"than which

the Blessed Virgin would have been greater if she had never been stained by the contagion of original sin. Therefore it was granted to her to be sanctified before her flesh was animated.[4]

3. As it has been stated earlier (3.27.1), no feast is celebrated except that of someone holy. But some keep the Feast of the Conception of the Blessed Virgin. Therefore it seems that in her very conception she was holy, and therefore that she was sanctified before animation.[5]

4. The Apostle says in Romans 11:16, "If the root be holy, so are the branches." But parents are the root of children. Therefore the Blessed Virgin could be sanctified even in her parents, before animation.

On the contrary: The things of the Old Testament were prefigurations of the New, according to 1 Corinthians 10:11, "All things happened to them in figure."[6] Now the sanctification of the tabernacle, of which it is written in Psalm 46:4—"The most high has sanctified his own tabernacle"—seems to signify the sanctification of the Mother of God, who is called "God's tabernacle," according to Psalm 19:4, "He has set his tabernacle in the sun." But of the tabernacle it is written in Exodus 40:31, 32, "After all things were perfected, the cloud covered the tabernacle of the testimony, and the glory of the Lord filled it." Therefore also the Blessed Virgin was not sanctified until all in her was completed, namely, the body and the soul.

I answer: The sanctification of the Blessed Virgin cannot be understood as having taken place before animation, for two reasons. First, because the sanctification of which we are speaking is nothing other than the cleansing from original sin, for sanctification is a "perfect cleansing," as Dionysius says in *On*

---

none greater can be conceived"—involved her being freed from sin at her conception, in a way distinct from and surpassing those others (e.g., Jeremiah or John the Baptist) who were thought to have been cleansed in the womb (see *De conceptione sanctae Mariae* 9).

4. This objection hints at an argument that Scotus would use later to argue for the fittingness of the immaculate conception: since Mary is "full of grace," God would bring about her redemption in the best way possible; it is better to be preserved from sin than to be cleansed from sin; therefore it is fitting that Mary would be preserved from original sin. As it is sometimes put: *Decuit, potuit, ergo fecit*—it was fitting; it was possible; therefore it was done.

5. In the controversy over the immaculate conception the liturgical question was as significant as the doctrinal question: should there be a feast of Mary's conception, and should this feast be designated as the Feast of the *Immaculate* Conception? A feast of the conception of Mary was kept in Palestine as early as the seventh century. After the time of Scotus (d. 1308), the observance of the feast as one celebrating the immaculate conception increased in popularity (though not without controversy). In 1476 Pope Sixtus IV allowed the liturgical celebration of the feast and dedicated a chapel to Mary as Immaculate Virgin in St. Peter's Basilica in Rome.

As the question is framed in the objection, only "saints" (i.e., those who are holy) have feast days; therefore if there is a feast of the conception of Mary, she must have been holy at the time of her conception. In the previous article (3.27.1) Aquinas uses this same sort of argument in the *sed contra* to argue that Mary was made holy before her birth: since the church observes the feast of the birth of Mary (in contrast to most other saints, who are commemorated on the date of their death), she must have been holy at the time of her birth.

6. See 1.1, note 39.

the Divine Names (chap. 12, no. 2). But sin cannot be taken away except by grace, the subject of which is the rational creature alone. Therefore before the infusion of the rational soul, the Blessed Virgin was not sanctified.[7]

Second, since only the rational creature can be susceptible to moral fault, before the infusion of the rational soul the offspring conceived is not guilty of a fault. And thus, in whatever way the Blessed Virgin would have been sanctified before animation, she could never have incurred the stain of original sin. Therefore she would not have needed redemption and salvation, which is through Christ, of whom it is written (Matthew 1:21), "He shall save his people from their sins." But this is unfitting [*inconveniens*], because Christ would not be the "savior of all people," as 1 Timothy 4:10 says.[8] It remains, therefore, that the Blessed Virgin was sanctified after animation.

Reply to 1: The Lord says that he "knew" Jeremiah before he was formed in the womb—that is to say, by the knowledge of predestination. But he says that he "sanctified" him, not before formation, but before he "came forth out of the womb," and so on.

As to what Ambrose says—that is, that the spirit of life was not yet in John the Baptist when he already had the Spirit of grace—by "spirit of life" we are not to understand the life-giving soul but the air that we breathe out [*respiratus*]. Or it may be said that in him there was not yet the spirit of life, that is, the soul, as to its manifest and complete operations.[9]

---

7. Here Aquinas simply applies the principle that a thing must be something before it can be some *sort* of thing. Thus Mary's rational soul had to exist before it could exist as either sinful or holy. Since only a rational soul can sin or bear the mark of sin, only a rational soul can be freed from sin, and therefore Mary could not have been freed from sin at any point prior to her animation. So, in Aquinas's view, Mary must have borne the mark of sin, if only for an instant, after her animation.

Duns Scotus will argue later, in what will eventually be seen as the definitive answer to this difficulty, that Mary's sanctification occurs neither before nor after her animation, but at the very instant when her soul was joined to her body.

8. This second argument follows from the first. If Mary were to have been "sanctified" prior to her reception of a rational soul, then "sanctified" must mean, in her case, something other than being freed from original sin. But if this were the case, then she would not be redeemed by Christ, who frees us from bondage to sin. This view is unacceptable to Thomas because of its "unfittingness." In other words, it does not cohere with the whole sweep of the story of salvation through Christ. Therefore, once again, Mary must have borne the mark of sin, if only for an instant, after her animation in order that she could receive Christ's redemption.

Again, Scotus will argue later for a different view, which will become part of the dogmatic definition of the immaculate conception. According to Scotus, in Mary's case "sanctified" *does* mean something other than being freed from original sin; it means being *prevented* from contracting original sin in the first place. However, this salvation is still through Christ; Mary's holiness is given to her so that she can be a fitting mother for the redeemer, and it is given on the basis of what Christ will do on the cross.

9. The quotation from Ambrose seems to suggest that John the Baptist received grace before he received a rational soul. Thomas offers two possible alternative readings of Ambrose: (1) John possessed a rational soul, but had not yet taken a physical breath; or (2) John possessed a rational soul, but it was not yet manifested through his actions.

Reply to 2: If the soul of the Blessed Virgin had never be touched by original sin, this would take away from the dignity that Christ has inasmuch as he is the universal Savior of all. Consequently, after Christ, who as the universal Savior did not need to be saved, the purity of the Blessed Virgin holds the highest place; for Christ did not contract original sin in any way whatever but was holy in his very conception, according to Luke 1:35, "The holy one that shall be born from you shall be called the Son of God." The Blessed Virgin, however, did indeed contract original sin but was cleansed from it before her birth from the womb. This is what is signified in Job 3:9, where it is said of the night of original sin, "Let it expect light," that is, Christ, "and not see it" (because "no defiled thing comes into her," as is written in Wisdom 7:25), "nor the rising of the dawning of the day," that is of the Blessed Virgin, who in her birth was immune from original sin.[10]

Reply to 3: Although the church of Rome does not celebrate the conception of the Blessed Virgin, it still tolerates the custom of certain churches that do keep that feast. Therefore such celebration is not to be entirely disapproved of. Nevertheless the celebration of this feast does not lead us to understand that she was holy in her conception. But since it is not known when she was sanctified, the feast of her sanctification, rather than the feast of her conception, is kept on the day of her conception.[11]

Reply to 4: Sanctification is twofold: [1] sanctification of the whole nature, inasmuch as the whole human nature is freed from all corruption of sin and punishment, which will take place at the resurrection; [2] personal sanctification, which is not transmitted to offspring brought forth by the flesh, because it has to do not with the flesh but with the mind. Consequently, though the parents of the Blessed Virgin were cleansed from original sin, nevertheless she contracted original sin, since she was conceived by way of fleshly desire and the intercourse of man and woman; for Augustine says in the book *On Marriage and Concupiscence* (bk. 1, chap. 12), "All flesh born of sexual intercourse is sinful."[12]

10. We can read this response as Thomas's preemptive rejoinder to the Scotist solution (see notes 4, 7, 8, above) to the difficulties outlined in the body of the article: if we locate Mary's sinlessness at the very moment of her conception, and see it as a "preventative" sinlessness, then nothing distinguishes her conception from that of Jesus. For Thomas, this view diminishes the honor shown to Christ.

11. Aquinas says that since we do not know precisely when in the womb Mary was made holy, some churches commemorate this mystery on the day of her conception, but conception and sanctification are not necessarily linked. Indeed, Aquinas says that what is commemorated on that feast day is the sanctification, not the conception. Since, as we have seen, Aquinas separates conception and animation, he would no doubt say that one thing we *do* know is that she was not sanctified at her conception.

12. Here Aquinas reflects the viewpoint of Augustine that it is the inordinate desire or "concupiscence" of the parents during the sexual act that transmits original sin. The redemption of "the flesh" is something that awaits the resurrection, so the parents of the Virgin Mary, although cleansed of original sin through faith in the redeemer who was to come, would not have been freed from concupiscence. Thus Mary was conceived in the ordinary human way: by two people who experienced bodily desire for each other.

QUESTION 40

CHRIST'S WAY OF LIVING

3.40.1

Whether Christ should have associated with people, or led a solitary life?[1]

It would seem that Christ should not have associated with people, but should have led a solitary life.

1. It was appropriate for Christ to show by his manner of life not only that he was a human being, but also that he was God. But it is not fitting that God should associate with human beings, for it is written in Daniel 2:11, "Except the gods, whose conversation is not with human beings"; and the Philosopher says in the *Politics* (bk. 1, chap. 2, 1253ᵃ) that one who lives alone is "either a beast"—that is, if one does this on account of savagery—"or a god"—if one does this on account of the contemplation of truth.[2] Therefore it seems that it was not fitting for Christ to associate with human beings.

1. The next few articles are from a section of the *Summa* that looks at the actual events of Jesus's life and inquires into their *convenientia* (see 3.1, note 1). Again, Thomas is in no sense trying to deduce rationally the way Jesus *had to* live. Rather, given that Jesus *did* live a certain sort of life, can we discern reasons for the way he lived?

2. The full quotation from Aristotle is: "He who is unable to live in society, or who has no need because he is sufficient for himself, must be either a beast or a god: he is no part of a state. A social instinct is implanted in all men by nature" (*Politics* 1253ᵃ). Aristotle's point is not, as the objection makes it appear, that living as a part of human society would be impossible for one who was divine; rather, human beings are, as Aristotle puts it, "social animals"—it is part of their nature to live in groups. Only a god or a beast could live outside of society.

2. While he lived in mortal flesh, Christ should have led the most perfect life. Now the most perfect life is the contemplative, as we have stated in the second part (2–2.182.1, 2).[3] But solitude is most suitable to the contemplative life; according to Hosea 2:14, "I will lead her into the wilderness, and I will speak to her heart." Therefore it seems that Christ should have led a solitary life.

3. Christ's manner of life should have been uniform, because it should have always given evidence of that which is best. But at times Christ avoided the crowd and sought lonely places; therefore Remigius,[4] commenting on Matthew, says, "We read that our Lord had three places of refuge: the ship, the mountain, and the desert; he went to one or other of these whenever he was pressed by the crowd." Therefore he should have always led a solitary life.[5]

On the contrary: It is written in Baruch 3:38, "Afterwards he was seen upon earth and conversed with human beings."

I answer: Christ's manner of life had to be in keeping with [*conveniret*] the purpose of his incarnation, on account of which he came into the world.[6] He came into the world, first, in order to manifest the truth; thus he says himself in John 18:37, "For this was I born, and for this I came into the world, that I should give testimony to the truth." Therefore he should not have hidden himself by leading a solitary life, but should have appeared openly and preached in public. For this reason in Luke 4:42–43 he says to those who wished to detain him, "I must preach the kingdom of God to other cities also; for that is the reason I am sent."

Second, he came in order to free human beings from sin; according to 1 Timothy 1:15, "Christ Jesus came into this world to save sinners." And therefore, as Chrysostom says, "Although Christ might, while staying in the same place, have drawn all people to himself, to hear his preaching, yet he did not do so; he thus gave us the example to go about and seek those who

---

3. Although the tendency of many Christians today is to think of active service for one's neighbor as the highest form of Christian life, this was not always the case. It was simply assumed in Aquinas's day that a life given over to thought, prayer, and the pursuit of the truth (i.e., the contemplative life) was superior to a life given over to bodily activity (i.e., the active life). At least since the time of Origen (d. ca. 254), the story of Mary and Martha from Luke 10:38–42 has been used to support this view; in the story Jesus commends Mary, who sits at his feet listening, rather than Martha, who is busy in the kitchen.

4. Remigius of Auxerre was a ninth-century monk and scholar. The original source of the quotation is unknown, but Aquinas quotes the same passage in connection with Matthew 5:1 in the *Catena aurea,* his collection of patristic comments on the Gospels. A similar statement can be found in Isidore of Seville's (ca. 560–636) *De Veteri et Novi Testamento quaestiones,* q. 36.

5. The objection is that *whichever* was better—action or contemplation—Jesus should have done *only* that thing.

6. Here we see one of the chief ways in which Thomas understands *convenientia*—as a way of describing the suitability of certain means to an end. To take an example he uses elsewhere, it might be possible to go on a twenty-mile journey on foot, but it is more "fitting" to use a horse (provided, of course, that the goal of the journey is to get to a certain destination and not to get exercise). Once one understands the goal of the action—to travel to a distant place—one can understand the fittingness of the means chosen.

perish, like the shepherd searching for the lost sheep, and the physician going to the sick."[7]

Third, he came in order that "by him we might have access to God," as it is written in Romans 5:2. And thus it was fitting that he should give people confidence in approaching him by associating familiarly with them. For this reason it is written in Matthew 9:10, "It came to pass as he was sitting . . . in the house, behold, many publicans and sinners came, and sat down with Jesus and his disciples." Jerome comments on this passage, saying, "They had seen the publican who had been converted from a sinful to a better life, and consequently they did not despair of their own salvation."[8]

Reply to 1: Christ wished to make his divinity known through his humanity.[9] And therefore, since it is proper to a human being to do so, he associated with people, at the same time manifesting his divinity to all by preaching and working miracles and by leading a blameless and righteous life among people.

Reply to 2: As stated in the second part (2–2.182.1; 2–2.188.6), the contemplative life is, absolutely speaking, more perfect than the active life, because the latter is taken up with bodily actions. But that form of active life in which someone, by preaching and teaching, delivers to others the fruits of contemplation is more perfect than the life that is solely contemplative, because such a life is built on an abundance of contemplation. And consequently such was the life chosen by Christ.[10]

---

7. Like the quotation from Regimus (see note 4, above), this quotation ascribed to Chrysostom is also found in Aquinas's *Catena aurea*, on Luke 4:42, though it is not found in any of Chrysostom's extant works.

One might also note that the second example does not work now that doctors do not make house calls.

8. Aquinas describes three "ends" or "goals" of the incarnation: (1) to manifest the truth; (2) to free people from sin; and (3) to open a path to life with God. He feels no compulsion to settle on the one "right" account of what God was doing in becoming human; Thomas recognizes that there are a number of effects of the incarnation and that these converge in order to bring human beings to salvation.

9. The objection presumes that if Christ were to act like a normal human being—in this case, living with other people—such actions would somehow "mask" his divinity. Aquinas, on the other hand, holds that the humanity of Christ, his human words and actions, are the means by which God is manifested. Like the first objection in 3.16.1, this objection presumes that humanity and divinity are *formae diversae* and that Jesus's being and acting fully human must be to the detriment of his being and acting fully divine. But as we have seen, Aquinas does not think of humanity and divinity as opposites in this sense (see 3.16, note 20).

10. Aquinas was a member of the Order of Preachers (the Dominicans), which, along with the Franciscans, represented an innovation in religious life. Prior to the advent of the Dominicans and Franciscans in the thirteenth century, "religious life" (i.e., men and women living under vows of poverty, celibacy, and obedience) primarily took the form of monks and nuns living in monasteries that were, at least in theory, devoted to the contemplative life and had limited contact with the world. The active work of Christian charity and preaching belonged to parish priests who were called "secular clergy" because they lived in the world (*saeculum*). What Dominic and Francis introduced was a form of religious community that sought to combine the contemplative and active lives, whereby members of the community would devote themselves to both prayer and service of the church.

Reply to 3: "Christ's action is our instruction."[11] And therefore, in order to give an example to preachers that they should not always be before the public, our Lord sometimes withdrew from the crowd. We are told of three reasons for his doing this. Sometimes it was for the sake of bodily rest; therefore in Mark 6:31 it is stated that our Lord said to his disciples, "Come apart into a desert place, and rest a little. For there were many coming and going, and they did not even have time to eat." Sometimes it was for the sake of prayer; thus it is written in Luke 6:12, "It happened in those days that he went out to a mountain to pray, and he passed the whole night in prayer to God." On this passage Ambrose remarks that "by his example he instructs us in the precepts of virtue" (*Commentary on Luke*, bk. 5). Sometimes he did so in order to teach us to avoid human approval. For this reason, commenting on Matthew 5:1—that Jesus, "seeing the multitude, went up into a mountain"—Chrysostom says, "By sitting, not in the city and in the market-place, but on a mountain and in a place of solitude, he taught us to do nothing for show and to withdraw from the crowd, especially when we have to speak of important things" (*Homilies on Matthew*, sermon 15).

3.40.3

Whether Christ should have led a life of poverty in this world?

It would seem that Christ should not have led a life of poverty in this world.[12]

As Thomas notes, he argues earlier in the *Summa* that although the contemplative life is superior to the active life (because thought or contemplation is the activity that makes human beings the distinctive kind of animals that they are), the *best* life would be one that combined the two, so that the benefits of contemplation could be shared with others.

11. This is a point Aquinas stresses repeatedly: Christ is to be our example. In this particular case, he is an example for preachers to teach not just by words but by example. Thomas is perhaps quoting Innocent III (1160–1216), *Sermon 22 de tempore*.

12. This may not seem to be a pressing christological question, but it was in fact a controversial issue in the thirteenth and fourteenth centuries. The new "mendicant" or "begging" orders—the Franciscans and Dominicans—both embraced poverty as an important part of their life, which distinguished them from earlier communities of monks, who typically owned land that earned an income for their monastery.

"Poverty" did not mean destitution but the renunciation of the ownership of property, not only by the individual members of the religious order (monks did not own any personal property) but by the order itself. Thus the houses the early Dominicans lived in were not owned by the Dominican order but by the church; they were then "loaned" to the Dominicans for their use (this practice continued, at least officially, until the fifteenth century).

The radicals among the Franciscans (knows as the "Spirituals") held that Christ lived a life of absolute poverty and that poverty was required for a perfect life. This view led to great controversy within the Franciscan order and within the church as a whole, and in the fourteenth century Pope John XXII condemned the proposition that Christ lived a life of absolute poverty. The Dominicans tended to have a more moderate approach to poverty. As we shall see, Aquinas

1. Christ should have taken up the most worthy form of life. But the most worthy form of life is that which is midway between riches and poverty,[13] for it is written in Proverbs 30:8, "Give me neither beggary [*mendicitatem*] nor riches; give me only the necessities of life." Therefore Christ should not have led a life of poverty, but of moderation.

2. External wealth is intended for bodily use, with regard to food and clothing. But in the matter of food and clothing, Christ led an ordinary life, following the way of life of those among whom he lived. Therefore it seems that he should also have observed the ordinary manner of life as to riches and poverty, and have avoided extreme poverty.

3. Christ invited people to imitate most particularly his example of humility, according to Matthew 11:29, "Learn from me, because I am meek and humble of heart." But humility is commendable most particularly in the rich; thus it is written in 1 Timothy 6:17, "Command the rich of this world not to be haughty." Therefore it seems that Christ should not have chosen a life of poverty.

On the contrary: It is written in Matthew 8:20, "The Son of Man has nowhere to lay his head," as if saying, as Jerome observes, "Why do you desire to follow me for the sake of riches and worldly gain, since I am so poor that I do not have even the smallest dwelling place, and I am sheltered by a roof that is not mine?" (*Commentary on Matthew,* bk. 1) And regarding Matthew 17:26, "That we may not scandalize them, go to the sea," Jerome says, "This incident, understood literally, edifies those who hear it; they are told that our Lord was so poor that he had not the means to pay the tax for himself and his apostles" (*Commentary on Matthew,* bk. 3).

I answer: It was appropriate for Christ to lead a life of poverty in this world. First, because this was in keeping with the duty of preaching, which he says in Mark 1:38 is the purpose for which he came, "Let us go into the neighboring towns and cities, that I may preach there also; because that is what I came for." Now in order that the preachers of God's word may be able to give all their time to preaching, they must be absolutely free from care of worldly matters, which is impossible for those who possess wealth. For this reason our Lord himself, when sending the apostles to preach, said to them, "Do not possess gold nor silver" (Matthew 10:9). And the apostles themselves say in Acts 6:2, "It is not reasonable that we should leave the word [of God] and serve tables."[14]

---

holds that poverty is not a good in itself but is the most "fitting" form of life for one who wishes to be a follower of Christ.

13. Though Aquinas goes on to cite the book of Proverbs, the real source behind this objection is Aristotle's notion of the "golden mean"—that is, the idea that virtue is to be found not in extremes but in the position between two extremes.

14. Here Aquinas is considering the practical usefulness of traveling preachers not having possessions. There is no mystique attached to poverty itself; it is simply that if one is constantly worrying about her investment portfolio, she is not going to have much time or energy for preaching the gospel.

Second, because just as he took bodily death upon himself in order to bestow spiritual life on us, so he bore bodily poverty, in order to enrich us spiritually, according to 2 Corinthians 8:9, "You know the grace of our Lord Jesus Christ: that he became poor for our sakes so that through his poverty we might be rich."[15]

Third, because if he were rich his preaching might be ascribed to greed. For this reason Jerome says about Matthew 10:9, that if the disciples had possessed wealth "they would have seemed to preach in order to gain money, not for the salvation of humankind" (*Commentary on Matthew,* bk. 1). And the same reason applies to Christ.

Fourth, so that the power of his divinity might be shown to be greater, to the degree that he seemed more lowly by reason of his poverty.[16] Therefore, in a sermon of the Council of Ephesus we read, "He chose all that was poor and despicable, all that was of small account and hidden from the majority, that his divinity may be recognized as having transformed the terrestrial sphere. For this reason he chose a poor maid for his mother, a poorer homeland, and lived in want. Learn this from the manger."

Reply to 1: Those who wish to live virtuously need to avoid both an abundance of riches and beggary, insofar as these are occasions of sin; for an abundance of riches is an occasion for being proud, and beggary is an occasion of thieving and lying or even of perjury. But since Christ was incapable of sin, he did not have the same motive as Solomon for avoiding these things.[17] Likewise, not every kind of begging is an occasion of theft and perjury, as Solomon seems to add (Proverbs 30:8), but only involuntary poverty, which a person will commit theft and perjury in order to avoid. But voluntary poverty is not open to this danger, and such was the poverty chosen by Christ.[18]

Reply to 2: One may live an ordinary way of life with regard to food and clothing, not only by possessing riches, but also by receiving the necessities of life from those who are rich.[19] This is what happened in regard to Christ. For it is written in Luke 8:2–3 that certain women followed Christ and "provided for him from their resources." As Jerome says against Vigilantius,[20] "It was a

15. The Vulgate reads, "that he became poor for your sakes that through his poverty you might be rich" (see 1–2.3, note 3). Here Aquinas seems to be attaching more than simply a practical value to poverty; it also has for him what we might call a symbolic value. The "poverty" that Christ takes on in becoming human—giving up his heavenly status in order to dwell with us on earth—is symbolized by the poverty of his earthly life.

16. This is again what we might call a "symbolic fittingness" of poverty. God's power is better manifested through humble people than through great ones.

17. King Solomon was traditionally thought to be the author of the book of Proverbs, which is quoted in the first objection.

18. Thomas makes clear in this reply that the poverty he is talking about is *voluntary* poverty, not the poverty that circumstances might force upon a person.

19. The Parma edition of the *Summa* reads "*from women* and from those who are rich."

20. The quotation is from Jerome's commentary on Matthew but addresses more or less the same issue as Jerome's polemical *Contra Vigilantium*: whether ministers of the church should be financially supported by the faithful.

Jewish custom and not thought wrong, following the ancient tradition of their nation, for women to provide their instructors with food and clothing out of their private means. But because this might give scandal to the Gentiles, Paul says that he gave it up" (*Commentary on Matthew,* bk. 4, on Matthew 27:55). Thus their communal living made it possible for them not to possess wealth, without their task of preaching being hindered by anxiety.[21]

Reply to 3: Humility is not greatly to be praised in one who is poor because of necessity. But in one who, like Christ, is poor willingly, poverty itself is a sign of great humility.[22]

3.40.4

Whether Christ abided by the Law?

It would seem that Christ did not abide by the Law.[23]

1. The Law prohibited any work being done on the Sabbath (Exodus 20:8, 31:13; Deuteronomy 5:12), since God "rested on the seventh day from all his work that he had done" (Genesis 2:2). But Christ healed a person on the Sabbath, and commanded him to take up his bed (John 5:5–9). Therefore it seems that he did not abide by the Law.

2. Christ did as he taught; according to Acts 1:1, "Jesus began to do and to teach." But he himself taught in Matthew 15:11 that "not everything that goes into the mouth defiles a person," and this is contrary to the injunction of the

21. Thus poverty, as Thomas means it here, does not involve necessarily going naked or hungry; rather it involves not possessing the means of obtaining food and clothing. As mentioned before (see note 12, above), for several centuries not only did individual Dominicans renounce personal ownership, but the Dominican order as a whole did not own property, having it, as it were, held in trust by the church. Of course, this system *can* turn poverty into a less-than-convincing facade, in which one owns nothing but lives quite comfortably—even luxuriously. One is reminded of the old joke in which a young man, upon looking at the lavish residence in which members of a religious order lived, commented, "If this is poverty, I can't wait to see chastity!"

22. Again, we see that what Thomas is talking about is voluntary poverty, not destitution. In sum, Thomas's remarks in this article suggest that he thinks it is fitting for Christ to have been poor: (1) for practical reasons—he could better accomplish his mission of preaching the Kingdom of God if he was not burdened with property; and (2) for "symbolic" reasons—Christ's poverty better manifested how the power of God is defined by Christ's humility. In both cases, we see that for Aquinas poverty is in no sense virtuous in and of itself. Indeed, poverty that is thrust upon people often causes them to become *less* virtuous. In the case of Jesus, his poverty was willingly taken on for the sake of his divine mission. And in the case of Christians, voluntary poverty frees one to be a follower and imitator of Christ, which is the path to holiness.

23. "Law" here refers, of course, to the Old Testament Law, the Torah. Thomas is not asking whether or not Christ was an obedient subject of the Roman Empire (or of any other empire). Indeed, the real issue is not whether Jesus's behavior was "lawful" in either the civil or religious sense. The real issue is the relationship between the Old Covenant that God established with Israel and the New Covenant established through Christ. Thomas is, in fact, extraordinarily interested in the Law of the Old Covenant, devoting seven questions to it (1–2.98–105) in the *Summa theologiae.*

Law, which declared that a person was made unclean by eating and touching certain animals, as stated in Leviticus 11. Therefore it seems that he did not himself abide by the Law.

3. One who consents seems to be judged in the same way as one who acts, according to Romans 1:32, "Not only those who do them, but also those who consent to those who do them." But Christ, by excusing his disciples, consented to their breaking the Law by plucking the ears of corn on the Sabbath, as is related in Matthew 12:1–8. Therefore it seems that Christ did not abide by the Law.[24]

On the contrary: It is written in Matthew 5:17, "Do not think that I have come to destroy the Law or the Prophets." Commenting on these words, Chrysostom says, "He fulfilled the Law . . . first, by transgressing none of the precepts of the Law; second, by justifying us through faith, which the Law according to the letter was unable to do" (*Homily on Matthew* 16).

I answer: In all things Christ abided by the precepts of the Law. As a sign of this, he even wished to be circumcised, for circumcision is a kind of declaration of one's intention of fulfilling the Law, according to Galatians 5:3, "I testify to every person accepting circumcising, that he is a debtor to do the whole Law."

Indeed, Christ wished to abide by the Law, in the first place to show his approval of the Old Law.[25] Second, that by obeying the Law he might perfect it and bring it to an end in himself, so as to show that he was the fulfillment for which it was ordained.[26] Third, to deprive the Jews of an excuse for slandering

---

24. The three objections, taken together, seem to cover all the ways in which one might violate a law: in thought (obj. 3), word (obj. 2), and deed (obj. 1).

25. Following Paul's statement in Romans 7:12, "The Law is holy, and the commandment is holy and just and good," Aquinas sees Christ's obedience to the Law as an affirmation of the fundamental rightness of the way of life laid down in the Torah. He says in 1–2.107.1 that both the Old Law and the New Law of Christ have one and the same goal: the subjection of human beings to God.

26. Though Aquinas affirms the Law, he also sees it as ultimately inadequate to the goal that it pursues. It can orient us toward obedience to God; but because it can direct only our outward actions, it cannot itself bring us to that obedience. Thus Christ, through his New Law, must "bring it to an end," in the sense of bringing it to the goal it seeks to obtain, which is the presence of the Holy Spirit in the believer through grace. Christ does this by means of his death and resurrection. Thus Christ is the "end" of the Law, not in the sense of terminating it or making it null and void, but in the sense that he is himself the goal toward which it aims and in accordance with which it is to be practiced.

For Aquinas this means, in practice, that Christians must obey the moral injunctions of the Law, summed up in the Ten Commandments, because these still serve to orient human beings to God. But Christians no longer obey the ceremonial injunctions of the Law, since all of these—including circumcision, the various sacrifices, and the regulations regarding food—served to point toward the coming of Christ. Now that Christ has come, it would be misleading to continue to practice these things because it would give the impression that one does not believe the Messiah has come. Likewise the judicial injunctions of the Law—those that regulated the common life of the nation Israel—are no longer binding because with the coming of Christ the distinction between Jew and Gentile has been abolished, thus abolishing the need for a law to regulate the life of the Jewish people as a distinctive community.

him. Fourth, in order to deliver people from subjection to the Law, according to Galatians 4:4–5, "God sent his Son . . . made under the Law, that he might redeem those who were under the Law."[27]

Reply to 1: Our Lord excuses himself from any transgression of the Law in this matter, in three ways. First, the command to keep the Sabbath holy does not forbid divine work, but human work, for though God ceased on the seventh day from the creation of new creatures, yet he always works by preserving and guiding his creatures. Christ's doing of miracles was a divine work; therefore he says in John 5:17, "My Father works until now; and I work."[28]

Second, he excuses himself on the ground that this precept does not forbid works that are necessary for bodily health. Thus he says in Luke 13:15, "Does not every one of you on the Sabbath untie his ox or his donkey from the manger and lead them to water?" And farther on (Luke 14:5), "Which of you has an ass or an ox fall into a pit, and does not immediately draw him out on the day of the Sabbath?" It is clear, however, that the miraculous works done by Christ related to health of body and soul.[29]

Third, because this commandment does not forbid works pertaining to the worship of God. Thus he says in Matthew 12:5, "Have you not read in the Law that on the Sabbath the priests in the Temple violate the Sabbath and are without blame?" And in John 7:23 it is written that "a man receives circumcision on the Sabbath." Now when Christ commanded the paralytic to carry his bed on the Sabbath-day, this pertained to the worship of God, that is, to the praise of God's power.[30]

---

27. Thomas derives this ambiguity of "subjection" to the Law from Paul. In one sense it is good to be subject to the Law, because through the Law one is subjected to God. In this sense, Christ willingly subjects himself to the Law. In another sense, one can be subject to the Law by being oppressed by it or, more precisely, by being oppressed by fear of it, because one has within oneself a contrary law that Paul calls "the law of sin" and that Aquinas identified as the tendency toward sin and away from God that medieval theologians called the *fomes peccati* (the "kindling" of sin). For Aquinas, Christ is subject to the Law in the first sense in order to release those who are subject to it in the second sense.

28. For Thomas, Christ's miracles differ from other miracles in that they are direct actions of God, not the actions of a human being who has been empowered by God. Thus he notes in several places that Christ does not pray before he works miracles, because he does not need to invoke divine power, being *himself* the power of God. Just as the ceaseless work God does in sustaining the world is not a violation of the Sabbath rest, so too the miraculous works of Christ are not a violation of that rest.

29. In this second "excuse" Thomas defends Christ's healing on the Sabbath from the opposite direction of the first defense (which invoked Christ's divinity): even if Christ were merely a human being, it is still allowable for a human being to do good works on the Sabbath.

30. The connection Thomas draws here between miracles and worship indicates that for him a miracle is not simply a suspension of the ordinary operations of the world (which he certainly thinks it is) but also an occasion of wonder, which is another meaning of the Latin word *miracula*. Christ works his miracles not only to get a job done—like a doctor healing a patient—but also to incite people to praise God—like a priest leading worship.

And thus it is clear that he did not break the Sabbath, although the Jews threw this false accusation in his face, saying in John 9:16, "This man, who does not keep the Sabbath, is not of God."

Reply to 2: Christ wished to show by those words that one is not made spiritually unclean by the use of any sort of foods considered according to their nature, but only according to some symbolic meaning [*significationem*] they have. Certain foods are called "unclean" in the Law due to some symbolic meaning, and thus Augustine says (*Against Faustus the Manichean*, bk. 6, chap. 7), "If a question be raised about pigs and lambs, both are clean by nature, since 'all God's creatures are good,' but, according to a certain symbolic meaning they have, lambs are clean and pigs unclean."[31]

Reply to 3: The disciples, being hungry, plucked the ears of corn on the Sabbath; but they also are to be excused from transgressing the Law, since they were compelled by hunger. In the same way, David was not a transgressor of the Law when, through being compelled by hunger, he consumed the loaves that it was not lawful for him to eat.[32]

---

31. In his writings against the Manichean bishop Faustus, Augustine says that lambs, because they chew their cud, symbolize people who meditate on and "chew-over" words of wisdom, regurgitated, as it were, "from the stomach of memory to the mouth of reflection." Pigs, on the other hand, symbolize those who take superficial pleasure in wisdom (pigs do, after all, enjoy eating) but do not later reflect on those words.

Like Augustine, Aquinas justifies Jesus's violation of the letter of the Law by a kind of appeal to the spirit: Jesus fulfills the inward intention of the Law in such a way that literal external obedience is no longer necessary. This is particularly the case with the parts of the Law regulating ceremonial and religious practice, though not with those parts regulating moral conduct.

32. This, of course, is the explanation Christ himself gives in Matthew 12:3–4.

Q U E S T I O N 42

CHRIST'S TEACHING

3.42.4

Whether Christ should have committed his teaching to writing?[1]

It would seem that Christ should have committed his teaching to writing.

1. Writing was invented to entrust a teaching to memory for the future. But Christ's teaching was destined to endure forever, according to Luke 21:33, "Heaven and earth shall pass away, but my words shall not pass away." Therefore it seems that Christ should have committed his teaching to writing.

2. The Old Law was a foreshadowing of Christ,[2] according to Hebrews 10:1, "The Law has a shadow of the good things to come." But the Old Law was put into writing by God, according to Exodus 24:12, "I will give you two tables of stone and the Law, and the commandments that I have written." Therefore it seems that Christ also should have put his teaching into writing.

3. It pertained to Christ, who came to "enlighten those who sit in darkness and in the shadow of death," as it is said in Luke 1:79, to remove occasions of error and to open up the road to faith. But he should have done this by put-

1. Again, this seems like a peculiar question. Part of Aquinas's genius is the way in which he can take a peculiar question and make an interesting theological point with it.

2. On the Old Law as the foreshadowing or "type" of the New Law, see 1.1, note 39. The objection seems to be arguing that if something is the case in a lesser matter (i.e., the Old Law was written) then it must be the case in a greater matter (the New Law should be written).

ting his teaching into writing, for Augustine says in *On Agreement among the Evangelists* (bk. 1, chap. 7), "There are some who wonder why our Lord wrote nothing, so that we have to believe what others have written about him. This is asked especially by those pagans who do not dare to blame or blaspheme Christ, and who attribute to him a most excellent, although merely human, wisdom. These say that the disciples made out the master to be more than he really was when they said that he was the Son of God and the Word of God, by whom all things were made."[3] And farther on he adds, "It seems as though they were prepared to believe whatever he might have written of himself, but not what others at their discretion preached about him." Therefore it seems that Christ himself should have committed his teaching to writing.

On the contrary: No books written by him are found in the canon of Scripture.[4]

I answer: It was fitting that Christ should not commit his teaching to writing.

First, on account of his dignity. For the more excellent the teacher, the more excellent should be his way of teaching. Consequently it was fitting for Christ, as the most excellent of teachers, to adopt that way of teaching that would imprint his teaching on the hearts of his hearers. Thus it is written in Matthew 7:29 that "he was teaching them as one having power." And so even among the Gentiles: Pythagoras and Socrates, who were most excellent teachers, were unwilling to write anything. For writings are a means to an end: imprinting a teaching on the hearts of the hearers.[5]

Second, on account of the excellence of Christ's teaching, which cannot be encompassed in a text; according to John 21:25, "There are also many other things that Jesus did, which, if they all were written, the world itself, I think, would not be able to contain the books that would have to be written." Augustine explains this passage by saying, "We are not to believe that the world could not contain them with respect to physical space . . . but that they could not be comprehended by the capacity of the readers" (*Homilies on the Gospel of John,* sermon 124, no. 8). But if Christ had committed his teaching to writ-

---

3. This argument is still current today. There are many people who claim that Jesus was simply a wise man and that it was his followers (especially St. Paul) who turned him into a God. Such people usually think they are being quite innovative.

4. Note that Aquinas does not explicitly cite an authority here, as is his normal practice. However, the authority he invokes implicitly is that of the church, which gathered together the list or "canon" of the books of Scripture.

The *sed contra* can also give us some insight into the nature of the *ex convenientia* form of argumentation: the initial response to the objection is simply that Jesus did not, in fact, write his teachings down, implying that he must have had good reasons for doing things this way. An argument *ex convenientia* is one that tries to understand those reasons.

5. Why is it "more excellent" to teach verbally than through writing? Aquinas sees an immediacy to verbal teaching, from which written teaching is one step removed. Speech imprints a teaching directly upon the hearer's heart, whereas writing seems to add a layer of mediation.

ing, people would have thought his teaching as no more profound than what appears on the surface of the writing.[6]

Third, so that his teaching might reach all in an orderly manner:[7] that is to say, he himself teaching his disciples directly, and they subsequently teaching others by speaking and writing. But if he himself had written, his teaching would have reached all immediately.[8] Therefore it is said of God's Wisdom in Proverbs 9:3 that "she has sent her handmaidens to summon to the fortress."

It is to be observed, however, that, as Augustine says, some of the Gentiles thought that Christ wrote certain books containing the magical art by which he worked miracles, which Christian discipline condemns. "And yet those who claim to have read those books of Christ do none of those things that they marvel at his doing according to those same books. Indeed, it is by a divine judgment that they are so far mistaken as to assert that these books were letters

6. Consider the difference between the place of sacred writings in Christianity and in Islam. Muslims believe the Qu'ran to be a direct dictation to the prophet Muhammad from God, through an angel. As such it is quite *literally* the word of God. For Christians, on the other hand, it is Jesus who is the Word of God, and Scripture is what bears witness to that Word. Scripture is always secondary. What Aquinas seems to be saying is that if Jesus had written his teaching down we might be tempted to think that the written text is what is of primary importance, rather than Jesus himself.

Thomas implies that the "personal" character of divine revelation in Christ is part and parcel of God's incomprehensibility. Since revelation is first and foremost the person of Christ and not a text, and since the act of existence of Christ's person is the divine act of existence (see 3.17.2), and since the divine act of existence cannot be comprehended by human beings (see 1–2.3, note 11), God's self-revelation is in fact a revelation that we can never fully grasp. At the end of his commentary on John's Gospel, Thomas writes, "To write about each and every word and deed of Christ is to reveal the power of every word and deed. Now the words and deeds of Christ are also those of God. Thus, if one tried to write and tell of the nature of every one, he could not do so; indeed, the entire world could not do this. This is because even an infinite number of human words cannot equal the one Word of God (chap. 21, lecture 6, §2660).

7. Note Aquinas's typical emphasis on hierarchical order. As always, however, the point of hierarchy is not for the higher to dominate the lower, but, to use a modern term, for the higher to empower the lower, to dignify and elevate it. Christ entrusts the writing-down of his teaching to his apostles not because it is a menial task that he delegates to subordinates, but because the apostles are ennobled by being given this role in the imparting of divine revelation. They are, as it were, "secondary causes" of revelation. Aquinas brings this out clearly in his commentary on John's Gospel, where he writes in reference to John the Baptist: "God wanted to have certain witnesses, not because he needed their testimony, but to ennoble those whom he appointed witnesses. Thus we see in the order of the universe that God produces certain effects by means of intermediate causes, not because he is himself unable to produce them without these intermediaries, but he deigns to confer on them the dignity of causality because he wishes to ennoble these intermediate causes. Similarly, even though God could have enlightened all men by himself and led them to knowledge of himself, yet to preserve due order in things and to ennoble certain men, he willed that divine knowledge reach men through certain other men" (chap. 1, lecture 4, §119).

8. The response to objection 1 helps clarify Aquinas's point here. Jesus relates to us not simply as individuals, but as members of a community—his body the church. The fact that we depend on the writings of the apostles bears witness to this communal character of the Christian faith.

addressed to Peter and Paul, because they saw them depicted in many places accompanying Christ. No wonder that the inventors were deceived by the painters; in fact, as long as Christ lived in the mortal flesh with his disciples, Paul was not a disciple of his" (*On Agreement among the Evangelists,* bk. 1, chaps. 9–10).[9]

Reply to 1: As Augustine says in the same book (*On Agreement among the Evangelists,* bk. 1, chap. 35), "All of his disciples are, as it were, members of the body of which Christ is the head. Consequently, when they put into writing what he showed and said to them, we must by no means say that he wrote nothing; for his members put forth that which they knew from his speaking as their head. Indeed, at his command they wrote whatever he wished us to read concerning his deeds and words, as if they were his hands."[10]

Reply to 2: Since the Old Law was given under the form of perceptible signs, it was also therefore fittingly written with perceptible signs. But Christ's teaching, which is "the law of the spirit of life" (Romans 8:2), should be "written not with ink, but with the Spirit of the living God, not on tablets of stone, but on the fleshly tablets of the heart," as the Apostle says in 2 Corinthians 3:3.[11]

Reply to 3: Those who were unwilling to believe what the apostles wrote of Christ would not have believed the writings of Christ himself, whom they thought to have worked miracles by magical means.

9. This passage from Augustine refers to pagan writers who claimed that Jesus wrote letters to Peter and Paul, thinking mistakenly that Paul had been a disciple of Jesus during his earthly life. These writers made the mistake because they had seen pictures that, according to early Christian practice, depicted Paul standing alongside Christ.

10. Here we see Aquinas taking over from St. Augustine a quite literal understanding of the church as a body of which Christ is the head. This view finds its ultimate origin in St. Paul (see Colossians 1:18: "He is the head of the body, the church"). For Augustine and Aquinas there is a real sense in which we can say that Christ *did* write down his teaching, because the church, which is his body, wrote down those teachings.

11. Here Thomas reiterates what he sees as the fundamental distinction between the Old Law of the Torah and the New Law of the Gospel: the former prescribes outward actions, whereas the latter is a new, internal principle of action.

QUESTION 46

THE SUFFERING OF CHRIST

3.46.1

Whether it was necessary for Christ to suffer for the deliverance of the human race?

It would seem that it was not necessary for Christ to suffer for the deliverance of the human race.[1]

1. The human race could not be delivered except by God, according to Isaiah 45:21, "Am not I the Lord, and there is no God else besides me? A just God and a savior, there is none besides me." But no necessity can compel God, for this would be contrary to his omnipotence. Therefore it was not necessary for Christ to suffer.

---

1. This article does not begin, as do so many in this section of the *Summa,* by inquiring into the *convenientia* of some aspect of the story of Jesus (see 3.1, note 1). Rather, Aquinas is asking about the *necessitas* of Jesus's suffering. Thomas has already discussed the sense in which the incarnation of God the Son is "necessary" (see 3.1.2); here he takes up the more specific topic of the necessity of the specific *form* in which the Son becomes incarnate: that of the Suffering Servant of God.

This article and the one following are important for examining the particular kind of necessity that is associated with "fittingness," which is discussed explicitly in the third article of this question (3.46.3). It is also important to note that these articles are inquiring about the relationship between the suffering of Christ and human deliverance or "liberation" from sin. Aquinas has already indicated (3.1.2) and will indicate again (3.46.3) that more is involved in human salvation than simple liberation from sin.

2. What is necessary is opposed to what is voluntary. But Christ suffered in accord with his own will, for it is written in Isaiah 53:7, "He was offered because it was his own will." Therefore it was not necessary for him to suffer.

3. As is written (Psalm 25:10), "All the ways of the Lord are mercy and truth." But it does not seem necessary on the part of the divine mercy that he should suffer, for it bestows gifts freely, and so would seem to forgive debts without repayment. Nor is it necessary on the part of divine justice, according to which humanity deserved everlasting condemnation. Therefore it does not seem necessary that Christ should have suffered for humanity's liberation.

4. The angelic nature is more excellent than the human, as is clear from Dionysius (*On the Divine Names,* chap. 4, no. 2). But Christ did not suffer to repair the angelic nature that had sinned. Therefore, apparently, neither was it necessary for him to suffer for the salvation of the human race.[2]

On the contrary: It is written in John 3:14, "As Moses lifted up the serpent in the desert, so must the Son of Man be lifted up, that whoever believes in him may not perish, but may have eternal life."

I answer: As the Philosopher teaches in the *Metaphysics* (bk. 5, chap. 5, 1015ª), the word "necessary" is used in several ways. In one way it means anything that by its nature cannot be otherwise, and in this way it is evident that it was not necessary for Christ to suffer, either on the part of God or on the part of humanity.[3]

In another way, a thing may said to be necessary from some cause quite apart from itself. If this is either an efficient or a moving cause, then it brings about the necessity of compulsion; for example, when someone cannot get away due to the force of someone else holding him.[4] But if the external factor that induces necessity is a goal, then it will be said to be necessary on account of presupposing such a goal—that is to say, when some particular goal either cannot exist at all, or cannot exist in a fitting manner, unless such an end be presupposed.[5]

---

2. If Christ could have saved the angels without suffering, he *certainly* could also have saved human beings.

3. We might call this "intrinsic necessity." For example, a human being *must* be a rational animal, because that is the nature (or definition) of a human being. For Aquinas, even God is subject to this sort of "necessity" inasmuch as God cannot be weak (since his nature is to be omnipotent) or ignorant (since his nature is to be all-knowing) or evil (since he is goodness itself). Aquinas does not see such necessity as a limitation on God; rather it is simply a matter of God being what he is (which we can try to grasp by denying him creaturely imperfections).

In the case of God's action in history, however, we cannot say that, *by definition,* God is a being who redeems the world through the suffering of his Son (not least because we do not have a definition of God), nor is being redeemed by the sufferings of Christ part of the definition of human beings.

4. On efficient (or "moving") causality, see 1.2, note 37.

5. The crucial difference Aquinas notes here concerns the kinds of necessity entailed in efficient (or "moving") and final causality (see 1.2, note 49). He also mentions a difference in

It was not necessary, then, for Christ to suffer from necessity of compulsion, either on the part of God, who determined that Christ should suffer, or on the part of Christ himself, who suffered voluntarily. Yet it was necessary from necessity of the goal.[6] This can be understood in three ways. First of all, on our part, who have been delivered by his suffering [*per eius passionem*],[7] according to John 3:14, "The Son of Man must be lifted up, that whoever believes in him may not perish, but may have eternal life." Second, on the part of Christ himself, who merited the glory of being exalted through the lowliness of his suffering. This is related to what is said in Luke 24:26, "Was it not necessary for Christ to suffer these things, and so to enter into his glory?" Third, on the part of God, whose determination regarding the suffering of Christ—foretold in the Scriptures and prefigured in the observances of the

---

the way that various means might be "necessary" to a particular end or goal. This distinction, between existing at all and existing in a fitting manner, is discussed in 3.1.2, above.

An efficient cause makes something necessary in the sense of "compulsory," whereas a final cause makes something necessary because certain means fit with certain ends. Take the example: "It is necessary to pay taxes." This statement could refer to the fact that the IRS would throw me in jail if I did not pay my taxes. In that case, the IRS would be an efficient cause compelling me to pay taxes. However, the statement could also refer to the fact that if we want our government to provide certain services to its citizens, then we had better pay taxes. In that case, the goal of having certain services provided would be the final cause, and paying taxes would be a fitting means to that goal. The necessity in this second case is different from that in the first, since it is not a matter of absolute compulsion. One could conceivably seek to reach the desired end by some other means: the government could raise money with an annual telethon; or the U.S. Navy could take up piracy and steal what we need from other countries. Paying taxes is simply the most "fitting" (*conveniens*) way for a government to fund itself.

6. That is, the suffering of Christ was the fitting means of reaching a particular goal (or goals).

7. The Latin word *passio* does not have the same meaning as our modern English word "passion." Most generally, *passio* is something that happens to us rather than to something that we do; a passion is the antithesis of an action. More specifically, *passio* refers to any feeling or emotion; in Aquinas's terminology, sadness, anger, and sexual desire are all "passions." Most specifically, *passio* means "suffering," and this is the sense in which Aquinas uses it here. I have chosen in most cases to translate *passio* as "suffering" for two reasons. First, in common English usage "passion" denotes strong emotion and, more specifically, sexual desire. For those who know only of "passionate kisses" and such, the term might be initially misleading. This, of course, is a fairly superficial concern, one that could be cleared up by a simple explanation. My second reason carries more weight. For some people "the passion" has an exclusively religious meaning that can be misleading when reading Aquinas, insofar as "the passion" denotes a series of "religious" events—those recounted in the "passion narratives"—rather than Jesus's experience of *suffering itself*. It is all very well and true to say that the events of Good Friday are key to human salvation, but Aquinas's point is, I think, more specific. It is the *suffering* of Christ, what is done to him, his *pathos*, that is key. If this sense of *passio* is lost, then much of the offense is removed from what Thomas has to say, and one might well wonder why he has to wrestle so ferociously with the notion of Christ's passion. But if we keep in focus that Thomas is trying to understand the necessity and fittingness of God incarnate *suffering* for us, then his teaching can regain some of its shocking vividness.

Old Testament—had to be fulfilled. And this is what is said in Luke 22:22, "The Son of Man is going his way according to that which is determined"; and in Luke 24:44, "These are the words that I spoke to you while I was still with you, that all the things that are written in the Law of Moses, and in the prophets, and in the psalms concerning me must be fulfilled"; and in Luke 24:46, "Thus it is written and thus it was necessary for Christ to suffer and to rise again from the dead."[8]

Reply to 1: This argument is based on the necessity of compulsion on God's part.

Reply to 2: This argument is based on the necessity of compulsion on the part of Christ as a human being.[9]

Reply to 3: It was in conformity with [*conveniens*] both Christ's mercy and his justice that humanity should be delivered by his suffering. With justice, because by his suffering Christ made repayment for the sin of the human race, and so the human race was set free by Christ's justice. With mercy, for human beings could not themselves repay for the sin of all human nature, as was said earlier (3.1.2), and therefore God gave his Son to repay on behalf of the human race, according to Romans 3:24–25, "Being justified freely by his grace, through the redemption that is in Christ Jesus, whom God has set forth as a reconciling offering, through faith."[10] And this came from a mercy more abundant than if he had forgiven sins without repayment. Therefore it is said in Ephesians 2:4, "God, who is rich in mercy, on account of his immeasurable charity by which he loved us, even when we were dead in sins, made us alive together in Christ."

Reply to 4: Unlike human sin, the sin of the angels was irreparable, as is clear from what was said earlier, in the first part (1.64.2).[11]

8. Thomas thinks that there are three different goals we might think of for which Jesus's suffering served as the means: (1) our salvation, (2) his own glorification, and (3) the fulfillment of God's plan as revealed in the rituals and prophecies of the Old Testament. Here we see again the logic of *conveniens*—these different goals "come together" in being served by the single means of Christ's suffering.

9. In his replies to objections 1 and 2 Aquinas says, in essence, that the objections are correct if one is speaking of necessity in the sense of compulsion. However, they are inadequate inasmuch as neither God nor Christ is compelled in this matter, and inasmuch as the objections fail to recognize that there is another meaning that can be given to the statement "Jesus had to suffer"—namely, that the suffering of Jesus was the most fitting means to an end.

10. Here Aquinas argues that Jesus's suffering was in fact a fitting means to the goal of human salvation (the first of the three goals Aquinas identifies with regard to Jesus's suffering; see note 8, above). The objection argued that to save humanity in this way would seem to be something like a bribe offered to God, an attempt to buy his mercy or to get him to overlook the strictness of his justice. How the suffering of Christ fits with both God's mercy and justice is discussed further in 3.48.2, below.

11. According to an earlier argument of Aquinas's, the wills of the angels are already immovably attached to either good or evil. So Christ does not suffer for the salvation of the angels because the fallen angels—that is, Satan and his demons—do not have the possibility of salvation.

3.46.2

Whether there was any other possible way of human deliverance besides the suffering of Christ?[12]

It would seem that there was no other possible way of human deliverance besides Christ's suffering.

1. Our Lord says in John 12:24, "Unless the grain of wheat falling into the ground dies, it remains alone; but if it dies, it brings forth much fruit." Regarding this verse, St. Augustine observes that "Christ called himself the seed" (*Homilies on the Gospel of John,* sermon 51, no. 9). Consequently, unless he suffered death, he would not otherwise have produced the fruit of our liberation.

2. In Matthew 26:42, our Lord says to the Father, "My Father, if this cup cannot pass me by, but rather I must drink it, your will be done." But he spoke there of the cup of suffering; therefore Christ's suffering could not pass away. Thus Hilary says (*Commentary on Matthew,* chap. 31), "Therefore the cup cannot pass unless he drinks of it, because we cannot be restored except through his suffering."

3. God's justice required that Christ should repay by suffering in order that humanity might be delivered from sin. But Christ cannot let his justice perish, for it is written in 2 Timothy 2:13, "If we do not believe, he remains faithful; he cannot deny himself." But he would deny himself were he to deny his justice, since he is justice itself. Therefore, it seems impossible for humanity to be delivered in some way other than by Christ's suffering.

4. There can be no falsehood underlying the faith. But the fathers of old believed that Christ would suffer.[13] Consequently, it seems that it had to be that Christ should suffer.

On the contrary: Augustine says in *De Trinitate* (bk. 13, chap. 10), "The way in which God deigns to deliver us through the mediator between God and humanity, the human being Jesus Christ, is both good and appropriate to the divine dignity; but let us also show that other possible means were not lacking on God's part, to whose power all things are equally subject."

I answer: A thing may be said to be possible or impossible in two ways: in one way, simply and absolutely; in the other way, based on an assumption.[14]

---

12. Thomas now takes up the question of the "necessity" of Christ's suffering from the opposite direction. Having argued in the previous article that there is a sense in which Christ's suffering was necessary (in the sense of the best means to an end), he asks here whether this sense of "necessity" means that there was absolutely no other way for God to redeem humanity.

13. By "fathers of old" Thomas means the holy people of the Old Testament.

14. To use a somewhat weak analogy, it may not be necessary, absolutely speaking, for me to return home by 6:00 p.m., but presupposing that I have promised my wife that I will be home for dinner, there is a real sense in which I *have to* be home by 6:00, or else be untrue to my word. God, of course, cannot be untrue to his word because this would be a defect, and God is perfect.

Therefore, speaking simply and absolutely, it was possible for God to liberate humanity by some way other than the suffering of Christ, because, as is said in Luke 1:37, "no word is impossible with God." Yet, once a certain assumption is granted, it *was* impossible. Since it is impossible for God's foreknowledge to be deceived and his will or decree to be frustrated, it was not possible, supposing God's foreknowledge and decree regarding Christ's suffering, for Christ not to suffer and, at the same time, for humanity to be delivered in some way other than by Christ's suffering. And the same argument holds for all things foreknown and foreordained by God, as was shown in the first part (1.14.13).[15]

Reply to 1: In this passage our Lord presumes God's foreknowledge and predetermination, according to which it was resolved that the fruit of humanity's salvation should not follow unless Christ suffered.

Reply to 2: We must understand what is quoted in the second objection in the same way [as in the first]. "If this cup cannot pass me by, but rather I must drink it,"—that is to say, because you have so ordained it—therefore he adds, "your will be done."

Reply to 3: Even this justice that requires from the human race satisfaction for sin depends on the divine will; for if he had willed to free humanity from sin without any satisfaction, he would not have acted against justice. For a judge cannot pardon a wrong without penalty while still preserving justice, if his task is to punish wrongs committed against another—for instance, against another person, or against the state, or any leader in higher authority. But God has no one higher than himself, for he is himself the supreme and common good of the whole universe. Consequently, if he forgives sin, which has the character of wrongdoing in that it is committed against him, he injures no one, just as anyone else acts mercifully and not unjustly in overlooking an offense committed against them without any repayment.[16] And so David exclaimed

---

15. Thomas's basic point here is that nothing *compels* God to save us through the sufferings of Christ—this is his freely chosen means of saving us. However, it is an *eternal* choice, not one that God makes at some point in world history. For us, "choosing" to do something involves a process of deliberation that issues in an act of will at a particular moment. But since God exists outside of the flow of time, this cannot be the case with God's choosing.

16. Judges are normally under an obligation to serve the needs of another, whether this be the ruler or, as in the case of democracies, the people themselves. So a judge cannot simply let a bank robber go free because she or he is feeling particularly merciful at that moment. To do so would violate the duty that the judge has to the robber's victims, as well as to society. God, however, is under no such obligation, since God is the one against whom the sin has been committed. Thus God can justly have mercy upon the sinner, since God is the "victim."

There is a deeper point underlying what Aquinas says here. Human judges are always beholden to something that stands above them and by which their own actions can be judged—the law, and ultimately justice itself. However, God is not like a human judge because he is himself the standard by which we judge justice and injustice. Therefore his mercy could never violate his justice because God is justice itself.

when he sought mercy, "Against you only have I sinned" (Psalm 51:4), as if to say, "You can pardon me without injustice."

Reply to 4: Both human faith and the divine Scriptures upon which faith rests are based on the divine foreknowledge and plan. And the same reason holds for that necessity that comes from holding something on faith and for the necessity that arises from the divine foreknowledge and will.[17]

3.46.3

Whether there was any more suitable way of delivering the human race than by Christ's suffering?

It would seem that there was some other more suitable way of delivering the human race than by Christ's suffering.

1. Nature in its operation imitates the divine work, since it is moved and regulated by God. But nature never does anything with two things that could be done with one. Therefore, since God could have liberated humanity solely by his divine will,[18] it does not seem fitting that Christ's suffering should have been added for the liberation of the human race.

2. That which is done through nature is accomplished more fittingly than that which is done through force, because force is a destruction of or lapse from what is according to nature, as is said in the book *On the Heavens*.[19] But Christ's suffering brought about his death by violence. Therefore it would have been more fitting if, instead of suffering, Christ had died a natural death for humanity's liberation.

3. It seems most fitting that whoever keeps something by force and unjustly should be deprived of it by some superior power. Therefore Isaiah 52:3 says, "You were sold for nothing, and you shall be redeemed without money." But the

---

17. Aquinas's basic point in this reply is that humans holding on faith that something will occur does not impose necessity on it anymore than God's foreknowledge of it does. On divine foreknowledge, see 3.1, note 38.

18. See 3.46.2, above, especially the reply to objection 3.

19. See Aquinas's commentary on Aristotle's *On the Heavens* (bk. 2, *lectio* 23), commenting on bk. 2, chap. 13, 294^b-295^a in Aristotle.

I have translated Aquinas's *violentia* as "force" rather than "violence" because the term has a much broader meaning than our modern word "violence." Any force that makes something go against its natural inclination—that is, "a severance or lapse from what is according to nature"—is, in Thomas's terms, "violent." For example, the natural inclination of a stone is to travel downward (Aquinas, of course, knows nothing of gravity, and therefore thinks of "downward tendency" as a property of the stone); therefore, the action of throwing the stone into the air is a "violent" one, in Aquinas's sense of the term. A human death is violent not because it involves shooting or stabbing, but because one does not die a "natural death," such as when one's body simply wears out. If one is killed by a lethal injection and gently drifts off into the Great Beyond, this would still, by Aquinas's definition, be a violent death, even if the injection was administered by a compassionate physician in order to end the suffering of a terminally ill patient.

devil possessed no right over humanity, which he had deceived by guile and held subject in slavery by a sort of force.[20] Therefore it seems most fitting that Christ should have deprived the devil solely by his power and without suffering.

On the contrary: St. Augustine says in *De Trinitate* (bk. 13, chap. 10), "There was no other more fitting way of healing our misery" than by the suffering of Christ.

I answer: Among different means to an end, the more fitting one is that by which various things come together that are themselves helpful to the end.[21] Through the liberation of humanity by Christ's suffering, many things came together for humanity's salvation, beyond deliverance from sin.[22]

First, through his suffering human beings know how much God loves them, and are thereby stirred to love him in return, which is the perfection of human salvation.[23] Therefore the Apostle says in Romans 5, "God reveals his love toward us, for while we were his enemies, Christ died for us."[24] Second, because through

20. The objection attacks a view of the death of Jesus that is sometimes known as the "ransom" theory of the atonement. This view is found in certain early Christian writers who draw upon New Testament texts such as Mark 10:45 ("the Son of Man came not to be served but to serve, and to give his life a *ransom* for many") and 1 Timothy 2:6 ("For there is one God; there is also one mediator between God and humankind, Christ Jesus, himself human, who gave himself a *ransom* for all"). In speaking of Christ as a "ransom," some of these writers seemed to imply that because of human sin the devil had, as it were, taken the human race hostage and Christ was the ransom paid to the devil. Most writers tried to avoid this reading because it seemed to imply that the devil had won something from God.

21. Here Thomas speaks of "fittingness" as *concurrere,* meaning to run or flock together. Once again we see *convenientia* in its root meaning of come (*venire*) together (*con*): a means to an end is fitting if it can gather a number of means together. See 1.3, note 1.

22. Aquinas does not want to tie the death of Christ to a single meaning; the suffering of Jesus on the cross works in a number of ways, which come together to bring about human salvation. Salvation involves having our sins forgiven, but not *only* that. As he has argued in the previous article, God could simply have forgiven our sins by an act of will. But it is fitting that God saves us through Jesus's passion, because it accomplishes more than simply the forgiveness of sins.

23. Christ's willingness to suffer tells us something about the depth of God's love for us and inspires us to try and love God in return. This is the significance of the cross that the philosopher and theologian Peter Abelard (1079–1142) had focused on. Rejecting the notion that God had to buy humanity back from the devil, Abelard saw the death of Jesus as simply a sign of God's love, which worked its effect in the depths of the human heart. Abelard writes: "By the faith which we hold concerning Christ, love is increased in us, by virtue of the conviction that God in Christ has united our human nature to himself and, by suffering in that same nature, has demonstrated to us that perfection of love of which he himself says 'Greater love than this no man has,' etc. So we, through his grace, are joined to him as closely as to our neighbor" (*Commentary on Romans,* bk. 2).

Oversimplified accounts of medieval theology often portray Abelard and Anselm as having diametrically opposed theories of salvation, with Abelard stressing the subjective moral influence exerted by Christ's death and Anselm stressing its nature as an objective act of "satisfaction" or repayment (see 3.48, note 1). However, Thomas, like most medieval theologians, incorporated elements of both of these approaches, without seeing them as contradictory.

24. Here Aquinas is apparently conflating verses 8 and 10 of Romans 5. On Thomas's somewhat free quotation of biblical texts, see 1–2.3, note 3.

his suffering he set us an example of obedience, humility, constancy, justice, and the other virtues that are necessary for humanity's salvation. Therefore it is written in 1 Peter 2:21, "Christ has suffered for us, leaving you an example, that you might follow in his footsteps."[25] Third, because Christ by his suffering not only freed humanity from sin, but also merited justifying grace for us and the glory of perfect happiness, as shall be shown later (3.48.1; 3.49.1, 5).[26] Fourth, because by Christ's sufferings human beings are all the more bound to refrain from sin. As 1 Corinthians 6:20 says, "You are bought with a great price; glorify and bear God in your body." Fifth, because Christ's suffering results in a greater dignity [for humanity]; for just as a human being was overcome and deceived by the devil, so also it should be a human being that overthrows the devil; and just as a human being merited death, so also a human being, by dying, should conquer death.[27] Therefore it is written in 1 Corinthians 15:57, "Thanks be to God who has given us the victory through our Lord Jesus Christ."

It was therefore more fitting that we should be freed by Christ's suffering, rather than simply by God's will.[28]

Reply to 1: Even nature uses several things for one purpose in order to do something more fittingly, as with two eyes for seeing; and the same thing can be observed in other cases.[29]

25. Because he was a Dominican, the notion of following in the steps of Christ was particularly important to Aquinas. Both the Dominicans and the Franciscans sought to live their lives in as close an imitation of Christ as possible, and they took literally the idea that Christ said to his apostles "follow me." In suffering on the cross Jesus shows us the virtues he wishes his followers to have: obedience, humility, constancy, and justice.

26. Simply being freed from sin is inadequate for human salvation. Aquinas understands salvation to be the eternal vision of God, something that we, in our created nature, are not suited for. So even if we were sinless, we could not be saved without the additional gift of God's grace, which transforms us so as to make us fit for eternal life with God. By his suffering—and, more importantly, by the virtues displayed in that suffering—Christ "merits" that grace for us. In other words, Christ acts on behalf of humanity to make God's favor something that can really belong to humanity.

27. Following St. Anselm, Aquinas wants to stress here that Jesus's suffering and death on the cross are the acts of a human being, which is important because *God* does not need to win any victory over Satan; *humanity* does. So Jesus acts on behalf of humanity to win the victory over sin and death, a victory that God has no need to win, since God is not subject to sin and death.

28. Notice that in these five points Aquinas speaks not about why *God* needs the suffering of Christ, but about why *we* do: to convince us of God's love; to give us an example of virtue to follow; to merit grace for us; to help us refrain from further sin; and to endow our human nature with the dignity of having triumphed over Satan, our ancient foe. This alignment of necessity with humanity is significant, because it indicates that for Aquinas what is involved in human salvation is not a change on *God's* part—as if God were angry with us, but with the death of Christ this anger is somehow mollified—but a change on *our* part—we are transformed into the kinds of creatures who can live in God's presence. Given Aquinas's conviction that God is unchanging, it would be impossible for him to claim that the death of Christ brings about a change in God.

29. That is, the objector is simply wrong in saying that nature never uses two things where one would suffice. We could certainly see with only one eye, but we see *better* with two.

Reply to 2: As Chrysostom says, "Christ had come in order to destroy death, not his own (for since he is life itself, death could not be his), but the death of human beings. Therefore it was not by reason of his being bound to die that he laid his body aside, but because the death he endured was inflicted on him by human beings. But even if his body had sickened and dissolved in the sight of all people, it was not fitting that he who healed the infirmities of others should have his own body afflicted with the same. And even had he laid his body aside without any sickness, and had then appeared, people would not have believed him when he spoke of his resurrection. For how could Christ's victory over death appear, unless he endured it in the sight of all, and so proved by the incorruption of his body that death was destroyed?"[30]

Reply to 3: Although the devil attacked humanity unjustly, nevertheless, on account of sin, humanity was justly left by God under the devil's bondage. And therefore it was fitting that Christ, through justice, should free humanity from the devil's bondage by making a repayment, through his suffering, on humanity's behalf. This was also a fitting means of overthrowing the pride of the devil—who is "a deserter from justice" and "a lover of power"—inasmuch as Christ should defeat the devil and liberate humanity not merely by the power of his divinity, but also by the justice and lowliness of suffering, as Augustine says in *De Trinitate* (bk. 13, chaps. 13, 14).

3.46.4

Whether Christ should have suffered on a cross?

It would seem that Christ should not have suffered on a cross.[31]

---

30. The quotation is actually not from Chrysostom but from Athanasius, *On the Incarnation of the Word,* chaps. 22, 23.

31. In my experience, some readers find this a frustrating, not to say ridiculous, question. But such readers make the mistake of approaching Aquinas as someone who is trying to *prove* the many doctrines of the Christian faith, and in this case they read him as somehow trying to prove that Christ has to die on a cross, which is not at all what Thomas is trying to do; rather, he is trying to show the fittingness of the crucifixion.

In contrast to the immediately preceding articles, the point of this article is not the *fact* of Christ's suffering, but the *form* of his suffering. Here we have a somewhat different use of the argument *ex convenientia* (see 3.1, note 1). As in the other instances, Thomas is taking a contingent fact—namely, that Jesus died by crucifixion rather than by stoning or drowning or beheading or burning—and asking why this should be the case. However, in this article his answers have more to do with showing what one might call the "symbolic fittingness" of this form of death than with showing how this contingent fact was the best way of achieving the desired end.

Implicit in Thomas's whole discussion in this article is a view of the world as a sort of "text"—a collection of signs that one who has been trained properly can "read." Thus he would not be satisfied with the typical modern answers to the question of why Jesus died by crucifixion—for example, that he was executed as a criminal by the Romans, and crucifixion was the way Romans executed non-Roman criminals. Aquinas believes that God can arrange the contingent facts of

1. Truth should conform to its prefiguration.[32] But in all the sacrifices of the Old Testament that prefigured Christ the animals were put to death with a sword and afterward consumed by fire. Therefore it seems that Christ should not have suffered on a cross, but rather by the sword or by fire.

2. John of Damascus says (*On the Orthodox Faith,* bk. 3, chap. 20) that Christ should not take on "dishonorable afflictions." But death on a cross was most dishonorable and ignominious; therefore it is written in Wisdom 2:20, "Let us condemn him to a most shameful death."[33] Therefore it seems that Christ should not have suffered death on a cross.

3. It was said of Christ, "Blessed is he that comes in the name of the Lord," as is shown in Matthew 21:9. But death upon a cross was a death that implied a curse, as we read in Deuteronomy 21:23, "Cursed by God is the one who hangs on a tree." Therefore it does not seem fitting for Christ to have been crucified.[34]

On the contrary: It is written in Philippians 2:8, "He became obedient unto death, even the death of the cross."

I answer: It was most fitting that Christ suffered the death of the cross.

First, as an example of virtue. In fact, Augustine writes in *On Eighty-three Various Questions* (q. 25), "God's Wisdom became a human being to give us an example in righteous living. But it is part of righteous living not to stand in fear of things that should not be feared. But there are some people who, although they do not fear death in itself, are still troubled over the manner of their death. In order, then, that no type of death should trouble a righteous person, *this* person's cross had to be set before him, because, among all kinds of death, none was more hateful, more fear-inspiring, than this."[35]

---

history in any way he wants, and therefore we can ask plausibly what God was trying to convey to us by choosing one arrangement of events rather than another, much as we might ask what a poet is trying to say to us by choosing one arrangement of words rather than another. Thus in asking whether Christ should have died by crucifixion, Aquinas approaches the question much as a literary critic might approach a poem, looking for nuances of meaning in the details of historical events.

32. See 1.1, note 39. If the death of Christ is the fulfillment of the animal sacrifices of the Old Law, then he should die in the same manner as those animals.

33. The objection is quite correct that, historically, crucifixion was considered an extremely dishonorable way to die, so dishonorable that Roman citizens could not be executed by crucifixion. To claim that such an ignoble act could be ennobling, not simply for the one who is subjected to it but also for the whole human race, would, as Paul says in 1 Corinthians 1:23, be "folly" to Gentiles.

34. This association between crucifixion and being cursed by God is, again, quite correct historically. It is what leads Paul to say that the cross of Jesus is a "scandal" or stumbling block to the Jews (1 Corinthians 1:23).

35. Thomas is already beginning to answer the second objection, regarding the dishonorable nature of Christ's death. In describing such a death as an example of virtue, Thomas, following Augustine, turns the ancient Greek and Roman idea of virtue on its head. Whereas writers like Aristotle understood virtue (which is rooted in the Latin word *virtus,* meaning "power" or "manliness") in terms of self-mastery, the example of the crucified Christ seems to say that

Second, because this kind of death was especially suitable as repayment for the sin of our first parent, which was the plucking of the apple from the forbidden tree against God's command. And so, to repay for that sin, it was fitting that Christ should suffer by being fastened to a tree, as if restoring what Adam had stolen; according to Psalm 69:4, "Then I paid that which I did not take away." Therefore Augustine says in a sermon on the passion, "Adam despised the command, plucking the apple from the tree; but all that Adam lost, Christ found upon the cross."[36]

Third, as Chrysostom says in a sermon on the passion (*The Cross and the Thief,* homily 1, no. 2), "He suffered upon a high tree and not under a roof, in order that the nature of the air might be purified. And the earth felt a similar benefit, for it was cleansed by the flowing of the blood from his side." And in addition to that, regarding John 3:14—"The Son of Man must be lifted up"—he writes, "When you hear 'lifted up,' understand his hanging on high, that he who had sanctified the earth by walking upon it might sanctify the air."[37]

Fourth, because by dying on the cross he prepares for us an ascent into heaven, as Chrysostom says.[38] Therefore Christ himself says in John 12:32, "If I am lifted up from the earth; I will draw all things to myself."

Fifth, because it corresponds to the universal salvation of the entire world. Therefore Gregory of Nyssa observes (*On the Resurrection of Christ,* oration 1) that "the shape of the cross, extending out into four extremes from their central point of contact, signifies that the power and the providence of him who hung upon it is diffused everywhere." Chrysostom also says that upon

---

true virtue is not found in self-mastery, but in self-abandonment. At the same time, Thomas does not break all ties with the ancient understanding of virtue, because he also says that this self-abandonment is the truest manifestation of the courage so prized by the ancients. It is by trusting in God that we can overcome not only fear of death, but even fear of a death that is dishonorable in the eyes of others.

36. Thomas is invoking the early Christian and medieval understanding of the cross as a tree, indeed, both as the tree of life and as the tree of the knowledge of good and evil. In his *Legenda aurea,* the thirteenth-century writer Jacobus de Voragine writes that the cross was made from a branch of the tree beneath which Adam and Eve sinned, which Seth, the son of the dying Adam, had begged from the archangel Michael, who promised that when the branch bore fruit Adam would be restored. Seth planted this branch over his father's grave, where it took root and, after centuries of adventures, was eventually used to make the cross of Jesus. The imagery of the cross as a tree can also be found in medieval stained glass windows, where the cross is often colored green, to symbolize that it is a source of life.

It is not clear which of Augustine's sermons Aquinas is quoting, though with reference to Matthew 27:35 he quotes the same passage in the *Catena aurea,* his collection of patristic commentaries on the Gospels. The basic idea, though nothing approaching the exact wording, can be found in the probably spurious sermon 32, one of the sermons attributed to Augustine in the *Patrologia Latina* (Paris, 1844–1855), vol. 39.

37. This quotation is not in fact from Chrysostom, but from the commentary on John's Gospel by the eleventh-century Byzantine writer Theophylact, who, like Aquinas himself, draws heavily from Chrysostom for his commentary.

38. Thomas appears to be referring not to Chrysostom but to Athanasius's *On the Incarnation of the Word,* chap. 25.

the cross "he dies with outstretched hands in order to draw with one hand the people of old, and with the other those who are from the nations."[39]

Sixth, because of the various virtues denoted by this kind of death. Therefore Augustine, in his book (epistle 140) on the grace of the Old and New Testaments, says, "It was not without purpose that he chose this kind of death, so that he might be a teacher of that breadth, and height, and length, and depth," of which the Apostle speaks (Ephesians 3:18), "for breadth is in the beam, which is fixed crosswise above; this pertains to good works, since the hands are stretched out upon it. Length is the tree extending from the crosspiece to the ground where it is planted—that is, it stands and abides—which is symbolic of patience. Height is in that remaining portion of the tree, which extends from the transverse beam upward to the top, and this is at the head of the crucified, because he is the heavenly longing of those who have perfect hope. But that part of the tree that is hidden in the earth to hold it fixed, and from which the whole springs, denotes the depth of grace freely given." And, as Augustine says elsewhere (*Homilies on the Gospel of John,* sermon 119, no. 2), "The tree to which his suffering limbs were fixed was also the chair of the master teaching."[40]

Seventh, because this kind of death corresponds to many prefigurations. As Augustine says in a sermon on the passion,[41] an ark of wood preserved the human race from the waters of the flood; at the exodus of God's people from Egypt, Moses used a wooden staff to divide the sea, overthrow Pharaoh, and save the people of God; also Moses dipped his staff into the water, changing it from bitter to sweet; at the touch of a wooden staff a saving spring gushed forth from a spiritual rock; likewise, in order to overcome Amalek, Moses stretched forth his arms with staff in hand; finally, God's Law is entrusted to the wooden Ark of the Covenant. All of these things are like steps by which we come to the wood of the cross.

Reply to 1: The altar of burnt offerings, upon which the sacrifices of animals were offered, was constructed of timbers, as is set forth in Exodus 27, and in this respect the truth corresponds to the prefiguration. But "it is not necessary for it to be alike in every respect, otherwise it would not be a likeness but the reality," as John of Damascus says (*On the Orthodox Faith,* bk. 3, chap. 26).[42] In particular, as Chrysostom says,[43] "his head is not cut off, as was done to John, nor was he sawed in two like Isaiah, so that his body might undergo

---

39. The "people of old" and "those who are from the nations" are the Jews and the Gentiles, respectively. See previous note.

40. Note how this reason differs from the first reason Aquinas gives, which also deals with the virtues. There he is speaking on the literal level of which virtues one can learn from Christ's particular form of death. Here he reads the cross as a kind of allegory for the virtues necessary for the Christian. Perhaps of more significance is the second quotation from Augustine, where Christ's cross is compared to a teacher's chair. For Thomas the Dominican, Christ never ceases to be a teacher, even in his death on the cross.

41. The reference is actually to the Pseudo-Augustinian sermon 32 (see note 36, above).

42. A symbol does not need to be identical to that which is symbolizes; indeed, if it were, it would cease to be a symbol and be a copy.

43. See note 38, above.

death whole and undivided, so that there might be no excuse for those who want to divide the church."[44] Moreover, in Christ's burnt offering the material fire was replaced by the spiritual fire of charity.[45]

Reply to 2: Christ refused to undergo the dishonorable sufferings that pertain to defects of knowledge or grace, or even virtue, but not those injuries inflicted from outside.[46] Indeed, as is written in Hebrews 12:2, "He endured the cross, despising the shame."

Reply to 3: As Augustine says in *Against Faustus the Manichean* (bk. 14, chap. 4), sin is accursed, and thus so are death and mortality, which come from sin. "But Christ's flesh was mortal, 'having the likeness of sinful flesh.'" Therefore Moses calls it "accursed,"[47] and in the same way the Apostle calls it "sin," saying in 2 Corinthians 5:21, "He made him to be sin who knew no sin"—namely, because of the penalty of sin.[48] "Nor is there greater ignominy on that account, because he said, 'He is accursed of God.' For unless God had hated sin, he would never have sent his Son to take our death upon himself, and to destroy it. Acknowledge, then, that it was for us that he took the curse upon himself, whom you confess to have died for us." Therefore it is written in Galatians 3:13, "Christ has redeemed us from the curse of the Law, being made a curse for us."

44. Christ's undivided body symbolizes the undivided church.

45. This almost casual comment at the end of this reply indicates some of the depth of Thomas's understanding of the crucifixion. Whereas many ancient understandings of sacrifice focused on the destruction of the victim that was offered or on appeasing the deity to whom the offering was made, the prophets of the Old Testament focused on the disposition of the one making the sacrifice. As the psalmist says, "The sacrifice acceptable to God is a broken spirit" (Psalm 51:17). The prophets rejected any notion of sacrifice as the human ability to coax God into granting favor; rather, the truly acceptable sacrifice is one that is a sign of one's steadfast love for God, particularly as expressed through acting justly toward one's neighbor. What is being offered in a sacrifice is in the end not the animal or other valuable object, but oneself. However, as long as there is a separation between the one offering and the thing that is offered—between the giver and the gift—there remains the danger that the sacrifice can become an attempt to control God, rather than an act of surrendering oneself to God in love.

When Thomas depicts Christ as the offering that is consumed by the fire of his own love, he is depicting him as triumphing over this separation between giver and gift. The crucifixion is not an attempt to appease God's anger or offer him something he needs. It is simply our shared humanity being offered to God by being ignited with the fire of Christ's love. See 3.48, note 11.

46. Christ's honor consists in the perfection of his humanity and in his sinlessness, not in his protection from external events. Implicit here is the idea that it is not what befalls a person that is honorable or dishonorable, but rather their character as a person.

47. Aquinas is referring back to the passage from Deuteronomy quoted in the objection; he presumes Deuteronomy to have been written by Moses.

48. The "penalty of sin" or *poenam peccati* is not an "external" punishment imposed by God in an act of retribution. Rather it is the effect of sin upon human nature—the way in which human nature is "disordered" by sin and becomes subject to suffering and death—an effect that is in accordance with God's justice (see 1–2.85.5). Thus Christ is "accursed" in the sense that he shares this "penalty" with the rest of humanity, not because he is an object of divine wrath. Cf. 3.1, note 9.

QUESTION 47

THE EFFICIENT CAUSE
OF CHRIST'S SUFFERING

3.47.1

Whether Christ was killed by someone else or by himself?

It would seem that Christ was not killed by someone else, but by himself.[1]

1. He himself says in John 10:18, "No one takes my life from me, but I lay it down." But someone is said to kill someone else who takes away that person's life. Consequently, Christ was not killed by others, but by himself.

2. Those killed by others fail gradually from an exhausted nature, and this is strikingly apparent in people who are crucified. As Augustine says in *De Trinitate* (bk. 4, chap. 13), "Those who were crucified were tormented with a lingering death." But this did not happen in Christ's case, since "crying out, with a loud voice, he yielded up the spirit," as Matthew 27:50 says. Therefore Christ was not killed by others, but by himself.

---

1. The question this article addresses grows out of the shape of the story of Jesus itself. For example, in Peter's first sermon in the book of Acts, he says that Jesus was "handed over to you according to the definite plan and foreknowledge of God, crucified and killed by the hands of those outside the law" (Acts 2:23). The Gospels portray the death of Jesus simultaneously as part of the divine plan with which Jesus willingly cooperated, and as an unjust act committed by sinful humanity. So the question, as the objections make clear, is whether and to what degree Jesus gives up his life willingly.

3. Those killed by others suffer a violent death, and therefore die unwillingly, because "violent" is the opposite of "voluntary."[2] But Augustine says in *De Trinitate* (bk. 4, chap. 13) that "Christ's spirit did not desert the flesh unwillingly, but because he willed it, when he willed it, and in the way that he willed it." Therefore Christ was not killed by others, but by himself.

On the contrary: It is written in Luke 18:33, "After they have whipped him, they will put him to death."

I answer: A thing may cause an effect in two ways. In one way, by acting directly so as to cause something. And in this way Christ's persecutors killed him because they inflicted a sufficient cause of death on him, and they did it with the intention of killing him, and the effect followed, that is to say, death resulted from that cause.[3] In another way, someone is said to cause something indirectly, that is, by not preventing it when he can do so—as if one person were said to get another person wet because he did not close the window through which rain is entering. In this way, Christ *was* the cause of his own suffering and death, for he could have prevented his suffering and death. First, by holding back his enemies, so that they would not have been eager to kill him, or would have been powerless to do so.[4] Second, because his spirit had the power of preserving his bodily nature from suffering any injury. Christ's soul had this power because it was united in unity of person with the divine Word, as Augustine says in *De Trinitate* (bk. 4, chap. 13).[5] Therefore, since Christ's soul did not fend off the injury inflicted on his body, but rather willed his bodily nature to succumb to such injury, he is said to have "laid down his life," or to have died voluntarily.[6]

2. On "violence," see 3.46, note 19.

3. The various elements Aquinas lists here indicate that he is interested particularly in the kind of causality unique to intelligent beings, not any sort of brute, mechanistic causality, the way a boulder in an avalanche might cause someone's death. He is interested in the crucifixion as what we might call a "moral" act. Thus he notes that Christ's persecutors did not simply cause his death by their actions but intentionally committed those actions, and with the intention of causing his death. One of the important points here is that those who killed Christ were not simply puppets, acting out the script that God had written for them. Rather, they were genuine moral agents whose actions flowed from within themselves.

4. As Jesus says in Matthew's account of his arrest, "Do you think that I cannot appeal to my Father, and he will at once send me more than twelve legions of angels?" (Matthew 26:53). Jesus could have countered his persecutors' violence with his own, forcibly restraining them.

5. Even if Jesus had not forcibly restrained his persecutors, he simply could have refused to die, perhaps like St. Denis, who, after having been beheaded, picked up his head and walked into town. The deeper theological point is that all of Christ's bodily weaknesses, including things like hunger and thirst, were things he willingly took on for our sake.

6. Thomas is trying to read the story of the crucifixion in such a way that it displays for us two contrasting instances of human willing: the will of Christ's persecutors, which is the will to destroy, and the will of Christ himself, which is the will to suffer and redeem. The drama of human salvation is played out in the confrontation between these two fundamental forms of human willing, which might be characterized, respectively, with terms from Augustine's *City of God*: *amor sui* (love of self) and *amor Dei* (love of God). Both must be genuine acts of will; neither Christ nor his persecutors can be unwilling participants in this drama.

Reply to 1: When it is said, "No one takes away my life from me," it should be understood as meaning "against my will"; for something is properly said to be "taken away" when one takes it from someone who is unable to resist.[7]

Reply to 2: In order for Christ to show that the suffering inflicted by violence did not take away his life, he preserved the strength of his bodily nature, so that at the last moment he was able to cry out with a loud voice. In this way, his death should be counted among his other miracles. Accordingly it is written in Mark 15:39, "Now when the centurion, who stood facing him, saw that in this way he breathed his last, he said, 'Truly this man was God's Son!'"

It was also a matter of wonder in Christ's death that he died sooner than the others who were afflicted with the same suffering. Therefore John 19:32–33 says that "they broke the legs of the first, and of the other that was crucified with him," that they might die more speedily. "But when they came to Jesus and saw that he was already dead, they did not break his legs." Mark 15:44 also states, "Pilate marveled that he should be already dead"; for just as by his own will his bodily nature kept its strength to the end, so likewise, when he willed, he suddenly succumbed to the injury inflicted.[8]

Reply to 3: At the same time that Christ died because he suffered violence, nevertheless, he died voluntarily, because the violence inflicted on his body prevailed over it only to the degree that he willed it.[9]

---

7. Here, and in all the responses, Thomas seems to be agreeing with the objections: Christ caused his own death. But, as usual, Thomas is really rejecting the flat-footedness of the objections. In this instance, he wants to say that Christ willingly hands his life over, but that it is also genuinely taken away from him, because his willingness to lay down his life does not affect the motivation of his killers at all.

8. Here we see Aquinas's tendency to ascribe to Christ on the cross a measure of equanimity and control that is dismissed by many theologians today as at best incredible and at worst undermining Christ's true humanity, showing him to be more a superhero than one who shared our human condition. Thomas, however, shared with all theologians of his day (and of the centuries prior to him) the belief that Christ not only maintained his composure on the cross, but even continued to enjoy the beatific vision (see 3.46.8). In other words, the human soul of Christ experienced the highest form of happiness possible during the crucifixion.

Before we dismiss Aquinas's view as incredible, or even harmful, we should note two things. First, despite Thomas's tendency to stress Christ's composure on the cross, he also clearly maintains that Christ's suffering was intense—indeed, Christ experienced the most intense pain possible (see 3.46.6). Second, we should remember that this deeply traditional view is not the result of idle speculation about Christ's divinity, but grows out of Jesus's teaching in the Beatitudes: "Blessed are those who are persecuted for righteousness sake" (Matthew 5:10). Christ promises blessedness to his followers in the very moment of their persecution, and not simply as a subsequent reward. On the cross, he embodies the blessedness he promises. Of course, this should imply to us that the blessedness involved in *beatitudo* is something rather different from what we are accustomed to call happiness.

9. In other words, in the case of Christ, "violent" and "voluntary" are not opposed. The question remains, is this unique in the case of Christ because of the powers conferred on his humanity by union with his divinity? Is the death of a martyr who could have escaped by renouncing her faith also not at the same time violent and voluntary?

Q U E S T I O N 48

What Christ's Suffering Did

3.48.2

Whether Christ's suffering brought about our salvation by way of repayment?

It would seem that Christ's suffering did not bring about our salvation by way of repayment.[1]

1. The Latin word *satisfactio* indicates a payment or offering that is given to make amends for an offense one has committed against another. I have chosen to translate it as "repayment" rather than "satisfaction," not least because in modern English the word "satisfaction" seems to refer to a subjective feeling and not to an exchange between two or more parties. At the same time, "repayment" is not an entirely unproblematic translation, since it can imply a purely financial transaction, whereas Aquinas wishes to stress *satisfactio* as an act undertaken to restore a relationship that has been broken. Because the notion of *satisfactio* may be alien to many today, I offer at the outset an overview of this notion and how Aquinas relates it to what Jesus accomplished through his suffering and death.

The term *satisfactio* is first used by Tertullian in association with the sacrament of penance (or "reconciliation," as it is usually called today). Originally, after having confessed his or her sin, a person would perform some "work of satisfaction" (or "penance," as it is usually called), such as extra praying or fasting, after which God's forgiveness would be pronounced by the priest in the absolution. With the passage of time, the order became reversed, so that absolution was pronounced prior to the penitent performing the work of satisfaction. In many ways, this was a happy development, since it made clear that God's love and mercy is not conditional upon some action that we perform; indeed, God never ceases to love the sinner. But if it is not a means of earning God's love and mercy, then what is the point of the work of satisfaction? The answer lies in the fact that our salvation is not a matter of a change in God's stance toward

1. It seems that making the repayment belongs to the one who commits the sin. This is clear in the other parts of penance, because the one who has done the wrong must be sorry over it and confess it.[2] But Christ never sinned,

---

us, but of a change in our stance before God (see 3.46, note 28). Therefore, in the sacrament of penance the work of satisfaction is the way in which the Holy Spirit brings about a change in the penitent, so as to restore his or her status as an adopted child of God.

The term *satisfactio* is first used in reference to the atoning work of Christ on the cross by Ambrose of Milan, but it is really Anselm of Canterbury, writing some eight hundred years after Ambrose, who works out in detail—in his *Cur Deus Homo?*—an account of Christ's death as an act of satisfaction or repayment, done on behalf of the human race. Thomas's account of *satisfactio* draws heavily on Anselm, but at the same time he does not simply parrot Anselm. As I shall note along the way, Thomas makes several significant changes and shifts in emphasis.

Thinking about the notion of "satisfaction" in general, one might say that the purpose of offering satisfaction in the case of an offense committed against a human being is threefold: (1) to mollify the offended party; (2) to restore the right order of things (i.e., if I have taken two dollars from you, I must give you two dollars in order to return matters to their proper state); and (3) to allow the one who committed the offense to engage in a (potentially) transforming act of repayment. In the case of an offense committed against God, God does not need to be mollified. However, the other two purposes of satisfaction still apply: the right order of things must be restored, and those who have committed the offense must engage in the practice of making amends so that their relationship with the offended party (i.e., God) may be restored.

These general mechanisms of satisfaction must be kept in mind when speaking of Jesus's suffering and death as a work of satisfaction or repayment. Since Jesus is God's Son by nature and not by adoption (see 3.16, note 9), he cannot lose his status as God's child (i.e., he cannot sin). Therefore, purpose 3 in the previous paragraph cannot apply to Jesus himself. However, purpose 2 still applies: the right order of things must be restored. So we ask, what is it that human sin has taken from God that rightly belongs to him? As Aquinas (following Anselm) sees it, human sin robs God of our love and loyalty. What is needed to set things right, then, is for a human being, acting on behalf of humanity as a whole, to give to God the love and loyalty that is rightfully God's. This is what Jesus does on the cross. He is a human being who does not withhold from God—even at the cost of his life—any of the love and loyalty that God deserves. And once Jesus, acting on our behalf, has set things in their proper order, we are enabled to participate in that restored order of things, provided that we are made fit for such participation through being transformed by the Holy Spirit by means of baptism and, after baptism, works of satisfaction (purpose 3).

I should add that Thomas's understanding of Christ's suffering as a repayment for sin is not the whole of his understanding of how Christ saves humanity. There are also the important issues of "merit" (see 1–2.109, note 7) and "sacrifice" and "redemption." But *satisfactio* remains for Thomas the key to understanding how the suffering of Christ reconciles us with God, and it is therefore also the key to understanding the other ways in which Christ's suffering and death operate.

By choosing to translate *passio* as "suffering" and *satisfactio* as "repayment," I have sought somewhat to distance Thomas's teaching on the death of Christ from language that seems too "religious." In some ways these translations can make Thomas harder to understand, since we do not like to think of Christianity in terms of pain and commerce; but they also makes the challenge of interpreting Thomas clearer.

2. The language of *satisfactio* grows out of the sacrament of penance (see previous note), where it was considered one of the three "parts" of the sacrament (the other two being sorrow or contrition and the act of confessing itself). The objection argues that just as acts of contrition and confession must be done by the one who has actually committed the sin, so too repayment.

according to 1 Peter 2:22, "who did no sin." Therefore he made no repayment by his personal suffering.[3]

2. No repayment is made to another by committing a greater offense. But in Christ's suffering the greatest of all offenses was perpetrated, because those who killed him sinned most severely, as stated earlier (3.47.6). Therefore it seems that repayment could not be made to God by Christ's suffering.[4]

3. Repayment implies equality with the offense, since it is an act of justice. But Christ's suffering does not appear equal to all the sins of the human race, because Christ did not suffer according to his divinity, but according to his flesh; for as 1 Peter 4:1 says, "Therefore Christ has suffered in the flesh." But the soul, where sin resides, is superior to the flesh. Therefore Christ did not make repayment for our sins by his suffering.[5]

On the contrary: Psalm 69:4 says in the person of Christ,[6] "Then I paid the debt for that which I did not take away." But one has not paid a debt who does not repay fully. Therefore it appears that Christ, by his suffering, has fully repaid for our sins.

I answer: To properly make repayment for an offense, one offers something that the offended one loves as much as, or even more than, he hated the offense. But by suffering out of love and obedience, Christ gave more to God than was required to compensate for the offense of the whole human race. First, because of the greatness of the charity on account of which he suffered.[7] Second, on account of the worth of his life that he laid down in repayment, for it was the life of God and of a human being. Third, on account of the extent of the suffering, and the greatness of the sorrows endured, as stated earlier (3.46.6). And therefore Christ's suffering was not only sufficient, but was an excess repayment for the sins of the human race; according to 1 John 2:2, "He is the reconciling sacrifice for our sins, and not for ours only but also for the sins of the whole world."

Reply to 1: The head and limbs are like one mystic person; and therefore Christ's repayment extends to all the faithful as being his members.[8] Also, insofar

3. The implication here is that Christ's sinlessness makes it singularly *un*suitable to see his death as a kind of "repayment." How can Christ make restitution for sins that he did not commit?

4. The objection makes the rather obvious point (a point made less obvious, in the case of Jesus's death, by years of pious conditioning) that two wrongs do not make a right: that is, committing an offense that is worse than the original one seems an unlikely way of making amends.

5. The objection presumes as background Anselm's claim that an offense against God has an "infinite" character (since God himself is infinite). How, then, can something that happens to Christ's human nature, which is finite, make amends for an infinite offense? Moreover, the death of Christ occurs in his body, not his soul, and the body is of even less account than the human nature as a whole.

6. Like all medieval theologians, Thomas, in many cases, reads the psalms as the voice of Christ speaking prophetically in the Old Testament.

7. It is perhaps significant that this is the point Thomas lists first. His emphasis is consistently on the inner attitude with which Christ takes up his suffering. See note 11, below.

8. On the relationship between Christ (the head) and his body (the church), see 3.8.1, above. In this reply, we see another place where Thomas indicates the place of the church in

as any two people are one in charity, the one can make repayment for the other, as shall be shown later.[9] But the same reasoning does not hold for confession and contrition, because repayment consists in an outward action, for which aids [*instrumenta*] may be used, among which friends are to be counted.[10]

Reply to 2: Christ's charity was greater than the malice of his crucifiers. Therefore the value of his suffering as repayment surpassed the murderous offense of those who crucified him: so much so that Christ's suffering was sufficient—and even excess—repayment for his murderers' sins.[11]

---

salvation. Because Christ is the head of the body of which Christians are the "members" or "limbs," he can act on their behalf. This same theology of the church as Christ's body is used by Aquinas in the article immediately before this one (3.48.1) to discuss how Christ can "merit" on our behalf: his actions are not simply his alone; they in some way belong to all those who are "incorporated" or (to coin a barbarous neologism) "in-bodied" into the community of his followers. Thomas writes: "Christ's works are referred to himself and to his members in the same way as the works of any other person in a state of grace are referred to that person." Thus, as one who suffers persecution for justice's sake, Christ merits salvation (see Matthew 5:11–12); but because Christians form part of the one body of Christ, they merit salvation on the basis of the meritorious act of Christ; they share in his reward.

The effect of Christ's suffering—whether we understand this effect primarily as the meriting of salvation or as the making of repayment—is not applied invisibly, as if by magic, to individuals; rather it operates within the field of force that the Holy Spirit generates through the beliefs and practices of the Christian community, in particular the sacraments. This integration of his understanding of the church with his understanding of Christ's act of *satisfactio* is one of the ways in which Thomas significantly develops Anselm's account. Anselm never really addresses the question of how Christ's reconciling repayment of love affects the rest of humanity. Here Aquinas indicates that because Christ acts as the head of the body, of which we are members, his offering is our offering, though not in a mechanical way, since becoming one with Christ in his body involves not only outward sacramental actions, but also inward transformation, by which the passionate love of Christ becomes our passion (see note 11, below). That being said, it is also important to note that Aquinas does not restrict the effects of Christ's suffering to the visible members of the church because (1) all human beings are at least potentially limbs of Christ's body, and (2) "the Spirit blows where it chooses" (John 3:8).

9. A discussion can be found in *Supplementum* 13.2. On the *Supplementum,* see 1–2.4, note 12.

10. On "instrumental causality," see 1.45, note 10. Earlier I noted the significance of Thomas's use of John of Damascus's claim that Christ's humanity was an "instrument" of his divinity (see 3.8, note 14). Here Thomas speaks in terms of Christ being an "instrument" by which humanity makes repayment to God.

11. Note especially one of the points Aquinas makes here. People sometimes speak of the sacrificial death of Christ as if God must punish someone for human sin, and so Christ offers himself as a victim to be punished in our place. This view is sometimes called the "penal substitutionary" view of redemption, which is emphatically *not* Aquinas's view. In this reply to the second objection, Thomas makes clear that what Christ offers to God is not the external fact of his death, but the "interior" reality of his love and loyalty. Although the death of Jesus is a part of God's plan to save humanity, Aquinas does not seem to think of it as a punishment that God inflicts upon Jesus (at least not in our modern sense of "punishment"; see 3.46, note 7). Indeed, here the death of Jesus appears to be the result of a sinful human action, which is redemptive only because Christ's love is greater than the hatred of those who killed him.

But *why* does the love of Christ take the form of suffering at the hands of sinful humans? Thomas seems to imply here and elsewhere that Christ's suffering is the result of the fact that

Reply to 3: The worth of Christ's flesh is not to be determined solely according to the nature of flesh, but also according to the person assuming it—that is, inasmuch as it was God's flesh. And from this it had infinite worth.[12]

---

the cure must be suitable for counteracting the disease. Thus, on one level, Christ's obedience counteracts human disobedience. But human disobedience to God is rarely if ever outright rebellion; it is more often misdirected or half-hearted seeking of the good, and it is this misdirection and half-heartedness for which Christ's suffering or "passion" is the cure.

Here we might return to *passio,* the Latin word Thomas uses for Christ's suffering. Think of our modern English usage, in which "passion" means being swept up into something or, in the case of love, someone. Christ's passion is both his human soul's whole-hearted response to God, and the visible manifestation of the Son's eternal act of existence, in which he is swept up, through the Holy Spirit, in love for the Father. We might say that Christ's whole life is his "passion," but, because of sin, in the end such passion must take the form of suffering, for two reasons: (1) because this passion is violently rejected by those who fear that it will mean the end of their illusory independence from God, and (2) because his suffering and death disengage his soul from that which fallen humanity takes at ultimate: bodily life. For these two reasons, the suffering of Christ is a fitting means of undoing the sin of Adam and Eve, in which they turned away from God and turned toward bodily things.

In the end, for Thomas it is "passion"—in the sense of all-consuming love—that makes repayment; but in the context of human sin, the medicine of the passion takes the bitter form of suffering. Thus the "external" fact of Christ's suffering on the cross cannot simply be dispensed with, for the rejection of such suffering in favor of the more "spiritual" offering of love could well be just another act of human half-heartedness and misdirection.

12. Aquinas's reply presumes what he has said about Christ being a single logical subject (*suppositum*) possessed of two natures, divine and human. The same logic that authorizes one to say "God is a human being" also allows one to say that the flesh that is crucified is God's flesh (*caro Dei*) and is thus of infinite worth. See 3.16.1, esp. note 14.

Q U E S T I O N **53**

CHRIST'S RESURRECTION

3.53.1

Whether it was necessary for Christ to rise again?

It would seem that it was not necessary for Christ to rise again.[1]

1. John of Damascus says (*On the Orthodox Faith,* bk. 4, chap. 27), "Resurrection is the rising again of a living being, which was disintegrated and fallen." But Christ did not fall by sinning, nor was his body disintegrated, as is clear from what was stated earlier (3.51.3). Therefore, it is not properly fitting for him to rise again.[2]

2. Whoever rises again is promoted to a higher state, since to rise is to be lifted. But after death, Christ's body continued to be united with divinity, therefore it could not be promoted to any higher condition.[3] Therefore, it was not appropriate for it to rise again.

1. On the different ways in which the word "necessary" can be used, see 3.46.1, especially note 5.

2. In the previous question, Aquinas argues, on the authority of Psalm 16:10 ("You will not let your holy one see corruption"), as interpreted by John Chrysostom, that Jesus's body did not decay in the tomb. The integrity of Jesus's body was a manifestation of his divine power and a sign that his death was not due to any weakness of his nature (which weakness would be indicated by the decay of his body) but was something that he accepted willingly. Following up on this argument, the objection seems to be saying that resurrection, as a restoration of bodily integrity, would be a misleading sign.

3. As with the previous one, this objection draws on an argument Aquinas makes earlier (3.50.2), namely, that Christ's body remained united to his divinity, though not to his human soul while in the tomb.

3. Everything that happened concerning Christ's humanity is intended for our salvation. But Christ's suffering was sufficient for our salvation, since by it we were liberated from guilt and punishment, as is clear from what was said earlier (3.49.1, 3). Consequently, it was not necessary for Christ to rise again from the dead.[4]

On the contrary: It is written in Luke 24:46, "It is proper for Christ to suffer and to rise again from the dead."

I answer: It was necessary for Christ to rise again, for five reasons.[5]

First, for the praise of divine justice, to which it belongs to exalt those who humble themselves for God's sake, according to Luke 1:52, "He has put down the mighty from their seat, and has exalted the humble."[6] Consequently, because Christ humbled himself, even to the death of the cross, out of char-

---

4. Whereas the first two objections indicate ways in which the resurrection of Jesus could be misleading, this third objection argues somewhat differently: since we are freed from sin through Christ's suffering and death, the resurrection is unnecessary. Of course, Thomas has already argued (3.46.1, above) that, strictly speaking, God could save us without the suffering of Christ—indeed at the outset of this part of the *Summa* (3.1.2) he argues that God could save us without becoming incarnate at all. But the objection here seems to be making a slightly different point: the resurrection does not accomplish anything with regard to our salvation. In other words, the resurrection is not simply "unnecessary" in the sense that the incarnation and passion are—that is, what God accomplishes through it *could* be accomplished in some other way; rather, the resurrection in fact accomplishes *nothing* with regard to our salvation.

This objection reflects a major strand in Christian theology, particularly in the West, in which it is the passion of Christ that is the "cause" of our salvation, whereas the resurrection serves some other purpose, such as strengthening the faith of the apostles. During the patristic period, in both East and West, writers tended to understand the suffering–death–resurrection of Jesus as a single event by which God redeems the world. In the fifth century, some writers began to speak of the passion of Christ as the unique cause of our forgiveness and thus of our salvation. For these writers, the resurrection was the greatest of miracles, but it was not different in kind from any other miracle. Over the course of the Middle Ages, this view came to dominate in the West: the resurrection was not ignored or seen as unimportant, but it was given no role to play as a cause of our salvation.

In his earlier writings, such as his commentary on the *Sentences* of Peter Lombard, Aquinas seems to have followed this prevailing view. However, in the *Summa theologiae,* he appears to have shifted his position somewhat, as we shall see in this article, so that the resurrection acquires once again its own distinctive role in the event of human salvation.

5. The fact that Aquinas offers five different reasons for why it was necessary (*necessarium fuit*) that Christ rise from the dead signals to us that we are dealing with the kind of necessity discerned by arguments *ex convenientia* (see 3.1, note 1). As he has already argued (3.46.1–3), this is not a necessity that imposes any sort of compulsion on God.

6. In presenting the resurrection of Jesus as an act of divine justice, vindicating the cause of Jesus, Thomas seems to anticipate a theme that would be stressed in the last part of the twentieth century by advocates of the so-called "Theology of Liberation." Like these later theologians, Thomas sees in Mary's song of praise from Luke's Gospel a summary of God's characteristic way of favoring the poor and the weak and the humble over the rich and the powerful and the proud: "He has put down the mighty from their seat, and has exalted the humble." In the resurrection of Jesus, this characteristic "preferential love for the poor" is manifested in an ultimate way, thus its fittingness.

ity and obedience to God, it was proper that he be exalted by God even to a glorious resurrection. Therefore it is said in his person in Psalm 139:2,[7] as the gloss interprets it,[8] "You have known (i.e., approved) my sitting down (i.e., my humiliation and suffering) and my rising up (i.e., my glorification in the resurrection)."

Second, for the building up of our faith,[9] since our belief in Christ's divinity is confirmed by his rising again. According to 2 Corinthians 13:4, "Although he was crucified through weakness, yet he lives by the power of God." And therefore 1 Corinthians 15:14 says, "If Christ be not risen again, then our preaching is empty, and our faith is also empty." And in Psalm 30:9, as the gloss interprets it, "What benefit is there in my blood (i.e., in the shedding of my blood) while I go down (as if by various degrees of evils) into corruption? (As though he was to answer: 'None; for if I do not rise again at once, but rather my body is corrupted, I shall proclaim to no one, I shall gain no one.')."

Third, to lift up our hope; for in seeing Christ, who is our head,[10] rise again, we hope that we too shall rise again. Therefore it is written in 1 Corinthians 15:12, "If Christ is preached as risen from the dead, how do some among you say that there is no resurrection of the dead?" And it is said in Job 19:25, 27, "I know" (i.e., with certainty of faith) "that my Redeemer" (i.e., Christ) "lives," having risen from the dead; and therefore "in the last day I shall rise out of the earth. . . . This my hope is held in my breast."

Fourth, to shape the lives of the faithful, concerning which Romans 6:4 says, "Just as Christ is risen from the dead by the glory of the Father, so we also may walk in newness of life." And farther on, "Christ, rising from the dead, now dies no more. . . . In this way you also should consider yourselves dead to sin, but alive to God" (Romans 6:9, 11).[11]

7. See 3.48, note 7.

8. On the "gloss," see 1.12, note 7.

9. The Latin reads *ad fidei nostrae instructionem,* which could be translated as "for our instruction in the faith." However, as Jean-Pierre Torrell points out (*Le Christ en ses mystères,* 543, n. 6), the word *instructio* and the related verb *instruo* carry implications of "building" and "construction." In English this same convergence of meanings is found in the slightly archaic word "edification." So the resurrection is not simply God trying to convey some "fact" about Jesus to us (i.e., that he is divine); rather, it is a means by which we become more sure of Christ's divinity and thus adhere more resolutely to this truth.

10. See 3.48, note 8.

11. Since the second reason has to do with faith and the third with hope, we might expect the fourth reason to deal with love or charity (*caritas*), rounding out the trio of "theological virtues" found in 1 Corinthians 13:13 (see 1–2.15, note 5). Indeed, it seems surprising that Thomas does not mention love here. But a closer reading of the article reveals that our expectation is not in fact misplaced. Thomas says that the resurrection should "shape" or "inform" the lives of those who believe and hope. We should take "form" here in the sense of that which makes something what it is, just as "cowness" is the form of each cow (on form, see 1.12, note 1). Elsewhere (2–2.23.8), Thomas says that charity is the "form" of the virtues—it is that which makes them virtues at all. So, for example, "courage" without charity is not a virtue. When Thomas says that the resurrection was necessary in order "to *shape* the lives of the faithful," he

Fifth, to complete our salvation. Just as it was for this reason that, in dying, he endured evil things that he might deliver us from evil, so he was glorified in rising again in order to advance us toward good things; according to Romans 4:25, "He was handed over for our sins, and rose again for our justification."[12]

Reply to 1: Although Christ did not fall by sin, he fell by death, because just as sin is a fall from righteousness, so death is a fall from life. Therefore the words of Micah 7:8 can be understood as though spoken by Christ: "Do not rejoice over me, my enemy, because I am fallen; I shall rise again." Likewise, although Christ's body did not disintegrate by returning to dust, yet the separation of his soul from his body was a kind of disintegration.

Reply to 2: Christ's divinity was united with his flesh after death by the personal union, but not by a natural union—that is, the way that the soul is united with the body as its form, so as to constitute human nature. Consequently, by the union of the body and soul, the body was raised to a higher natural condition, but not to a higher personal condition.[13]

Reply to 3: Christ's suffering brought about our salvation, properly speaking, by removing evils; but the resurrection did so as the beginning and exemplar of all good things.

---

means that for Christians, the fact that Jesus was raised from the dead should "inform" all their actions, such that they may "walk in newness of life" and be "alive to God." The resurrection of Jesus is the key to the Christian moral life because it is the definitive act of God's love in history, and is thus a sign of both the Spirit of love shared between the Father and Son, and the love of God for all humanity. Lives that are "informed" by this great sign of charity are lives of true virtue. Thus it seems that Thomas is talking about charity after all.

12. Aquinas's fifth reason for Christ's resurrection is somewhat different from the first four, in that here (and in the response to the third objection) he makes it clear that the resurrection has a *causal* role in our salvation; it serves to "complete" the process of salvation. Thomas was rooted in the Western medieval tradition of treating cross and resurrection separately (see note 4, above); therefore, here he distinguishes between them and assigns them distinct roles in the process of salvation. He does not seem to think that the resurrection has any relationship to the forgiveness of sins; rather, it is, as he says in the reply to the third objection, "the beginning and exemplar of all good things." Still, Thomas clearly sees the resurrection of Jesus as a *cause* of our salvation, and not simply as some miraculous add-on to what was accomplished on the cross. Thomas says earlier (see 3.1, note 13) that in thinking of human salvation we need to think of it in terms of our "withdrawal from evil" and our "furtherance in good." Thus the cross, which frees us from sin, and the resurrection, which advances us in goodness, are both causal factors in the one process of salvation.

13. Christ's body was a better body after the resurrection than when it lay in the tomb, because body and soul were reunited, which is more in keeping with the natural condition of the body. But it was not the body of a more esteemed person, since it remained the body of the Son of God even while it lay in the tomb.

CHRIST'S POWER AS JUDGE

3.59.5

Whether after the judgment that takes place in the present time, there remains yet another general judgment?

It would seem that after the judgment that takes place in the present time, there does not remain another general judgment.[1]

1. A judgment serves no purpose after the final assigning of rewards and punishments. But rewards and punishments are assigned in this present time, for in Luke 23:43 our Lord said to the thief on the cross, "This day you shall be with me in paradise,"[2] and in Luke 16:22 it is said that "the rich man died and was buried in hell." Therefore it is useless to look forward to a final judgment.

2. According to an alternative version of Nahum 1:9, "God shall not judge

---

1. Aquinas is asking whether there will be a final judgment at the end of time, in addition to the judgment that is passed on us at the time of our death. In order to understand the discussion, it is important to keep in mind three things that constrain the argument. First, certain passages in the New Testament, such as those cited later in this objection, speak of a definitive judgment that is passed at death. Second, based on the New Testament and the creeds, Aquinas is committed to the proposition that Jesus will return at some point in the future "to judge the living and the dead," at which time the bodies of the dead will be raised and reunited with their souls. Third, in Aquinas's day, it was a deeply rooted church practice to invoke the prayers of the saints, who were seen as those who were already enjoying the vision of God. Taken together, these three factors seem to leave Christians in the position of saying that there are two judgments, one at the time of death and the other at the time of Christ's return. Aquinas is not trying to *prove* that there are two judgments—he presumes that Christians take this as an article of faith—but he is trying to show the reason why this might be the case.

2. Note, the emphasis should fall on "*this day.*"

the same thing a second time."[3] But in the present time God judges both worldly and spiritual matters. Therefore, it does not seem that another final judgment is to be expected.[4]

3. Reward and punishment correspond to merit and demerit. But merit and demerit do not pertain to the body except inasmuch as it is the instrument of the soul.[5] Therefore neither reward nor punishment is due to the body except through the soul. Therefore, no other judgment is required at the end in order to reward or punish a person in the body, besides that judgment in which souls are now punished or rewarded.[6]

On the contrary: It is said in John 12:48, "The word that I have spoken, the same shall judge you in the last day." Therefore there will be a judgment at the last day besides that which takes place in the present time.

I answer: Judgment on something changeable cannot be rendered fully before its consummation. Thus judgment cannot be rendered fully regarding the quality of any action before its completion, both in itself and in its results, because many actions appear to be advantageous, which by their effects are shown to be harmful.[7] Similarly, judgment cannot be fully rendered regarding any person before the close of their life, since one can be changed in many respects from good to evil, or from evil to good, or from good to better, or from evil to worse.[8] Therefore the Apostle says in Hebrews 9:27, "It is appointed for mortals to die once, and after that the judgment."

3. The "alternative version" in question is the Septuagint, which was the ancient Greek translation of the Hebrew Bible and the basis of the pre-Vulgate Latin translation of the Old Testament. The Vulgate version of this verse is quite different: *non consurget duplex tribulatio* (a double tribulation shall not arise).

4. In other words, no double jeopardy.

5. That is, the body is not, of itself, deserving of either praise or blame. If I save the life of the president because I happen to be standing between the president and an oncoming bullet, it is not a meritorious act; indeed, it is not a human act at all. For a bodily action to deserve praise or blame it must be an action prompted by the soul, such that the soul has moved the body to act. On "merit" in general, see 1–2.109, note 7.

6. The objection is anticipating an argument like this: the soul is judged at the time of death, and the body is judged when it is raised at Christ's return. This is, in fact, the argument Aquinas makes in several of his other works (e.g., *Summa contra Gentiles* 4.96; *Quodlibetal questions*, bk. 10, q. 1.2; *Compendium theologiae,* chap. 242). Interestingly enough, this is not the focus of his explanation in this article. Nor does he offer the argument that he employs in his earlier commentary on Peter Lombard's *Sentences* (bk. 4, distinction 47, q. 1, a. 1, subquestion 1), namely, that the judgment made at the time of death is an individual one, whereas the judgment made at the end of time is a collective one. As we shall see, Thomas's argument in this article is more complex and, perhaps as a result, less clear.

7. For example, we might make the judgment that Ty Cobb swings the bat beautifully. But we would have to revise our judgment if the bat subsequently connected with the back of an opposing player's head.

8. In *Confessions* 10.36 Augustine writes, "Anyone who could change from the worse to the better can also change from the better to the worse." For Augustine, this mutability of the human person places severe restrictions on self-knowledge, with the result that we do not have enough information even to judge ourselves.

But it must be observed that although a person's earthly life in itself ends with death, it nevertheless remains to some degree dependent on what comes after it in the future. In one way, one's life continues on in people's memories, in which, sometimes contrary to the truth, good or evil reputations linger on.[9] In another way, one lives on in one's children, who are, as it were, something of their parent. According to Sirach 30:4, "His father is dead, and he is as if he were not dead, for he has left one behind him that is like himself." And yet many good people have evil sons, and vice versa. In a third way, one lives on to a degree in the result of one's actions, as in the case of how, from the deceit of Arius and other false leaders, unbelief continues to flourish down to the end of the world, just as faith will continue to derive its progress until then from the preaching of the apostles. In a fourth way, one lives on as regards the body, which is sometimes buried with honor and sometimes left unburied, and finally turns completely to dust. In a fifth way, one lives on in the things on which one's heart is set, such as worldly concerns, some of which are ended quickly, while others endure longer.[10]

All these things are submitted to the evaluation of the divine judgment. Consequently, a definitive and public judgment cannot be made of all these things during the course of this present time. For this reason, there must be a final judgment at the last day, in which everything concerning every human being in every respect shall be fully and openly judged.[11]

9. The writing of history constitutes a kind of judgment upon the lives of those who are remembered in such histories, even if it is not a true or faithful judgment.

10. For example, if one devoted one's entire life to a cause, sacrificing other things for the sake of that cause, and after one's death and with the passage of time that cause turned out to be evil or trivial, one's life would be judged accordingly.

11. What Thomas is saying here is, frankly, a little confusing. It may help to take it step by step. First, he notes that, as with an action, one cannot pass judgment on a person until a state of completion is attained. In one sense, we attain this completion at our death. Thomas believes, along with most of the Christian tradition, that at death our eternal fate is fixed and we are consigned either to heaven with the saints, to hell with the damned, or to purgatory, where those who have been judged to be among the saved but whose lives are still marked by sin are purified. From this moment on there can be no change in our ultimate destination.

However, Thomas notes that in another sense we have a sort of "afterlife" that is purely *natural* and not to be confused with the continued existence of the soul after death. In this "natural afterlife" people live on, for example, through their children or reputation or continuing influence. Thus, Aquinas notes, there is a sense in which our lives on earth are *not* finished at the time of our death. For Aquinas, then, the final judgment is the point at which God offers the final evaluation of our lives, incorporating the "natural afterlife" of our influence on history. However, this judgment is *not*, as Aquinas sees it, a second chance, a court of appeals for those who lost the first time around and ended up in hell. That judgment is made at the time of death.

What, then, we might well ask, is the purpose of this judgment? One of the purposes of judgment is to assign praise and blame; and, as Aquinas indicates when he says that people's memories are "sometimes contrary to the truth," praise and blame are not always justly apportioned by history. Thus the final judgment is a kind of public manifestation of God's true judgment, correcting and supplementing the imperfect judgment that human beings have made. To use a loose analogy, the final judgment is akin to the hearings of the Truth and Reconciliation Commission in South Africa, whereby both the victims and the perpetrators of decades of violence and deceit were granted a public venue in which to tell the truth about their lives

Reply to 1: Some people have held the opinion that the souls of the saints shall not be rewarded in heaven, nor the souls of the lost punished in hell, until judgment day.[12] The falsity of this opinion is evident from what the Apostle says in 2 Corinthians 5:8, "We are confident and would like instead to be absent from the body, and to be present with the Lord"—that is, not to "walk by faith" but "by sight," as appears from the context. But to "walk by sight" is to see God in his essence, in which "eternal life" consists, as is clear from John 17:3.[13] Therefore it is manifest that the souls separated from bodies are in eternal life.

Consequently, it must be maintained with regard to all that concerns the soul that a human being enters into an unchangeable state after death, and therefore there is no need for postponing judgment regarding the reward of the soul. But since there are other things having to do with a person that go on through the whole course of time, and that are not outside of the divine judgment, all of these things must be brought to judgment at the end of time. For although one neither merits nor demerits in regard to such things, they still, to a degree, accompany one's reward or punishment.[14] Therefore all these things must be weighed in the final judgment.

Reply to 2: "God shall not judge the same thing a second time," that is, in the same respect. But it is not unfitting for God to judge twice according to different respects.[15]

Reply to 3: The reward or punishment of the body depends upon the reward or punishment of the soul. Nevertheless, since the soul is changeable only accidentally on account of the body, once it is separated from the body it enters into an unchangeable condition and receives its judgment.[16] But the body remains subject to change down to the close of time, and therefore it must receive its reward or punishment then, in the last judgment.

---

under apartheid (my thanks to David Toole for this example). It is in the final judgment that dictators who may have been revered for their skill in statecraft are revealed as the tyrants that they were, and that the martyrs who died unknown and unburied are shown to be the true heroes of history.

12. This is a view that Thomas elsewhere (e.g., *De rationibus fidei* 1) ascribes to the "Greeks and Armenians"—that is, Eastern Orthodox Christians. To this day, however, it remains unclear exactly what the nature of the disagreement is between the Orthodox East and the Catholic West on the state of the soul after death and prior to resurrection. Some theologians on both sides see the differences as vast; others see the differences as almost entirely semantic.

13. "And this is eternal life, that they may know you, the only true God, and Jesus Christ whom you have sent."

14. This clause might also be translated as "they somehow have something to do with his reward or punishment." Thomas does not specify *what* exactly. Perhaps what he means is that the revelation of the good or evil wrought in one's "natural afterlife" will be part of one's eternal reward or punishment.

15. To use an example Thomas himself mentions: Arius, at his death, could be judged for his erroneous beliefs about the Trinity; at the final judgment he could also be held accountable for the evil effects of his teachings on later generations would also be revealed.

16. The soul by its nature is unchangeable. However, its union with the body makes it changeable, so that, for example, it can acquire good or bad habits. Once it is separated from the body it can no longer change.

QUESTION 61

THE NEED FOR THE SACRAMENTS

3.61.1

Whether sacraments are necessary for human salvation?

It seems that sacraments are not necessary for human salvation.

1. The Apostle says in 1 Timothy 4:8, "Bodily activity is of little profit." But the use of sacraments involves bodily activity, because sacraments are carried out through the signification of things and words that can be perceived by the senses, as has been said.[1] Therefore sacraments are not necessary for human salvation.

2. In 2 Corinthians 12:9 the Apostle was told, "My grace is sufficient for you." But it would not be sufficient if sacraments were necessary for salvation. Therefore sacraments are not necessary for human salvation.[2]

3. Given a sufficient cause, nothing more seems to be required for the effect. But Christ's suffering is the sufficient cause of our salvation, for the Apostle says in Romans 5:10, "If, when we were enemies, we were reconciled to God

---

1. In 3.60.6 Thomas argues that sacraments are acts of signification (or what we might call "acts that convey meaning") involving both words and signs (e.g., gestures, objects, etc.) that can be apprehended through the senses. On the significance of Thomas's developed views on sacraments as signs, see note 8, below.

2. This objection anticipates the argument of some of the more radical Protestant groups of the sixteenth century, who rejected the notion of sacrament because they felt that the church had turned sacraments into a kind of "good work" by which one earned one's salvation—instead of relying on God's grace.

by the death of his Son, much more surely, being reconciled, shall we be saved by his life." Therefore sacraments are not required for human salvation.[3]

On the contrary: Augustine says in *Against Faustus the Manichean* (bk. 19, chap. 11), "It is impossible to keep people together in one religious denomination, whether true or false, unless they are united by means of visible signs or sacraments."[4] But it is necessary for human salvation that people be united together in the name of the one true religion.[5] Therefore sacraments are necessary for human salvation.

I answer: Sacraments are necessary for human salvation for three reasons.[6] The first is taken from the condition of human nature, which is such that it has to be led by bodily and perceptible things to spiritual and intellectual things.[7] It is characteristic of divine providence to provide for each thing according to the requirements of its condition. And therefore divine wisdom fittingly provides human beings with aids to salvation in the shape of bodily and perceptible signs that are called sacraments.[8]

---

3. This objection appears at first glance to be virtually identical to the previous one, with the word "passion" substituted for the word "grace." However, there does seem to be a difference between grace as a cause and Christ's passion as a cause. "Grace" refers to a disposition or quality within the soul, and thus is something like a formal cause; on the other hand, the passion is a historical event, and in this sense more like an efficient cause. On the various types of causality, see 1.2, note 37.

4. It is interesting to note that here Aquinas quotes from Augustine's response to the Manichean bishop Faustus. The Manicheans held that the material world was inherently evil, and thus that such material things as sacraments could not help one toward salvation. In Thomas's day, criticism of the sacraments was associated with the Cathar heresy, which was thought to be a revival of Manicheanism.

5. Here Thomas alludes to a point that is central for his thinking about the church and the sacraments: salvation is inextricably tied up with our unity in Christ; the church is a manifestation of that unity; and the sacraments are the "tools" by which God builds up the church. Aquinas does not think of the sacraments simply as instruments for imparting grace to individuals, but as the ligaments of the mystical body of Christ.

6. In the three reasons that follow, Aquinas draws upon a standard medieval notion that sacraments were instituted (1) on account of instruction, (2) in order to humble, and (3) to direct human religious activity (see, for example, Hugh of St. Victor, *On the Sacraments of the Christian Faith* 1.9.3). However, Thomas gives something of a historical twist to these traditional categories: instruction is something needed even prior to the fall (though human beings did not need instruction through sacraments prior to the fall; see 3.61.2); humbling is needed after the fall; and, with the giving of the Law to Israel, God seeks to provide appropriate ritual activity to his people.

7. See 1.1, note 33.

8. In a previous question (3.60) Aquinas discusses the way in which sacraments are "signs" (*signa*). In Aquinas's day it was normal to first discuss sacraments as causes of grace rather than as signs. The earlier approach of Augustine, who began with the notion of sacraments as "signs," fell under a cloud of suspicion in the eleventh century because it was used by Berengar of Tours to critique an overly "physical" approach to the Eucharist (i.e., that there was something akin to a "chemical" change in the bread and wine by which they became the body and blood of Christ). Berengar's position that the bread and wine were "signs" of Christ's body and blood was widely perceived as a denial that they were truly Christ's body and blood. As a result, the

The second reason is taken from the state of human beings, who in sinning subjected themselves by their desires to bodily things. Now the healing remedy should be given to a person so as to reach the part affected by

---

view of Hugh of St. Victor that a sacrament was a material "container" of God's healing grace
came to eclipse Augustine's account of sacraments as signs. Only with Peter Lombard did the
Augustinian view begin to make a comeback, but even in Lombard the sacrament-as-sign was
subordinated to the sacrament-as-cause.

Although Thomas believes that the sacraments of the New Covenant are causes of grace
(see 3.62.1), this is not his starting point in the *Summa theologiae* (though it was in his early
commentary on Peter Lombard's *Sentences*). Following the lead of Augustine, he first discusses
sacraments as a kind of sign—not to deny that they are also causes of grace, but to suggest
that they are causes *on account of* their being signs; they cause by signifying. His early statement in his *Sentences* commentary that sacraments are "in the genus of cause and sign" (bk.
4, distinction 1, q. 1, a. 1) is replaced in the *Summa* with the statement that they are "in
the genus of sign" (3.60.1). Careful attention to the fact that Aquinas places the sacraments
under the primacy of the category "sign" allows us to say four things about his understanding the sacraments.

First, as John Yocum has pointed out, by defining sacraments as "signs" Aquinas is able to
include the Christian sacraments and the sacraments of the Old Testament (i.e., the rituals
enjoined by the Law) under one heading, thus showing the unity of the two covenants and the
consistency of God's "sacramental" dealing with humanity. What distinguishes the sacraments
of the Old Covenant from those of the New is that whereas the former are signs, the latter are
both signs and causes or, better, signs that cause. See John Yocum, "Sacraments," in *Aquinas
on Doctrine*, ed. Thomas Weinandy, Daniel Keating, and John Yocum (London: T & T Clark,
2004), 159–81, esp. 160–63.

Second, Thomas's mature opinion that the sacraments of the New Covenant are signs that
cause—and not signs *and* causes, as if the actions of meaning and causing were separable—gives
some hint of the kind of sign that Thomas thinks a sacrament is. Sometimes we think of signs
as pointers to something that is absent (as in "Las Vegas: 450 mi."), but signs are also signs of
presence (as when light on the horizon is a sign that Las Vegas is just ahead). Even more, there are
some signs that not only indicate the presence of something but also bring that thing about. For
example, when a judge says "I condemn you to twenty years in prison," the words are not mere
signs or indicators of condemnation; they *bring about* or *cause* that condemnation. The words
spoken when the president takes the oath of office or when a man and a woman make wedding
vows function in a similar way. However, we must always bear in mind that such examples are
simply analogies for the utterly unique way in which sacramental signs are causes.

Third, because for Thomas sacraments are causal signs they are not so much objects as actions.
The bread and wine of the Eucharist become sacramental signs only when they are consecrated,
and consecration involves the actions of words and gestures. Thus the sacraments are human
activities, ritual actions that human beings engage in. Moreover, Aquinas also maintains that if
the sacraments are to be causes of *grace* (which only God can give), then they must also be actions
of God in Christ. Indeed, Aquinas thinks that the sacraments are one of the chief ways in which
the sanctifying activity of Christ is extended into our own day. As Timothy McDermott puts it,
"The [sacramental] rituals are tools the cutting edge of which is their symbolic representation
of Christ's sacrifice, tools actually being wielded by Christ to incorporate men into his own
life. The sacraments are visible historical gestures of Christ in the present world." See Timothy
McDermott, *Summa Theologiae: A Concise Translation* (Allen, Tex.: Christian Classics, 1989),
544. For more on sacraments as "tools," see the next article (3.62.1).

Fourth, and finally, the primacy of the category of "sign" in Thomas's mature theology of the
sacraments can help us understand why it is that he says there will be no sacraments in heaven

disease.[9] Consequently, it was fitting that God should provide human beings with a spiritual medicine by means of certain bodily signs, for if one were offered unveiled spiritual things, one would be unable to apply one's mind to them, because it would be taken up with the material world.

The third reason is taken from the general inclination of human action toward bodily things. Therefore, so that it should not be too hard for human beings to be drawn away entirely from bodily actions, bodily activity was offered to them in the sacraments, by which they might be trained to avoid superstitious practices (consisting in the worship of demons) and all manner of harmful action (consisting in sinful deeds).[10]

Therefore it follows that through the institution of the sacraments human beings, in a way consistent with their nature, are instructed through perceptible things; they are humbled, through confessing that they are subject to bodily things, seeing that they receive assistance through them; and they are even preserved from bodily injury by the saving use of the sacraments.[11]

(see 1–2.101.2). As much as Thomas values the sacraments, he sees them as provisional. Just as the rituals of the Old Covenant were sacramental signs pointing toward Christ and the New Covenant, so too the sacraments of the New Covenant are signs pointing toward the marriage of heaven and earth in the New Jerusalem, where there will be "no temple in the city, for its temple is the Lord God the Almighty and the Lamb" (Revelation 21:22).

9. That is, you have to apply the medicine to the wound. The "wound" that has been inflicted upon human nature, according to Aquinas, is the loss of "original justice" (see 1–2. 109, note 3). In the state of original justice human beings were not led astray by their senses, but with the loss of original justice we have become subject to temptation through the senses. One might say that our senses are the main chink in our defensive armor. It is therefore fitting that the remedy be applied by sensual means, that is, through the sacraments.

10. Thomas is not unduly troubled by the resemblance between Christian sacramental worship and various forms of superstition: both appeal to the human person's need for symbolic, embodied worship. However, he recognizes that ritual activity can be harmful (spiritually, morally, or even physically; one need think only of various modern bacchanalia—fraternity parties come to mind—to see how this might be the case), so God graciously provides us with rituals by which we are led to true human flourishing.

11. All three of Thomas's reasons are linked by his conviction that God provides us with sacraments because he does not expect us to live like the angels. We are bodily creatures, and so God reaches out to us in a bodily way. Here we see again Aquinas's view that "grace perfects nature" (see 1.1, note 28). Human beings are by nature embodied creatures who know through their senses. In acting upon us, grace does not need to override our embodied nature.

Although the three reasons Thomas offers here are rooted in *our* nature, not in God's, in *Summa contra Gentiles* 4.56 Thomas offers another reason why sacraments are a fitting means of our salvation, and in this case he is thinking not about us but about God: "Instruments must be proportioned to the primary cause; and the prime and universal cause of human salvation is the Word Incarnate; it was fitting therefore that the remedies through which that universal cause reaches human beings should resemble the cause in this, namely, that divine power works invisibly through visible signs." Here, Thomas finds it fitting that the saving work of Christ, the Father's Word—or, we might say, the Father's "Sign"—should be applied to human beings by means of signs. This passage can perhaps provide a fruitful starting point for thinking about the way in which Christ himself is a "sacrament" of God's presence and activity.

Reply to 1: Bodily activity, as such, is not very profitable; but activity through the use of the sacraments is not merely bodily, but to a certain extent spiritual, that is, in its signification and in its causality.

Reply to 2: God's grace is a sufficient cause of human salvation. But God gives grace to human beings in a way that is suitable to them. In this way the sacraments are necessary to human beings, so that they may obtain grace.

Reply to 3: Christ's passion is a sufficient cause of human salvation. But it does not follow that the sacraments are not also necessary for human salvation, because they obtain their effect through the power of Christ's suffering;[12] and Christ's passion is, so to speak, applied to human beings through the sacraments, according to the Apostle in Romans 6:3, "All we who are baptized in Christ Jesus are baptized in his death."[13]

12. At first glance, Thomas seems to have involved himself in contradiction here: how can sacraments be necessary to human salvation if something else (i.e., the suffering of Christ) is sufficient for human salvation? However, as Thomas has already pointed out, in addition to absolute necessity, there is a kind of relative necessity, by which something is obtained in the most fitting way possible (see 3.46, note 5). Clearly the necessity of which he speaks here is "necessity" in this second, weaker sense.

13. It is one thing to say that we are saved through the death of Christ on the cross. It is another thing to ask *how* that death bears any relationship to us, since we are separated from it by the intervening events of history. For Aquinas, the answer to this question is that Christ is the head of the church (see 3.8.1, above), and therefore there is a kind of organic unity of the church and Christ: what is true of the head is also true of the body. Moreover, for Aquinas the church is essentially a sacramental reality; the sacraments are the tools by which the head builds up the body. So it is chiefly through the sacraments that the saving action of Christ upon the cross is "applied" to human beings.

QUESTION 62

THE SACRAMENTS' PRINCIPAL EFFECT, WHICH IS GRACE

3.62.1

Whether the sacraments are the cause of grace?

It seems that the sacraments are not the cause of grace.[1]

1. It seems that the same thing is not both a sign and a cause, since the nature of a sign appears to be more in keeping with an effect.[2] But a sacrament is a sign of grace. Therefore it is not its cause.

---

1. As noted earlier (see 3.61, note 8), the typical medieval starting point for thinking about the sacraments was to think of them as causes, as things that bring something about (i.e., grace). In the *Summa,* Thomas modifies this starting point by placing the sacraments under the single category of "sign." At the same time, Thomas does not abandon all talk of causality; and in fact gives a strong account of sacramental causality in this article.

Some modern theologians have found Thomas's sacramental theology seriously lacking precisely because of this emphasis on sacraments as "causes"; see especially Louis-Marie Chauvet, *Symbol and Sacrament* (Collegeville, Minn.: Liturgical Press, 1995). According to these critics, an overemphasis on causality grows out of a theology in which God and creation stand over and against each other in a relationship that is essentially that of two distinct entities (this view is generally referred to as "onto-theology"). Sacraments then become the means by which these two entities seek to "influence" each other. Additionally, the language of "causality" seems to make the workings of the sacraments approach too closely the model of physical change, underplaying their nature as signs or "symbols." One can judge for oneself how well these criticisms fit Thomas's theology.

2. That is, fire produces smoke, which is a sign of the presence of the fire.

2. Nothing bodily can act on a spiritual thing, since "the agent is to be esteemed more than the patient," as Augustine says (*The Literal Interpretation of Genesis,* bk. 12, chap. 16).[3] But the subject of grace is the human mind, which is something spiritual. Therefore the sacraments cannot cause grace.

3. That which belongs to God should not be ascribed to a creature. But it belongs to God to cause grace, according to Psalm 84:11, "The Lord will give grace and glory." Since, therefore, the sacraments consist in certain words and created things, it seems that they cannot cause grace.[4]

On the contrary: Augustine says (*Homilies on the Gospel of John,* sermon 80, no. 3) that the baptismal water "touches the body and cleanses the heart." But the heart is not cleansed except through grace. Therefore baptism causes grace, and in a similar manner so do the other sacraments of the church.

I answer: It is necessary to say that the sacraments of the New Law, in some way, cause grace; for it is evident that through the sacraments of the New Law a person is incorporated into Christ. Thus the Apostle says regarding baptism in Galatians 3:27, "As many of you as were baptized into Christ have clothed yourselves with Christ." But a person is not made a member of Christ except through grace.[5]

Some people, however, say that the sacraments are not the cause of grace by their own action, but insofar as God causes grace in the soul when the sacraments are employed. Such people give as an example someone who presents a lead coin and receives, by the king's command, a hundred Euro.[6] It is not as though the metal coin, by any action of its own, caused this person to be given that sum of money; rather, this occurs only because of the will of the king.[7] Therefore, Bernard

3. In other words, the doer of an action ("the agent") is greater than that which receives the action ("the patient"). For example, in the building of a table, the carpenter is more important than the wood from which the table is built.

4. In effect, these objections focus on three different aspects of sacraments that seem to make them unsuitable as causes of grace. First, as signs, sacraments seem unsuitable not only as causes of grace but as causes generally. Second, their material nature seems to make them unsuitable for any kind of spiritual effect, of which grace is one. Third, their nature as creatures seems to make them unsuited as causes of something that God alone can do, which is to give grace.

5. Thomas's initial response depends upon the preceding tradition's nearly unanimous affirmation of the connection between sacramental rituals and incorporation into Christ's body. Since this incorporation is an act of grace, it would seem that there is a close connection between the sacraments and the reception of God's grace. However, as A. M. Roguet notes, Thomas shows great prudence in recognizing that this conclusion regarding the link between the sacraments and grace does not in itself specify the *way* in which the sacraments cause grace. The tradition of the church is simply that they do so, as Aquinas puts it at the beginning of his reply in this article, "in some way" (*per aliquem modem*). Thomas's task as a theologian is to specify further this relationship between the sacraments and grace—that is, to identify the understanding of causality that best accords with and accounts for the shared faith of the church. See A. M. Roguet, *Les Sacrements* (Paris: Les Éditions du Cerf, 1945), 220.

6. *Centum libras*: one may substitute here their favorite form of modern currency.

7. Although we might speak of a shared Christian conviction regarding the "close connection" between the sacraments and grace (see note 5, above), this conviction varied in its details. The

says in the sermon *On the Lord's Supper* (no. 2), "Just as a canon is invested by means of a book, an abbot by means of a crosier, a bishop by means of a ring, so by the various sacraments various kinds of grace are conferred."

But if we examine the question properly, we shall see that according to this way of understanding them the sacraments are mere signs; for the lead coin is nothing but a sign of the king's command that this person should receive money. Similarly, the book is a sign of the conferring of the office of canon. Therefore, according to this opinion, the sacraments of the New Law would be mere signs of grace; yet we have it on the authority of many saints that the sacraments of the New Law not only signify but also cause grace.[8]

We must therefore say something different, namely, that an efficient cause can be of two types, principal and instrumental. A principal cause works by the power of its form, and the effect is made similar to the form, as in the case of fire, which by its own heat makes something hot.[9] In this way nothing but God can cause grace, since grace is nothing other than a shared likeness of the divine nature, according to 2 Peter 1:4, "He has given us most great and precious promises, that we may be partakers of the divine nature."

But an instrumental cause does not work by the power of its own form, but only through the motion given to it by the principal agent. Therefore the effect is not made to be like the instrument but like the principal agent; for instance, the couch is not like the ax, but like the knowledge that is in the craftsman's mind. And it is in this way that the sacraments of the New Law cause grace, for they are instituted by God to be employed for the purpose of conferring grace.[10] Therefore Augustine says in *Against Faustus the Manichean*

---

approach described here, which in the Middle Ages was characteristic of Franciscan theologians such as Bonaventure and Duns Scotus, is sometimes referred to as "occasionalism." There is nothing in the nature of sacraments themselves that causes grace; they are "causes" only because of God's promise. They are the "occasion" for God's action. This approach stresses the will of God in order to guarantee that the grace of God is in no way manipulated by human beings.

8. As Thomas sees it, "occasional causality" (see previous note) is no causality at all; rather it reduces the sacraments to "mere signs" that have no intrinsic connection to the gift of grace. Note that Aquinas has no argument for why one should find this kind of causality inadequate other than "the authority of many saints." This seems like a weak argument, until one realizes that by invoking the authority of the saints Thomas is painting a kind of holistic picture of the Christian tradition. The authoritative teaching of the saints is not to be found in books but in the total life of the church down through history. In essence, Thomas is saying that the occasionalist position, by making the connection between the sacraments and grace an extrinsic one, cannot account for the indispensable role that the sacraments have played in the life of the church throughout history. He spells out his differences with occasionalism in more detail in the reply to objection 2.

9. Recall that a form (see 1.12, note 1) is that which makes something the kind of thing it is. So when Thomas says that a principal cause "works by its form" to make an effect similar to its form, he means that it works in such a way that it shares its way of existing with something else; thus fire makes other things fiery.

10. Strictly speaking, God is the only cause of grace, because grace conforms us to God. The sacraments, however, are like tools in God's hands and therefore can in some sense be

(bk. 19), "All these things," that is, pertaining to the sacraments, "are done and pass away, but the power," that is, of God, "that works through them remains forever." But something is properly called an instrument when someone works through it; therefore it is written in Titus 3:5, "He saved us through the washing of regeneration."

Reply to 1: A principal cause cannot properly be called a sign of its effect, even if the effect is hidden and the cause itself is perceptible and manifest.[11] But an instrumental cause, if it is manifest, *can* be called a sign of a hidden effect. The reason for this is that it is not merely a cause but also to a degree an effect, insofar as it is moved by the principal agent.[12] And in this sense, the sacraments of the New Law are both causes and signs. And this is why, to use the common expression, "they effect what they signify."[13] From this it is clear that they perfectly fulfill the conditions of a sacrament, since they are related to something sacred, not only as a sign but also as a cause.

Reply to 2: An instrument has a twofold action: first, its instrumental ac-

---

thought of as causes of grace, just as creatures can be "secondary causes" (see 1.45, note 10). To use Thomas's analogy of the carpenter: if we ask about the "cause" of a table (i.e., "Why does this table exist?"), the proper answer is, "Because a carpenter made it." In Thomas's terms, the carpenter is the "principal cause" of the table, and it resembles the idea in his mind. However, we could also answer truthfully, "Because the ax cut the wood" (though the table does not resemble the ax) because it was through the distinctive form of the ax as a cutting tool that the carpenter acted. Yet it would seem strange to say "The ax made the table," since it is the ax only as wielded by the carpenter that makes a table.

11. A carpenter cannot be a sign of a hidden piece of furniture because we could well have a carpenter without there being any actually existing piece of furniture (i.e., if the carpenter's shop had just burned down, taking his entire stock with it).

12. Thomas's logic is clear enough: the action of an instrumental cause is itself a sort of effect, since it is acted upon by the principal cause; therefore, it is not excluded from being a sign. At first, an example seems hard to find. Certainly an ax just lying around is in no way a sign of a hidden piece of furniture. However, Thomas is not talking about the instrument simply as an object lying around, but as an object "in act" under the influence of the carpenter. Thus a carpenter wielding an ax on a piece of wood, might be a sign of a piece of furniture that the carpenter has envisioned and that is now in the process of being made, even if the wood has not yet taken the shape of a piece of furniture.

If we apply this analogy to the sacraments, we see why the form (i.e., the words of the ritual) and the matter (i.e., bread and wine, water, oil, etc.) are necessary for there to be a sacrament. The terms "form" and "matter" were used in sacramental theology well before Aquinas, but he gives these terms new meaning when he speaks (see, for example, 3.60.7) of the words and material element of a sacrament in a way that is at least analogous to Aristotle's description of the actualization of matter by form. Only when the matter of the sacrament is given form by the words, and is therefore "in act," does the sacrament become a sign of its effect, just as the ax can be a sign of a table only when it is being wielded by a carpenter whose intention it is to craft a table. Dropping the technical scholastic vocabulary, we can say that the material elements must be located within the sacramental ritual in order to become signs of the hidden action of God's grace—that is, in order to be sacraments at all.

13. This claim that sacraments "effect what they signify" is a key phrase in Catholic sacramental theology. Note that Thomas does not say that "they effect *and* they signify," as if the two things are unrelated properties of a sacrament; rather, they cause *by* signifying.

tion, and in this respect it works not by its own power but by the power of the principal agent; and second, its own action, which belongs to it on account of its own form. Thus an ax cuts something in two by reason of its sharpness, but it makes a couch because it is the instrument of a craft. However, its instrumental action is accomplished only by the exercise of its own action, for it is by cutting that the ax makes a couch. Similarly, the bodily sacraments, by their own operation, which they exercise on the body they touch, accomplish an instrumental operation on the soul by means of divine institution. For example, the water of baptism, in terms of its own power, cleanses the body, and thereby, inasmuch as it is the instrument of divine power, cleanses the soul, since soul and body together make a unity. And thus it is that Augustine says that it "touches the body and cleanses the heart."[14]

Reply to 3: This argument considers that which causes grace as principal agent, and this belongs to God alone, as stated above.

14. Here Aquinas spells out in more detail how his own position differs from occasionalism (see note 7, above). For the occasionalist position, the specific natural qualities of the sacramental signs have nothing to do with the operation of grace. The sacraments depend entirely upon God's decision to use them as the occasion for grace. But for Thomas, "grace perfects nature" (see 1.1, note 28), so he sees the natural qualities of the signs being taken up and transformed when they are used by God as means of imparting grace. Just as the skilled carpenter, in cutting wood, uses the instrument whose qualities are most suited to that task (an ax, say, rather than a hammer), so too God uses the signs whose natural qualities are most suited for the particular action of grace. Thus water is used in baptism for spiritual cleansing, and bread and wine in the Eucharist for spiritual feeding, and so forth (see 3.65.1, below). This natural foundation for the supernatural effect of the sacraments is important to Thomas, as it was for Augustine, who wrote, "If sacraments did not have a resemblance to the things of which they are sacraments, they would not be sacraments at all" (epistle 98.9). Just as the vision of God is something that we naturally yearn for but can achieve only through God's grace, so too with the sacramental signs. We might even go so far as to say that just as the human person is fulfilled by attaining the vision of God, so too water is fulfilled in becoming the means of spiritual washing, and food and drink are fulfilled by becoming the body and blood of Christ.

THE OTHER EFFECT OF THE SACRAMENTS, WHICH IS A SEAL

3.63.1

Whether a sacrament imprints a seal on the soul?
It seems that a sacrament does not imprint a seal on the soul.[1]

1. After discussing grace as one effect of the sacraments, Thomas turns to the sacramental "seal" (*character*), which he takes to be the other effect of the sacraments. Here, and elsewhere when it is used with regard to the sacraments, I have translated the Latin word *character* as "seal," rather than with the English cognate "character." There are advantages and disadvantages to this choice. Perhaps the main disadvantage is that "character" is the English translation used commonly in sacramental theology (e.g., the English translation of the current *Catechism of the Catholic Church,* nos. 1121, 1272). On the other hand, although the image of a seal impressed in wax is not necessarily any more familiar today than the word "character," it seems to me to have the advantage of better conveying Thomas's meaning, as well as of avoiding confusion with the notion of "character" current in moral philosophy.

The roots of Thomas's understanding of the sacramental seal can be traced back to two main sources: Augustine and Dionysius the Areopagite. In his controversy with the Donatists, Augustine forged a theology of baptism, to which Aquinas refers when he quotes Augustine at the end of his response. Though the theological issues in the Donatist controversy were more complex than the single issue of sacramental efficacy (to which the controversy had been reduced in Thomas's day), the practical issue was the question of whether those who had received schismatic baptisms should be baptized upon becoming Catholics. Augustine's rejection of such rebaptism led him to articulate the position that baptism, even baptism by a schismatic group, constitutes a "seal of holiness," and that to rebaptize such a person "is unquestionably a sin" (epistle 23.2). In other words, baptism places an indelible mark upon a person that cannot

1. The word "seal" seems to signify some kind of distinctive sign. But Christ's members are distinguished from others by eternal predestination, which does not imply anything in the predestined, but only in God as the one predestining, as we have said in the first part (1.23.2). For it is written in 2 Timothy 2:19, "The sure foundation of God stands firm, having this mark the Lord knows those who are his." Therefore the sacraments do not imprint a seal on the soul.[2]

2. A seal is a distinctive sign, for a sign, as Augustine says in *De doctrina Christiana* (bk. 2, chap. 1), "is that which conveys something else to the mind, besides the outward appearance that it impresses on the senses."[3] But nothing in the soul can impress an outward appearance on the senses. Therefore it seems that no seal is imprinted on the soul by the sacraments.[4]

3. Just as the believer is distinguished from the unbeliever by the sacraments of the New Law, so was it under the Old Law. But the sacraments of the Old Law did not imprint a seal, which is why they are called "justices of the flesh" by the Apostle in Hebrews 9:10; therefore it seems that the sacraments of the New Law do not either.

On the contrary: The Apostle says in 2 Corinthians 1:21–22, "He . . . who has anointed us is God, who also has sealed us, and given the pledge of the Spirit in our hearts." But a seal means nothing else than a kind of marking. Therefore it seems that by the sacraments God imprints his seal on us.

---

be erased by subsequent sin. By the thirteenth century, largely due to the influence of Peter Lombard, the Latin term *character* was used to convey the notion that baptism, along with confirmation and ordination (which like baptism were not repeatable), imparted a indelible sacramental seal upon the soul.

The other source for Thomas's theology of the sacramental seal is Dionysius the Areopagite, particularly the *Ecclesiastical Hierarchy* 5, from which Aquinas derives the idea of a seal that grants one a participation in the priesthood of Christ. The three sacraments that confer this seal make one suited to a particular role in the church, which is essentially a "cultic" community—that is, a community of worship. Thus baptism confers a seal such that the baptized are both suited to worship God through receiving the sacraments, and obliged to offer worship to the Father along with Christ, the great high priest. Confirmation confers the seal that allows one to honor God by publicly witnessing to God before the world. And ordination confers the seal that grants one the status to worship God not only by receiving the sacraments, but also by ministering them.

2. The force of this objection is that what distinguishes God's people from other people is something in God, not something in his people.

3. The word translated here as "outward appearance" is *species,* a Latin word with a wide range of meanings.

4. The somewhat convoluted (but not invalid) logic of this objection is as follows:
1. Baptism brings about an effect in the soul.
2. Things in the soul are spiritual.
3. A seal (*character*) is a kind of sign.
4. A sign is something that makes an impression on the senses.
5. Things that make an impression on the senses must be perceptible, not spiritual.
6. Therefore, the effect of baptism cannot be the imparting of a *character.*

I answer: As is clear from what has been stated already (3.62.5), the sacraments of the New Law are intended for a twofold purpose, namely, as a remedy against sins and to perfect the soul in things having to do with the worship of God according to the rituals of the Christian life.[5] Now whenever anyone is assigned to some definite purpose it is normal for that person to receive some outward sign of this assignment. Thus, in antiquity, soldiers enlisted in military service used to be signified by certain marks on the body, on account of being appointed to something bodily. Since by the sacraments people are appointed to a spiritual service pertaining to the worship of God, it follows that by means of the sacraments the faithful receive a certain spiritual seal. For this reason Augustine says in *Against the Letter of Parmenian* (bk. 2, chap. 13), "If a deserter from the battle, through fear of the mark of enlistment on his body, throws himself on the emperor's mercy and, having sought and received mercy, returns to the fight, is that seal renewed when the man has been set free and reprimanded, or is it not acknowledged and approved instead? Are the Christian sacraments, by any chance, of a less lasting nature than this bodily mark?"

Reply to 1: The seal of divine predestination destines the faithful of Christ to the reward of the glory that is to come. But they are appointed to acts befitting the church in the present by a certain spiritual mark that is set on them, and this is called a seal.[6]

Reply to 2: The seal imprinted on the soul is a kind of sign insofar as it is imprinted by a perceptible sacrament, for we know that someone has received the baptismal seal because he has been washed by perceptible water. Nevertheless, anything that assimilates one thing to another, or discriminates one

5. Here we can see some of the structural similarities between Thomas's thinking about the incarnation and his thinking about the sacraments. Both the incarnation and the sacraments have a two-fold purpose: (1) a negative one—to draw us away from sin; and (2) a positive one—to draw us toward the good (see 3.1, note 13). The good toward which Christians are drawn in the sacraments is the worship of God. But to participate in the worship of God is to participate in Christ's priesthood, as Thomas will make clear in a later article (3.63.3). So it is through the gift of the sacramental sealing of baptism, confirmation, and ordination that Christians are made capable of receiving and sharing the benefit of worshiping God. Behind this understanding of the sacramental seal is a profoundly biblical understanding of the church as a "a chosen race, a royal priesthood, a holy nation, God's own people" (1 Peter 2:9); the Christian community has been chosen and marked by God as a priestly people, who offer worship to God on behalf of all humanity.

6. Here Thomas makes a distinction between that which has to do with our future (divine predestination) and that which has to do with our present (the sacramental seal by which we participate in Christ's priesthood). Behind this distinction lies the view that not all people who are sealed by God in baptism or confirmation or ordination will necessarily be saved. The sacramental seal is indelible, because it is a power deriving from Christ's eternal priesthood, but grace is not (as Thomas argues in 3.63.5 *ad* 1), because the human soul is changeable in this life. Thus an unbelieving person who is baptized does receive the sacramental seal but does not receive grace (3.68.9 *ad* 1). However, with the sacrament of penance, the full effects of baptism can be received after the fact (3.68.10).

thing from another, even though it is not perceptible, can be called a seal or a mark on account of a kind of likeness; thus the Apostle calls Christ "the figure" (in Greek, *charakter*) "of the substance of the Father" (Hebrews 1:3).[7]

Reply to 3: As stated earlier (3.62.6) the sacraments of the Old Law did not have in themselves any spiritual power of producing a spiritual effect. Consequently, in those sacraments there was no need of a spiritual seal, and bodily circumcision sufficed, which the Apostle calls a "mark" in Romans 4:11.

7. Thomas quotes this verse from Hebrews several times in his discussion of the sacramental seal, which would indicate that it provides something of a key to his understanding of *charakter*. The visible rite of baptism *does* make an impression on the senses, but this is not the heart of what Thomas means by the sacramental seal. To stay with the metaphor of "impression," we might say that the sacramental seal is not a matter of making an impression upon our senses, but of God "impressing" Christ (who is the *charakter* of God) upon the soul, like a signet ring making an impression in wax. In this way, Christians are quite literally "conformed" to Christ—spiritually molded and shaped in his likeness.

Thomas is also alluding here to his view that the sacramental seal is the *res et sacramentum*. On the categories of *sacramentum tantum*, *res et sacramentum*, and *res tantum*, see 3.66, note 4.

QUESTION 65

THE NUMBER OF THE SACRAMENTS

3.65.1

Whether there should be seven sacraments?[1]

It seems that there should not be seven sacraments.[2]

1. The sacraments derive their efficacy from divine power and from the power of Christ's passion. But the divine power is one and Christ's passion is one, since "by one offering he has perfected for ever those who are sanctified," as Hebrews 10:14 says. Therefore there should be only one sacrament.[3]

2. A sacrament is intended as a remedy for the defect caused by sin, which is twofold: penalty and guilt [*poena et culpa*].[4] Therefore two sacraments would be enough.

1. In Thomas's day the official numbering of the sacraments at seven—baptism, confirmation, Eucharist, penance (confession or reconciliation), extreme unction (anointing of the sick), marriage, and ordination—was comparatively recent. Various theologians in the twelfth century offered different enumerations; some of them omitted such things as marriage or ordination, whereas others included such things as the use of holy water or the taking of monastic vows (Abelard had five sacraments and Bernard of Clairvaux had ten). The theologian Peter Lombard, in his *Sentences,* numbered them at seven (bk. 4, distinction 2, chap. 1), and it was largely because of the influence of this text that seven was accepted as the definitive number of sacraments.

2. Note that the objections move progressively from arguing for only one sacrament (obj. 1) to arguing for six sacraments, omitting marriage (obj. 5).

3. In some ways the first objection is the most powerful, because it asks why there should be *any* diversification of the sacraments, given that they all have the same effect of imparting grace.

4. In other words, in sinning we both incur a penalty (*poena*) by which our natures are damaged and damage our relationship with God by incurring guilt (*culpa*). However, one needs

3. Sacraments belong to the actions of the ecclesiastical hierarchy,[5] as Dionysius explains. But, as he says, there are three actions of the ecclesiastical hierarchy, namely, to purify, to enlighten, and to perfect (*The Ecclesiastical Hierarchy,* chap. 5, no. 3). Therefore there should be no more than three sacraments.

4. Augustine says in *Against Faustus the Manichean* (bk. 19, chap. 13) that the sacraments of the New Law are less numerous than those of the Old Law. But in the Old Law there was no sacrament corresponding to confirmation and extreme unction. Therefore these should not be counted among the sacraments of the New Law.

5. Lust is no more serious than other sins, as we have made clear in the second part (2–2.74.5; 2–2.154.3). But there is no sacrament instituted as a remedy for other sins; therefore neither should marriage be instituted as a remedy for lust.

On the contrary: It seems that there should be more than seven sacraments.[6]

6. Sacraments are a kind of sacred sign. But in the church many blessings are by perceptible signs, such as the blessing of water, the consecration of altars, and other similar things. Therefore there are more than seven sacraments.

7. Hugh of St. Victor (*On the Sacraments of the Christian Faith* 1.12.4) says that the sacraments of the Old Law were offerings, tithes, and sacrifices.[7] But the sacrifice of the church is one sacrament, called the Eucharist. Therefore offerings and tithes also should be called sacraments.

8. There are three kinds of sin: original, mortal, and venial. Baptism is intended as a remedy against original sin, and penance against mortal sin. Therefore, besides the seven sacraments, there should be another against venial sin.

I answer: As stated earlier (3.63.1), the sacraments of the church were instituted for a twofold purpose, namely, in order to help human beings develop fully [*perficere*] in things having to do with the worship of God according to the rituals of the Christian life,[8] and to be a remedy against the defects caused

---

to understand that by "penalty" Thomas does not mean a punishment arbitrarily applied by God. See 3.46, note 28.

5. That is to say, the priesthood.

6. Note that here Aquinas deviates from the usual pattern of an article. After five objections arguing that seven sacraments are too *many,* he now offers three objections—introduced by his usual phrase *sed contra* ("On the contrary" or "On the other hand")—arguing that seven sacraments are too *few.*

7. That is, offerings of things; percentage offerings (tithes); and offerings of animals (sacrifices).

8. *Perficere* can, of course, be translated as "to perfect," and in other places I have translated it this way. But, as noted above (see 1.45, note 14), for Thomas "perfection" really means "full actualization," which we might also describe as "full development." Since in this article Aquinas speaks of the role of the sacraments in terms of the analogy of human physical and social development, it seems that "develop" better conveys his meaning here. It is important, however, to recall that for Thomas something develops in a certain way only under the influence of something else that is already developed in that way.

by sin.[9] And in either way it is fitting that there should be seven sacraments; for spiritual life has a certain resemblance to the life of the body, just as other bodily things have a certain likeness to spiritual things.

In bodily life one develops in two ways: first, in regard to one's own person; second, in regard to the whole community of the society in which one lives, for a human being is by nature a social animal.[10]

With regard to oneself, a person develops in the life of the body in two ways: first, directly [per se], that is, by acquiring something that brings a certain development to life; second, indirectly [per accidens], that is, by the removal of hindrances to life, such as sickness or the like.

The life of the body is developed directly in three ways. First, through generation, by which a person begins to be and to live, and corresponding to this in the spiritual life there is baptism, which is a spiritual regeneration, according to Titus 3:5, "By the washing of regeneration," and so on. Second, through growth, by which a person is brought to their full size and strength, and corresponding to this in the spiritual life there is confirmation, in which the Holy Spirit is given to strengthen us.[11] For this reason the disciples, who were already baptized, were told in Luke 24:49, "Stay in the city until you are clothed with power from on high." Third, through nourishment, by which life and strength are preserved in a person, and corresponding to this in the spiritual life there is the Eucharist. Therefore it is said in John 6:54, "Unless you eat of the flesh of the Son of Man, and drink his blood, you shall not have life in you."

And [these three sacraments] would suffice if a person could have a life free from bodily and spiritual suffering; but since people are subject at times both to bodily weakness and to spiritual weakness (i.e., sin) they therefore need a cure for their weakness. This cure is twofold. First is healing, which restores health, and corresponding to this in the spiritual life there is penance. According to Psalm 41:4, "Heal my soul, for I have sinned against you." Second is the restoration of former vigor by means of suitable diet and exercise, and corresponding to this in the spiritual life there is extreme unction, which removes the remainder of sin and prepares a person for final glory.[12] Therefore it is written in James 5:15, "And if he has sins, they shall be forgiven him."

9. See 3.63, note 5. Thomas spends most of his time in this article discussing how sacraments perfect human beings in the worship of God. He also offers two brief discussions of how one might think of sacraments as remedies for sin. Given this mismatch of allotted space, it seems that Aquinas prefers to think about the sacraments as things that perfect or fulfill us spiritually, rather than as things that function as remedies for sin.

10. This precise articulation of the view that human beings are by nature social is one that Aquinas takes over from Aristotle, though the view itself was one almost universally accepted in the Middle Ages.

11. Notice that Aquinas thinks of confirmation as a sacrament of growth, not, as is common today, as a sacrament of some sort of intellectual "maturity."

12. In the Middle Ages the anointing of the sick was usually reserved for those at the brink of death—thus the name "extreme unction" (lit. "final anointing"). Aquinas therefore thinks

In regard to the whole community, a person develops in two ways. First, by receiving power to rule the community and to carry out public acts, and corresponding to this in the spiritual life there is the sacrament of ordination. Accordingly, it says in Hebrews 7:27 that priests offer sacrifices not for themselves only, but also for the people. Second, in regard to natural procreation, which is accomplished by marriage, both in the bodily and in the spiritual life, since it is not only a sacrament but also a function of nature.[13]

We may likewise gather the number of the sacraments according to their being intended as a remedy against the defects caused by sin:[14] baptism is intended as a remedy against the absence of spiritual life; confirmation, against the weakness of soul found in those of recent birth; the Eucharist, against the soul's tendency to sin; penance, against actual sin committed after baptism; extreme unction, against the remainders of sins—that is, of those sins that are not sufficiently removed by penance, whether through negligence or through ignorance; ordination, against divisions in the community; matrimony, as a remedy against sinful desire in the individual and against the decrease in numbers that results from death.

Finally, some incline toward numbering the sacraments according to a certain adaptation to the virtues and to the defects and penalties resulting from sin.[15] They say that baptism corresponds to faith, and is intended as a remedy against original sin; extreme unction corresponds to hope and is intended as a

---

of it as a sacrament preparing one for the vision of God, not as a sacrament designed to bring about physical healing; however, he does say in *Summa contra Gentiles* 4.73 that "by this spiritual remedy bodily sickness is sometimes cured, when it is expedient for salvation." In terms of his analogy of health or vigor, penance is like an operation to remove a tumor or, perhaps better, the resuscitation of someone whose heart has stopped, whereas extreme unction is like physical therapy, which restores us to our former (spiritual) strength.

13. Aquinas's discussion in the preceding paragraphs is perhaps easier in outline form. Remember, he is drawing an analogy between what one needs to develop in bodily existence and what one needs to develop in spiritual existence. Thus we have:

    I. Fulfillment as an individual
        A. directly (*per se*): by the provision of what aids in fulfillment
            1. birth (baptism)
            2. growth (confirmation)
            3. nourishment (Eucharist)
        B. indirectly (*per accidens*): by the removal of what hinders fulfillment
            4. healing (penance)
            5. recuperation (extreme unction)
    II. Fulfillment as a member of a community
            6. receiving power to rule and act publicly (ordination)
            7. propagating (marriage)

14. Here Aquinas turns to sacraments as ways of withdrawing from sin. First he looks at them as specific kinds of medicines for specific spiritual ills. Then he draws a connection between the seven sacraments and the three theological virtues (faith, hope, and charity) and four cardinal virtues (prudence, justice, temperance, and fortitude), and the corresponding vices of each.

15. For example, see Alexander of Hales (*Summa universae theologiae* 4.8.7.2) and Bonaventure (*Breviloquium* 6.3.2–3).

remedy against venial sin; the Eucharist corresponds to charity and is intended as a remedy against the tendency toward hatred; ordination corresponds to prudence and is intended as a remedy against ignorance; penance corresponds to justice and is intended as a remedy against mortal sin; marriage corresponds to temperance and is intended as a remedy against sinful desire; confirmation corresponds to fortitude and is intended as a remedy against weakness.

Reply to 1: The same principal agent uses diverse instruments to bring about diverse effects, in accordance with the thing to be done. In the same way, the divine power and the passion of Christ work in us through the diverse sacraments as through diverse instruments.[16]

Reply to 2: There is a diversity of guilt and penalty, both according to what they are—inasmuch as there are various kinds of guilt and penalty—and according to people's various states and conditions. And in this respect it was necessary to have a number of sacraments, as explained above.[17]

Reply to 3: In hierarchical actions we must consider the agents, the recipients, and the actions. The agents are the ministers of the church, and to these the sacrament of ordination belongs. The recipients are those who approach the sacraments, and these are brought into being by marriage. The actions are purifying, enlightening, and developing [*perfectio*].[18] But purification, considered in isolation, cannot be one of the sacraments of the New Law, which confer grace; rather, it belongs to certain sacramentals, namely, instruction in the faith and exorcism. But purification along with enlightenment, according to Dionysius, belongs to baptism; and for one who falls back into sin, it belongs secondarily to penance and extreme unction. Developing with regard to an ability—which is something like a formal perfection—belongs to confirmation,[19] whereas, as regards the attainment of the end, it belongs to the Eucharist.

16. In this response Aquinas does not address directly the question of why there needs to be more than one sacrament, but his answer is implied in the body of the article. It is important to remember that sacraments are for *our* benefit and are not necessary from God's perspective. Similarly, the *diversity* of the sacraments is for our benefit. Just as the single goal of bodily fulfillment requires a diversity of particular goods (birth, nourishment, reproduction, etc.), so too the single goal of spiritual fulfillment requires a diversity of "instruments" (on "instrumental causality" in general, see 1.45, note 10; on sacraments as "instruments," see 3.62, note 11). A single carpenter can make a table; the carpenter, however, uses various tools—a saw, a plane, a hammer, and so on—as is required by the material that she is working with. Similarly, although there is a single principal cause of grace—God—there are a diversity of instrumental causes as required by the material upon which God is working, namely, the embodied human person.

17. Aquinas grants the objection's claim that the sacraments can be diversified according to sin, but the relevant categories are not the effects of sin (guilt and penalty) but the kinds (*species*) of sin, which he addresses in the body of the article.

18. See note 8, above.

19. Thomas speaks hear of perfection with regard to a *virtus,* which could be translated as "virtue" or "power" or "capacity," but which I have translated as "ability" in light of his description of it as a *quasi perfectio formalis.* In other words, to acquire an ability is something like acquiring a new form—that is, becoming a new kind of thing. Thus one who acquires skill

Reply to 4: In the sacrament of confirmation we receive the fullness of the Holy Spirit in order to be strengthened, whereas in extreme unction a person is prepared so that they may take in God's unveiled glory,[20] and neither of these two purposes was suited to the Old Testament. Consequently, nothing in the Old Law could correspond to these sacraments.[21] Nevertheless, the sacraments of the Old Law were more numerous, because of the various kinds of sacrifices and ceremonies.

Reply to 5: There was need for a special sacrament to be applied as a remedy against sinful sexual desire [*concupiscentiam venereorum*]: first, because not only

---

in archery becomes an archer, and one who acquires skill in pottery becomes a potter. But the word *virtus* also carries a moral connotation, inasmuch as Aquinas defines "virtue" as an ability to act well.

20. I have translated *ut recipiat immediate gloriam* loosely, interpreting it as referring to the unmediated nature of the vision of God, not the temporal immediacy of that vision. However, Thomas could be saying that those who receive the sacrament of extreme unction, being cleansed of venial sins, do not need purification in purgatory and thus see God without delay.

21. The fullness of the Holy Spirit is not given until the day of Pentecost, after Jesus's ascension into heaven, and so a sacrament signifying this reception of the Spirit would not be appropriate to the Old Testament. Likewise the attainment of the direct vision of God's glory is possible only after the death of Christ. Until the death of Christ, holy people could not attain the vision of God and awaited Christ's coming in a place of departed spirits. This realm, sometimes called *limbus patrum* (limbo [from the Latin for "edge"] of the fathers), is an ancient Christian belief that is closely related to the Jewish notion of Sheol, which was the place in which the righteous dead awaited resurrection on the last day. Something like limbo is perhaps alluded to in Ephesians 4:9, which says that Christ "also descended into the lower parts of the earth," or in 1 Peter 3:18–19: "[Christ] was put to death in the flesh, but made alive in the spirit, in which also he went and made proclamation to the spirits in prison." A similar allusion can be found in Ignatius of Antioch's (ca. 35–ca. 107) Epistle to the Magnesians 9:2, and in Irenaeus (ca. 140–200) we find an explicit statement that "the Lord went down under the earth to proclaim to them [i.e., the righteous dead] his coming, the remission of sins for those who believe in him" (*Against Heresies,* bk. 4, chap. 27.2). The so-called *Gospel of Nicodemus,* probably written in the fourth century, gives a vivid account of Christ breaking down the gates of hell and rescuing Adam, Eve, and all the just from the clutches of Satan.

The *limbus patrum* is distinguished from the *limbus infantium* or *puerorum* (limbo of infants or children), which is the realm of those who were never baptized and never attained the age of reason. There they enjoy a limited, natural happiness, being deprived of the supernatural vision of God because they lack the grace of baptism (whether water baptism, or baptism of desire; see 3.68, notes 6 and 7). This idea arose as a mitigation of the teaching of Augustine that unbaptized infants were damned to hell (where, he notes, their punishment is lenient; see *Enchiridion on Faith, Hope, and Love,* chap. 93). The *limbus puerorum,* which Aquinas accepted (see *Scriptum super libros Sententiarum,* bk. 4, distinction 45, q. 1, a. 2, subquestion 3), never became part of official church teaching, despite its nearly universal acceptance by theologians. In recent decades, it has fallen out of favor, perhaps because it seems to restrict God's saving will too narrowly. The current *Catechism of the Catholic Church* states, "Indeed, the great mercy of God who desires that all men should be saved (1 Timothy 2:4), and Jesus' tenderness toward children which caused him to say: 'Let the children come to me, do not hinder them' (Mark 10:14), allow us to hope that there is a way of salvation for children who have died without Baptism" (par. 1261).

the person but also the nature is corrupted by this desire;[22] second, because of its intensity, by which it enthralls reason.

Reply to 6: Holy water and other consecrated things are not called sacraments because they do not produce the effect of a sacrament, which is the receiving of grace.[23] They are, however, a kind of disposition to the sacraments, either by removing obstacles—thus holy water is intended against the snares of the demons and against venial sins—or by making things suitable for the conferring of a sacrament—thus the altar and vessels are consecrated on account of reverence for the Eucharist.

Reply to 7: Offerings and tithes, both in the law of nature and in the Law of Moses, were intended not only for the sustenance of the ministers and the poor, but also as prefigurations; and it is for this reason that they were sacraments.[24] But now they no longer remain as prefigurations, and therefore they are not sacraments.

Reply to 8: The infusion of grace is not necessary for the blotting out of venial sin.[25] Therefore, since grace is infused in each of the sacraments of the New Law, none of them was instituted directly against venial sin, which is taken away by certain sacramentals, for instance holy water and similar things. Some people, however, hold that extreme unction is intended as a remedy against venial sin; but of this we shall speak in its proper place.[26]

22. It is not entirely clear what Aquinas means here. Perhaps he is referring to the Augustinian view that original sin (i.e., the corruption of human nature) is transmitted through the sinful desire that inevitably accompanies sexual intercourse.

23. Earlier writers, such as Hugh of St. Victor, had used the term *sacramentum* very broadly to speak of all the mysteries of the Christian faith, and, as noted (see note 1, above), for at least the first millennium the use of the term was not fixed. Thomas is trying to bring greater precision to the term by marking the difference between the seven sacraments of the church and those other rituals of blessing employed by Christians (what he calls *sacramentales*). He makes this distinction in terms of their effect: the seven sacraments are instrumental causes of grace, whereas these other rituals of blessing create the fitting context for the bestowal of grace but are not themselves instrumental causes of grace. To use the example of a carpenter: the carpenter might do better work while listening to music, but we would not normally describe her radio as one of her tools.

24. On prefigurations or "figures," see 1.1, note 43. Aquinas calls the rituals commanded by the Old Law "sacraments," though they are in fact more like the *sacramentales* discussed in the previous objection because they are not themselves causes of grace.

25. In contrast to a mortal sin, a venial sin is not a definitive turning away from God; therefore it does not require a new imparting ("infusion") of grace in order for it to be overcome.

26. Thomas died before actually getting to the discussion of the sacrament of extreme unction in the *Summa;* a discussion can be found in question 30, article 1 of the *Supplementum* (see 1–2.4, note 12). In his early commentary on the *Sentences* of Peter Lombard (from which the discussion in the *Supplementum* was taken), Aquinas holds the view that although the removal of venial sins is not the *principal* effect of extreme unction (i.e., the effect for which it was instituted), it may be, as it were, a "side effect."

QUESTION 66

THE SACRAMENT OF BAPTISM

3.66.1

Whether baptism is the act of washing itself?

It seems that baptism is not the act of washing itself.[1]

1. The washing of the body is something transitory, but baptism is something permanent. Therefore baptism is not the act of washing itself; rather it is "the regeneration, the seal, the safeguarding, the enlightenment," as John of Damascus says (*On the Orthodox Faith*, bk. 4, chap. 9).[2]

2. Hugh of St. Victor says (*On the Sacraments of the Christian Faith* 2.6.2) that "baptism is water sanctified by God's word for the blotting out of sins." But the act of washing itself is not water, but a certain use of water.[3]

3. Augustine says in his *Homilies on the Gospel of John* (sermon 80, no. 3), "The word is added to the element, and this becomes a sacrament." But the

1. There are two essential points at issue in this question. The first is whether we should think of sacraments as consecrated "objects" (e.g., water, oil, bread) or as "actions." The second point addresses the need for clarity when speaking about the sacramental sign, the reality being signified and brought about, and the ultimate effect at which the sacrament aims.

2. This objection addresses the question of whether the sacrament should be thought of as the transitory sign or as the permanent effect that is brought about. In other words, is baptism about being washed in water, or is it about rebirth, the conferring of a seal, and so on?

3. This objection and the following one raise the issue of sacraments as "objects" versus sacraments as "actions."

element is the water, and therefore baptism is the water and not the act of washing.

On the contrary: It is written in Sirach 34:30, "One who washes himself [*baptizatur*] after touching the dead, if he touches him again, what does his washing avail?" It seems, therefore, that baptism is the act of washing or bathing.

I answer: In the sacrament of baptism, three things may be considered: that which is "sacrament only" [*sacramentum tantum*]; that which is "reality and sacrament" [*res et tantum*]; and that which is "reality only" [*res tantum*].[4]

That which is sacrament only [*sacramentum tantum*] is something visible and outward—namely, the sign of the inward effect, which is the very definition of a sacrament. And this outward thing that can be perceived by the senses is both the water itself and its use, which is the washing.[5] Therefore some people have thought that the sacrament is the water itself, which seems to be the meaning of the passage quoted from Hugh of St. Victor [objection 2], for in the general definition of a sacrament he says that it is "a material element,"

4. It was Augustine, in his *De doctrina Christiana,* who introduced the language of "sign" (*signum*) and the "thing" (*res*) to which the sign pointed. In terms of sacramental theology, the sign or sacrament is the visible element of the rite, whereas the "thing" is the effect brought about by the sacrament. After the controversy over the teachings of Berengar in the eleventh century (see 3.61, note 8), theologians, seeking to avoid the position that sacraments are "mere signs," began to develop the notion of a middle term between the sacrament itself (*sacramentum tantum*—i.e., the outward sign) and the thing itself (*res tantum*—i.e., the ultimate effect of the sacrament). This middle term was understood as the immediate effect of the sacrament, which linked the sign and its ultimate effect. Hugh of St. Victor and Peter Abelard both spoke of this immediate effect of the sacrament as being both "thing and sacrament" (*res et sacramentum*). At the beginning of the thirteenth century, Pope Innocent III endorsed this terminology.

This set of distinctions became a standard tool in later medieval sacramental theology. In this article, Aquinas applies the distinctions to baptism: the *sacramentum tantum* is the rite of washing with water; the *res et sacramentum* is the sacramental seal that is conferred; and the *res tantum* is the justification or "making righteous" of the sinner. In terms of the Eucharist, Aquinas sees the *sacramentum tantum* as the bread and wine, the *res et sacramentum* as the body and blood of Christ, and the *res tantum* as unity in and with Christ.

Note that the *res et sacramentum* is unfailingly brought about by the proper performance of the sacramental rite (*ex opera operato*): in baptism the sacramental seal is conferred; in the Eucharist the body and blood of Christ become present. However, the *res tantum*—the ultimate purpose of the rite—is *not* unfailingly brought about. It can be hindered by sin on the part of the one who receives the sacrament. Thus although all who are baptized receive the seal of Christ, they are not all made righteous. And although all who receive the Eucharist receive the body and blood of Christ, they are not all united in and with Christ. Therefore the sacraments do not work mechanically.

5. Thomas employs the notion of *sacramentum tantum* to make clear that what he is speaking of here is the sacramental rite, which includes both the water and its ritual use. Thus for Thomas a sacrament is not a sacred object but a sacred *action* that involves material objects; he therefore seems to have preserved some of the ancient Christian sense of the intimate connection of sacraments and liturgy. Although he does not generally begin his sacramental theology by looking at the rites according to which the sacraments are celebrated (which was common in the patristic period and is making something of a comeback today), he does not totally ignore the ritual element of the sacraments.

and in defining baptism he says it is "water." But this is not true;[6] for since the sacraments of the New Law bring about a certain sanctification, the sacrament takes place where the sanctification takes place. But the sanctification does not happen in the water; rather, a certain instrumental sanctifying power, which is not permanent but transient, flows from the water into the human person, who is the subject of true sanctification. Consequently, the sacrament does not occur in the water itself, but in applying the water to a human being, that is, in the washing.[7] Therefore the Master in his book of *Sentences* (bk. 4, distinction 3) says that "baptism is the outward washing of the body done together with the prescribed form of words."

The reality and sacrament [*res et sacramentum*] is the baptismal seal, which is both the thing signified by the outward washing, and a sacramental sign of the inward justification.[8] In this sacrament, this justification is the reality only [*res tantum*]—namely, the reality signified and not signifying.[9]

Reply to 1: That which is both sacrament and reality—that is, the seal—and that which is reality only—that is, the inward justification—remain: the seal remains and is indelible, as stated earlier (3.63.5); the justification remains, but can be lost. Consequently, John of Damascus defined baptism not with regard to what is done outwardly, which is the sacrament only, but with regard to what is inward. Therefore he sets down two things as pertaining to the seal, namely, "mark" [*sigillum*] and "safeguarding," since the seal, which is called a mark, so far as it is concerned in itself, safeguards the soul in good. He also sets down two things as pertaining to the ultimate reality of the sacrament, namely, "regeneration," which refers to the fact that a person, by being baptized, begins the new life of righteousness, and "enlightenment," which refers especially to faith, by which a person receives spiritual life, according to Habakuk 2 (Hebrews 10:38; cf. Habakuk 2:4), "The just one lives by faith."[10] Baptism is a sort of declaration of faith, and for this reason it is called the "sacrament of faith."

6. For Aquinas, this is an unusually bald statement of disagreement with a theological authority. Earlier (3.62.3) he had conceded, on Hugh's theological authority, that the sacraments of the New Covenant can be said to "contain" grace. However, Thomas still worries that this view can be taken in too material a sense, as if the material object itself constituted the sacrament. Hugh compares sacraments to jars that contain medicine, an analogy that is quite alien to Thomas's way of thinking about sacraments. Here Thomas makes clear that sacraments "contain" grace only inasmuch as they *confer* grace through the use of visible signs in a ritual context.

7. In other words, the purpose of baptism is not to make holy water, but to make holy people.

8. It is interesting that Thomas calls the "character" or "seal" conferred by baptism a "sign," since it is not something that is apprehensible by our senses in the normal way. However, because it is something unfailingly brought about by the sign of washing with water, it shares, as it were, in the "sign" qualities of that washing.

9. That is, in contrast with the *res et sacramentum,* which is both something signified (by the ritual of baptism) as well as itself a sign (of justification).

10. In Thomas's terms, John of Damascus is speaking of the *res et sacramentum* (the "mark" and the "safeguarding" of the sacramental seal) and the *res tantum* (the "regeneration" and the

Similarly, Dionysius defined baptism by its relation to the other sacraments, saying in *The Ecclesiastical Hierarchy* (chap. 2, no. 1) that it is "like the source of the most holy commands of the sacred action, which forms in the soul the dispositions for their reception"; and again by its relation to heavenly glory, which is the universal goal of all the sacraments, when he adds, "preparing the way for us, by which we mount to the repose of the heavenly kingdom"; and again as to the beginning of spiritual life, when he adds, "the handing on of our sacred and most Godlike regeneration."[11]

Reply to 2: As already stated [in the reply above], the opinion of Hugh of St. Victor on this question is not to be followed. Nevertheless, the saying that "baptism is water" may be accepted as true insofar as water is the material principle of baptism. This would be a case of "causal predication."[12]

Reply to 3: When the words are added, the element becomes a sacrament, not in the element itself, but in the person to whom the element is applied by being used in washing him. Indeed, this is signified by those very words that are added to the element, when we say, "I baptize you," and so on.[13]

"enlightenment" of being made righteous by God), whereas Thomas himself is speaking of the *sacramentum tantum*. Of course, this is not the conceptual framework within which John worked.

11. Though Dionysius is not mentioned in the objection, Thomas deals with him in the reply. He does so in much the same way as he deals with John of Damascus, by analyzing what he says in terms of the categories of *res et sacramentum* (the seal disposes one to reception of the other sacraments) and *res tantum* (heavenly glory).

12. In other words, a case of speaking of baptism in terms of its causes. In this case, water is the material cause of the sacramental sign. Aquinas seems to think that this might be technically correct (thus Hugh's statement is not heretical), but it is ultimately a misleading way in which to speak about baptism.

13. Thomas notes that the words used in the administration of baptism are addressed to the recipient, not to the water. The water is, of course, blessed before it is used, but the sacrament does not take place until that use.

QUESTION 68

THOSE WHO RECEIVE BAPTISM

3.68.2

Whether a person can be saved without baptism?

It seems that no person can be saved without baptism.

1. Our Lord said in John 3:5, "Unless one is born again of water and the Holy Spirit, it is not possible to enter the kingdom of God." But only those who enter God's kingdom are saved. Therefore no person can be saved without baptism, by which one is born again of water and the Holy Spirit.

2. In the book *De ecclesiasticis dogmatibus* (chap. 41),[1] it is written, "We believe that no catechumen,[2] even one who dies with good works, will have eternal life, except in the case of martyrdom, in which everything in the sacrament of baptism is fulfilled."[3] But if it were possible for anyone to be saved

1. A work by Gennadius of Marseilles, who lived in the fifth century. During the Middle Ages it circulated in collections of works by Augustine, and many people attributed it to him. Thomas usually quotes it without ascribing an author, though in two places he ascribes it to Augustine (see *Lectura super Matthaeum* 6.3 and *Scriptum super libros Sententiarum,* bk. 4, distinction 14, q. 2, a. 5 *ad* 5).

2. A catechumen is one who is preparing for baptism; the term comes from the Greek word for one who "hears."

3. The idea that martyrs are "baptized in blood" is an ancient one in Christianity. Cyprian (d. 258), for example, speaks of "the most glorious and most sublime blood-baptism" (epistle 73.22). Thomas himself writes in 3.66.11 that one who is martyred "without baptism of water receives the sacramental effect from Christ's passion, insofar as he is conformed to Christ by suffering for him."

without baptism, this would be the case especially with catechumens who are credited with good works, for they seem to have the "faith that works through love" (Galatians 5:6). Therefore it seems that no person can be saved without baptism.

3. As stated earlier (3.68.1; 3.65.4), the sacrament of baptism is necessary for salvation. But something is necessary if "without it something cannot be," as it is said in the *Metaphysics* (bk. 5, chap. 5, 1015ª). Therefore it seems that no person can obtain salvation without baptism.

On the contrary: Augustine says regarding the book of Leviticus (*Questions on the Heptateuch*, bk. 3, q. 84) that "some have received the benefits of invisible sanctification without visible sacraments; truly it is possible to have the visible sanctification conferred by the visible sacrament without the invisible sanctification, but it will bring no benefit."[4] Since, therefore, the sacrament of baptism pertains to the visible sanctification, it seems that a person can obtain salvation without the sacrament of baptism by means of an invisible sanctification.

I answer: Someone may lack the sacrament of baptism in two ways.[5] First, in both reality and in desire, as in the case with those who neither are baptized, nor wished to be baptized. In the case of those who have the use of the free-will, this clearly indicates contempt of the sacrament. Consequently, those who in this sense are unbaptized cannot obtain salvation, since are they neither sacramentally nor mentally incorporated into Christ, through whom alone can salvation be obtained.

4. In other words, the visible sacrament of baptism does not unfailingly bring about salvation; only the invisible sanctification of grace does so. This distinction between the visible and invisible is important to the Augustinian conception of the church. Augustine says elsewhere, "As long as she is a stranger in the world, the city of God has in her communion, and bound to her by the sacraments, some who shall not eternally dwell in the lot of the saints." Similarly, some citizens of God's city are not yet bound to the church by the visible sacraments, but by an invisible sanctification. Thus, "in truth, these two cities are entangled together in this world, and intermixed until the last judgment effects their separation"(*City of God,* bk. 1, chap. 35).

5. What Aquinas says in the following response is based on the scholastic distinction between (1) *sacramentum tantum,* (2) *res et sacramentum,* and (3) *res tantum* (see 3.66, note 4); in baptism, these terms would correspond to (1) the outward washing with water in the name of the Trinity, (2) the conferring of the inward baptismal seal (*character*), and (3) the justification or "making righteous" of the sinner. His essential argument is that one can have the last without the first—the *res* without the *sacramentum*—because desire for the sacrament is sufficient to bring about its ultimate effect in those cases where the outward sign is, for whatever reason, truly unavailable. However, an explicit refusal of the outward sign would, in Thomas's eyes, make it impossible to receive its ultimate effect, because it would constitute a lack of charity.

When Thomas says that one may lack the sacrament of baptism in two ways, he is not in fact exhausting all of the possibilities available to him. One might, as he will point out, lack both the visible sign *and* its ultimate effect, or one might lack the visible sign but *not* its ultimate effect. However, one might also have the visible sign, but still lack its ultimate effect, as in the case of those who place an obstacle in the way of God's grace through receiving the sacrament with insincerity or hard-heartedness.

Second, someone may lack the sacrament of baptism in reality but not in desire, as is the case when someone wishes to be baptized but for some reason dies before receiving baptism. Such a person can obtain salvation without being actually baptized, on account of the desire for baptism, which comes from the "faith that works through love." By this love, God, whose power is not tied to visible sacraments, sanctifies a person inwardly.[6] Therefore Ambrose says of Valentinian,[7] who died while still a catechumen, "I lost him whom I was to regenerate, but he did not lose the grace he prayed for" (*De obitu Valentiniani consolatio,* nos. 29, 30).

Reply to 1: As it is written in 1 Kings 16:7, "People see those things that appear, but the Lord beholds the heart." Now one who desires to be "born again of water and the Holy Spirit" by baptism is regenerated in heart, though not in body. Thus the Apostle says in Romans 2:29 that "circumcision of the heart is spiritual, not literal; whose praise is not from people but from God."[8]

Reply to 2: No person obtains eternal life unless he is free from all guilt and debt of punishment. But this complete absolution is given when one receives baptism, or suffers martyrdom; for this reason is it said that in martyrdom "everything in the sacrament of baptism is fulfilled," that is, with regard to

---

6. This notion of "baptism of desire" was used by Catholics in former generations who wished to make allowance for the possible salvation of those who were outside the visible bounds of the Roman Catholic Church due to a physical or moral impossibility of their obtaining the sacrament. Sometimes this phenomenon was also called the "baptism by the Holy Spirit" or "baptism of flames" (*baptismus flaminis*—a kind of patristic pun on *baptismus fluminis* or "baptism in a river"). The latter designation in particular indicated both of the fire of the Spirit and the person's burning desire for the sacrament. The possibility of baptism of desire is an official teaching of the church.

Until recently, debates about baptism of desire centered on questions concerning what constituted a "moral impossibility" and how "burning" this desire had to be. For example, if one was raised a Muslim or a Buddhist or an atheist, and if conversion was literally inconceivable given one's cultural background, then was baptism a moral impossibility? Similarly, if one was raised in a non-Christian religion or anti-Christian environment and therefore could not form an explicit desire for baptism, did an implicit desire (i.e., one *would have* desired it if one had been raised in different circumstances) suffice? Historically, those who wished to cast the net of salvation as widely as possible tended to give a positive answer to these questions, and they sometimes cast the net so widely that one might wonder what circumstances would *not* have counted as a moral impossibility and what disposition toward baptism would *not* have counted as an implicit desire. On the other hand, those who wanted the door to salvation all but closed to non-Christians (and non-Catholics) tended to interpret "moral impossibility" and "desire" so strictly as to admit very few. It seems fairly clear that Aquinas inclined toward the latter view. In recent decades, discussion of the salvation of non-Christians has largely abandoned the framework of baptism of desire.

7. That is, Emperor Valentinian II, who converted from Arianism to Catholic Christianity, but was assassinated in 371, before he could be baptized.

8. It may not be immediately apparent how this reply answers the first objection, since Thomas does not respond to the specific biblical passage cited. Instead he draws on different passages from Scripture to suggest the spiritual, not physical, effect of baptism. His implicit point is that just as purification of the heart is not tied to visible circumcision, so too it need not be tied to the visible rite of baptism.

the full liberation from guilt and punishment. Suppose, therefore, that a catechumen has the desire for baptism (otherwise, he could not be said to die with good works, for such works cannot be without "faith that works through love"); such a one, were he to die, would not come immediately to eternal life but would suffer punishment for his past sins; "but he himself shall be saved, but only by fire," as is stated in 1 Corinthians 3:15.[9]

Reply to 3: The sacrament of baptism is said to be necessary for salvation insofar as a human being cannot be saved without baptism, at least baptism of desire, "which, with God, counts for the deed" (Augustine, *Explanations of the Psalms* 57:3).[10]

3.68.9

Whether children should be baptized?

It seems that children should not be baptized.[11]

1. The intention to receive the sacrament is required in one who is being baptized, as stated earlier (3.68.7). Children cannot have such an intention, since they do not have the use of free-will. Therefore it seems that they cannot receive the sacrament of baptism.

2. Baptism is "the sacrament of faith," as stated above (3.66.1 *ad* 1).[12] But children do not have faith, which consists in an act of the will on the part of the believer, as Augustine says in the *Homilies on the Gospel of John* (sermon 26, no. 2). Nor can it be said that their salvation is implied in the faith of their parents, since the latter are sometimes unbelievers, and their unbelief would

9. Both martyrdom and baptism by water free one from the guilt of sin *and* subsequent punishment (see 3.46, note 48, and 3.65, note 4). However, baptism of desire frees one only from guilt. Thus a catechumen who dies must be saved "by fire"—that is, by undergoing purification in purgatory (as do those who incur sins after being baptized in water). Thus Thomas interprets the text cited in the objection as saying that only those who are baptized in water or blood can obtain eternal life *immediately.*

10. Here Thomas simply expands the meaning of "baptism" to include baptism of desire.

11. The practice of infant baptism seems to have developed in the church over the course of time, perhaps beginning with the first generation of Christians. Only with the Radical Reformers or Anabaptists of the sixteenth century did widespread criticism and rejection of the practice emerge. However, for Aquinas the question is not purely theoretical. In the twelfth century, figures such as Arnold of Brescia and Peter de Bruis had argued against infant baptism, and in the thirteenth century the Cathars had rejected baptism by water entirely, substituting for it a "baptism" through the laying on of hands called the *consolatum,* which was performed only on adults (and often not until they were at the point of death).

12. Aquinas states repeatedly that baptism is the *sacramentum fidei* (a term first found in Tertullian), and most of what he says about baptism seems to presume that the person being baptized is an adult. The objection uses Aquinas's own approach to baptism against him, as it were, since for Aquinas adult baptism seems to be the theological norm. Thus the objection seems to say that Thomas must either disavow the practice of infant baptism, or cease calling baptism the "sacrament of faith."

more likely lead to the damnation of their children. Therefore it seems that children cannot be baptized.

3. It is said in 1 Peter 3:21 that "baptism saves, not as removing the filth of the flesh, but as the examination of a good conscience toward God." But children have no conscience, either good or bad, since they do not have the use of reason; nor can they be fittingly examined, since they do not understand.[13] Therefore it seems that children should not be baptized.

On the contrary: Dionysius says in the last chapter of *The Ecclesiastical Hierarchy* (chap. 7, no. 3.11), "Our heavenly guides," that is, the Apostles, "approved of infants being admitted to baptism."

I answer: As the Apostle says in Romans 5:17, "If by the transgression of one, death reigned through that one," namely, Adam, "much more will they who receive abundance of grace and gift and justice reign in life through one, Jesus Christ." Now children contract original sin from the sin of Adam; this is made clear by the fact that they are subjected to death, which "passed upon all" on account of the sin of the first human, as the Apostle says in the same passage (Romans 5:12). Much more, therefore, can children receive grace through Christ, so as to reign in eternal life.[14] But our Lord himself said in John 3:5, "Unless one is born again of water and the Holy Spirit, he cannot enter into the kingdom of God." Consequently, it became necessary to baptize children, so that, as in birth they incurred damnation through Adam, in a second birth they might obtain salvation through Christ.

Furthermore, it was fitting that children should receive baptism so that in being nurtured from childhood in things pertaining to the Christian way of life, they might more firmly persevere in them,[15] according to Proverbs 22:5, "A young person, once set on his path, will not depart from it, even when old." This reason is also given by Dionysius (*The Ecclesiastical Hierarchy*, bk. 7, no. 3.11).

Reply to 1: The spiritual regeneration brought about by baptism is in some respects like fleshly birth, inasmuch as the child in the mother's womb does not receive nourishment independently but through the nourishment of its mother. Likewise, children before the use of reason, being as it were in the womb of their mother the church, receive salvation not by their own act

---

13. This objection reflects the medieval baptismal rite, in which questions were put to the infant being baptized, and in which the godparent answered the questions on the child's behalf. In a sense, the objection points to the incongruity of using a baptismal rite designed for adults when baptizing infants.

14. The logic here is not immediately apparent. Aquinas's point, which he makes more explicitly in the reply to objection 2, seems to be that salvation is something we *receive*, not something we achieve. Just as in our generation we receive the sin of Adam, so too in our *re*generation we receive the grace of Christ.

15. In addition to showing that the baptism of infants is possible, Thomas wants to indicate here that it is good pastoral practice. The idea that young people need the grace of baptism fits well with the importance Thomas places on the role of grace in moral formation and the cultivation of the virtues.

but by the act of the church.[16] Therefore Augustine says in *On the Merits and Forgiveness of Sins and on Infant Baptism* (bk. 1, chaps. 25, 19), "The church, our mother, offers her maternal mouth for her children, that they may be instructed in the sacred mysteries; for they cannot as yet believe with their own hearts so as to gain righteousness, nor confess with their own mouths so as to gain salvation. . . . And if they are rightly said to believe, because in a certain fashion they make their profession of faith by the words of their sponsors, why should they not also be said to repent, since by the words of those same sponsors they show their renunciation of the devil and this world?" For the same reason they can be said to intend [to receive baptism], not by their own act of intention (since at times they struggle and cry) but by the act of those who bring them to be baptized.[17]

Reply to 2: As Augustine says, writing to Boniface (*Against Two Letters of the Pelagians*, bk. 1, chap. 22), "In the church of our savior little children believe through others, just as they contracted from others those sins that are forgiven in baptism." Nor are they hindered in their salvation if their parents are unbelievers, because, as Augustine says, writing to the same Boniface (epistle 98, no. 5), "Little children are offered that they may receive grace in their souls, not so much from the hands of those that carry them (yet from these too, if they themselves are good and faithful) as from the whole company of the saints and the faithful. For it is right to understand that they are offered by those who are pleased at their being offered, and by whose charity they are united in communion with the Holy Spirit." The unbelief of their own

---

16. Certain metaphors or images of baptism seem to fit better than others with the practice of baptizing infants. For example, to say that baptism is like "fleshly birth" is to say that just as a child is born without giving its consent, so too is it reborn in baptism without its consent. With the help of Augustine, Thomas develops another aspect of the metaphor: just as a child, after conception, is nurtured in the womb by what the mother eats, so too the child reborn in baptism remains sheltered and nourished within the womb of Christ's bride, the church, feeding on the faith of the church.

17. Augustine's argument (which Thomas is adopting) is perhaps difficult for us to grasp, given the pervasive individualism of modern culture. We tend to presume that one cannot intend or believe or answer for another, whereas Thomas seems to think it is obvious that parents and guardians can do these things for their children. Of course, he expects that as the capacity for free choice and intention develops in children they will come to "own" their faith, but he also expects that the faith they profess will be a faith that belongs not to them but to the whole church.

It is instructive to compare what Aquinas says here with what he says about the role of intention in adult baptisms. In 3.68.7 he writes that just as "one who has the use of free will must, in order to die to the old life, 'will to repent of his old life' (Augustine, sermon 351), so must he, of his own will, intend to lead a new life, the beginning of which is precisely the receiving of the sacrament." The role of intention is crucial in the case of adults because they can form intentions for *and against* certain actions; and explicit intention is required on the part of an adult precisely because of the possibility of forming a counterintention. Because a child cannot form its own intentions, it cannot oppose or inhibit the workings of grace (despite the fact that they sometimes struggle and cry when brought to the baptismal font).

parents, even if they strive to infect them with the worship of demons after baptism, does not hurt the children; for as Augustine says in the same place (epistle 98, no. 1), "Once the child has been begotten by the will of others, he cannot subsequently be held by the bonds of another's sin so long as he does not consent with his will, according to Ezekiel 18:4: 'As the soul of the father, so also the soul of the son is mine; the soul that sins—that one shall die.' Yet he contracted from Adam that from which he was released by the grace of this sacrament, because he was not as yet endowed with a separate existence." But the faith of one, indeed of the whole church, benefits the child through the operation of the Holy Spirit, who unites the church together and communicates the goods of one member to another.[18]

Reply to 3: Just as a child, when being baptized, believes not through himself but through others, so too he is examined not through himself but through others, and the ones asked confess the church's faith in the child's place, who is included in this faith by the sacrament of faith. And the child acquires a good conscience in himself by the grace that makes one righteous—not, of course, a fully realized good conscience, but the disposition to one.[19]

18. In this reply Aquinas makes it clear that it is the faith of the church, not the faith of the parents, that is determinative. Indeed, godparents serve as reminders that baptism is not a family affair but an act of the whole church. At the same time, Thomas says in the next article (3.68.10) that children of unbelievers should not be baptized over the objections of their parents. Although the baptism would be valid, it would be pastorally ineffective and would distort the natural obligation of obedience and respect that children have toward their parents.

19. Baptism is the sacrament of faith, but it is not a sacrament simply conferred on those who already have a fully formed faith; indeed, if one had a fully formed faith (i.e., faith motivated by love), one would presumably not need the sacrament of baptism, since it is a sacrament whose purpose is to lead to the formation of fully formed faith.

THE CONVERSION OF
THE BREAD AND WINE

3.75.1

Whether the body of Christ is in the sacrament of the Eucharist truly, or only in a figure or as in a sign?

It seems that the body of Christ is not in the sacrament of the Eucharist truly, but only in a figure or as in a sign.[1]

1. It is written in John 6:54 that our Lord uttered the words "Unless you eat the flesh of the Son of Man, and drink his blood," and so on. When hearing this, "Many of his disciples said, 'This is a hard saying.'" Our Lord responded, "It is the spirit that gives life; the flesh profits nothing," as if he were to say, according to Augustine's exposition of Psalm 4,[2] "Give a spiritual meaning to what I have said. You are not to eat this body that you see, nor to drink the blood that they who crucify me are to spill. It is a mystery that I put before you; in its spiritual sense it will give you life, but the flesh profits nothing."

1. Having argued earlier (see 3.61, note 8) that sacraments are a kind of sign (or, as we might say, a "symbol"), Aquinas asks here whether the sacrament of the Eucharist is *merely* a sign or symbol of Christ's presence. Thomas obviously has Berengar in mind. We might think about this question in this way: Granted that Christ, in instituting this sacrament, said of bread and wine, "This is my body" and "This is my blood," what reason do we have for thinking that he was speaking literally and not figuratively? After all, he also said, "I am the good shepherd," and we do not take this to be a description of his employment.

2. *Explanations of the Psalms* 98:9.

2. Our Lord said in Matthew 28:20, "Behold, I am with you all days, until the consummation of the world." In explaining this, Augustine makes this observation (*Homilies on the Gospel of John,* sermon 30, no. 1), "The Lord is on high until the world is ended; nevertheless the truth of the Lord is here with us. For the body, in which he rose again, must be in one place, but his truth is spread abroad everywhere." Therefore, the body of Christ is not in this sacrament in actual truth, but only as in a sign.

3. No body can be in several places at the same time;[3] indeed, this is not fitting even to an angel, since this would mean that it could be everywhere.[4] But Christ's body is a true body, and it is in heaven. Consequently, it seems that it is not in the sacrament of the altar in truth, but only as in a sign.

4. The church's sacraments are intended for the benefit of the faithful. But according to Gregory in a certain homily (*Homilies on the Gospels,* sermon 28), the ruler is criticized "for demanding Christ's bodily presence." Furthermore, the apostles were prevented from receiving the Holy Spirit because they were attached to his bodily presence, as Augustine says (*Homilies on the Gospel of John,* sermon 94, no. 2) about John 16:7, "Unless I go, the Paraclete will not come to you." Therefore Christ is not in the sacrament of the altar according to his bodily presence.

On the contrary: Hilary says in *On the Trinity* (bk. 8, no. 14), "There is no room for doubt regarding the truth of Christ's body and blood, for now by our Lord's own declaration and by our faith his flesh is truly food and his blood is truly drink." And Ambrose says in *On the Sacraments* (bk. 6, chap. 1), "As the Lord Jesus Christ is God's true Son, so is it Christ's true flesh that we take and his true blood that we drink."

I answer: The presence of Christ's true body and blood in this sacrament cannot be detected by the senses but only by faith, which rests on divine authority. Therefore, regarding Luke 22:19—"This is my body that shall be delivered up for you"—Cyril says, "Do not doubt whether this is true, but rather take the Savior's words with faith; for since he is the truth, he does not lie" (*Commentary on Luke*).[5]

---

3. Part of what it means to be a body is to occupy a particular place.

4. The mention of angels in the objection is quite cryptic, almost to the point of being unintelligible. The objection seems to be saying that since angels, which are disembodied intelligences, cannot be in multiple locations at the same time, it is even more the case that bodies cannot occupy multiple locations at the same time. Aquinas discusses the angels' relation to place in 1.52.

5. In the hymn *Adoro Devote,* which is traditionally ascribed to Thomas (though this ascription is disputed), we find a poetic expression of the view he states in this paragraph:

> Seeing, touching, tasting are in thee deceived;
> How says trusty hearing? that shall be believed:
> What God's Son has told me, take for truth I do;
> Truth himself speaks truly or there's nothing true.
> (from the translation of G. M. Hopkins)

Thomas holds the view (which is the orthodox Catholic view to this day) that the bread and wine undergo a transformation such that they cease to be bread and wine and become the body

This is fitting,[6] in the first place, for the perfection of the New Law; for the sacrifices of the Old Law contained only prefigurations of the true sacrifice of Christ's passion, according to Hebrews 10:1, "The Law has a shadow of the good things to come, not the image itself of the things." And therefore the sacrifice of the New Law instituted by Christ should have something more—namely, that it should contain the suffering one himself, not only as a sign or prefiguring, but also in actual truth.[7] And therefore, as Dionysius says in *The Ecclesiastical Hierarchy* (chap. 3, no.1), this sacrament, which really contains Christ himself, "perfects all the other sacraments," in which there is a participation in Christ's power.

Second, this accords with Christ's charity, out of which he took on a true body of our nature for our salvation. And because it is the special feature of friendship to live together with friends, as the Philosopher says in the *Ethics* (bk. 8, chap. 5, 1157[b]), he promises us his bodily presence as a reward, saying in Matthew 24:28, "Where the body is, there shall the eagles be gathered together." Yet meanwhile in our pilgrimage he does not deprive us of his bodily presence, but unites us with himself in this sacrament through the truth of his body and blood.[8] Therefore he says in John 6:57, "The one who eats my

---

and blood of Christ. As Thomas understands this transformation, the reality (or "substance") of the bread and wine is transformed into the reality of Christ's body and blood. However, the appearances (or "accidents" or "species") of bread and wine remain. This view of how Christ is present in the Eucharist is usually known as "transubstantiation" (a term Thomas wholly approves of, but which he feels compelled to use only five times in the *Summa theologiae*).

Contrary to what some people believe, Aquinas does not think he can "prove" that in the Eucharist the bread and wine are transformed into the body and blood of Christ, since, as the first paragraph of his response makes clear, the transformation is not one that the senses can detect. To prove something, we must argue either from self-evident first principles (and as a contingent event, the transformation of bread and wine cannot be a self-evident first principle) or from effects that are evident to our senses back to the cause of those effects. Of course, Thomas does not think that the transformation of the bread and wine *needs* proving, since Christ, who is Truth itself, says of the bread "This is my body" and of the wine "This is my blood."

6. *hoc autem conveniens est:* Although Aquinas does not believe that the transformation of the bread and wine can be proved, he does think that, once faith assents to such a transformation, he can show why it is "fitting" (on *convenientia* in general, see 3.1, note 1). In what follows, Thomas offers three reasons that, taken together, offer something like a cumulative case for why one should believe that Christ is speaking literally and not figuratively when he says, "This is my body" and "This is my blood."

7. Aquinas's point is that the sacrifices commanded in the Old Law were *already* signs of the sacrifice of Jesus on the cross (see 1.1, note 43), and therefore if the Eucharist were meant *only* as a sign or symbol there would not be much point to it; one might as well continue the animal sacrifices of the Old Law. But note also that Thomas does not deny that the Eucharist is a sign; rather, it is something *more* than a sign.

8. Following Aristotle, Aquinas thinks it is strange to speak of someone as a "friend" when you do not interact with them on a regular basis, and the most fitting mode of interaction for us as human beings is through the medium of our bodies (e-mail is a poor second to face-to-face contact). Therefore, if you think, as Thomas does, that we are called to be Christ's friends (see John 15:13–15), then it is only fitting that Christ provide a way to be present to us bodily.

flesh and drinks my blood abides in me, and I in him." Therefore this sacrament is the sign of supreme charity and lifts up our hope, on account of such a familiar union of Christ with us.

Third, this accords with the completeness of faith, which concerns Christ's humanity as much as it does his divinity; according to John 14:1, "You believe in God, believe also in me." And since faith is in things unseen, just as Christ shows us his divinity invisibly, so too in this sacrament he shows us his flesh in an invisible manner.[9]

Some, not considering these things, have claimed that Christ's body and blood are not in this sacrament except as in a sign. This is a view to be rejected as heretical, since it is contrary to Christ's words. Therefore Berengar, who had been the first inventor of this heresy, was later forced to withdraw his error and to acknowledge the truth of the faith.[10]

Reply to 1: The heretics spoken of before have found in this authority an occasion of error by misunderstanding Augustine's words;[11] for when Augustine says, "You are not to eat this body that you see," he does not intend to exclude the truth of Christ's body, but only that it was not to be eaten in the appearance [*species*] in which it was seen by them.[12] And by the words "It is a mystery

9. Christ's divinity is an object of faith because it is hidden in his humanity. But this humanity itself becomes an object of faith in the Eucharist because it is hidden under the appearances of bread and wine. This is again given poetic expression in *Adoro Devote* (see note 5, above.):
> On the cross thy godhead made no sign to men;
> Here thy very manhood steals from human ken:
> Both are my confession, both are my belief,
> And I pray the prayer of the dying thief.

10. Berengar was made to sign two separate oaths. The first, from 1059, said: "The bread and wine that are laid on the altar are, after consecration, not only a sacrament. They are also the true body and blood of our Lord Jesus Christ, and they are physically taken up and broken in the hands of the priest and crushed by the teeth of the faithful not only sacramentally, but in truth." Berengar quickly recanted, and one can hardly blame him. This oath prescribes a kind of hyperrealism about the Eucharist that does not fit well with the tradition of the church, making Holy Communion sound like an act of cannibalism.

Twenty years later, in 1079 at the synod of Rome, Berengar signed another oath, framed in more moderate language than the first: "I, Berengar, believe in my heart and confess with my lips that the bread and wine that are placed on the altar are, by the mystery of the sacred prayer and the words of the redeemer, substantially changed into the true and proper and life-giving body and blood of Jesus Christ our Lord; and that after consecration, they are Christ's true body, which was born of the virgin and hung on the cross, being offered for the salvation of the world, and which sits at the right hand of the Father; and Christ's true blood, which was poured forth from his side; not only by way of sign and by the power of the sacrament, but in their true nature and in the reality of their *substantia.*"

11. As mentioned before (3.61, note 8), Augustine speaks of sacraments as "signs," and Aquinas agrees with Augustine on this point. The heretics, whom Aquinas mentions just above at the end of his reply, make their mistake, according to Aquinas, in thinking that Augustine believes that sacraments are *merely* signs.

12. Here and elsewhere in Aquinas's discussion of the Eucharist, *species* means "outward appearances."

that I put before you; in its spiritual sense it will give life to you," he intends not that the body of Christ is in this sacrament merely according to mystical signification, but "spiritually," that is, invisibly, and by the power of the Spirit.[13] Therefore, in commenting on John 6:64—"the flesh profits nothing"—he says, "But only in the way that they understood it; for they understood that the flesh was to be eaten in the way that a dead body is torn into pieces, or as it is sold in the meat market, not as it is given life by the spirit. Let the spirit draw near to the flesh, and the flesh profits very much; for if the flesh profited nothing, the Word would not be made flesh, that it might dwell among us" (*Homilies on the Gospel of John*, sermon 27, no. 5).[14]

Reply to 2: That saying of Augustine, and all others like it, is to be understood to be about Christ's body as it is seen in its normal outward appearance, in the same way that our Lord himself says in Matthew 26:11, "But you will not always have me." Nevertheless, he is invisibly under the outward appearances of this sacrament wherever this sacrament is performed.

Reply to 3: Christ's body is not in this sacrament in the same way that a body is in a place, such that its size corresponds to the place, but in a special way that belongs to this sacrament. Therefore we say that Christ's body is upon many altars, not as being in different places, but as being present "sacramentally," and by this we do not understand Christ to be there only as in a sign—even though a sacrament is a kind of sign—but that Christ's body is here according to a way proper to this sacrament, as stated above.[15]

---

13. In other words, when Augustine says that Christ's body is "spiritually" present, he is not denying that it is *really* present but that it is *visibly* present in the way that Christ's body was present to his disciples. Thomas's reply to the next objection makes essentially the same point.

Note as well that Thomas says Christ is present through the power of the Spirit (*per virtutem Spiritus*). In his commentary on the *Sentences*, Thomas says even more explicitly that "the power of the Holy Spirit alone brings about this conversion" (bk. 4, distinction 8, q. 2, a. 3, *ad* 1). Western theology, particularly Scholastic theology, is sometimes accused of ignoring the role of the Spirit in the Eucharist. But the Spirit was widely held by medieval Western theologians to be the agent of the Eucharistic change, even though the Canon (the prayer during which the Eucharistic consecration took place, used in the West from at least the time of Gregory the Great) contains no petition for the Holy Spirit to consecrate the bread and wine. For ample documentation, see Yves Congar, O.P., "The Holy Spirit and the Eucharist in the Western Tradition," in *I Believe in the Holy Spirit*, vol. 3, *The River of the Water of Life Flows in the East and in the West*, trans. David Smith (New York: Seabury Press, 1983), 250–57.

14. For Aquinas, as his use of this quotation from Augustine indicates, the logic of objections that say that Christ's words must be understood as spiritual—such that the bread is only symbolically Christ's body—can just as easily be applied to the incarnation. In other words, the same mind-set that denies Eucharistic realism also tends to deny the realism of the incarnation.

15. Thomas denies that Christ is present only symbolically in the elements of the Eucharist, but he also denies that Christ's presence is a *physical* one—that is, that Christ's body is present, for example, in the same way in which it was present in Mary's womb or on the cross. If this were the case, then Christ's body could not be present on many altars at the same time. Nonetheless, Thomas still wants to claim that the body that is present in the Eucharist is the same one that was in Mary's womb and that hung on the cross. This apparent contradiction is the result of a distinction Thomas makes between *what*—or, better, *who*—is present, and in

Reply to 4: This argument holds good for Christ's bodily presence as he is present in the manner of a body, that is, as it is in its visible appearance, but not as it is spiritually, that is, invisibly, after the manner and by the power of the Spirit.[16] Therefore Augustine says in his *Homilies on the Gospel of John* (sermon 27, no.6), "If you have understood in a spiritual way" Christ's words concerning his flesh, "they are spirit and life to you; if you have understood them in a fleshly way, they are also spirit and life, but not to you."

3.75.8

Whether this proposition is false: "The body of Christ is made out of bread"?

It seems that this proposition is false: "The body of Christ is made out of bread."[17]

1. Everything that something else is made "out of" [*ex quo*] is that which is made into the other; but the reverse is not the case. For we say, "out of something white, something black is made," and "something white is made black," and we may even say that "a person becomes black," but we still do not say that "a black thing is made out of a person," as is shown in the *Physics* (bk. 1, chap. 5, 188ᵇ). If it is true, then, that Christ's body is made out of bread, it will be true to say that "bread is made the body of Christ." But this seems to be

---

how this presence occurs. What Thomas wants to say is that Christ's presence in the Eucharist is *neither* purely symbolic *nor* physical; rather it is a way of being present that is unique to the sacrament of the Eucharist.

16. In other words, the objection holds, if we are speaking about Christ's body as it was visible, walking around Palestine. So long as the disciples were attached to the visibility of Christ's body, the Spirit—and the way of seeing associated with the Spirit, namely, faith—could not come. The presence of Christ is not less real for being spiritual, and "spiritual" should not be taken to mean "purely symbolic."

17. Much of what Thomas says in this article is a summary and application of what he has said in the seven preceding articles in question 75, and in particular in article 4, which addresses the question of whether bread can be converted into the body of Christ. Here, he draws together all that he has said in this question by inquiring into the acceptability of a particular verbal formulation, an approach that is reminiscent of 3.16.1, above. There, however, the word in question was the copula "is"; here it is the preposition "out of" [*ex*].

As in the case of the earlier, christological discussion, this is more than a matter of simply fretting about words. At issue is the best model to use in understanding the sort of "change" that is involved in transubstantiation. Thomas is sometimes accused of simply grafting Christian theology onto Aristotelian philosophy, or of using Aristotle's metaphysics to explain Christian mysteries. This accusation is often supported with reference to Thomas's use of the language of "substance" and "accidents" in his discussion of the Eucharist. This article, however, shows that Aquinas's understanding of Eucharistic conversion is primarily rooted not in Aristotle's metaphysics, but in a biblical metaphysics of creation from nothing, something that is quite alien to Aristotle's philosophy.

false, because the bread is not the subject of the making, but rather its term.[18] Therefore, it is not said truly, "The body of Christ is made out of bread."

2. The process of becoming reaches its conclusion in something existing [*esse*], or in something having been made to exist. But this proposition is never true: "Bread is the body of Christ"; or "Bread is made the body of Christ"; or again, "Bread will be the body of Christ."[19] Therefore it seems that not even this is true: "The body of Christ is made out of bread."

3. Everything that something else is made "out of" is converted into that which is made from it. But this proposition seems to be false: "Bread is converted into the body of Christ," because such conversion seems to be more miraculous than the creation of the world, of which it is not said that nonbeing is converted into being.[20] Therefore it seems that this proposition is likewise false: "The body of Christ is made out of bread."

4. That which something else is made "out of" is capable of being that thing. But this proposition is false: "Bread is capable of being the body of Christ." Therefore this is likewise false: "The body of Christ is made out of bread."

On the contrary: Ambrose says in the book *On the Sacraments* (bk. 4, chap. 4), "When the consecration takes place, the body of Christ is made of bread."

I answer: This conversion of bread into the body of Christ has something in common both with creation and with natural change,[21] and in some respects differs from both.[22] One thing that is common to all three is the order of the terms—that is, that after one thing there is another: in creation there is existence after nonexistence; in this sacrament there is Christ's body after the

18. In the statement "The brunette was made into a redhead," both "brunette" and "redhead" are "terms" (i.e., beginning and ending points) of the change, but they are not the subject that undergoes the change (i.e., that "from which something else is made"). We might say, "Jane was made into a redhead," so long as we do not imply that Sally has ceased to exist (being replaced by a redhead), when in fact she is the subject that has undergone the change. The redhead is still Jane. Thus the force of the objection is that the proposition "The body of Christ is made out of bread" treats "bread" as if it were the subject undergoing a change, which would mean that the body of Christ is still bread, just as the redhead is still Jane.

19. The objection seems to be that when we speak of a process of becoming, we can reformulate it as a statement of existence. Thus the statement "The brunette becomes a redhead" entails that "the brunette is a redhead."

20. In 1.45.2 Thomas denies that creation is properly described as a "change," since this would imply that there is some subject that undergoes the change, whereas creation is the bringing of things into existence without a preexisting subject.

21. Under "natural change" [*transmutatione naturali*] Thomas includes both changes of appearance (or "accidental change"), such as Jane changing from a brunette to a redhead, and changes in the kind of thing that something is (or "substantial change"), such as the change in the matter from which Jane is composed when she ceases to be a human being and becomes a corpse.

22. Another way of putting this would be to say that "change" is an analogous term. On analogy, see 1.13.5, above.

substance of bread; in a natural change there is white after black, or fire after air. Also, these terms just mentioned do not exist simultaneously.[23]

The conversion of which we are speaking has this in common with creation: that in neither of them is there any common subject belonging to both extremes.[24] This is the opposite of what is seen to be the case in every natural change.[25]

However, this conversion does have something in common with natural change in two respects, although not in the same way. First, in both cases one of the extremes passes into the other, such as bread into Christ's body, and air into fire (whereas [in creation] nonbeing is not converted into being).[26] But this change comes to pass differently in the two cases; for in this sacrament the whole substance of the bread passes into the whole body of Christ, whereas in natural change the matter of the one receives the form of the other, the previous form being laid aside.[27] Second, they have this in common: that in both cases something remains the same (whereas this does not happen in creation). Yet this happens differently in the two cases, for in natural change the same matter or subject remains, whereas in this sacrament the same accidents remain.

23. In other words, in all three cases you first have A and then B; at no point do you have A and B simultaneously.

24. "Extremes" here is synonymous with "terms." See note 18, above.

25. For Thomas's account of how creation differs from other sorts of change, see 1.45.5, above. Here the key point is that in both creation and the Eucharist there is no X such that "the X that is A" becomes "the X that is B"; or, to return to Jane (see note 18, above), there is no "Jane who is a brunette" who becomes "Jane who is a redhead." Unlike Aristotle, who understood "creation" as something that happens when God gives form to an eternally existing "prime matter," Aquinas holds that creation is simply God bringing things in their totality (both matter and form) into existence (on matter and form, see1.12, note 1). In other words, there is no "matter that is unformed" that becomes "matter that is formed." Similarly, Aquinas holds that in the Eucharist there is no "X that is bread" that becomes "X that is the body of Christ." Yet although we can formulate this matter negatively, by denying the persistence of a subject in both creation and the Eucharist, it is difficult to come up with a positive statement of Eucharistic change. As with the mystery of God, so too with the mystery of Eucharistic change: what it is not is clearer than what it is (see 1.1, note 41).

26. Part of the problem Thomas confronts is a certain imprecision of language. The Christian tradition has spoken of creation ex nihilo (from nothing), but not in the sense of "nothing" as something that is converted into something else; rather, "nothing" is not any kind of thing at all. So in the phrase *creatio ex nihilo,* the preposition *ex* really indicates nothing more than the order of the terms in the proposition. We cannot even really say that in creation we first have nonbeing and then being, since this would seem to ascribe some sort of (albeit shadowy) existence to nonbeing, which is absurd. It would also imply a temporal succession of being following upon nonbeing, which is equally absurd, since there is not time prior to creation, and thus no "before" God's creative act. Thus creation is different from any other sort of change (so much so that it can be called a change at all only improperly), including the Eucharistic conversion, in which one first has bread and then has the body of Christ.

27. A substance, in the case of physical realities, is composed of matter and substantial form. When one kind of thing becomes another kind of thing, matter takes on a new form, with the subsequent form replacing the former. For Thomas, this is not the kind of change that occurs in the Eucharist. In this instance (and, seemingly, *only* in this instance), there is a

From these observations we can gather the various ways of speaking about such matters;[28] for in none of the previously mentioned three things do the extremes exist simultaneously, and therefore in none of them can one extreme be predicated of the other by the substantive verb of the present tense—that is, we do not say: "Nonbeing *is* being," or "Bread *is* the body of Christ," or "Air *is* fire," or "White *is* black."[29] Yet, on account of the relationship of the

---

different sort of change: rather than one form replacing another, one entire substance—matter *and* form—replaces the other.

It is worth asking *why* Thomas believes the Eucharist requires a change of the entire substance and not simply a change of form. After all, if wood becomes fire by taking on a new form, why could bread not become the body of Christ in the same way?

Thomas's answer to this question seems circular—it cannot be a natural change because this would not be a change of substance. But *why* must it be a change of substance? Thomas gives something approaching an answer in the *Summa contra Gentiles* 4.61.3, where, in noting (as he does above at 3.65.1) that the Eucharist corresponds on a spiritual level to bodily nourishment, he says that "nutriment must be conjoined to the one nourished in substance." Thomas contrasts this with baptism, which corresponds on a spiritual level to physical birth. Birth does not involve my being personally conjoined to my parents—indeed, one might say that birth is precisely the end of that conjunction. However, in order for food to nourish me, its substance must come into contact with mine. But this analogy still does not tell us why the presence of Christ's substance must involve a complete conversion of one substance to another.

We might approach this question using resources borrowed from Thomas; although he himself does not utilize them with regard to this question. In particular, we might emphasize that it is Christ in his personal totality who is present in this sacrament, which means that Christ is present as human as well as divine. Full human presence is bodily presence, because it is my particular matter that differentiates my human nature from that of others (see 1.45, note 16). So if Christ is to be present in this sacrament in his humanity, this must involve his body in its own proper materiality, though this is the transformed bodily presence of the risen Christ that Paul describes as a "spiritual body." Thomas makes clear that this is an utterly unique sort of bodily presence, since it is not a local presence (i.e., it is not a question of occupying a particular place).

28. We might try to envision the array of similarities and differences that Thomas has just mapped out by using a table:

Creation, Natural Change, and Eucharistic Conversion

	A certain order of terms: extremes do not exist simultaneously	A common subject of change	One extreme passes into another	Something remains throughout the change
Creation	Yes: nothing then something	No	No	No
Natural change	Yes: person then corpse (substantial change) or brunette then redhead (accidental change)	Yes: matter (substantial change) or substance (accidental change)	Yes: a change of form (either substantial or accidental)	Yes: the matter (substantial change) or substance (accidental change) does not change
Eucharistic conversion	Yes: bread then the body of Christ	No	Yes: a change of substance	Yes: the accidents do not change

29. On "predicated," see 1.3, note 2.

extremes, in all of them we can use the preposition *ex* [out of], which denotes order; for we can truly and properly say that "being is made out of nonbeing," and "out of bread, the body of Christ," and "out of air, fire," and "out of white, black."[30]

However, because in the case of creation one of the extremes does not pass into the other, we cannot use the word "conversion" in speaking of creation, so as to say that "nonbeing is converted into being." We can, however, use the word in speaking of this sacrament, just as in natural change.[31] But since in this sacrament the whole substance is converted into the whole substance, on that account this conversion is properly termed "transubstantiation."[32]

Again, since there is not any subject of this conversion, the things that are true in natural conversion by reason of the subject are not to be granted in this conversion. Indeed, it is evident in the first place that the potential of something to be the opposite of what it is, is a consequence of there being a subject, and for this reason we say that "a white thing can be black," or that "air can be fire." However, the latter statement is not as correct as the former; for the subject of whiteness, which is potentially black, is the whole substance of the white thing, since whiteness is not a part of it, whereas the subject of the form of air is part of it. Therefore we can say truly, "Air can be fire," because the part is taken for the whole by means of synecdoche.[33] But in this conversion [i.e., transubstantiation], and similarly in creation, because there is no subject it is not said that one extreme can be the other, so as to say that "nonbeing can be being," or that "bread can be the body of Christ." And for the same reason it cannot be said properly that "being is made of [*de*] nonbeing," or that "the body of Christ is made of [*de*] bread," because this preposition "of" [*de*] denotes a cause that is the same substance as the effect, and, in the case of natural changes, this common substance of the extremes is meant according to something common in the subject.[34] And for the same reason it is not

30. See note 26, above.

31. That is, we use the word "conversion" (*conversionis*) to speak of natural and Eucharistic conversion because in both of these cases one thing "passes into another" (*transit in alterum*): wood becomes fire, and bread becomes the body of Christ.

32. In 1.75.4 Thomas writes: "This conversion is one not of form but of substance. Neither is it a kind of natural motion; rather it can be spoken of by its own special name [*proprio nomine*]: transubstantiation." One might say that Thomas sees the term "transubstantiation" as a kind of negative place holder that distinguishes Eucharistic conversion from both creation and natural change.

33. The difference Thomas marks here is between accidental change and substantial change. Strictly speaking, we can say, referring to an accidental change, that "a white table can be a black table" (i.e., by being painted); however, if we were to speak properly, we would not say that "air can be fire" but rather that "the matter that constitutes the substratum of air can be the substratum of fire." In other words, in substantial change the substratum is not a "thing" (i.e., a substance) but only part of a thing (i.e., its matter). But, using synecdoche—the form of speech by which a part is taken for the whole—we say "air can be fire" or (perhaps more commonly) "the tree can be a table."

34. That is, it is the common subject shared by the extremes.

granted that "bread will be the body of Christ," or that it "becomes the body of Christ," just as it is not granted in creation that "nonbeing will be being," or that "nonbeing becomes being," because this manner of speaking is true in the case of natural changes on account of the subject, as when we say that "a white thing becomes black," or "a white thing will be black."

Nevertheless, since after the change something remains the same in this sacrament—namely, the accidents of the bread, as stated earlier (3.75.5)—some of these expressions may be acceptable in a certain sense.[35] On might say, "Bread is the body of Christ," or "Bread will be the body of Christ," or "The body of Christ is made of [de] bread," provided that the word "bread" is not understood as the substance of bread, but in general "that which is contained under the species of bread," under which species there is first contained the substance of bread, and afterward the body of Christ.[36]

Reply to 1: That which something else is made "out of" sometimes implies the subject along with one of the extremes of the change, as is the case when it is said, "A black thing is made out of a white one."[37] But sometimes it implies only the opposite or the extreme, as when it is said, "Out of morning comes the day." And so it is not granted that the latter becomes the former, that is, "that morning becomes the day."[38] So likewise in the matter in hand, although it may be said properly that "the body of Christ is made out of bread," yet it is not said properly that "bread becomes the body of Christ," except in a certain sense, as was said above.[39]

Reply to 2: That which something else is made "out of" will sometimes be spoken of as that thing because of the subject that is implied.[40] And therefore, since there is no subject of this [Eucharistic] change, the comparison does not hold.

---

35. Thomas must do a bit of back pedaling here, since the Roman Canon (the prayer in which the Eucharist is consecrated) asks that the offering of bread and wine "may become for us the body and blood of your most beloved Son, our Lord Jesus Christ" (*nobis corpus et sanguis fiat dilectissimi Filii tui, Domini nostri Iesu Christi*). It is difficult to see how these words differ from those Thomas has just disallowed: "it becomes the body of Christ" (*fiat corpus Christi*).

36. Thomas's answer to the difficulty mentioned in the previous note is that we might sometimes speak of Eucharistic conversion as if it were natural change because the "species," which in this context means the outward appearance of bread, functions, at least grammatically, something like a subject that undergoes change. Thus the words of the Roman Canon might be understood as, "May that which is contained under the appearances of bread and wine cease being bread and wine and begin to be the body and blood of Christ."

37. This would be the case with the statement "A redhead is made out of a brunette," since Jane is implied as the subject (see notes 18 and 21, above).

38. This would be the case with the statement "Jane replaced John as the head of the company," since there is no independent thing called "the head of the company" that was transformed from John into Jane.

39. That is, when "bread" is understood to mean the outward appearance of bread.

40. "The brunette is a redhead" is a logical (if somewhat confusing) implication of "The brunette becomes a redhead," only because "the brunette" is an oblique way of speaking about Jane (see notes 18 and 21, above).

Reply to 3: In this change there are many more difficulties than in creation, in which there is only the difficulty that something is made out of nothing, insofar as this belongs to the mode of production unique to the first cause, which presupposes nothing else. But in this [Eucharistic] conversion, not only is it difficult for this whole to be changed into that whole, so that nothing of the former may remain (which is not the ordinary mode of production of any cause); this conversion has the further difficulty that the accidents remain while the substance is destroyed, and many other difficulties of which we shall treat hereafter (3.77). Nevertheless, the word "conversion" is accepted in the case of this sacrament, but not in the case of creation, as stated above.[41]

Reply to 4: As was observed above, potentiality belongs to the subject, whereas there is no subject in this conversion. And therefore it is not granted that bread is capable of being the body of Christ, for this conversion does not come about by the passive potentiality of the creature, but solely by the active power of the Creator.[42]

41. Thomas acknowledges with admirable candor the difficulties of understanding the change involved in transubstantiation, compared to which creation is quite easily graspable. He mentions two difficulties here: first, in creation ex nihilo there is no prior substance that must be converted; second, the persistence of the appearances of the bread and wine must be accounted for, which presents a problem because they have no substance to which they are attached.

42. Our ability to say "The body of Christ is made out of bread" is not dependent on our ability to say "Bread is able to be the body of Christ" but on our ability to say "God is able to bring it about that the body of Christ is made out of bread." In other words, the Eucharistic conversion is in no sense a natural change but is, rather, a miracle wrought by God's power.

QUESTION 80

RECEIVING THE EUCHARIST

3.80.1

Whether one should distinguish two ways of eating Christ's body?

It seems that two ways of eating Christ's body should not be distinguished, namely, sacramentally and spiritually.[1]

1. Just as baptism is spiritual regeneration—according to John 3:5, "Unless one be born again of water and the Holy Spirit," and so on—so also this sacrament is spiritual food. Therefore our Lord, speaking of this sacrament, says in John 6:64, "The words that I have spoken to you are spirit and life." But there are not two distinct ways of receiving baptism, namely, sacramentally

---

1. The backdrop for this article are the distinctions between *sacramentum tantum, res et sacramentum,* and *res tantum* (see 3.66, note 4). In his little work *De articulis fidei et ecclesiae sacramentis,* Thomas spells out succinctly how these terms apply to the Eucharist: "Thus, therefore, there is in this sacrament something that is the *sacramentum tantum,* that is to say, the appearances of bread and wine; and something that is *res et sacramentum,* that is, the true body of Christ; and something that is *res tantum,* that is to say, the unity of the mystical body, the church, which this sacrament both signifies and causes" (cf. *Summa theologiae* 3.73.6).

The remainder of question 80 is composed of eleven articles that are both speculative and practical. Perhaps the most famous speculation appears in 3.80.3 *ad* 2, where Thomas addresses the question of whether a mouse that eats the consecrated bread receives the body of Christ. Practically, Thomas addresses questions such as whether the priest should deny communion to a sinner. Many of the questions, both practical and speculative, find their resolution in the application of the distinction between spiritual and sacramental eating.

and spiritually. Therefore this distinction should not be made regarding this sacrament either.

2. When two things are related such that one exists on account of the other, they should not be divided from one another, because the one derives its species from the other. But sacramental eating is intended to have spiritual eating as its goal. Therefore sacramental eating should not be separated from spiritual eating.

3. Things that cannot exist without one another should not be contrasted with each other. But it seems that no one can eat spiritually without eating sacramentally; otherwise the ancient fathers would have eaten this sacrament spiritually.[2] Moreover, sacramental eating would be pointless if spiritual eating were possible without it. Therefore it is not fitting to distinguish a twofold eating, namely, sacramental and spiritual.[3]

On the contrary: Regarding 1 Corinthians 11:29—"He that eats and drinks unworthily," and so on—the gloss says, "We hold that there are two ways of eating: the one sacramental, and the other spiritual."[4]

I answer: There are two things to be considered in the receiving of this sacrament, namely, the sacrament itself and its effect, and we have already spoken of both.[5] The perfect way, then, of receiving this sacrament is when

---

2. The objection presumes that the holy people of the Old Testament did *not* eat Christ spiritually.

3. The three objections all argue against distinguishing or dividing the two forms of eating Christ's body, but they seem to have different interests in doing so. The first objection makes spiritual eating primary, so much so that sacramental eating is not really a way of eating Christ's body at all. The second objection seems to acknowledge a genuine sacramental eating of Christ's body, but its purpose remains the spiritual eating, and so the two forms of eating are bound together so closely that there is no reason to distinguish between them. The third objection emphasizes sacramental eating, as if to say that to eat Christ's body sacramentally is always to eat it spiritually. As usual, Thomas seeks a path between erring alternatives: a solely spiritual understanding of the Eucharist in which the bread and wine are mere symbols (objection 1) and a hyperrealist account that borders on the mechanical or magical (objection 3).

4. On the gloss, see 1.12, note 7.

5. Thomas here speaks of the twofold division between the sacrament itself (*ipsum sacramentum*) and the effect itself (*effectus ipsius*) that he discusses in questions 73–79 of the third part. It is not immediately apparent how this division relates to the threefold division of *sacramentum tantum, res et sacramentum,* and *res tantum* (see note 1, above). Indeed, Thomas seems to speak about the "effect" in different ways in different places. In *De articulis fidei et ecclesiae sacramentis,* Thomas speaks of a twofold effect of the sacrament of the Eucharist: the first effect is "the consecration of the sacrament itself," that is, the changing of bread and wine into the body and blood of Christ; the second effect occurs not in the elements of bread and wine but "in the soul of the one who eats worthily"; this effect "is the joining of that person to Christ." This makes it appear that both the *res et sacramentum* and *res tantum* are grouped together as "effects," and that the "sacrament itself" refers only to the sacramental "species" or appearances of bread and wine (cf. *Summa theologiae* 3.80.4, where he speaks of the twofold *res,* of which the "sacrament" is the sign). If we followed this way of speaking, then we would say that one who ate "sacramentally but not spiritually" would simply eat the *sacramentum tantum,* that is, the accidents of bread and wine. However, Thomas's

one takes it so as to partake of its effect. Now, as was stated earlier (3.79.3, 8), it sometimes happens that someone is hindered from receiving the effect of this sacrament, and such reception is an imperfect one.[6] Therefore, as the perfect is contrasted with the imperfect, so sacramental eating, in which the sacrament alone is received without its effect, is contrasted with spiritual eating, in which a person receives the effect of this sacrament so that one is spiritually united with Christ through faith and charity.[7]

Reply to 1: A similar distinction is made regarding baptism and the other sacraments; for some receive the sacrament only, whereas others receive the sacrament and the reality of the sacrament. However, there is a difference. Other sacraments are accomplished in the use of the material element; the receiving of the sacrament is the completion of the sacrament. But this sacrament is accomplished in the consecration of the material element, and its uses—whether for sacramental or for spiritual eating—follow from the sacrament. In baptism and in the other sacraments that imprint a seal, those who receive the sacrament receive some spiritual effect, that is, the seal, which is not the case in this

---

use of *ipsum sacramentum* in this article (and in those following it) makes it clear that he is referring not simply to the bread and wine, but to the *res et sacramentum,* that is, the body and blood of Christ. Thus in 3.80.3, arguing against those who would say that sinners do not receive the body and blood of Christ, but only the appearances of bread and wine, he states explicitly that "sacramental eating" is the eating of Christ's body and blood, whether it is done by a sinner or a saint.

6. This hindering would normally occur because of mortal sin, which makes it impossible to eat Christ's body spiritually, since this is nothing other than being united to Christ in love. So one in a state of mortal sin would eat Christ's body sacramentally, but would eat to his or her condemnation. As Thomas puts it in his hymn *Lauda Sion:*

> Both the wicked and the good
> eat of this celestial food:
> but with ends how opposite!
> With this most substantial bread,
> unto life or death they're fed,
> in a difference infinite.

7. In 3.80.3 *ad* 3 Thomas muddies the water somewhat by speaking of a third form of eating: "accidental eating." He notes that although consecrated bread eaten by a mouse or dog would not cease to be Christ's body, we still should not speak of a mouse or dog eating Christ's body "sacramentally," since it is "incapable of using it as a sacrament." We should speak rather of a nonhuman animal as eating only the accidents—the *sacramentum tantum,* as it were. He goes on to note that a human being who ate consecrated bread without knowing it was consecrated would also eat only accidentally and not sacramentally.

This third possibility restores the threefold division of *sacramentum tantum, res et sacramentum,* and *res tantum,* but it also presents some confusion because it might appear that Christ's presence is somehow dependent on human understanding. However, Thomas seems quite clear that Christ is present in the sacrament whether a human being (or a mouse) knows it or not. But only when one can "use" the sacrament as a sacrament can one eat "sacramentally," and the ability to "use" the sacrament seems to depend on the ability to know it is a sacrament. As Thomas says in 3.80.3 *ad 2,* an unbeliever (in this case, one who does not believe that Christ is present in the sacrament) receives Christ in the sacrament but does not feed on him sacramentally.

sacrament.[8] And therefore, in the case of this sacrament, the sacramental use is distinguished from the spiritual use more than in the case of baptism.

Reply to 2: The sacramental eating that is also a spiritual eating is not contrasted with spiritual eating, but is included under it. But the sacramental eating that does not secure the effect is contrasted with spiritual eating, just as the imperfect, which does not attain the perfection of its species, is contrasted with the perfect.[9]

Reply to 3: As stated earlier (3.73.3), the effect of the sacrament can be secured by anyone inasmuch as one receives it in desire, though not in reality. Consequently, just as some are baptized with the baptism of flames, through their desire of baptism, before being baptized in the baptism of water,[10] so likewise some eat this sacrament spiritually before they receive it sacramentally.

This happens in two ways. First, because of a desire to receive the sacrament itself, and in this way those who desire to receive these sacraments once they have been instituted are said to be baptized, and to eat spiritually and not sacramentally.[11] Second, because of a prefiguration; thus the Apostle says in 1 Corinthians 10:2 that the ancient fathers were "baptized in the cloud and in

8. Some modern authors have criticized Aquinas for his view that the sacrament of the Eucharist is "accomplished" (*perficiantur*) through the consecration of the matter and not through its reception. Such authors take this to mean that the real "point" of the Eucharist is to consecrate bread and wine, and that Holy Communion is a sort of optional add-on. One might be forgiven for this criticism, since much late medieval and early modern Eucharistic practice proceeded in exactly this way: at most masses only the priest would receive communion, while lay devotion was focused on the adoration of Christ present in the Eucharist. But if one looks at what Thomas has to say as a whole about the Eucharist, it is clear that for him the purpose of this sacrament is the nourishment of Christians through the reception of Holy Communion.

Thomas's point is simply that the *res et sacramentum* occurs, as it were, in the conversion of the bread and wine, whereas in baptism and the other sacraments in which the *res et sacramentum* is a "character" or "seal" (see 3.63.1), the *res et sacramentum* is accomplished only with the conferral of the seal. Thomas's point is not that after the consecration nothing further is to be done. Thus: "In the sacrament of the Eucharist, what is both *res et sacramentum* is in the matter itself, but what is *res tantum*, namely, the grace bestowed, is in the recipient; whereas in baptism both are in the recipient, namely, the seal, which is *res et sacramentum*, and the grace of pardon of sins, which is *res tantum*" (3.73.1 *ad* 3).

9. When we speak of those who eat Christ's body "spiritually," we are not distinguishing them necessarily from those who eat his body "sacramentally." Indeed, those who with faith and love eat his body sacramentally most certainly eat it spiritually as well. The distinction is between those who eat spiritually (whether or not this includes sacramental eating) and those who eat it *only* sacramentally.

10. See 3.68, note 6.

11. This sentence refers to what later Catholic tradition would call "spiritual communion," in which someone unable to receive Holy Communion would seek to unite themselves with Christ through faith in and desire for Christ as he is present in the sacrament. An "act of spiritual communion" might take the following form (this one by St. Alphonsus Ligouri): "My Jesus, I believe that you are present in the most holy sacrament. I love you above all things, and I desire to receive you into my soul. Since I cannot at this moment receive you sacramentally, come at least spiritually into my heart. I embrace you as if you were already there and unite myself wholly to you. Never permit me to be separated from you. Amen."

the sea," and that "they did eat . . . spiritual food, and . . . drank . . . spiritual drink."[12] Nevertheless sacramental eating is not pointless, because the actual receiving of the sacrament produces the effect of the sacrament more fully than the desire for it does, as stated earlier concerning baptism.[13]

12. "Prefiguration" refers to the way in which the holy people of the Old Testament ate Christ spiritually through faith in God's promised redeemer, a faith that they professed through ritual foreshadowings of Christ, such as the Passover feast (see 1–2.103.3). Thus Thomas simply disagrees with the presumption of the objection that they did not eat spiritually.

13. In 3.69.4 *ad* 2 Thomas says: "One receives forgiveness of sins prior to baptism inasmuch as one desires baptism, whether explicitly or implicitly, and yet in actually receiving baptism a fuller forgiveness of sins occurs, with respect to being freed of all penalty." One cannot apply this statement to the Eucharist directly, since the ultimate effect of the Eucharist is not forgiveness of sins, as with baptism, but union with Christ. Thomas's point seems to be that a more complete union with Christ is achieved through worthy sacramental eating than through spiritual eating alone.

Also note the more general remarks that Thomas makes about why human beings need sacraments (see 3.61.1, above).

QUESTION 83

THE RITE OF THIS SACRAMENT

3.83.1

Whether Christ is sacrificially offered in this sacrament?

It seems that Christ is not sacrificially offered [*immoletur*] in the celebration of this sacrament.[1]

1. It is written in Hebrews 10:14 that "Christ by one offering has perfected forever those who are sanctified." But that offering was his sacrificial offer-

---

1. Thomas uses *immolatio* in this article (rather than *sacrificium*), which carries the connotation of an offering that involves the death of that which is offered. Thomas does not use this term because he thinks Christ is killed in the celebration of the Eucharist; rather, the term simply makes clear that the Eucharistic sacrifice involves the representation of Christ's death on the cross.

Thomas says in a number of places (e.g., 3.79.7) that the Eucharist "not only is a sacrament but also a sacrifice." Although he has a fairly systematic exposition of how, in the consecration and reception of Christ's body and blood, the Eucharist is a sacrament, his remarks on its nature as a sacrifice are more scattered and unsystematic, in part for historical reasons: the controversy surrounding Berengar of Tours had contributed greatly to the development of the theology of Christ's presence in the Eucharist, whereas in Thomas's day there had not yet been significant controversy over the sacrificial nature of the Eucharist (which would come in the sixteenth century with the Reformation).

ing.[2] Therefore Christ is not sacrificially offered in the celebration of this sacrament.

2. Christ's sacrificial offering was made upon the cross, on which "he delivered himself for us, an offering and a sacrifice to God for an odor of sweetness," as is said in Ephesians 5:2. But Christ is not crucified in the celebration of this mystery.[3] Therefore, neither is he sacrificially offered.

3. As Augustine says in *De Trinitate* (bk. 4, chap. 14), in the sacrificial offering of Christ, the priest and the victim are one and the same. But in the celebration of this sacrament, the priest and the victim are not the same. Therefore, the celebration of this sacrament is not a sacrificial offering of Christ.

On the contrary: Augustine is quoted in Prosper of Aquitaine's *Book of Sentences,* "Christ was sacrificed once in himself, and yet he is sacrificed daily in the sacrament."[4]

I answer: The celebration of this sacrament is spoken of as Christ's sacrificial offering for two reasons.

First, because, as Augustine says in *To Simplicianus* (bk. 2, chap. 3), "The images of things are called by the names of the things of which they are the images, as when, looking upon a picture or a fresco, we say, 'This is Cicero, and that is Sallust.'" But, as was said earlier (3.79.1), the celebration of this sacrament is a sort of image representing Christ's suffering, which is his true sacrificial offering.[5] Therefore Ambrose says, in commenting on Hebrews 10:1, "In Christ a sacrifice capable of giving eternal salvation was offered up. What then do we do? Do we not offer it up every day in memory of his death?"[6]

Second, it is called a sacrifice in regard to the effect of his suffering—namely, because by this sacrament we are made partakers of the fruit of our Lord's

2. The objection here is one that recurs in the sixteenth-century disputes over the sacrificial nature of the Eucharist: the one sacrifice of Christ on the cross makes any further sacrifice unnecessary and therefore precludes the Eucharist being a sacrifice.

3. The objection is that the Mass does not represent the particular manner of Christ's death.

4. This quotation is not actually in the *Sentences* of Proper of Aquitaine (ca. 390–ca. 455), which was a kind of distillation of quotations from Augustine. It is, however, found in Gratian's *Decretum* (bk. 3, distinction 2, chap. 52), where it is ascribed to Prosper's *Sentences.* The quotation itself is not exactly that of Augustine but is Lanfranc's account of Augustine's view. However, Augustine himself says something very much like this in epistle 98, no. 9.

5. One might ask exactly *how* the celebration of the Eucharist is an "image" of Christ's suffering on the cross. In 3.83.5 Thomas offers some allegorical interpretations, of the sort typical in medieval expositions of the Mass, of the priest's actions. Thus in *ad* 3 he says that the various signs of the cross represent various events in Christ's passion, and in *ad* 5 he says that the priest's extended arms after the consecration, which was a distinctive Dominican practice, represent Christ's extended arms on the cross. But Thomas means more here than that the Eucharist is a sort of passion play: its representation of the suffering and death of Christ is tied to the very act of Eucharistic consecration itself, as the second reason Thomas offers makes clear.

6. The quotation is actually found in John Chrysostom's *Homilies on the Epistle to the Hebrews,* homily 17, no. 6. It is ascribed to Ambrose in Gratian's *Decretum,* bk. 3, distinction 2, chap. 53.

suffering. Therefore in one of the Sunday Secrets it is said, "Whenever the commemoration of this sacrifice is celebrated, the work of our redemption is enacted."[7]

Consequently, according to the first reason, it could be said that Christ was sacrificed even in the prefigurations of the Old Testament; therefore Revelation 13:8 speaks of those "whose names are not written in the book of life of the Lamb that was slain from the beginning of the world." But, according to the second reason, it is only in this sacrament [of the Eucharist] that Christ is sacrificially offered in its celebration.[8]

Reply to 1: As Ambrose says in the same place, "There is but one victim"—namely that which Christ offered and which we offer—"and not many victims, because Christ was offered only once, and this latter sacrifice is the pattern of the former; for just as what is offered everywhere is one body, and not many bodies, so also is it but one sacrifice."[9]

---

7. The *Secreta* or "Secret" is the prayer said in the Mass after the bread and wine have been prepared and before the Eucharistic Prayer begins. In the Mass as reformed after the Second Vatican Council this prayer is call the Prayer over the Gifts. In the Dominican rite of Mass of Thomas's day, the particular prayer quoted here was used on the seventh Sunday after the Octave of Trinity; in the reformed rite of Mass, it is used on the second Sunday in Ordinary Time.

Because a sacrament is both a sign and a cause, the kind of "representation" we speak of with regard to the Eucharist goes beyond merely picturing something absent. Rather, it is a representation that makes present that which it represents. And the Eucharist does not simply represent Christ-in-general, but Christ in his self-offering to God the Father. So just as we might speak of the real presence of Christ in the Eucharist, we might speak of the real presence of Christ's sacrifice. Theologians today appeal to the Greek term *anamnesis* (which in the Gospels is the term Jesus uses at the last supper, often translated as "remembrance") to convey this idea of a ritual recalling that makes present.

Thomas appears to hold the view that it is through the separate consecration of Christ's body and blood that Christ's sacrifice is present, because it is a sacramental representation of the separation of Christ's body and blood on the cross. This view is not developed systematically, and must be gleaned from scattered remarks. In 3.80.12 *ad* 3 he says that "the representation of the Lord's passion is brought about in the very consecration of this sacrament, in which one should not consecrate the body without the blood." In 3.76.2 *ad* 1 he says that the body and blood of Christ are consecrated in the separate species of bread and wine because "this serves the representation of the passion of Christ, in which the blood was separated from the body."

This view that the consecration *itself* constitutes the Eucharistic sacrifice might be contrasted with some other late medieval theories that Christ becomes present through the consecration of the elements and is then offered by the priest. This was the view that so enraged reformers like Luther, and rightly so, since it makes it appear that the Eucharist is our offering of Christ to God the Father—something we do in addition to Christ's offering of himself on the cross—rather than our sacramental representation of Christ's own self-offering, which is unique. The close link Thomas presumes between presence and sacrifice—both being effected through the consecration of the elements—helps guard against such views, making it clear that Eucharistic sacrifice, no less than Eucharistic presence, is a divine and not a human action.

8. The contrast drawn here parallels what Aquinas says generally about the difference between the sacraments of the Old Law and those of the New (see 3.62.1).

9. We might say that just as the Eucharistic conversion of the bread and wine into the body and blood of Christ is not a new incarnation, so too the Eucharistic sacrifice is not a new passion.

Reply to 2: As the celebration of this sacrament is an image representing Christ's suffering, so the altar is representative of the cross itself, upon which Christ was sacrificially offered in his own outward appearance.

Reply to 3: For the same reason (cf. reply to objection 2) the priest also bears Christ's image, in whose person and by whose power he pronounces the words of consecration, as is evident from what was said earlier (3.82.1, 3). And so, in a way, the priest and victim are one and the same.[10]

---

10. The priest does not offer Christ; rather Christ offers himself through the instrument of the priest's ministry.

Glossary of Names

Ambrose (339–97) was bishop of Milan, whose preaching influenced St. Augustine at the time of his conversion. Along with Jerome, Gregory, and Augustine, he is one of the four doctors (i.e., authoritative teachers) of the Latin-speaking church.

Anselm (ca. 1033–1109) was a Benedictine monk in France and later Archbishop of Canterbury in England. His *Proslogion* offered the so-called ontological argument for the existence of God (which Aquinas rejects in *Summa theologiae* 1.2.2), and his *Cur Deus Homo* interpreted the saving work of Christ in terms of "satisfaction."

Arius (d. 336) was a Christian theologian who taught that the Word proceeded from the Father in the same way as other creatures and was thus not of the same being or essence (in Greek *ousia*, in Latin *substantia*) as God the Father. This meant that Christ was not, properly speaking, divine. His position was condemned at the Council of Nicea in 325, which affirmed that Christ was of the "same being/essence" (*homoousious*) as God the Father.

Athanasius (ca. 296–373) was the bishop of Alexandria in Egypt. He was an important figure in establishing the Christian doctrine of the Trinity, in particular for arguing against Arius that the Son was equal in divinity with the Father. Frequently when Thomas cites Athanasius he is quoting from the so-called "Athanasian Creed," which was not actually written by Athanasius.

Augustine of Hippo (354–430) is one of the most important Christian theologians of all time and is a major influence on Aquinas, as well as on Western Christianity as a whole. It is rare to find Thomas in outright disagreement with Augustine on theological matters. Though Thomas's Aristotelianism leads him to qualify some of Augustine's more Platonic views, his commitment to Augustine's views on creation do as much, if not more, to qualify Aristotle.

Avicenna (980–1037), also known as **Ibn-Sina**, was a Muslim philosopher and physician who, like Aquinas, was influenced by both Aristotle and Neoplatonism (though his thought is more Neoplatonic than Thomas's). He is the source of a number of important distinctions Thomas employs, particularly the distinction between essence and existence.

Berengar of Tours (ca. 1010–1088) was a theologian who, at least by some accounts, maintained that Christ was present in the Eucharist only symbolically. Berengar was made to swear two oaths professing his faith in Christ's presence in the Eucharist, the second of which became a touchstone of Catholic orthodoxy (see 3.75.1).

Boethius (ca. 480–524) was a Roman philosopher and politician who transmitted a good deal of Greek philosophy to the Latin-speaking West, particularly on questions of logic. Boethius was a Christian, though what today is his most famous work, *The Consolation of Philosophy,* contains little that is explicitly Christian. In his commentary on Boethius's *De Trinitate* (*On the Trinity*) Aquinas offers some of his most fully developed remarks on the nature of theological inquiry.

Dionysius the Areopagite (fl. ca. 500), sometimes referred to as Pseudo-Dionysius, was an authority much referred to by Aquinas and other medieval theologians. The original Dionysius is a figure in the book of Acts whom Paul converts to Christianity while visiting Athens (see Acts 17:34). However, the Dionysius to whom Thomas refers—probably a Syrian monk—was the author of a body of theological writings under the name of the Dionysius of the book of Acts. In his writings, this anonymous monk addressed certain fundamental questions about human knowledge of God and was heavily influenced by Neoplatonic philosophy. During the Middle Ages, it was assumed that these writings were in fact penned by the Dionysius of Acts, and because this Dionysius was thought to be someone who had been converted (and, presumably, instructed) by Paul himself, his writings had an authority for medieval theology that was close to that of Scripture itself.

Gregory I (ca. 540–604), also known as Gregory the Great, was a monk who became pope and is considered—along with Ambrose, Augustine, and Jerome—one of the four traditional doctors (i.e., authoritative teachers) of the Latin-speaking church. His commentary on the book of Job, known as the *Moralia,* greatly influenced medieval biblical interpretation.

Hilary of Poitier (ca. 315–ca. 367) is sometimes known as the "Athanasius of the West," on account of his defense of the teaching of the Council of Nicea against the Arians in the West. He features prominently as an authority in Thomas's discussion of the Trinity in both his *Sentences* commentary and the *Summa theologiae.*

Hugh of St. Victor (d. 1142) wrote a lengthy overview of Christian faith and practice entitled *De sacramentis Christianae fidei,* which, despite its title, was not solely on the sacraments, but presented a more or less comprehensive overview of Christian theology, structured according to the story of salvation (i.e., beginning with creation, moving through fall and redemption on to the last judgment).

Jerome (ca. 345–420) was the translator of the Vulgate, which was the standard Latin translation of the Bible in the Middle Ages. He wrote many biblical commentaries and was known for his rather acerbic personality.

John Chrysostom (ca. 347–407) was bishop of Constantinople (modern day Istanbul) and was renowned for his preaching ("Chrysostom" means "golden mouthed"). He features prominently in the *Catena aurea,* the collection of patristic comments on the four Gospels that Thomas compiled at the request of Pope Urban IV.

John of Damascus (ca. 675–ca. 749) was a Greek theologian who lived in an area ruled by Muslims. His work *De fide orthodoxia* (which is the third part of a larger work entitled *Source of Knowledge*) is a comprehensive account of Christian belief from an Eastern Christian perspective. It was available in the medieval West in a Latin translation, and he was one of the primary sources through which Aquinas was influenced by the Eastern Christian tradition.

Moses Maimonides (1135–1204), whom Thomas normally calls "Rabbi Moses," was a Jewish thinker who wrote primarily in Arabic and was strongly influenced by the Aristotelian philosophy that flourished in the Arabic-speaking world. His major work, the *Guide for the Perplexed,* influenced Thomas, particularly in his development of the essence–existence distinction.

Origen (ca. 185–ca. 254) was probably the most important early Christian theologian. A number of his more speculative ideas were condemned as heretical after his death. Thomas associates him with trinitarian heresy because he spoke at times, in Platonist fashion, of Christ as an emanation from God the Father, and thus as having a lower level of existence.

Nestorius (d. ca. 451) was the bishop of Constantinople who held that Jesus was truly divine and truly human, but that there was no "union" between these two natures. For Nestorius the relationship of humanity and divinity in Jesus is akin to the way God indwelled the temple in Jerusalem: the temple's destruction in AD 70 did not lead to the conclusion that God had been destroyed. In a similar way, for Nestorius the "is" in "God is man" does not indicate the sort of union that would authorize one to say "God was born" or "God died on the cross"—two statements that Nestorius explicitly denied. It was for this denial that his views were condemned at the Council of Ephesus in 431.

Peter Lombard (ca. 1100–1160) wrote a work known as the *Sentences,* which was the standard textbook for teaching theology in Aquinas's day. In the

Sentences Lombard collated various authoritative opinions (*sententia*) from Scripture and previous theologians on a wide variety of theological questions and then sought to offer a resolution to their disagreements. In Thomas's day it was expected that one would write a commentary on the *Sentences* in order to become a Master (roughly equivalent to a professor) of Theology—that is, the commentary on the *Sentences* served the purpose of the modern dissertation.

Sabellius (fl. ca. 220) was a Christian theologian about whom little is known. His name became attached to the view that the Father, Son, and Spirit spoken of in the New Testament were simply three different "names" or "modes of appearing" of the one God. Thus when God is in heaven we call God "Father"; when God is incarnate in Jesus we call God "Son"; and when God is present to the church we call God "Spirit." One way of putting the matter is to say that for Sabellius the names "Father," "Son," and "Spirit" refer to how God relates to the world, not to relations within God. The opponents of Sabellius maintained that the Father, Son, and Spirit were numerically distinct and mutually related *personae* or *hypostases,* and not simply appearances.

Theodoret of Cyrrhus (ca. 393–ca. 460) was a supporter of Nestorius who later came to support the view put forward by the Council of Chalcedon (451), which sought a mediating position between Nestorius, who emphasized the distinctness of Christ's two natures, and Cyril of Alexandria, who emphasized the unity of Christ's person.

SUGGESTIONS
FOR FURTHER READING

Thomas's own writings are voluminous, and the secondary works on him continue to be produced at what might be called an alarming rate (at least for those who feel compelled to read even a fraction of them). Below I list just a few works, concentrating (though not exclusively) on what is available in English and not too inaccessible to a reader of Aquinas who is still something of a novice.

THE WORKS OF AQUINAS

Jean-Pierre Torrell, in his biography of Thomas (see below), provides a comprehensive list of all of Thomas's works, along with information on the best editions.

The Leonine edition of Thomas's works is intended to be the definitive edition, but it is not yet complete, in spite of having been launched in 1882. The other major editions of Thomas's complete works are the Piana edition (1570), the Parma edition (1852–1873), and the Vives or Paris edition (1871–1880). Critical editions of a number of individual works have been published by Marietti in Turin. Thomas's works in Latin are now available online, in the collection originally assembled by R. Busa from a variety of editions, at http://www.corpusthomisticum.org.

Many of Thomas's works have been translated into English, and the English translation of Torrell's biography of Aquinas lists them up to 1996. There is an excellent online bibliography of English translations of Aquinas's works maintained by Thérèse Bonin of Duquesne University at http://www.home.duq.edu/~bonin/thomasbibliography.html.

The complete *Summa theologiae* is available in two English translations:

The Summa theologica. Translated by the Fathers of the English Dominican Province. 2nd, rev. ed. 22 vols. London: Burns, Oates & Washbourne, 1912–36. Reprinted in 5 vols. Westminster, Md.: Christian Classics, 1981. This version contains the questions that constitute the *Supplementum,* which Thomas's followers assembled after his death—using his commentary on Lombard's *Sentences*—in order to complete the projected plan of the *Summa.* It is now in the public domain and is widely available online (see, e.g., http://www. newadvent.org/summa/). It offers a fairly literal translation of the Latin.

Summa theologiae. Translated by Thomas Gilby et al. 60 vols. London: Eyre and Spottiswoode; New York: McGraw-Hill, 1964–73. This translation, commonly known as the "Blackfriars edition," contains the Leonine edition of the Latin on facing pages with an English translation that tends (in varying degrees, depending on the particular translator) to be free. Some of the volumes come with helpful appendices. It does not include the *Supplementum.*

In addition, Timothy McDermott has produced a volume entitled *Summa Theologiae: A Concise Translation* (Allen, Tex.: Christian Classics, 1989). In this case, "concision" means eliminating all of the objections and most of the replies, and "translation" really means paraphrase. However, McDermott's rendering of Thomas often brilliantly conveys his meaning in the way that a more literal translation can fail to do, so the book is well worth consulting as a kind of companion to the *Summa.*

Biographies

Chesterton, Gilbert Keith. *St. Thomas Aquinas: The Dumb Ox.* New York: Sheed and Ward, 1933. This book is dated in terms of historical scholarship, but probably unsurpassed for literary style. It is a good beginning biography to give to people who might not be already interested in Aquinas.

Foster, Kenelm, O.P., ed. and trans. *The Life of St. Thomas Aquinas: Biographical Documents.* Baltimore, Md.: Helicon Press, 1959. The most important medieval sources for the life of Thomas. A must-read for those who want pious anecdotes.

Torrell, Jean-Pierre, O.P. *Saint Thomas Aquinas.* Vol. 1, *The Person and His Work.* Translated by Robert Royal. Washington, D.C.: The Catholic University of America Press, 1996. Torrell's work is the state-of-the-art biography of Thomas, and the first volume in a two-part interpretation of Aquinas.

Tugwell, Simon, O.P. "The Life and Works of Thomas Aquinas." In *Albert and Thomas: Selected Writings.* Classics of Western Spirituality. Translated and edited by Simon Tugwell, O.P. New York: Paulist Press, 1988. For those who do not have the time or inclination to read a full biography, Tugwell offers a relatively brief and up-to-date mini-biography of Aquinas. His account departs from Torrell's on a number of points, and so makes an interesting counterpoint.

OVERVIEWS OF AQUINAS'S THOUGHT

Chenu, Marie-Dominique, O.P. *Toward Understanding St. Thomas.* Translated by A.-M. Landry, O.P., and D. Hughes, O.P. Chicago: Henry Regnery Company, 1964. Though now dated, this remains a classic introduction to Aquinas that helped counter the then prevailing tendency to view Thomas as more a philosopher than a theologian.

Davies, Brian, O.P. *The Thought of Thomas Aquinas.* Oxford: Clarendon Press, 1992. This book offers a clear and, on the whole, accurate overview of Thomas's work, as well as explanations of Thomas's positions on key questions. The book generally follows the pattern of the *Summa theologiae,* though it tends to focus on questions more of interest to philosophers than to theologians (e.g., over half of it is devoted to the first part of the *Summa*). Davies, however, by no means ignores theology. For students, this is probably the most useful one-volume companion to Aquinas's thought as a whole, not least because Davies provides examples for Thomas's arguments, something Thomas himself habitually fails to do.

Healy, Nicholas M. *Thomas Aquinas: Theologian of the Christian Life.* Burlington, Vt.: Ashgate, 2003. Though it presents itself as a general introduction, this book in fact offers a fresh interpretation of Thomas as a theologian whose overriding concern was to help his fellow Christians follow Christ. Particularly notable is the fact that the author not only says that Thomas's biblical commentaries should be read, but appears to have in fact read some of them.

Kerr, Fergus, O.P. *After Aquinas: Versions of Thomism.* Oxford: Blackwell, 2002. Though one can read this book as an introduction to Aquinas's thought, what distinguishes it from other introductions is the attention it pays to subsequent interpretations of Thomas, particularly in the last one hundred years. If you want to know what Thomists are arguing about today, this is the book to read.

Torrell, Jean-Pierre, O.P. *Saint Thomas Aquinas.* Vol. 2, *Spiritual Master.* Translated by Robert Royal. Washington, D.C.: The Catholic University of America Press, 2003. The companion volume to Torrell's biography of Aquinas, this book opens to view the connections between Thomas's theology and what some today would call his "spirituality." This book is useful for those who have difficulty getting past Thomas's rather dry language to see the passionate love of Christ that motivates his theology.

Weinandy, Thomas, O.F.M., Cap., Daniel Keating, and John Yocum. *Aquinas on Doctrine: A Critical Introduction.* New York: T&T Clark International, 2004. With essays on the major topics in systematic theology, this is a good starting point for those readers who are interested in examining Thomas's views on particular doctrines in more detail.

SPECIALIZED STUDIES

Burrell, David B., C.S.C. *Knowing the Unknowable God: Ibn-Sina, Maimonides, Aquinas.* Notre Dame, Ind.: University of Notre Dame Press, 1986. This book on the human capacity to know God is notable because it locates Thomas within a sector of his medieval context that has been too-often ignored: the intersection of Christian, Muslim, and Jewish thought. The writing is dense and not for the intellectually faint of heart.

Cessario, Romanus, O.P. *The Godly Image: Christ and Salvation in Catholic Thought from Anselm to Aquinas.* Petersham, Mass.: St. Bede's Publications, 1990. Despite the title, this book is less a survey than it is an account of Thomas's understanding of salvation through the death of Christ. The author argues that Thomas's mature theology focuses not on some sort of mechanical repayment for sin, but on the restoration and perfection of God's image in human beings.

Emery, Gilles, O.P. *Trinity in Aquinas.* Ypsilanti, Mich.: Sapientia Press, 2003. This book collects essays by an important contemporary interpreter of Aquinas on the Trinity. The essays fit together well, producing a comprehensive account of Thomas's trinitarian theology, as well as its background in medieval theology.

Jenkins, John I., C.S.C. *Knowledge and Faith in Thomas Aquinas.* Cambridge: Cambridge University Press, 1997. Jenkins revisits the well-plowed field of the relationship of faith and reason in Aquinas to argue that Thomas does not keep the two so neatly separated as some have thought. Jenkins also provides a helpful account of what Thomas means by *scientia* and of the kind of *scientia* that theology is.

Leget, Carlo. *Living with God: Thomas Aquinas on the Relationship between Life on Earth and "Life" after Death.* Leuven: Peeters, 1997. This book is an examination of the way in which Thomas weaves the theme of "life" through his theology, beginning with the divine life and culminating with eternal life. As such, the book would be particularly useful for those interested in Thomas's eschatology in the context of his thought as a whole. The book also provides a good introduction to the Thomism associated with the Thomas Instituut te Utrecht in the Netherlands, with its emphasis on Thomas as an apophatic and scriptural theologian.

Rouget, A.-M., O.P. *Les Sacraments.* Éditions dé La Revue des jeunes. Paris: Les Éditions du Cerf, 1945. The first half of this work is the Latin text with French translation of *Summa theologiae* 3.60–65. The second half consists of explanatory notes on the text, as well as a lengthy essay offering a comprehensive discussion of Thomas' sacramental theology. I include it here because I know of no work in English that offers an equivalent account of Thomas's sacramental theology in general.

Torrell, Jean-Pierre, O.P. *Les Verb Incarné.* 3 vols. Éditions dé La Revue des jeunes. Paris: Les Éditions du Cerf, 2002. The three volumes cover *Summa theologiae* 3.1–26, with each volume containing the Latin text, French translation, extensive explanatory notes, and interpretive essays. Together they constitute a comprehensive account of Thomas's theology of the person of Christ. I include it here because I know of no English equivalent.

Williams, A. N. *The Ground of Union: Deification in Aquinas and Palamas.* Oxford: Oxford University Press, 1999. Williams argues that Aquinas has more in common with Eastern Christian thought (represented by Palamas) than has traditionally been thought. Specifically, she argues that for both Thomas and Palamas the entire goal of theology is union with God. The book is especially useful for those interested in the nature of theological inquiry and in theological anthropology. It is a good antidote for those who see an unbridgeable gulf between Eastern and Western Christianity, as well as for those who think of Thomas as a philosopher who occasionally indulged in theology as a hobby.

Journals

For English speakers interested in Thomas's theology, *The Thomist* is the preeminent journal. *New Blackfriars,* the journal of the English Dominicans, does not focus exclusively on Thomas but often has articles on current thought and events that are written from what might broadly be called a "Thomist" perspective. The journal *Angelicum* is published by the Pontifical University of Saint Thomas Aquinas in Rome, with articles in a variety of European languages, including English. For those who read French, the *Revue Thomiste* often publishes important essays, as well as offering useful surveys of current literature.

Index to the Introduction and Notes